EYEWITNESS

EYEWITNESS

A Personal Account

of a Tumultuous Decade 1937–1946

by ROBERT PAYNE

Doubleday & Company, Inc., Garden City, New York

1972

Other books by Robert Payne:

THE WHITE PONY

FOREVER CHINA

MAO TSE-TUNG

THE CIVIL WAR IN SPAIN

A PORTRAIT OF ANDRÉ MALRAUX

THE WORLD OF ART

Library of Congress Catalog Card Number 79-180097
Copyright © 1972 by Robert Payne
All Rights Reserved
Printed in the United States of America
First Edition

For Rose *and* Mireille

CONTENTS

ILLUSTRATIONS

(between pages 182 and 183)

The author, Rangoon, December 1941
Correspondents with General Lister near Mora de Ebro, July 1938
The author with General Lister
The author, Chungking, March 1942
Japanese prisoner at Changsha, January 1942
Chialing River near Peipei
Gateway in Kunming
Wen Yi-tuo

(between pages 206 and 207)

Marshal Feng Yu-hsiang
Hsiung Hsi-ling and Madame Hsiung Hsi-ling
Rose Hsiung, circa 1938
Rose Hsiung, Peipei, in 1942
Jacqueline, 1946
Valley of Yenan, woodcut by a Chinese Communist artist
The author at a dinner with Mao Tse-tung, July 1946
Rose Hsiung's scroll painting of the author disguised as Ming
  Dynasty scholar

EYEWITNESS

NOTES ON A GREEN DRAGON

When I was a child I was haunted by a green dragon. Where he came from and what he was doing in my life were mysteries I did not attempt to unravel, but I had no doubt of his existence and I was certain that he watched over my welfare. When I attempt to reconstruct his origins, I realize that he was inseparable from an early fascination with China. I remember wallpaper covered with a pattern of dragons in the house of an old woman who possessed a cabinet of Chinese figurines, and no doubt the wallpaper dragons had something to do with the shape he always assumed. I suspect that he originally came about as the result of a dangerous experiment played by nearly all children when they discover that by pressing their fists against their eyeballs they can produce a wonderful display of sparks accompanied by a fierce roaring in the ears. By the time I was seven or eight the green dragon who came flaring out of the dark was my familiar companion, and I believed that all children were accompanied by dragons. It did not surprise me that they rarely mentioned the existence of their dragons because it is in the nature of children to be secretive about their most prized possessions.

The green dragon was a possession, something owned, like a pet dog or a pet rabbit, but there was a remarkable difference. He would do whatever I wanted him to do, however impossible. When I was in trouble, I would summon him by pressing my eyeballs or simply by staring into the dark and he would come in a rush of green flame to do my bidding. If a knee was bruised, he would heal it. If lessons went badly, he saw that they miraculously improved. If my father rebuked me, the green dragon had his own mysterious ways of rebuking my father. He was not only an instrument of punishment and healing and the overseer of my lessons, but he was also the author of many minor blessings. I had a passion for walking about with my shoelaces untied, and the green dragon was always there to prevent me from falling. I had also a passion for climbing trees, and the green dragon saw to it that even the outlying branches would support my weight. In London winters I suffered atrociously from chilblains, but for some reason the green dragon regarded my bleeding feet as unworthy of his consideration. This was his only error of omission.

On all larger matters the green dragon could be relied upon to behave with exemplary patience and promptness. He had long ago acquired form and features, resembling an immense flaming serpent with the face of a tiger, winged and scaly, the emerald green body shading into yellow and gold; and as we grew older together, the expression became more kindly and more forgiving. He could do anything he pleased or anything I wanted, and sometimes I was dimly aware that this was dangerous. The danger lay in the superb powers granted to the dragon, for there was simply nothing he was incapable of doing. I learned to be very careful about cursing people, because when I did curse them they died atrociously. Did I want power and vast possessions, the green dragon was ready to supply them. At a very early age I was haunted by China, and the green dragon announced imperiously that I would go to China, marry a Chinese princess and live in a vast palace, a prospect which seemed perfectly natural to the London schoolboy with the scuffed shoes and the trailing shoelaces.

The greatest danger, of course, lay in the realm of power, which the green dragon possessed in abundance and in a bewildering variety of forms. I did not ask to become Prime Minister, perhaps because I was sufficiently aware that this was an arduous and killing profession, but I did ask that I should be able to talk to all the kings and prime ministers of this world. The schoolboy reading about Caesar was quite consciously looking forward to the day when he would encounter living Caesars far more powerful than any Roman emperors. The green dragon would open the palace gates and usher me into the presence of the great, and there would be a solemn conclave. Wherever I wanted to travel—and this was chiefly in the Far East—the green dragon would take me. If I asked for wealth, he would give it to me, and if I was content to be poor he would remain by my side ready at a moment's notice to save me from the importunities of poverty. If I was in mortal danger, he would immediately rescue me, and if I was heartbroken, he would immediately heal the wound. I had only to call and he would come racing across the vast spaces of the sky, glowing against the darkness, to do whatever service I demanded of him.

I suspect that many children have similar fantasies and outlive them, but this fantasy obstinately refused to be outlived. When childhood and early youth came to an end, the green dragon was still present, though no longer the chief artificer and protector of my dreams. He became Greendragon, which is not quite the same as a green dragon. He still wore his tiger's mask, but I was growing increasingly aware that the mask concealed another mask, and however often I tore away the masks I would never see his real face. Once he had been very simple: now he luxuriated in dazzling complexities. Once he could be trusted implicitly and was almost tangible, but now I found myself wondering about his purposes and he was no longer the close companion of my childhood days. I no longer had long conversations with him before falling asleep. He had become almost an abstraction of vast and splendid powers, gliding serenely across the heavens in perfect silence, rather than the engine of destruction and creation with glittering green scales who came with the terrifying roar of an express train. Dragons, apparently, have no objection to becoming abstractions provided they are permitted to appear in their physical dress whenever they want to, and even as an abstraction he wore an appearance of majestic power.

No one in his senses ever throws a dragon away, and so he remained with me long after my dragon-haunted childhood. It was always pleasant to have a dragon in attendance and to believe rightly or wrongly that he could strike people dead, confound all my enemies, and obey my most impossible commands. Also, he was very decorative.

In the following pages I have told the story of my wanderings in Europe and the Far East. If the reader sometimes detects the presence of a green dragon lurking in the background, he should not be alarmed. This dragon never breathed fire, his claws rarely tore people apart, and he was nearly always peaceful.

BRIEF ENCOUNTERS

Nineteen thirty-seven was the year of Hitler, the year when Europe began to slide helplessly into the abyss.

When I look back on that year, I wonder how it was possible for so many people to be so innocent. The strange white face of Hitler stared out from all the newspapers, the raucous voice was heard on the radio, threats and ultimatums followed one another in quick succession, and very few believed that he would carry out his threats and even fewer believed that he would drag the whole world into war. My own innocence seems totally inexplicable. I look at photographs of myself taken in 1937, when I was twenty-five, and ask myself: Why didn't you know? How is it possible that you did not know? What were you doing in the world?

The young face seems to belong to another age, another dispensation of time. The blue eyes are untroubled, the brow unfurrowed, the expression carefree. It might be an actor's face, or the face of a young priest secure behind the walls of his seminary. I had worked in a shipyard, traveled widely, attended four universities, written four books, and should at least have possessed some knowledge of the tragic times I was living through. Stalin was murdering millions of his countrymen, Hitler had set up his concentration camps, Mussolini had just conquered Abyssinia, the Japanese were setting fire to the towns and villages of the Yangtze Valley, but these things scarcely concerned me. The Spanish Civil War was raging, but for all I knew it might have been raging on another planet.

My father was a naval architect, and so I knew a good deal about shipyards and warships in England and South Africa, where we were stationed for three years. These ships and shipyards were objects of great beauty, and I thought of them as the shield of England's shores. No doubt they sometimes engaged in battle, but the outcome was always predictable: Britain

ruled the seas. I had lived among sailors nearly all my life and
I could not imagine a time when our ships would ever relin-
quish their command of the seas. The most beautiful sight I had
ever seen was the battle cruiser *Hood* gliding at dusk out of
the Tamar into Plymouth Sound with all her pennons flying.
She was an abstract shape of vast and terrible power, but her
lines were so clean-cut, so elegant, that she gave an impression
of imperious grace: as though the goddess Athena had emerged
from the coast of Cornwall and was advancing slowly toward
her destiny.

I was born into the Royal Navy and expected to spend
all the rest of my life in it, probably as a naval architect.
When the family returned from South Africa in 1929 I worked
as a shipwright at Cammell Laird's Shipbuilding Company in
Birkenhead, where I did very much as I pleased, wandering
about the shipyard every afternoon to admire the girders and
bulkheads rising from the keel plates. It was the height of the
depression, with workmen being laid off every day and the
blackest misery was descending on Merseyside. I spent a good
deal of time on the mold loft floor, where the ships' lines were
drawn on wooden panels stretching across an area as large as
a football field. One day, on the mold loft floor, I encountered
my friend Scottie in tears. He was a small proud man from
Glasgow with a spiky white beard and watery blue eyes, and
I had learned more from him than from anyone else. He had
just received the little white card terminating his employment.

"What will happen to the mold loft floor when you are
gone, Scottie?" I asked.

"Aye, mon, they can do without me," he said. "They've got
all the young 'uns I've trained, and they won't miss me. I've
spent fifty years on the floor, and I know every inch of it,
and love it, and now it's the end of me."

So it was, for I used to see him in his small stone house
just outside of Birkenhead, where he lived with his wife on
the dole. He received no pension and not even a half-hunter
gold watch with his name engraved on it for all his years of
service, and he died of a broken heart six weeks later.

The two years I spent as a shipwright were supposed to be
preparation for a career as a naval architect, but I was no
longer sure I wanted to spend my life among ships. In winter

especially, while the chill winds swept up the Mersey estuary, the workmen moving like gray shadows in the mist, with here and there the brilliant red glare of an acetylene flame, the shipyard looked like a modern version of hell. There was despair on the faces of the men who were still working, and a greater despair on the faces of the men who huddled outside the employment exchanges. Scottie's death appalled me. I was beginning to realize that England was suffering from a disease for which there was perhaps no cure.

Every Saturday afternoon I took the ferry to Liverpool and wandered around the Walker Art Gallery, and worked in the Hornby Library with its treasures of incunabula and finely printed books. It was another world, as far as possible removed from the shipyard. The Hornby Library, just behind the art gallery, was an Italianate building, all marble and gold, crammed with books in leather bindings, rare manuscripts and marble statues, and for some reason very few people entered it and sometimes I would have the library to myself all Saturday afternoon and evening. Here I found colored reproductions of the frescoes in the Ajanta caves and equally magnificent reproductions of the wall paintings in the Tun-huang caves of North China; and late in the evening, wandering around Liverpool in a daze, my head filled with the happy discoveries made in the Hornby Library, dreaming of India and China, I would remember the green dragon and the long epic called "The Adventures of Sylvia, Queen of Denmark and China," which I had written when I was seven years old.

The thought of becoming a naval architect faded during the long cold winters of Birkenhead. One day Mr. Johns, in charge of the drawing office, summoned me to his small office with a splendid view of the shipyard.

"You seem to be very restless," he said. "You're twenty years old. You ought to know what you are going to do with your life. You have all the advantages—a father who will help you to become a naval architect, and all your uncles are naval architects. What's the matter with you?"

A few weeks later I entered Liverpool University. The difficulty was to know what to study. Two departments had no students at all, and there were obvious advantages in having a department for oneself. Dr. John Garstang was in charge of the

Department of Egyptian Archaeology, had in fact been in charge of it since the turn of the century. I was interviewed by him as he stood among his mummy cases, and he pronounced that I had the makings of an archaeologist. I went to see him three or four times, and each time he painted a picture of the archaeologist's life as one of glowing happiness, though he was himself unhappy, and his mouth was turned down at the corners. Dr. Bruce Boswell was in charge of the Slavonic Department, and he also wanted students desperately, even one student. He promised to teach me Russian and Polish, and hinted that if I worked well enough I would become a Slavonic scholar. He was a fat, jolly man, and beamed merrily. I became his student, and for month after month I sat at one end of a long mahogany table while he sat at the other end with a mountain of typewritten cards in front of him. In three months I came to the conclusion that the complexities of the Polish language were driving me to madness, and I concentrated on Russian. The Russian library consisted of about three hundred books hidden away in one of the red brick towers of the university. One day I came upon Boris Pasternak's book of poems *Themes and Variations,* and for the first time felt the excitement that lies within the Russian language. I took courses in German and Italian. The teacher of Italian was Leonora Eyles, who was so beautiful that the small class of male students learned nothing at all. We gaped at her, admired and adored her, and were tongue-tied whenever in her innocence she asked us questions.

After my second year at Liverpool University my father thought I should get a job, and I took the examination for entering the Ministry of Labour. There were about three thousand candidates and two hundred positions to be filled. I came low down on the list of two hundred, and learned that the last fifty places were reserved for the Internal Revenue Service. In this way I became an assistant inspector of taxes and was posted to Guildford in southern England. Any shipyard was more beautiful than a tax office, and I soon came to the conclusion that there was nothing I less wanted to be than an inspector of taxes.

Every Wednesday I traveled to London to attend an advanced course on taxes at Somerset House. I remember absolutely nothing abut the tax course, but the journey to London was made enjoyable by Charles Williams, the poet and novelist, who was a friend of my father's. I would meet him at the Oxford University Press and we would go off to a small restaurant on Ludgate Hill. He must have had pity on me, for these meetings continued for a whole year, and every Wednesday saw the arid horror of Somerset House and the heaven of Williams' presence. He talked about God as though God was present at his side, and about the angels and about the English poets: he knew them well, from Chaucer to Shakespeare and Dylan Thomas. God and English poetry, he said, was enough for one lifetime. I had been translating Yuri Olesha's novel *Envy* from Russian, and he sent me off to Leonard Woolf, who published it at the Hogarth Press. I was writing a novel about an uprising in England called *The War in the Marshes,* and he sent me off to T. S. Eliot, who published it at Faber and Faber. "All things are possible under the Mercy," he said. The Mercy often wore the face of Charles Williams.

There was something strangely angelic about Charles Williams, as though he scarcely belonged to the earth. He believed firmly in the presence of angels and even more firmly in God's abundant intervention in the workings of history. One day he remarked that no one had ever written the history of the individual human soul through the ages. "It can't be done," he said, "but at least one could make a stab at it. I have a feeling that the high moments of poetry would tell the story. Surely the human soul has a history, for it grows, it changes, it is never the same, and it has nothing to do with changing dynasties, Acts of Parliament, or indeed anything recorded in the history books."

For a year of Saturday afternoons I burrowed in the British Museum, making occasional discoveries which were reported to him. We planned the book together and gradually it began to assume another dimension. It became a history of the soul in its pride and abasement, in its moments of greatest torment. The notes accumulated, and survived the war and his death. Many years later a large envelope with his signature found me in San Francisco. The book wrote itself from the notes and was finally published under the title of *Hubris.*

Suddenly, after a year of working as an assistant inspector of taxes, the string snapped. Without a word to my superiors I took the train to Devonport, where my father was manager of the dockyard. I announced firmly that I would not look at another tax form, unless it was my own, for the rest of my life. My father was alarmed, but sympathetic. In his beautiful Queen Anne house overlooking the Tamar, with the dockyard at my feet, I began writing a long novel about the battles in Mongolia at the end of the World War. It was a bloodcurdling novel full of scarcely imaginable horrors made endurable only because it was written in the Russian way, quietly, dispassionately, without any straining for effect. When I had finished it, I sent it to Charles Williams, who placed it squarely in the hands of Herbert Read, who was then a reader for Heinemann. It was published during the week when Hitler invaded Austria.

My father doubted whether it was possible for anyone to make a living as a novelist. I was a failed shipwright and a failed tax inspector, and presumably would become a failed novelist. I translated Søren Kierkegaard's Fear and Trembling from Danish, and my father warned me against hoping to make a fortune out of translations. An uncle, who despaired that I would ever be able to make anything of my fragmentary life, gave me a hundred pounds on condition that I spent a Wanderjahr in Europe "to learn the facts of life." I decided to go to Munich, Vienna, Budapest, Prague and Cracow.

Munich in the autumn of 1937 was at once pleasant and terrifying. All day the Stormtroopers marched and sang through the cobbled streets, the blood-red swastika flag waved in the wind, and from the Brown House, Hitler's headquarters near the vast Königsplatz, jackbooted Nazi officers marched out with set jaws on errands that were never errands of mercy. The most terrifying thing in Munich was the great granite tomb, overlooking the Brown House, which had been built to honor the remains of the Nazis who fell in the abortive putsch of 1923, when Hitler made his first desperate attempt to seize power. At the four corners of the tomb stood four soldiers in massive helmets and heavy greatcoats, their heads bowed, their rifles reversed. Ominous and motionless, they seemed to be made of the same granite as the tomb.

There was also another Munich of Gemütlichkeit and music, of gardens, museums and baroque churches, which existed independently of the National Socialist movement. Over the door of the Brown House, Hitler ordered that there should be carved the words DEUTSCHLAND ERWACHE!, but this other Munich did not ask to be awakened, because it was already awake. When the Stormtroopers marched along the ugly, sprawling Briennerstrasse, they gave an impression of menacing power because they were no more than an extension of the brutality of the street, but when they marched beneath the churches and palaces near the Englischer Garten, they were dwarfed by the buildings erected by the Wittelsbach kings and looked out of place, like a rabble of schoolchildren shouting in a cathedral. There were whole areas of Munich where the Stormtroopers rarely penetrated.

My mother was sent as a young girl to study German in a convent school just outside of Munich and I went to see the nuns, who had been known for three centuries as the Englische Fräulein. The convent at Berg am Rein had been founded by some English noblewomen, whose names were still remembered, but all the nuns were now German. They wore heavy black habits and enormous white caps, but I never saw them walking. They tripped, they danced, they ran about like schoolgirls. They remembered my mother vividly and they mimicked her French accent enchantingly, and they even remembered her father, the gruff bearded doctor from Vienne in the south of France, who wore a high collar and a black frock coat and strode about as though he owned the earth. But what they especially remembered was my mother's very French beauty, her gaiety, her facility in learning to read and write German, so that in a few weeks she was writing the terrible dark angular script, like tangles of barbed wire, as though she was born to it. All the older nuns remembered her and described what they remembered, until without the slightest difficulty it was possible to recreate an image of her, fifteen years old, with a red ribbon in her hair, smiling her smile of pure dazed happiness.

An old baroness, whom my mother had known as a girl, was living in Munich, and I went to call on her. She was reputed to be a martinet, the wielder of a silver-mounted cane, with fierce opinions on everything. Hermann Goering, wounded in the Odeonsplatz during the abortive putsch, had made his way to her house, where he remained in hiding for several weeks until his wound healed and he was smuggled to Sweden. The baroness complained that the Stormtroopers made too much noise outside her window, and "fat Hermann" had never made a speech she could understand, while Hitler was quite intolerable when he ranted on the radio, though he could be charming in an Austrian way when he was being courted by the ladies of Munich. She spoke of his sweet voice, his *süsse Stimme*, and his strange power over the weather, for when he planned a parade or made a speech before thousands of his followers there was never any rain. But on the whole she disapproved of him and she would have preferred Germany to be ruled by some antique general like Hindenburg or Ludendorff because, as she said, "only strong men can rule Germans." She did not think Hitler was strong enough.

One of those who thought Hitler was strong enough was Rudolf Hess. I had a letter of introduction to him, but for some reason decided not to send it. I had no particular reason for seeing him and knew little about him except that he was the Deputy-Führer and Hitler had dictated *Mein Kampf* to him in prison. One day, having spent most of the morning and the early afternoon in the State Library vainly attempting to understand why the wrong books kept coming to my desk, I wandered into the nearby Englischer Garten in a furious temper. I had no plans for the rest of the afternoon. It was a miserable cloudy day, the rain was beginning to fall, and the children were running to shelter. Wandering through the rain, I decided that I was sick of Munich and the Stormtroopers marching through the streets and the blood-red swastika flags that hung from too many windows. I told myself that I would take the night train to Vienna. Then I remembered the letter of introduction and found myself walking in the direction of Hess's apartment simply because there was nothing else to do. A maidservant opened the door, took the letter, and then closed the door again. It occurred to me that I had probably come to the wrong address, because there were no armed guards standing outside the house and there was nothing to suggest that an important dignitary lived there. About two minutes later the door opened wide, and there was Hess himself in his brown shirt and riding breeches, smiling broadly and waving the letter. The photographs, which emphasized the beetle brows and the cleft chin, had not done him justice. He looked remarkably healthy, his eyes were clear, he had an enchanting smile, and he spoke

English without an accent. He took me into his study, where
there was a small silver-framed portrait of Hitler on the desk,
but otherwise the room resembled the quiet study of a studious
man. It was filled to the ceiling with books, at least half of them
in English. There were comfortable leather sofas and hand-
woven carpets on the floor.

For a while we talked about the mutual friend in London who
wrote the letter of introduction. He had a short barking laugh,
which was distracting, and he talked in sudden spurts of four
or five sentences which ended abruptly, but the general impression was of a man who was genuinely anxious to please and
had studied the art of putting people at ease. Was there anything
he could do for me? Was there anybody in Germany I would
like to meet? How long was I staying? Only once did he talk
about Hitler, saying that a great miracle had taken place and
the name of the miracle was Hitler. At that moment his face
grew hard and defiant, bristling with a strange energy and
ruthlessness, so that I was reminded of the sudden jerky gestures
of the Stormtroopers as they marched in the streets. But Hess's
moment of portentousness passed, and once more he was the
kindly host talking about everything under the sun, while the
rain whistled against the windowpane looking out over the
dark courtyard. Suddenly, while he was talking about the pleasures of gliding, the telephone rang and he sprang up and answered it, speaking in the sharp and strident voice which he
evidently used whenever he reminded himself that he was the
Deputy-Führer. At last he put the telephone down, swung
round, and said: "How very fortunate! Come, we are going to
see the Führer!"

I thought this was absurd, for I had come to a strange house
with no expectation of seeing anyone except perhaps Hess's
secretary, and indeed I had rather hoped I would see no one. Hess
seemed to be rushing about the room collecting papers and
documents. I must have looked startled, for he suddenly said in
his barking voice: "Are you coming or not coming?" A moment
later we were racing down the steps two at a time, and guards
mysteriously appeared in the street, and we all climbed into a
waiting Mercedes-Benz. We were crowded together, knees jutting against knees, and there were enough guns in the car to fill
a small armory. The car raced through the streets and came to a

sudden halt outside the Hotel Vierjahrenzeiten. We marched into the hotel with the Stormtroopers on both sides of us, in front and behind, and Hess was saying that the Führer would probably like to talk about England.

Hitler was sitting at a small table in an alcove of an enormous empty dining room. He did not resemble the pictures in the newspapers. The strange white face was not white: he had ruddy cheeks, the mustache was brown, not black, the eyes were blue, and the forelock was not obtrusive. He was talking to an airforce general and had his back to the wall, so that he could see anyone coming across the room. There were two or three waiters hovering over him, and two SS guards stood watchfully against the curtains, hands on their belts. Hess presented me, and I made a short bow, for it was clear that there was going to be no shaking of hands. Then Hitler smiled up at Hess, and made a curious circular movement with his hand, indicating that we should both sit down at the table while he finished his interrogation of the air-force general, who was answering questions briefly, succinctly, as though he had trained himself to answer in sentences five words long.

At last the conversation with the air-force general came to an end, and Hitler began talking rapidly to Hess in a low voice, presumably about me, but I was much too busy studying his face to pay any attention to what he was saying. Hitler was drinking milk, the air-force general was drinking tea, and soon a plate and a teacup appeared beside me. Hitler was nodding approvingly. "*Ein Englander,* a writer, staying in Munich, yes, of course . . ." Then an extraordinary thing happened, for Hitler turned toward me and slowly pointed his fork at me, and I wondered what on earth one is supposed to do when a dictator prods you with a very sharp fork. Hess was laughing and pointing to the enormous silver plate full of cakes and tarts in the center of the table. Hitler was saying: "Which cake would you like?" I pointed to a strawberry cake, and he neatly speared it with the fork and placed it on my plate.

He said: "I very much admire the English people, and if God is willing, I hope one day to visit England."

I said in my very best German that I was delighted, and I hoped he would visit the best parts of England—Devon and Cornwall.

"What is that?" Hitler said, looking up at Hess. "What is he saying?"

"Devon and Cornwall," Hess said, giving the words the proper Teutonic intonation.

"That is the part of England that juts out toward America," I said. "It would give me great pleasure to show them to you."

He smiled politely. I doubt whether he had given much thought to Devon and Cornwall. He speared a cream cake and placed it on his own plate, and I prepared myself for a lengthy discussion about England. Suddenly an SS officer came across the dining room, whispered something in Hitler's ear, and Hitler shot up from his chair. While the SS guards, Hess and the air-force general made the Hitler salute, Hitler himself was striding across the room.

"Unfortunately, something very important," Hess was saying apologetically. "I will try to arrange a meeting for you at Berchtesgaden, when we shall have more time."

For a few minutes longer we stayed around the table, talking desultorily. I told myself that I had spent about six minutes by Hitler's side, the baroness was right when she spoke of his pleasant voice, and the newspapers were wrong when they showed him white-faced with a black mustache. It had been a trivial meeting, and I had learned nothing about him. Three days later I took the train to Vienna, and it never occurred to me that it might have been worth while to wait for a summons from Berchtesgaden.

THE INVASION OF AUSTRIA

I spent the winter of 1937 in sporadic wanderings, and when spring came I decided that Vienna was a wonderful jumping off point for further adventures. I reached Vienna from Paris on March 6, 1938. I did not know and could not guess that Hitler would come a few days later.

I found an apartment in the Johann Straussgasse owned by two young Jews, Willi and Gerda Sussmayer. They were both in their late twenties, but looked younger because they spent most of their free time skiing or playing tennis. The brother was an upholsterer, the girl worked as a secretary in an insurance business near the Ringstrasse, and they owned two or three apartments in the same building. I liked my new apartment with its heavy dark Austrian furniture and peasant embroideries hanging on the walls, and I liked my two landlords. Neither of them showed the slightest interest in politics. "In Vienna," Gerda said, "politics is a cesspool, and we can only remain sane by escaping from it altogether." I had the feeling that they lived only for the open air and regarded Vienna as a prison from which they could slip away every weekend.

I intended to keep the apartment for six months, perhaps longer. The books were unpacked, the empty traveling cases were stored away, an old desk of exactly the right size was found in an attic, and I was beginning to enjoy the feeling that comes when an apartment which was strange and unfamiliar a few days before begins to look as though one has inhabited it for many weeks. Gerda and Willi could not have been more helpful, and Vienna in those spring days could not have looked more beautiful.

On March 9, three days after I arrived in Vienna, Dr. Kurt von Schuschnigg, the Chancellor, announced that a plebiscite would be held four days later to decide whether Austria would be free and independent or whether it would become a satellite of Germany, for Hitler had claimed that the vast majority of Austrians wanted to join Germany. Since the vast majority of Austrians obviously did not want to become part of the Third Reich, Dr. Schuschnigg's announcement of a plebiscite was greeted without much fanfare. It was felt that he had reached a sensible decision and that the plebiscite would take place in an orderly fashion. In the outskirts of Vienna there had been some street fighting between Austrian Nazis and members of Schuschnigg's Fatherland Front, but these street fights had been going on for a long time. Trucks were arriving at the Hotel Bristol in the center of the city and unloading crates of propaganda posters and leaflets from Germany, while a small crowd of ardent Nazis applauded the arrival of each crate, but this too had been going on for some time. The atmosphere was calm. Willi Sussmayer was saying that there was simply nothing to prevent him from going off on his skiing holiday.

Nevertheless he did not go, putting off the journey from hour to hour. A new note of music could be heard, a high-pitched, scarcely audible note, which could not be written down in any known musical notation. At first it revealed itself in a vague uneasiness, like the first faint warnings of the coming storm. The lovers were wandering arm in arm in the Wienerwald, the shops in the Kärntnerstrasse were full of eager purchasers, the trams made their familiar clanging noise as they swept along the Mariahilferstrasse, the sun shone on all the flowering gardens, and all the time we had an obscure presentiment that something had gone terribly wrong. During the evenings especially we kept close to the radio.

As it happened, Willi Sussmayer's radio had broken down, and in the early evening of March 11 he was sitting with his sister and a few friends around the radio in my room. Suddenly, at 7:30 P.M., the announcer said that the Chancellor was about to address the Austrian people on a grave and urgent matter. Then there was a long pause while we gazed at one another uncomprehendingly, for though there might be many grave and urgent matters we could not guess which one the Chancellor had in mind. Then the voice of the Chancellor broke the silence, a deep and measured voice, yet lifeless, as though all emotion had been wrung from it, the voice of a man utterly exhausted and without hope. He announced that Hitler had issued an ultimatum to the Austrian government to dissolve itself and to permit the formation of a new government of National Socialists obedient to Hitler, and to Hitler alone. If the Chancellor refused to accept the ultimatum, then Hitler would throw the whole weight of the Wehrmacht against Austria. The Chancellor was talking slowly. as though he wanted more time, and still more time, to elucidate the unalterable complexities of the day. Hitler had been saying that Austria was in a state of anarchy, and the Chancellor replied: "I state before the world that the accounts that have been broadcast through Austria of trouble breaking out among the workers, of rivers of bloodshed, of a government no longer master of the situation and incapable of restoring order have been fabricated from A to Z." They were brave words, and they sealed his own fate. Finally he said: "I take leave of the Austrian people with a wish that springs from the heart: 'May God protect Austria.'"

We waited for a few moments, expecting the voice would go on, for much had been left unsaid, many problems remained unexplored. We knew him as a rather severe, totally humorless, unglamorous man, a scholar of political science rather than a politician, whose chief comfort was his Catholic faith. Everything he said was unexpected, but even more unexpected was his dignity. The Austrian national anthem was being played slowly like a funeral march, while we all gazed at the radio, which resembled a small coffin lying on the velvet tablecloth. In the silence Willi said: "This is the end!" and I could see his fists clenching and unclenching, his knuckles shining white.

Suddenly through the open windows there came a confused roar from the center of the city. We had not the least doubt what the roar signified: the triumph of the Nazis. I went out into the streets to find Vienna transformed. Already on the Johann Straussgasse three or four Nazi flags were flying, and as I went down to the Ringstrasse more and more flags came out. There was a wild excitement in people's faces: everyone had gone mad—with fear or with triumph—and this madness was somehow symbolized by the blood-red curtains of flags, for at the heart of the city the flags were everywhere. The peddlers who had been selling shoelaces a few hours ago were selling Nazi armbands. A few trucks full of shouting boys wearing armbands were racing along the streets; the same trucks kept returning, and they were evidently attempting to make us believe that there was a whole army of trucks. None of the boys carried guns. That would come later.

Outside the Opera three large megaphones like guns pointed at the crowds gathered below. From the megaphones came the eerie chanting of the "Horst Wessel," which was almost the Nazi national anthem. At intervals people shouted: *"Ein Reich, ein Volk, ein Führer,"* and sometimes the crowd fell silent, as though oppressed by a momentary fear.

In spite of the regimented shouting, there was much in the extraordinary excitement gripping the center of the city that was spontaneous. It was a tribute not to Hitler, but to the weeks of uncertainty that had now come to an end. From the very first everyone must have been dimly aware that a fight between Hitler and Schuschnigg could end only with the victory of the Führer. Now the weeks of uncertainty were over, and relief was written on nearly all the faces we saw in the Opern-Ring.

The roads were impassable. The whole of the square in front of the Opera was filled with people gazing up at the megaphones, from which news bulletins came at regular intervals. Men who had worn the ribbons of the Fatherland Front all day now wore Nazi badges in their lapels. A long line was forming outside the Hotel Bristol, where a large portrait of Hitler stood in the window of the travel bureau. There were heaps of flowers below the portrait, and people were gazing at it with that look of intense worship, fear and perplexity which is usually reserved for the contemplation of religious figures. In the middle of the crowd a pale-faced boy suddenly began to chant hysterically: *"Hitler ist hier!"* For the first time I saw mass conversion, in an atmosphere of relief and hysteria, taking place before my eyes.

Of course there was regimentation; of course the Nazis were under orders to fill the streets with boys wearing armbands to give the impression that the whole city was in their power. The revolutionary marshals were in the side streets directing the revolutionary traffic. Bakunin used to say: "You can't have a revolution until you capture the town hall." Now all the traffic seemed to be moving in the direction of the Chancellery, which was already in Nazi hands. Torches were being handed out by the marshals, who wore especially wide Nazi armbands, and gradually about a thousand boys and youths were formed into a column six abreast to march on the Chancellery. I joined the head of the column and marched with them, because there was no better way to see what was happening, but in fact I saw very little and watched myself becoming dazed and suffocated by the rhythm of the march and the pounding cries of "*Sieg Heil!*" and "*Ein Reich, ein Volk, ein Führer!*" The torches, too, helped one to enter a mindless trance, for with their golden flames and black curling smoke and fearful shadows, they created a strangely distorted world. Everything became gold and black, and the shadows and the flames raced up and down the buildings lining the way to the Chancellery.

This was the first of many triumphal marches through Vienna, and though it generated excitement, it also generated a curious sullen despair. Once the marchers reached the Chancellery, there was nothing more to do. I suspect that all triumphal marches end in the same way—the victorious soldiers break out of the parade and go home, wondering what all the excitement was about.

Willi and Gerda Sussmayer did not sleep that night. They had decisions to make—very weighty decisions. Exactly what those decisions were I did not know until later in the evening of the next day when they came to my room and said very quietly: "Of course there will be a pogrom. They are already arresting people, mostly Jews. We can't wait!" I thought they were talking about leaving Austria, and said something about how lucky they were to be good skiers—they could slip over the frontier on skis. Gerda was standing near the radio and looking at me fixedly. "It is not a question of escaping," she said.

"Then what is it?"

"It is a question of doing the best we can now—of showing that this masquerade must come to an end!"

Twenty-four hours had passed since Schuschnigg had admitted defeat. There was no masquerade: Vienna was firmly in the hands of the Nazis, and now they were armed. During the afternoon I watched trucks full of armed boys and youths rolling into Vienna from Steiermark and Carinthia to swell the number of Nazis in the center of the city. Later I had seen an automobile coming to a screeching halt outside a house in the Kärntnerstrasse, and four Stormtroopers poured out with their guns at the ready. One of them smashed in the door of the house with his boots, and then they all went into the house. Less than a minute later there came screams from upstairs. From the expressions of the passers-by it was easy to understand that it was not an unusual occurrence. On the plate-glass windows of the shops the letters "J.V." (*Jude, verrecke!*) appeared in blood-red paint. Immense gray Junker planes marked with the swastika were flying low overhead, proof, if any proof was needed, that German military power was being employed to terrorize the Austrians into submission. This was not a masquerade. This was the real thing.

"You can't possibly call it a masquerade," I said, "and it is not going to end."

"It will come to an end if we kill Hitler," Gerda said. "As for the masquerade—that is exactly what it is! He is bluffing all the time. The bluff works, because the politicians haven't got the guts to stand up to him. So we are going to kill him."

She spoke very quietly, very insistently, exactly as though she was saying: "We are going out for a walk."

"We have the guns," Willi said. "More than we need, probably. Would you like to see them?"

They were almost like children in their delight in showing off the guns, which had been smuggled into the house and concealed in the basement after the abortive uprising in 1934. There were Mausers, pistols, about twenty rifles, and three or four little Hungarian revolvers. They had been dug out of the basement during the morning and taken up to the apartment where Gerda and Willi lived. They were covered with grease, and there were small boxes of ammunition. I thought the rifles were useless—one could not possibly take a rifle out in the streets and shoot at Hitler when he came riding in triumph through Vienna—but I had considerable respect for the revolvers. While we were talking, four friends of Gerda and Willi appeared. They were members of the Fatherland Front, and also members of the ski circle, magnificently bronzed and fit. They were not Jewish, and if you put a Nazi armband on any of them, he would be taken for a Nazi. The strange thing was that everyone spoke in a perfectly natural voice. There were some loose floorboards in my apartment, and it was decided that the guns would nestle very nicely under the floorboards, which were then covered by a carpet.

If the Nazis came to examine the apartment, it was unlikely that they would pay very much attention to my room.

The new newspapers came out blazoned with eagles and swastikas, the megaphones shrilly announced that the German army was pouring over the frontier, and more and more trucks filled with shouting boys drove wildly through the center of the city. Willi and Gerda were both completely fearless, but they did not leave the house. They spent most of the day on the telephone, talking in the strange language that everyone seemed to have invented simultaneously, believing that the telephone exchange was not yet full of Nazi eavesdroppers, and indeed they had good reason to believe that for a few more days Austria would still be in the hands of the old, tolerant and rather muddle-headed officials. There were, for example, very few Nazis at the railroad stations and many people on the Nazi death lists were able to slip out of the country without too much difficulty. Once Hitler arrived, the terror would begin in earnest.

The Johann Straussgasse was one of those long wide residential streets inhabited largely by doctors, lawyers, small-business men and retired officials. Although quite close to the Ringstrasse, it was a quiet street, and no boys with Nazi armbands came marching along it and certainly there were no trucks full of shouting youths waving the Nazi flag. In this quiet backwater Willi and Gerda quietly planned to kill Hitler, and they were not alone. There must have been twenty people involved in the conspiracy. Meanwhile they pored over maps, listened to the radio, and interminably discussed the best way of shooting him as he stood in his Mercedes-Benz during his triumphal progress through Vienna, for they had not the least doubt that he would offer himself as a target. "And if we kill him, that will be the end of the whole rotten Nazi swindle," Gerda said. "The whole edifice will come crashing down, because he controls everything. He is an Austrian, and he will meet his fate in Austria."

On the day before Hitler entered Vienna, the new Nazi government issued a decree that any unauthorized person found in possession of guns would be shot without trial. Neither Willi nor Gerda was disturbed by the decree: they had their small armory of guns, they could fight it out, and they did not really expect to survive the attack on Hitler, although they had made careful plans for escaping over the Italian frontier. They did not in the least resemble storybook conspirators; they were quite non-chalant and went about their affairs as though there had been no invasion of Austria, as though Hitler was a fly that had to be swatted and would soon be a thing of the past.

That day the Nazis began their house-to-house search for guns. At one o'clock in the morning Gerda heard on the telephone that Frau Goerdeler was coming for the washing. This meant that the search had already begun on the Johann Straussgasse and that we would probably have to do something about the guns. Someone went up on the roof and reported that there were Stormtroopers *at both ends of the street.* There were eight of us sitting around my bedroom, discussing what could be done. We decided to leave the house, taking the guns with us. It was a dark night, and we thought we would take the street facing the house, another long street that led to the Ostbahnhof. We slipped out of the house one by one, but we had not gone far when we saw an army truck coming slowly along the street facing the house, and we assumed there were Stormtroopers in it. There was a telephone box nearby. I was carrying two rifles under my greatcoat and there were four revolvers in my pockets. It was an unusually large telephone box, and I laid the rifles down on the ground with the revolvers. Gerda and Willi did the same, and so did two or three of the others. The telephone box was an ideal hiding place for the weapons, for no one was likely to go there during the night, and we intended to retrieve the guns later. Two of Gerda's friends simply wandered off into the night with their guns, reached their own homes without any trouble, and telephoned the next day to say that they had come to the conclusion that nothing could be done because the streets where Hitler would make his triumphal progress were already filled with soldiers. Meanwhile we returned to the house, while one of Gerda's friends kept watch from the roof. Just before dawn I strolled across the road to the telephone box. All the guns had vanished. There was a light frost on the ground, but there was no sign of any footsteps.

In this ghostly fashion Gerda's conspiracy against Hitler came to its miserable end, and she turned her attention to other matters: she had excellent connections, warned people when they were in danger, organized a courier service and arranged, with the help of some railroad officials, to lead a party of skiers across the frontier. That afternoon from a perch on a lamppost I saw Hitler parading along the Ringstrasse. He looked curiously small in the huge Mercedes-Benz, and seemed to be in a state of delirium, for he made strange fluttering salutes and his head jerked spasmodically from side to side, so that he resembled a marionette on a string. He did not in the least resemble the man who had offered me a strawberry cake.

John Lehmann, the editor of *New Writing*, had been living in Vienna for some time. He knew everybody, and he too spent many hours sitting at his telephone listening post. He had the look of a young proconsul, very debonair, wearing fashionable clothes and giving the impression that he was at ease in polite society and uneasy elsewhere. In fact he was playing the role of the Scarlet Pimpernel. We met once or twice a day in his apartment or at Sacher's Coffeehouse: he had compiled a long list of people who were in hiding and needed to be rescued, and was bitterly annoyed because the English had done so little, while the French had already rescued Madame Dollfuss, the widow of the Austrian Chancellor who had been murdered by the Nazis in 1934. They had put her in a car, covered her with a blanket, and rammed through the frontier post at Bratislava at seventy miles an hour. The French were issuing false passports, and it seemed possible that the British consulate might be induced to do the same. I called the consulate and asked a consular officer for a dozen blank passports for the most urgent humanitarian reasons. His face turned red, then scarlet, then magenta, then purple, and then he let out a great bellow of indignation and his hand leaped for the telephone. "I am going to call the chief of police!" he roared. "I am going to have you arrested!" The dark hairs on the back on his hand were quivering, and his whole body was shaking. I marched off to see the consul and was told in tones of icy disdain that English passports were reserved for Englishmen.

"But the French have been giving passports to people who are in mortal danger," I protested.

"The French are messing up everything!" he replied. "They are absolutely lawless! They don't know what they are doing!"

I reported my failure to the Scarlet Pimpernel. We were sitting in Sacher's Coffeehouse calmly discussing how we could rescue the people on his list when we noticed that a German colonel

in full uniform was sitting at the next table. We were talking in
a kind of code, but it was not a very good code. When we looked
up, the German colonel smiled, waved his gloved hand, and said:
"In Vienna everybody is very happy." We continued our discussion in the street.

The Scarlet Pimpernel's sympathies were divided between the
Fatherland Front and the Communists. Ilse Schott, the head of
the Communist Youth League, was in hiding and had to be
spirited out of the country as quickly as possible. "I'm told that
she is pretty, sensible and level-headed," the Scarlet Pimpernel
said. "You could take her out as your wife."

The plan gradually took shape. Two days later Ilse Schott
appeared at the apartment on the Johann Straussgasse, and for
once I learned that the Scarlet Pimpernel's sources of information were defective. She was small and dumpy, wore large spectacles with thick lenses, and was exhausted and frightened. She
spoke English well, which was an advantage, but she was terrified out of her wits and obviously not in the mood for making
a difficult and dangerous journey. She had brought a passport
photograph, and I stuck this on the square on my passport
reserved for a wife. Gerda, who was in touch with the railway-
men, arranged for the first class sleeping compartment to Paris.

Neither of us slept that night as the train roared across Austria.
For a while I tried to read *The Magic Mountain*, which I had
borrowed from the English Library on the Ringstrasse the day
before. For some reason she hated the book, and in her shrill
voice she announced that Thomas Mann was "an enemy of the
working class." I said the Nazis hated the book, too, and there
must be some merit in a book which is hated by both the Communists and the Nazis.

"Please don't read it," she said. "If they see you reading it,
they will arrest us!"

She was very pale, and there was a strange twitching around
the corners of her mouth.

"Please throw the book away, please get rid of it," she said
an hour later. "You don't want them to see us with it!"

It was impossible to argue with her. The book had become
a focus for all her anxieties. I asked what she had to fear, since
she was an Englishwoman traveling on an English passport, and
what more likely than that her husband should be reading an

English novel, or at least a German novel in an English translation. She would have none of it: the book must go. At any
moment the German inspectors would enter the compartment
and examine us, and when they saw the book they would become suspicious.

"Please do me a favor, please throw it away," she pleaded.
"Throw it out of the window!"

Because it was fruitless to argue with her and because she was
growing more nervous every minute, I pulled up the window
and threw the book out of the train. The pages opened out like
a white fan, catching the light from a neighboring compartment,
hovering briefly and then passing out of sight, sucked into the
darkness of the Austrian night. She seemed relieved, and for a
while she sat very quiet in her corner, and there was no more
clasping and unclasping of her hands.

After this she decided it would be better to turn out all the
lights and pretend to sleep, though she was sure she would not
sleep. But when we had put out the lights there remained a little
green gas jet overhead, and as the night wore on and our eyes
grew more accustomed to the ghostly green glow, it was as
though we were sitting in broad daylight. Someone once told me
there was a way of putting out the small gas flame on con-
tinental trains, and I spent some time trying to find the secret
switch that permitted one to sleep in darkness. The roaring of the
train was beginning to dull my senses, and though I searched
everywhere I could not find it.

For half the night she sat bolt upright with her hands on her
lap, gazing straight ahead. She was absolutely certain she would
be arrested, and very probably we would both be arrested. I
thought she was being unreasonable, for we had a very good
chance of reaching the Swiss frontier unharmed. I thought every
moment was bringing us closer to freedom, while she was convinced that every moment was bringing her closer to arrest.
"You don't know them, you don't know them!" she said, and I
knew that she meant the Stormtroopers.

We rehearsed what must happen if the Stormtroopers entered
the compartment. She must behave like a quiet, submissive and
loving wife, saying nothing whatsoever, under no conditions ut-
tering a word in German, and showing not the least sign of
nervousness. She must be casual, happy, and self-assured. All

Stormtroopers, by definition, possessed a sixth sense which enabled them to smell fear, and we must not permit them to smell fear. The crucial moment would come when they looked at the passport, and at that moment she should be very busy looking out of the window or rummaging through her luggage. I was being a heavy-handed schoolmaster, but this was the only way I knew to stem her rising hysteria.

As the night wore on, the hysteria became more and more palpable, resembling a silver fireball ricocheting around the compartment, gradually fading, then glowing again in some totally unexpected quarter high above the luggage rack or underneath the seats, and sometimes it seemed to be outside the train altogether. She had given birth to it, and now it seemed to possess an independent life. Until the dawn came up, this fireball of hysteria was a familiar companion.

She told me a little about her life, the words coming in whispered rushes. She was the daughter of a Viennese doctor, the eldest of seven children. At the age of fifteen she joined the Communist Party and in the following year she cut off all ties with her family. She had not seen them since then and had not the slightest interest in them; her family was the party. Year by year, as the result of hard work and a natural gift for organization, she had risen higher in the party hierarchy, and now at the age of twenty-two or twenty-three she was an associate member of the Central Committee of the Austrian Communist Party. She had visited Moscow and attended a reception given by Stalin. She was high on the Nazi blacklist, "somewhere near the top," and she could expect no mercy if they found her. The overwhelming event in her life was the 1934 uprising against Dollfuss. She had been one of those who fought in the Karl Marx Hof against Dollfuss' soldiers, and when that huge fortress-like apartment house was captured, she escaped through the cellars.

"And you went on fighting?"

"No, I went to Russia. That was when I met Stalin. I had a long holiday by the Black Sea and then I came back to Vienna."

A first-class compartment in an Austrian train smells of leather, linseed oil and fresh timber, and the entire design is calculated to suggest a quietly luxurious refinement. The Vienna-Zurich express was a superbly civilized train, and certainly I had never traveled in greater comfort. She did not think very highly of it, saying that the Russian trains were far more comfortable. You had to travel on the Moscow-Black Sea express to know the meaning of real luxury.

By three o'clock in the morning we were both in a strange state of exhaustion and torpor, drowsy and wide-awake, alert to all the sounds in the corridor. Whenever a door opened, whenever anyone walked along the corridor to the lavatory, we were instantly watchful, instantly aware of any unusual sounds, like animals who sleep with their ears cocked. She was still quivering, still terrified, when at last she lay down full length in her bunk and drew the sheets and blanket over her, fully dressed. She was still wearing her spectacles which glowed like little green discs in the light of the little gas flame. From time to time she asked questions: "Is the door properly closed?" or "When do we reach Switzerland?" She spoke in a queer unaccented English which somehow sounded like a foreign language.

The train roared and rattled through the Arlberg tunnel, and then we knew we were coming close to the frontier. When we came out of the tunnel, there were the first streaks of daylight, and soon the tops of the mountains turned yellow as crocuses and then a soft waxy white. Dawn was hurrying down the slopes of the mountains, cocks were crowing, peasants were at work in the shadowed fields, and the raw morning air filled the compartment, where the little green gas jet was still burning. I looked at the passport again, with the photograph of the girl neatly stuck to the place where it said: "Picture of Wife. Et de sa Femme." In the upper bunk she was groaning a little.

"Is it all right?" she said, and once again there was that same desperate nervousness in her voice.

"Yes, it is perfectly all right. For God's sake just stay there, and don't say anything!"

The light was thickening, and the gray shadows in the fields became people glowing with color from the dazzling light flowing down the mountains. I had parted the heavy curtains over the windows and was reveling in the clean mountain air, but she wanted the comfort of the darkness.

"Please close the curtains," she whimpered. "It's too bright."

I closed the curtains and wondered what in the world had led me to believe that Vienna was a place where I could usefully

spend a large part of my life. Obviously I had chosen it because
it lies at the geographical center of Europe, and was therefore
the logical jumping-off point for exploring the continent. What
puzzled me was that I had arrived at this conclusion so logically,
for I was not a creature of logic. Vienna was not my home, I had
no roots there, and though I spoke German and read it with some
facility, I heartily detested the language and had no particular
feeling for German or Austrian civilization. In Vienna I would
always be a stranger and a foreigner. Then what was I doing with
this absurd Viennese wife on my passport? It was the morning
of March 18, 1938, and far from spending the rest of my life
there, I was a refugee from Austria after only twelve days in the
country.

The train came to a sudden jolting stop at Feldkirch on the
Austrian frontier. The customs officials climbed onto the train,
and for a long time the train just stood there, puffing steam, while
workmen went up and down the line with their hammers, knocking on the wheels. It was one of the longest waits I had ever
known, but it could not have been more than ten minutes. I said:
"They will be coming soon. Remember what you have to do.
Just stay there in the bunk, don't say anything—above all, don't
say anything—and everything will be all right."

She said nothing, only a kind of thin nervous scream of
despair, and I could see her body moving under the heavy brown
blanket.

At last there came heavy footsteps down the corridor. The
customs and passport inspectors were making their way slowly
down the corridor followed by German police officers wearing
Nazi armbands. The customs and passport inspections were pro-
tracted, and the officials must have spent five minutes in the
first sleeping compartment and another five minutes in the second. Meanwhile the train with much clanking of axles and blowing of steam whistles was making its way to Buchs, just inside
the Swiss frontier. Suddenly it was dawn at its brightest, the
mountains gleaming white, the whole landscape glowing in a
crystalline light. We saw clean snow-swept villages, and children
in red woolen caps were waving to us.

We occupied the fifth compartment on the sleeper, and we
wondered how much longer it would be before we encountered
the full force of customs, passport and police. Evidently the

people in the other sleepers were being examined: there was a good deal of cursing, groaning, buffeting, and the sound of luggage being torn apart. Finally it was our turn, and we knew we were in for a rough time. The customs inspector tore into our luggage as though he were a famished wolf who expected to find meat, while the passport inspector held the passport to the light and growled that something was wrong—irremediably wrong—and went on to discuss his findings with the two German policemen in the corridor, who entered the compartment shouting: "*Schwein! Schwein!*" at the top of their lungs. They had heavy, lumpish faces, and were obviously enjoying themselves. They pulled the girl off her bed, set her down near the window, and one of them said the words I somehow never expected to hear from them. "Ilse Schott," he said.

In the long silence that followed, the girl slowly nodded her head, and there was on her face the expression of someone who is very weary but nevertheless looks eagerly toward martyrdom. I tried to explain that my wife was tired and unnerved by the long journey, and would they please leave us alone. Instead they pushed us out into the corridor, stuck guns in our backs, and spoke about what they were going to do with us. Suddenly the train made a sudden lurch and came to a halt, and the words *Buchs* swung across the window and then vanished. A little fat Swiss policeman with a Hitler mustache swung onto the train and stood in our path.

"What are you doing?" he barked at the Germans.

"We have just arrested these two swine!"

"You should have thought of it earlier," the Swiss said. "You are two hundred meters inside Swiss territory."

The Austrian passport inspector returned my passport with a bow, the customs inspector scowled, and the Germans cursed with the thick curses which are only possible in German.

We went back to the sleeper and continued our journey to Paris.

THE ARTISTS

In Paris the chestnut trees were still in flower, and nothing had changed. The tricolor flew over the Senate and the Palais Bourbon, and the crowds along the Boulevard St. Germain looked as though they had not a care in the world. Friends who had been sitting at the marble-topped tables of the Deux Magots two weeks before were still sitting there over glasses of beer—the same glasses, the same beer. Austria had fallen, and for them it was as though some obscure nameless oasis in the Sahara had sunk beneath the sands.

The overwhelming fact was that among my relatives and acquaintances the fate of Austria was a matter of absolutely no importance. When I visited my French cousins, I was told that Austria had always belonged to the German community and if it wished to be absorbed by Germany that was a matter to be decided by Germany and Austria alone without the intervention of other powers. They were rather proud of non-intervention. Non-intervention was working very satisfactorily in Spain, and no doubt it would work equally satisfactorily elsewhere. They hoped the serpent would take a long time to digest its prey, and then, softened by Austrian humanism, it would abandon any further conquests.

One of my cousins, Victor Constant, was president of the Municipal Council of Paris. He was a small, florid, well-meaning man with beady eyes and a huge paunch, who had once been a wine merchant in Le Puy. He entered politics when he was quite young, but first came to prominence when, already middle-aged, he was elected to parliament for Montmartre. It was a strange enough choice, for he had a thick southern accent that was not always intelligible to the Parisians. They said he was a good member of parliament, kept open house, listened to all complaints, helped the poor out of his own pocket, and fought hard to give Montmartre its proper place in the sun. At some point on the political ladder he encountered Pierre Laval and thereafter they were thick as thieves. Laval had twice been prime minister of France, and though he was now out of office, he was still a power to be reckoned with.

Victor Constant, mayor of Paris, sat in an enormous gilded chair at an enormous gilded table. His small chin jutted out a little, for he was very sure of himself and of his power, and he obviously enjoyed his gilded cage. Documents appeared on the table, he glanced at them, scratched a signature, and watched them being wafted away by frock-coated attendants who fluttered silently around him, like black butterflies.

"So you were in Vienna during the Anschluss? What was it like?"

I told him, while he signed documents and whispered to a *huissier*. All the time he was smiling benevolently.

"You speak of a rape, *mon cher cousin*, whereas the newspapers have reported that the Austrians welcomed Herr Hitler with delirious enthusiasm. Films, photographs, everything predisposes me to believe that the Anschluss was carried out in the most orderly fashion possible. You say the Austrians were terrorized into accepting Herr Hitler, whereas it is my belief that they welcomed him with open arms. For myself, I attach absolutely no significance to the Anschluss."

"None at all?"

"No, because it alters nothing. The balance of power remains exactly where it was before. The Austrians and Germans are allies, they have always been allies, they fought side by side in the Great War, and therefore Herr Hitler has gained nothing he did not already possess. France has nothing to fear from the German Reich."

My cousin rarely spoke with such breathless certainty, and I was a little puzzled. The airplanes flying low over Vienna, the tanks moving over the mountain passes, the display of massive concentrated force, and the terror in the streets, none of these left the slightest impression on him. All he remembered were the faces of the people welcoming Hitler into Austria, as they appeared in newspaper photographs and in the newsreels.

Because he was a kindly man and because I looked dejected, my cousin stopped signing the documents which were pouring onto his table and explained the political situation at some length.

Above all, there was nothing to fear. Secure behind the Maginot line, France stood as the guarantor of the peace of Europe. Hitler's energies were being exhausted by internal problems. His speeches were intended for internal consumption only. The French government and Hitler were well aware of each other's power—"*Ils s'entendaient bien*,"—and of course there were understandings, necessarily secret, between the two countries. He himself had known that the German army would enter Austria a week before it happened. The greatest danger arose when people panicked. It was necessary to judge Herr Hitler calmly, in the perspective of world politics. The Germans had their legitimate spheres of influence; so had the French; and the moment the Germans stepped across their legitimate boundaries, there would be trouble, but that moment was not likely to arise, since Herr Hitler was a realist.

"I think you would be well-advised to leave politics to the politicians," he said, when I objected that Genghiz Khan also had his legitimate spheres of influence. "The important thing is to understand the complexity of the situation, and this can only be done by the politicians. Have no fear. *On s'arrangera*—everything will be arranged!"

I think it was at this moment that I realized the Second World War was inevitable.

My cousin was a man who had spent his life "arranging" things, and no doubt he believed sincerely that it would always be possible to arrive at accommodations with Hitler. *On s'arrangera*, those words which he regarded as the key to all the insistent political problems of the time, were precisely the words that filled me with the greatest despair, and I left his office with the feeling that he knew as little as I did about the mysterious forces at work, which were inevitably drawing us into war.

Since Vienna was no longer habitable, I decided to remain in Paris and found an apartment in the Avenue de l'Observatoire, next door to the Closerie de Lilas, the restaurant where André Gide, Guillaume Apollinaire, Jean Cocteau and innumerable other writers and poets congregated before the First World War. What especially delighted me was the view from the eighth-floor apartment, looking down over the Luxembourg Gardens, all misty green during the long hot summer, and the silvery white dome of the Panthéon floating just outside the window.

This was my corner of Paris, for I had spent a good deal of my youth living with cousins in the Rue Madame, not a stone's throw away. The Luxembourg Gardens with their dusty pathways, rain-speckled statues of the queens of France and marionette shows had been my garden ever since I could remember. I knew the baker's shop on the Rue de Fleurus, the post office on the Rue de Vaugirard, and the windows full of painted religious gewgaws on the Place St. Sulpice with a sense of intimacy, and I could have walked blindfold through those streets smelling of fresh bread and faded incense. But I had never lived so high up, with such a spectacular view of the roofs of Paris. Vienna was a nightmare to be forgotten, and I was home again.

One day in April Herbert Read arrived in Paris. He was a Yorkshireman, the son of a farmer, with a face of weathered granite, slow in speech, with a gift of quietness and gentleness. He had written an autobiography, *The Innocent Eye*, and a short novel, *The Green Child*, which I regarded with awe, because he had wedded poetry to the most accomplished prose written for a generation. He was a poet, a literary critic, an authority on art, an expert on industrial design, and there was a beautiful wholeness and consistency about all his works. He was in a carefree mood, with four or five leisurely days in front of him. We sat at one of the tables outside the Coupole and watched the world go by.

Fame had touched him, but left him unspoiled. He was as pleased as a child when a passer-by recognized him, the face lighting up, the bell-like laughter pouring out of him. Young poets approached him with their poems, artists showed him their portfolios and invited him to their studios, art collectors would ask him what painter to buy. He especially enjoyed the company of the young and was quietly attentive to pretty girls.

At that time I knew very little about the world of art. I was taking lessons in sculpture at an art school in the Rue de la Vieille Chaumière, but without any notable success. A young Italian woman, golden-skinned and full-breasted, stood on a wooden dais in what appeared to be a state of catalepsy, while about fifteen students gazed at her with expressions of disbelief and bewilderment, for her very beauty made it difficult to render her in soft clay. The mechanics of sculpture were simple; the difficulty was to give to the clay figure the spark of life. We measured her, studied her from all angles, pirouetting around the modeling stand, advancing and retreating, but though we all made creditable figures fifteen inches high, there was not one that conveyed the excitement of her flesh. Even those of us who had never sculpted before turned out to be good craftsmen, and we all knew that it was not enough to be a good craftsman.

Herbert Read came to the art school to admire our work and our clay-spotted smocks. He thought there was a good deal to be said for the gregarious young artists and for a lifetime spent in the calm contemplation of the naked human figure, but wondered why we were not more adventurous like his friends Henry Moore and Barbara Hepworth. I explained that we might become more adventurous if we had a long-necked, bony, tubercular girl to model from. Our model was so perfectly proportioned that we were reduced to making three-dimensional photographs of her in clay, hating ourselves because we could not reproduce the golden glow of her flesh.

We were sitting outside the Coupole, basking in the sun and talking about the great art critics, the people who really knew about art, and he thought they could be counted on the fingers of one hand. In his view the greatest living critic was a little-known German refugee from Munich called Max Raphael, who had written brilliantly about Cézanne, Picasso, Doric temples and prehistoric paintings. If anyone was capable of hammering out a new aesthetic, it would be this obscure middle-aged man who was living in poverty. Herbert Read had the magician's touch, for he had scarcely mentioned the name when Max Raphael came hurrying along the Boulevard Montparnasse.

Max Raphael was a small man, almost a dwarf, with a heavy nose, a small mouth, and soft dark eyes. The precocious nose gave him something of the aspect of a long-billed South American bird, and there was something birdlike in his walk. His clothes were threadbare, and he spoke French with a heavy Germanic accent, but fastidiously, for he was well aware of the resources of the language. Beside Herbert Read, ruggedly handsome, calm and soft-spoken, with the manners of a mediaeval prince, Max Raphael looked like a red-faced peasant, ungainly and ill-at-ease, without any natural grace. But when he smiled, or when his powerful mind was set in motion, you became aware of an extraordinary presence. A sovereign intelligence

ruled. He was, or seemed to be, in total command of the world
of art.

During the following weeks I saw him nearly every day. He
lived in a small one-room apartment in one of the narrow streets
off the Boulevard Montparnasse. There was a bed, a bamboo
bookcase, a high desk for reading and writing, and a rickety
kitchen chair for the benefit of occasional visitors. There were
some postcards tacked to the bare whitewashed wall. They were
portraits of Flaubert, Baudelaire and Rimbaud, and there was
also a postcard photograph of a Gallo-Roman bronze head he had
seen in the museum at Lyons. To my astonishment, the bronze
head represented the tutelary goddess of Vienne, where my
mother was born. Max Raphael said it was the noblest head he
had ever seen, a distillation of all that was most beautiful in
Greece, Rome and France.

"Understand, penetrate!"

He liked to say these words often, for this was the creed by
which he lived. Works of art deserved to be studied minutely,
all the resources of scholarship should be brought to bear on
them, and it was necessary to know all that was knowable about
the social climate from which they had evolved. It was not
enough simply to study them in the light of contemporary style:
one must know the intentions of the artist, the artistic style of
the period, the debts that were being repaid. Thus the study of
a single etching by Rembrandt might involve a prolonged study
of the technique of etching, the religious life of Amsterdam, the
social forces working on the artist, the state of his bank account,
the state of his personal life, and what he owed to his collection
of etchings by other artists. The dignity of a work of art demanded that men should devote themselves to its elucidation
with relentless scholarship. Only after these studies were completed was it possible to penetrate into the heart of the mystery.

I went with him to the Louvre where he stood for half an hour
in front of Le Nain's painting of a peasant family, while he
probed, measured, analyzed, commenting on all those aspects of
the painting which I had failed to see. Sometimes it was heavy
going, for he had the German gift for intricate analysis, and
he delighted in running a theory past all its proper limits.
He liked to measure, and when he wrote his book on the Doric

Temple he very carefully measured the temples of Paestum and Agrigentum.

"You measured to the very last centimeter?" I asked.

"No, the very last millimeter," he replied. "Millimeters are important."

Long training had given him insights into art which went far beyond scholarship. The voice trembled, the long nose twitched with excitement, and his eyes glittered when he came upon a painting or a piece of sculpture that especially delighted him. It was as though a work of art imprisoned him and he had to fight his way out. At an exhibition of Cézanne's paintings he became a mass of quivering nerves which seemed to caress the paintings until they had revealed their secrets. He saw Cézanne's paintings of Mont St. Victoire as heroic adventures: a man was creating a mountain even more solid, more massive and more convincing than the mountain made by God.

We went to the studio of the sculptor Henri Laurens, filled with huge plaster casts of females with contorted tubular bodies, the sculptor moving among his statues with the air of a monk let loose in an engine room, and indeed his sculptures resembled engines, and Laurens himself was always surprised by his inven- tions. He had a long face of grave beauty, and limped heavily. Max Raphael talked—endlessly and brilliantly, relating the forms to the sculptures of Romanesque cathedrals and the works of the Renaissance. Three hours later, when the art critic had finished his exposition of the sculptor's works, Henri Laurens bowed politely and said: "Thank you, Max, for explaining to me what I am doing," and there was not the least trace of irony in his voice.

Jacob Epstein came to Paris with his plump, red-headed wife. An hour after he stepped off the train, he was sitting at the Coupole at the table next to Herbert Read. Many years had passed since he had been in Paris, and he looked around him with an expression of happy bewilderment. He had been over-working in London and had come to Paris for a rest, and was blissfully aware that there would be no rest. He had enormous hands, thickly veined and very powerful, with thumbs as large as a girl's hand, and soon he was breaking up pieces of bread and molding them into strange shapes, gargoyles and humped serpents and winged dragons. If there had been no bread, he would have made the same shapes out of handkerchiefs or tablecloths.

Epstein looked like a workman, rough-hewn, jowly, sure of himself. He had a workman's heavy walk, and he would shoulder his way through a crowd like an elephant shouldering its way through a teak forest. I used to think that his body and his intelligence were no more than the necessary scaffolding for the enormous hands and the prominent, slightly bulbous eyes. Fame had left no mark on him, unless it was to make him more self-assured, more certain of his powers; and when he growled at the hooligans who periodically defaced his statues with red paint, he did so with a kind of pained bewilderment, asking himself what he had done to offend them.

When he was young, he had lived in poverty in Paris. Modigliani was his close friend; they shared their last crusts together, and together they went out to the cafes to sell their drawings, usually with little success. Once a rich American tossed a franc to Modigliani for a drawing. The franc rolled under the tables, Modigliani went scrambling after it, someone thought it was amusing to kick him, and he came up with a bleeding forehead and a gash under his eye.

"Nowadays they tell you that Modigliani spent his time chasing women and drinking himself to death," Epstein said, "but it is not true. He was a sober dedicated artist, totally devoted to his art. Only he starved a great deal, and when you have had no food, a single glass of wine has a terrible effect on you. They said he took hashish, but he never did. As for women, he was very faithful to the woman he lived with, and had to fight off the women who were clamoring for him. He was the most handsome, generous, kindly, brilliantly gifted man I ever knew, and he had to die like a rat in the gutter."

"You know, it is not right to say he was unknown at the time of his death. He was very famous in the quartier, everyone knew he was a genius and that his works would one day be in the world's museums. But to give him enough money to live on— that was something else. They gave him a great funeral and about a thousand people followed him to his grave. The police thought it was the funeral of a very distinguished man and they saluted smartly."

Jacob Epstein came to Paris to rest, to bask in the sun, to

make leisurely visits to the museums. He told himself he would not work at all, and within forty-eight hours he had hired a beautiful young Negress to pose for him and was working twelve hours a day on his drawings, which he regarded as just as important as his sculptures. About all his drawings there was a curious heaviness, for he was essentially a sculptor working in masses and volumes with little feeling for line, and his drawings were sculptural. "Everything becomes sculpture in my mind," he said, and so it was. Even music became sculpture. One day while we were dining in a restaurant, some music coming over the radio startled him into immobility and after a while he began to draw on the back of a menu strange shapes and contours dictated by the music of Beethoven, saying that a certain relation of shapes that had tormented him for many years had at last become clear. When he looked at his sculptures he could remember the music that created them.

I was still working at the art school and thought it would be useful to have his opinion of my sculptures, which now included a portrait bust of the Italian model as well as the small nude figure. Normally voluble, he was very quiet as he surveyed all the figures standing so proudly on the modeling stands of twelve or fifteen students, all eager for his advice and especially for his commendation.

"I think you are all very good," he said, and then paused. "Good technicians, but not sculptors. You are all modeling from outside, but the sculptor models from within. A sculpture explodes. I see no explosions."

My career as a sculptor came immediately to an end, for his judgment was deserved. The other students went on modeling, but I tossed my two lumps of clay back into the clay box and never returned to the art school.

"You gave up very easily," he said, taunting.

"I'll never be able to make clay explode."

Epstein laughed, but since I was obviously downcast he proposed that I should accompany him through the Paris museums. The first museum we visited was the Musée Guimet, where the oriental sculptures, nearly all of them from French Indo-China, made him drunk. When he looked at a statue, he set himself solidly in front of it, legs apart and arms akimbo, his eyes opening wide as though they were mouths, and his tongue pushing against his cheeks, as though in some mysterious way he was recreating the statue in himself. The heavy, jowly face grew younger, and the blood rushed to his forehead. "They knew, no one knew better, how to release the power within the stone," he said, and he waved his arms, rolled his head, looked round the statue, pushed out his lips, went into all manner of mild contortions, and finally turned away with a look that was at once ecstatic delight and intolerable regret. "One should look deep within the statue," he said, "for the greater sculptor does not merely portray the skin. Deep, deep within the stone, where the power lies." I learned from him that "the greater sculptor" is not concerned with the outward appearance; he is concerned with the energy within.

While the Cambodian statues especially intoxicated him, some of the Indian bronzes produced the same effect on him. I knew how much he admired them by his sadness when he left them.

One day we went to see Rodin's Burghers of Calais, which had been set down in the open air near the Trocadero. It was raining, and the statues gleamed. In this dreariness, under the gray skies, the Burghers acquired a grave and unexpected dignity. He had not liked them before. Now, seeing them within arm's reach, solemn as music, he found himself kneeling in the mud to see what they would look like on a high plinth and pronounced them perfect.

We took shelter from the rain in a cafe, and a newsboy came by, chanting the headlines. It was another speech by Hitler. Epstein groaned and said: "Do you know what happens to sculptures in a war? They are all melted down to make guns."

So the days passed among sculptures and paintings, and sometimes but very rarely I worked on my books. A young Russian, Benjamin Goriely, helped me to revise my translations of Pasternak's short stories. Goriely means "burning," and a kind of incandescent melancholy had long ago settled on his features. He seemed to know all the Russian exiles in Paris, and one day he suggested that I should call on Marina Tsvetaeva, whom he regarded as the greatest of Russian poets.

I read her poems and marveled, for they possessed a sculptural quality and that "power within" that Epstein proclaimed as the sole test of "the greater sculptor." There were three great Russian poets—Pasternak, Anna Akhmatova and Marina

Tsvetaeva. No one could say one was greater than another, for they shared a towering eminence. They were lyrical poets, their roots in the nineteenth century, although their sensibilities were profoundly of our own time. All three were intensely distrusted by Stalin's government because they were incapable of writing odes in honor of Stalin. They were major poets in the sense that Rainer Maria Rilke, Paul Valéry and William Butler Yeats were major poets, but they lived in fear of the dictatorship. Some of the fierce energy of their poetry derived from the crushing atmosphere of fear in which they lived.

No sooner had Benjamin Goriely suggested that I should call on Marina Tsvetaeva than difficulties began to arise. She would see no one, she was living apart from the Russian community, a mysterious tragedy had taken place, she was being followed by the police, she wanted desperately to see people, she had shut herself up in her apartment like a nun, she was about to leave for Russia, she was in hiding, she was not in hiding. Almost daily there came bulletins from Benjamin Goriely announcing some new phase of her activities. I did not know then that her husband, Sergey Ephron, was one of Stalin's secret agents implicated in several murders including the murder of Trotsky's son. When Benjamin Goriely said: "She is being watched by the police," I assumed that he was merely giving way to conspiratorial enthusiasm. It was absurd that a major poet should be watched by the police.

A week, two weeks passed, and finally he announced that everything had been arranged. She was living in an apartment on the Boulevard Pasteur. At precisely four o'clock, not a minute sooner or a minute later, I was to knock five times on the door and say aloud, but not too loud: "The Holy Trinity." Then the door would open and she would be standing there in a white dress.

"This is stretching conspiracy a little too much," I objected.

"This is how it must be," he replied. "There is no other way. You must be there at exactly four o'clock and knock five times, otherwise she will not see you."

"What if I am delayed in the Métro?"

"You had better go by taxi."

Everything happened exactly as he said it would happen. The door opened, a woman in a white dress appeared, and I entered a small bare room largely occupied by a white bed. The shutters were closed, and a solitary electric lamp hung from the ceiling. On the bed a boy was kneeling. He was about sixteen, thick-boned, and fat, with a startling pallor. He looked terrified, but so too did the woman in the white dress, who did not in the least resemble the picture I had formed of her. She had a raw bony face, deep sunken eyes, heavy lips and straggling hair. She smoked incessantly, inhaling deeply until the smoke had settled in her lungs and then exhaling very slowly, as though she wanted to conserve the energy of the smoke within her. On the table there were the remnants of a meal: crumbs, an open sardine tin, two dirty plates.

It seemed incredible to me that she should be living in this small drab one-room apartment. She was speaking in short, jagged sentences, and what she said during these first moments was totally incomprehensible, chiefly because she was talking simultaneously to me and to the boy, who was still kneeling on the bed, panic-stricken.

"You don't have to pay any attention to him," she was saying. "He does not know how to behave—no manners at all! I've brought him up badly, it's my fault, but I cannot go on apologizing for his behavior."

I spent only five minutes in the apartment, for she suddenly announced that it was far too dangerous to talk there. Although it was a hot summer day she put on a heavy fur coat and we went out in the street, leaving the boy behind. There was a park nearby where a few children were playing. In the park her manner changed, she felt free, there was no more danger, no one was listening. I had the impression that she saw people very rarely, and now the words came out in a flood. She talked about poetry, "the kingdom of poetry," into which all could enter at will, and there were no signs saying: "Do not walk on the grass" and "Everything is forbidden." On the contrary, everything was permitted in the kingdom of poetry to those who came with open hands. In this kingdom there were no prisons, no executioners, no executions, for no one died in it. A man might seem to die, and he would lie quiet on the earth for a little while and then walk away.

I mentioned Pasternak, and her manner changed. Previously she had spoken in an exalted way; now she became grave, even reverent. She imitated his famous deep-throated voice, and even succeeded in imitating his appearance, his long face which gave him a strange resemblance to a thoroughbred horse. She recited his poems, and then repeated them in his voice, a slow, precise and incantatory voice that throbbed with energy and pain, the voice of a man deeply concerned with the world's suffering. It was as though she had summoned her beloved Pasternak out of the air and was happy in his company. She was laughing merrily, the years dropped away and she was young again.

Because I had translated Pasternak's poems, I became a friend to be trusted. Suddenly she said: "I have a terrible problem. Should I go back to Russia? Tell me what to do! You must help me!" Since I knew nothing about the real situation, I could only say that Russia seemed terribly dangerous. "You are telling me not to go back?" she said. "No," I replied, "I am saying only that Russia is terribly dangerous." She stood very still under the dusty plane trees and said: "Russia is only another word for danger."

When at last we walked back to the apartment, she reminded me of someone going to an execution. There remained for her the small room, the boy in the bed, the empty sardine tin. The air of doom, hysteria and quiet determination seemed to grow more menacing with every step toward the apartment. From time to time she looked over her shoulder to see whether she was being followed.

Whenever I mentioned her name, the Russian exiles in Paris who had most reason to admire her spoke of her scornfully. She was a poet, of course, and much may be excused in a poet, but she was insanely difficult, opinionated, and hysterical. Though she carried a Soviet passport, the Soviets distrusted her; the White Russians regarded her as a spy; some mysterious tragedy enveloped her and caused her to be shunned.

Her poetry, too, was uncompromising and terrifying: it did not lull the reader to sleep. Here is part of a poem she wrote in 1921, when Lenin still hoped to bring about a world revolution under Russian leadership:

> —In the name of the Lord!
> In the name of Reason!—
> What a festering sore we are!
> What a leprous canker we are!

Gleaming like wolves' eyes
Through the fur of the snowstorm,
The Star of Russia
Against the whole world!

Many years later I learned that the mysterious tragedy that afflicted her was a very simple one: she already knew, or guessed, that her husband had been killed on the orders of Stalin. A few months later she returned to Russia, hoping to make a living by her translations. In 1941 she hanged herself. Pasternak called her "the purest poet of our time."

No one could have been more different from Marina Tsvetaeva than the painter Jean Lurçat. He was rich, famous, well-liked by everyone. Tall and handsome, with an aquiline nose and the air of a *grand seigneur*, he regarded his success as the natural consequence of his talents. He had an adoring wife, a young son, a large house in a fashionable part of Paris, and he was doing exactly what he wanted to do. He was drawing cartoons for the Gobelins factory, and these drawings on thin sheets of paper were transformed into glowing tapestries, which were instantly recognizable as his work, so that it was scarcely necessary for him to add his signature. He would draw a phoenix in a nest of curling flames, and the finished tapestry, richly colored, was a work of splendor. He reveled in his talents, rejoicing in the lightning speed of his brush and pencil. Marina Tsvetaeva found no comfort in her genius and every poem came out of her like an agonizing birth.

Jean Lurçat was my political whetstone. I had gone to Austria without any political convictions, and it was now necessary to possess at least some rudimentary convictions. Jean Lurçat decided to educate me. He had been to Russia, and he had seen the future. He would say quite dispassionately, as though it was a matter beyond dispute: "Stalin is the only political genius of our time. Study him, study his writings, go to Russia. A new world is being created." In his vast study hung with his tapestries, he delivered a lecture on manifest destiny: the manifest destiny that Soviet Communism would inherit the world. Had I read the Webbs' book *Soviet Communism?* Had I read the official transcript of the trials of Bukharin and all the other traitors who had quite properly been put to death by Stalin?

Lurçat was elegant and immaculately tailored, his gold rings flashed, his beautiful hands made arabesques, he pranced about the room, and all the time he was marshaling an intricate array of arguments to prove that Stalin was the most democratic of rulers, the one man chosen by history to lead the world to salvation. The trouble about his arguments was that they resembled his tapestries, being richly colored, elegant, inventive, and totally unrelated to life. Those tapestries could only be hung in a rich man's room.

Occasionally we argued furiously. I was not convinced that the Webbs' *Soviet Communism* told the whole story, for the book said precious little about labor camps and the activities of the secret police. I read the official transcript of the trials and was sure they had been scrupulously edited to favor whatever case Stalin wanted to bring against his adversaries. The evidence was loaded, and the men in the dock were doomed before the trial began. "On the contrary," he said, "Stalin gave them the benefit of every doubt. The trial was scrupulously fair, and in addition it is a psychological document of extraordinary importance. One might be reading Dostoyevsky—"

"Or one might not?" I suggested. "One might be reading Racine's *Britannicus*, where everyone gets slaughtered for the wrong reasons."

"No, *mon cher*, you are wrong. In Russia one gets slaughtered for the right—for the proletarian—for the appropriate Marxist reasons."

The elegant game of political argument was interrupted with games of tennis. Lurçat's wife, a Rumanian woman of great beauty, was making a life-size sculpture of their nine-year-old son. It was a wonderful sculpture, filled with warmth and inner life, and therefore unlike her husband's decorative tapestries. I admired the beauty of the wife and the intellectual agility of the husband, but most of all I admired the statue as I watched it grow under her hands. Jean Lurçat had a theory that sculpture was a minor art, and that only in painting could an artist achieve the greatest heights. His wife said nothing, but continued to sculpt. She had heard his arguments so often that they no longer dazzled her.

The long summer of 1938 seemed to possess the quality of an

endless enchantment, as though summer had come to stay and no winter would follow. The women wore light dresses, the skies were a deep purple-blue, the flowers in the Luxembourg Gardens were sheets of glowing color around the marble statues of the queens of France. There was the illusion that nothing whatsoever would happen to dispel the atmosphere of peace. Occasionally Hitler spoke on the radio, and the earth trembled. Even Jean Lurçat believed in the formula: *"On s'arrangera."* We went to see the celebrations on July 14: the French tanks rumbled through the streets, the spahis in their red robes rode their sleek horses past the grandstand where the President of France took the salute, and that night the sky blossomed with a thousand fireworks. We were assured that there was not the slightest danger of war. France possessed the most powerful army in the world and stood impregnable behind her frontiers.

One evening at Jean Lurçat's house I heard myself saying: "What happens if the formula does not work? What if it was not intended to work? What if everyone goes mad? What if everyone is already mad?"

Jean Lurçat was appalled, for he had expected better things from his pupil. The world was rational: the traditional interests of nations remained unchanged: all problems, even the purges in Russia and the civil war in Spain, must ultimately submit to Cartesian logic. He began to talk about the civil war at great length, demonstrating that it had come about from the most logical reasons and would inevitably end with the victory of the Republican forces for the same logical reasons. It was a brilliant *tour de force,* illustrated with examples from Roman and French history: no one had ever displayed so convincingly the logic of history. He brought out maps of Spain to reinforce the arguments already established by pure reason. In his mind the civil war was already over: the people had triumphed, as they must always triumph, and it only remained to mop up the remnants of Franco's army.

"If you don't believe me, go to Spain and see for yourself," he said.

"How on earth does one go to Spain?"

"It is the simplest thing in the world. You have only to telephone the Spanish ambassador."

I was not accustomed to telephoning ambassadors.

"If you like, I will telephone him for you. I know him very well. You can have a visa tomorrow and be in Barcelona the next day."

He was as good as his word. He telephoned the ambassador, and there was no trouble in getting the visa. I went to London, met the editor of the *News Chronicle,* and learned that the newspaper had no correspondent in Barcelona. Would they let me be their correspondent? They would. As Jean Lurçat said, everything had become simple, logical and inevitable. But in Spain I learned that nothing was simple, logical and inevitable except defeat.

A STREET IN BARCELONA

The little single-engined L.A.P.E. airplane which took off from Toulouse airfield one day toward the end of July looked as though it had been put together with a few sheets of plywood, some ropes and sticking plaster. It had a strange bulbous shape, creaked merrily, and sometimes quite unaccountably made a prolonged tinkling sound like the bell of an alarm clock in slow motion. There were rents in the fabric, and the windows were cloudy and fly-spotted, so that one had to look round the fly-spots to see the strange landscape, like clotted milk, beyond. Decidedly it was not an airplane that inspired confidence.

One does not fly off to a war without a proper accompaniment of delays, ironies, and jubilations. The day was bright and warm, with a soft white haze curling off the grass. Someone had decided that the Spanish Republican airplane should be placed in a very obscure and distant part of the airfield, with the result that workmen would emerge from distant buildings low on the horizon and move toward us through the summer haze looking like insects. The mechanic, who was also the pilot, was stripped to the waist and most of the upper part of his body and all his face were covered with black grease. He said his name was Miguel, and we would be leaving soon, and not to worry.

Two hours later he was still working on the engine, and by this time the complete complement of four passengers had arrived, inspected the airplane, pronounced that it obviously would never fly, and sat down contentedly in the shade of the wings. One was a Mexican diplomat so fat that he would obviously require two seats, another was a saturnine attaché from the Spanish Republican embassy in Paris, and the third was a woman of about forty with red hair and high cheekbones who must once have been a dazzling beauty. She said she was the wife of one of the foreign aviators flying for the Spanish Republic. Of the four of us she was the most nervous about the airplane, perhaps because she knew more about them. From time to time Miguel would appear among us and explain in rapid Spanish that we would be off in a few minutes. The red-haired woman smiled charmingly, and Miguel asked her whether she would have dinner with him that night in Barcelona.

"They don't have anything to eat in Barcelona," she said, and again there was the slow mocking smile.

Jean Lurçat had given me explicit instructions: Take as much canned food, chocolate bars, and packets of Gauloises as you can carry. Take a revolver, if you like. It may come in useful. Also stockings, bolts of cloth, and women's underwear—they, too, might be useful. What puzzled me was how he knew, for he had not been to Spain. His advice was sensible, and all these things except a revolver were in my duffel bag.

I arrived at the airfield before noon, and around four o'clock Miguel announced that he was ready to go, but for some reason the navigator had not arrived. Simultaneously the French police ordered us to remove all our luggage from the airplane. There were arguments with the police, with much flaying of arms, and suddenly our luggage was thrown into the airplane, we were taxiing along the edge of the field, and a few moments later we flew over the foothills of the Pyrenees and the bright afternoon sun had contracted into bluish-white stains on the fly-spotted windows.

One question which absorbed us was whether the airplane, which resembled nothing so much as a lumbering farmcart even when it was airborne, would be able to climb over the Pyrenees. Another question, which we scarcely admitted to ourselves, was whether we would be shot down by Franco's airplanes once we were in Spain. We were very slow, very vulnerable, and very fragile. The airplane was unarmed, and apparently followed a more or less regular schedule: Franco's airmen could play with us as they pleased. Coughing and spluttering, the flying farmcart barely scraped over a pass in the Pyrenees, where the ice had melted on the iron-black slopes, while above us the white peaks glittered and swayed deliriously. Soon the Pyrenees fell away, and there were only a few fleecy clouds in the distance. This saddened us, for clouds are useful hiding places. Below us lay the reddish earth of Catalonia, the neat farms, groves of olive trees, beached fishing vessels, winding roads with no traffic on them, the quiet landscape slumbering in the summer sun.

All the way to Barcelona it was the same quietness and peace. There was not a single factory chimney belching smoke, not a single automobile on the road, no horses working in the fields. Sometimes in later years, flying in the Far East, I would find myself looking down on a landscape that seemed to be caught up in a dreaming stillness with no visible signs of life, seemingly flourishing without the aid of human hands, and so it was in Catalonia. Even when we flew into the airfield at Prat de Llobregat, taxiing up to a small shed, there was no sign of life, and there were no other airplanes in sight. Finally a small man emerged from the shed, smiled, shouted something to Miguel, clambered onto the airplane, examined our passports, and welcomed us with grave courtesy to Spain. The red-haired woman ran down the steps, shook out her hair, and laughed. A small Citroën came out of nowhere, and five minutes later we were on our way to Barcelona.

The Hotel Majestic on the Paseo de Gracia was built at the turn of the century when it was fashionable to build marble stairways and to decorate ballrooms with marble columns. The enormous picture windows, looking out on the tree-shaded street, were crisscrossed with white paper in a rather pathetic effort to prevent splinters of glass from killing everybody in the hotel if a bomb fell nearby. Otherwise the hotel looked exactly as it must have looked before the war. One could imagine an elderly duchess coming up to Barcelona from her country estate for a week of shopping and installing herself quite comfortably in this residential hotel. The old frock-coated receptionist would greet her with exquisite politeness, and he would himself accompany her to her suite. In those days the clock with the gilded angels over the stairway was still working. It was not working any more.

The Hotel Majestic possessed a faded grandeur, unlike the Ritz Hotel, a few blocks away, which proclaimed its contemporary magnificence and elegance. In the Majestic lived the foreign correspondents, although there was also a scattering of less amiable people—munitions salesmen, adventurers, perhaps spies. At the Ritz lived the diplomats, the fancy ladies, the wives and mistresses of the aviators flying for the Republic, and André

Malraux with his entourage of film-makers, for he was making a film based on his novel *L'Espoir*.

During nearly all the days I spent in Spain my home was a small room on the third floor of the Hotel Majestic. It was not much larger than a storage closet, but it had a wonderful view over the Paseo de Gracia. Nothing worked in the room, neither the electric light nor the telephone nor the bell for summoning the maid. It was a monk's cell, and therefore perfect for someone who hoped to be a war correspondent. I dumped my duffel bag, and walked downstairs. The first person I met was Louis Fischer, dark and saturnine, with a shock of thick black hair, and the rolling gait of a buccaneer. Jean Lurçat had sent him a telegram about my coming, and he was prepared to act the role of the friendly schoolmaster gently initiating me into the higher mathematics of bombardments and revolutions.

It was growing dark, candles were being stuck into wine bottles, and the public rooms downstairs gleamed with endless processions of flames in the reflecting mirrors. Already the hotel was assuming the look of a conspirators' lair. Huge shadows wandered across the ceiling, the waiters laid out the soup plates, the telephone on the reception clerk's desk was constantly ringing, and Louis Fischer was talking about his latest interview with Dr. Negrín, the President of the Republic. He was far more than a journalist: he was a manipulator of power, an *éminence grise,* all the more shadowy because he presented himself as a stocky, down-to-earth journalist. Lenin had written about "the mysterious beginnings of war." Louis Fischer was in love with mysteries. He was engrossed by secret treaties, secret understandings, secret journeys. In half an hour he painted a picture of Europe like a vast spider web with half a dozen spiders maneuvering for positions of vantage. He had met all the spiders and taken their measure.

Louis Fischer stood out from the other journalists and enjoyed his position of eminence. No one else had succeeded in interviewing Dr. Negrín, or was on such intimate terms with Alvarez del Vayo, the foreign minister. Even if he had never collected prime ministers and foreign ministers we would have been in awe of him, for he spoke with absolute authority.

Dinner consisted of little pieces of squid floating in a watery soup followed by some dried fish. There were bread cobs which tasted of sawdust and bottles of sweet Catalan wine. Coffee consisted of distilled wood shavings and horse chestnuts. The white-gloved waiters served these offerings with perfect aplomb, as though we all belonged to the minor nobility and deserved the most considerate service.

By nine o'clock we had finished dinner, and there was a trembling in the air. Without being told, everyone knew there would be an air raid. Usually the people of Barcelona had twenty minutes' warning before the Italian airplanes from Majorca flew over the city, while on moonlight nights they simply assumed that the airplanes would come without warning and took the proper precautions. The chief precaution was to avoid the area of the docks. People hid in cellars or in the *refugios* or went to the cinema to forget about the air raid. Louis Fischer thought the safest place was the open street. "I am damned if I am going to be crushed under a lot of beams," he said. "You should have a look at the port. There's nothing left, nothing but sunken ships and twisted derricks, but the ships keep on coming and the life of the port goes on."

Ten minutes later the searchlights came up over the port, sweeping in great arcs across the sky, hovering on the edge of a cloud, then moving rapidly in search of the airplanes coming from the east. When the searchlights finally caught the six silver Savoia-Marchettis flying in close formation, you had the impression that the airplanes had deliberately placed themselves in the center of the searchlights. The anti-aircraft guns were out of action. Like silver insects, the airplanes wandered across the sky, dipped their wings, as though saluting the city, and then veered sharply over the port area and dropped their bombs. There came a grinding hollow roar, a shuddering of the earth, a rending of the fibers, a sound so unearthly that it seemed to come from some unknown and never-to-be-comprehended source within the body or within the brain, and in the shock waves all the leaves of the trees in the Paseo de Gracia began to tremble and flash in the moonlight, as though there had been a snowfall. The bombs had fallen perhaps a mile away, but the whole city seemed to be shuddering in a cataleptic trance while the airplanes wheeled again and once more dropped their bombs.

"Your first bombing?" Louis Fischer asked.

"Yes."

"You'll get used to it."

"I'm damned if I'll ever get used to it."

"Yes, you will. In the end one gets used to everything, even this incredible war where nothing has happened according to the textbooks."

He seemed oddly amused, far away, lost in his thoughts. For a few more seconds the street was deserted, and then we saw people running in the shadows, heard cries, and listened to the strange shivering sound of the leaves as they trembled in another shock wave. Always after a bombardment there was the shivering of the leaves.

Louis Fischer went on talking about the nature of the war, the forces that made wars inevitable, the conspiratorial energies of man let loose to confound all human impulses, and all the time he was talking in abstractions, while I wondered what was abstract about bombs and watched the leaves slowly falling and fluttering on a midsummer night. From far away we heard the screaming of the ambulances, and ten minutes later there came the all clear.

When we returned to the Hotel Majestic, most of the correspondents were sitting at the tables in the dining room, strangely quiet. There was Boleslavskaya, the correspondent of *Pravda*, with her red hair piled high, her round plump face shining like an overripe fruit in the candlelight, and it was only when you came quite close to her that you observed the depths and intelligence in her green eyes. There was Herbert Matthews, the correspondent of the New York *Times*, tall and lean, resembling a professor on his sabbatical, so well-dressed, so American, that he seemed to belong to another world. There was Sefton Delmer, the correspondent of the London *Daily Express*, with his round cherubic face and eyes full of mischief, wearing tweeds as though he was on holiday. He had been the *Daily Express* correspondent in Berlin and was on fairly intimate terms with Hitler and Goering. Georges Soria of the French Communist newspaper *L'Humanité*, short and wiry, had the appearance of a wily fox and the intelligence of a professor at the Sorbonne. Marthe Huysmans, sleek and elegant, was the reporter of a left-wing Belgian newspaper. One could imagine her marching into battle, but one could also imagine her supervising a tea party in a town house in Brussels or Antwerp. She had enormous eyes which lit with fire and excitement whenever she was aroused by the agony of the war. Since she was nearly always aroused, her eyes continually gave off sparks, and it was easy to recognize her in the candlelit darkness.

That evening none of the correspondents went off to see the damage caused by the bombs. They had seen it so often before, and there was nothing to report. On the following day they learned from the newspaper *Vanguardia* that the port had been bombed and that twenty-one men, women and children had lost their lives.

All the correspondents were suffering from frustration. The Republican Army had crossed the Ebro and thrown back the much larger army of the enemy, but no one had yet been allowed to go to the front. There was not the least doubt that the Republicans had scored a great victory, but for some reason—perhaps the lack of transport or gasoline, or because the government was afraid that Franco would regroup his forces and throw back the Republican Army—the foreign correspondents were being told they would be allowed to go to the front only "when suitable arrangements had been made." Exactly what was meant by "suitable arrangements" was unknown. So they complained, made endless telephone calls to the Ministerio de la Guerra, visited hospitals, day schools and munitions factories, and wondered why so little was known about a victory which was certain but so far unrecorded except by military correspondents in the field.

The next morning I walked out into the blazing sunlight of Barcelona. The air was pure, the birds were singing, and the people were going about their affairs as though there was no war. The Paseo de Gracia wore an air of opulence. Fantastically beautiful baroque façades inlaid with seashells, plaster volutes and curling columns expressed the happy turbulence of the Catalan spirit. All the way down to the wide Plaza de Catalunya the sunlight poured through the trees, the butterflies hovered, the summer fragrance poured out of the sky. I wondered what had happened to the war. There was no traffic, no automobiles, no horses, only a few people, and most of them were old women or girls. The men had vanished from the world.

So it was everywhere in Barcelona: the men were at the front or in the factories. It had become a city of women and children, a few men with crutches, men with bandages, men with deep sunken eyes, hollow cheekbones and quivering mouths. You would go into a shop and discover that there was not a single male anywhere in sight. There were bookshops filled with women and girls poring over books in the Catalan language which had just come off the presses, for they smelled of fresh ink and fresh paper, but the rare men who entered the shops were like strangers. There were no dogs or cats: probably they had been eaten.

The Plaza de Catalunya was dominated by the Telefonica, which resembled a fortress. It had been fought over during the previous year by Communists, Trotskyists, anarchists and Catalan nationalists in a civil war within a civil war, and was scarred with bullet holes and shell holes, which had now weathered. The scars on the Telefonica seemed to have been cunningly arranged to form an appropriate decoration. Every lamppost had its bullet hole, every stone windowsill bore the scooped mark of a bullet. Barcelona was wearing its wounds proudly, and twenty years later, when I returned to the city, I recognized the same bullet holes, which no one had ever thought of mending.

In the Plaza de Catalunya there was a shoeshine boy with an eager face and dark glowing eyes. He was about ten years old, and wore long black trousers and a faded blue pullover. His shoes gleamed like diamonds. He cleaned my shoes until they shone with a spectacular radiance, and I paid him what he asked and added a tip for good measure. He flung the tip back at me, drew himself up to his full height, and said: "In the Republic no one accepts tips."

Beyond the Plaza de Catalunya was the Ramblas, a street as wide as the Paseo de Gracia, gay with flowers. Old women brooded over enormous bouquets, girls stopped to admire them, children played along the sidewalk, but no one bought the flowers. In the narrow side streets the washing hung on lines from every floor. Red blankets, pink chemises, green skirts, yellow blouses fluttered in the soft wind. I suspect that Cubism owed much to those broken shapes of color hanging in the narrow streets where Picasso walked in his youth. Those oval, olive-hued faces peering out of darkened doorways, these, too, I had seen before in Picasso's paintings.

In these streets humming like beehives, you saw houses that had been hit by bombs, sliced in two, an outer wall having collapsed, leaving chairs and beds exactly where they had been, the wallclocks still on the walls, the child's toy where he had left it, all the private possessions laid out obscenely for the benefit of every passer-by. In the summer of 1938 it was still possible to feel the enormity of the crime. You stood in front of these shattered houses, your heart racing, and you wondered how the world could possibly endure such an outrage and still survive.

In the Cathedral a bomb had crashed through the roof ten feet away from the high altar. Now a great glittering mound of rubble and broken glass lay at the foot of the altar, and the sun poured through the star-shaped hole in the roof. Banners, gray with dust and age, hung over the carved and painted stalls of long-dead Catalan knights. Here kings had prayed, and here Santa Eulalia, the patron saint of the Catalans, lay entombed. On the altar stood the crucifix which Don John of Austria had nailed to the prow of his ship at the battle of Lepanto. High up in a dark corner of the Cathedral there hung a blood-red Saracen's head with a heavy beard. It swayed gently in the wind coming from the broken roof.

I stayed for a while in the empty Cathedral, wondering how soon all the other Cathedrals in Europe would suffer the same fate, unable to take my eyes from the blood-red head which swayed so menacingly among the rafters, while the white doves flew through the empty windows and the mountain of rubble gleamed in the sunlight. On the Ebro front Franco's Moors panicked when the Republican Army passed over to the offensive. It was strange that Spaniards should still be fighting the Moors.

When I returned to the hotel, Jim Lardner was sitting quietly in the lobby, lost in some dream of his own. He had been a war correspondent for an American newspaper until he could no longer endure the role of a passive observer and joined the International Brigade. He had been wounded, and was now recuperating. He had a thin sensitive face, wore spectacles, and looked very frail and ghostly. On the previous evening I sat at table with him, but he seemed to be hovering somewhere in the remote distance, saying nothing and quietly observing.

"So what's new?" he said, and I told him what I had seen in a day's wandering around Barcelona.

"Will you file a report on what you have seen?" he asked.

"Probably not."

"Why not?"

"The *News Chronicle* probably isn't interested in the washing hanging in the lanes near the Ramblas."

He looked up sharply and said: "I wish to God they wouldn't write anything at all about Spain! I wish to God they would just go out and fight! What in hell is the good of writing in a time like this?"

"You don't want any reporters here?"

"No, just fighters. When you get to the front, you'll understand that. The future of everything—the whole world—depends on whether the Spanish Republican forces can sweep the Moors and the Italians and the Germans out of Spain, and there's only one way to get them out!"

His pallor and ghostliness seemed in some mysterious way to reinforce the passionate speech. During the following days he became a familiar presence, almost a Grand Inquisitor, warning us that civilization was a deadly peril and demanding that the reporters do their utmost to help the Spanish Republic. He was very quiet, very insistent, very determined. He was killed a few weeks later when he rejoined his battalion at the front.

The truth was that there was very little the war correspondents could do, because they were very rarely permitted to go to the front and their newspapers had lost interest in the war. For the French, the British and the Americans, the civil war in Spain resembled a bullfight. It had its moments of excitement, but did not seem to touch them deeply. From time to time they looked down from their seats on the grandstand at the magic circle of the bull ring, and they applauded the courage of the bull and the grace of the matadors.

I thought of Jim Lardner when I went to visit Antonio Machado, the greatest of Spanish poets, who was then living in a small house in the foothills of Tibidabo, the tortured mountain that rises above Barcelona. Here, according to the Catalan legend, Christ had stood with Satan and heard the words: "*Tibi dabo*—I shall give to you." The poet was sitting in a wild garden full of ferns and fruit trees. He was a heavy-set man, with heavy features, and he was leaning on a gnarled stick made from one of the broken branches. Although it was a very hot day, he wore a heavy overcoat.

"It is very simple," he said. "We must fight and win—there is nothing else. Spain cannot tolerate the shame of having German and Italian soldiers on our soil."

"And the Moors?" I asked.

"That is the shame of shames! No, we cannot tolerate this rape of our country! Everyone must help. One helps, I suppose, by writing poems, but bullets are better! Never in all her history has Spain suffered so much shame."

He spoke about his early years as a schoolteacher, about his first poems, and about the famous anthology of epigrams and meditations known as *Juan de Mairena*, but he always came back to Spain and the shame of the civil war. He was sixty-two, but looked much older. His younger brother, also a poet, kept a watchful eye on him, while a ten-year-old granddaughter with long thick pigtails and flashing eyes curled at his feet. Sometimes he looked like granite and sometimes he looked so frail that a puff of wind might have blown him over.

Many foreign universities had invited him to occupy their chairs of Spanish literature, but he refused to leave Spain. "I belong here," he said, digging the gnarled stick deeper into the soft earth of the garden. He said: "I understand now something I never understood before—that a young man will give his life happily for his country. Yes, he will give his life happily. He will run toward the enemy smiling and laughing."

I asked him to recite some of his more famous poems, and at first he refused, saying he was out of voice, and then that he could no longer remember them. Suddenly he threw back his head and began to chant a poem about the shame of the invasion, the voice quavering, the tears jerking down his worn cheeks, and he was waving the stick in the air to the beat of the poem.

In that wild garden, among the fruit trees, it was the voice of Spain singing.

MORA DE EBRO

On one of those brilliant blue days, the sky very high and the wind singing, we drove to the front in a truck with a spluttering engine, armed with official documents from the Ministerio de la Guerra. There were five correspondents, the driver, a guard, and Vicente Campos, the poet, who either came along for the ride or was in charge of us. We never discovered what his function was, and we never asked, because we were so happy to be with him. He told stories well, recited poetry at astonishing speed, and bounced about in the back of the truck like someone on holiday. He had a white skin and dark liquid eyes, and he had a way of raising his hand to emphasize a line of poetry or some statement about the war, and this gesture was accomplished so gracefully that we were always silent at such moments. He was a real poet, working under the protective eye of Antonio Machado, and we had read some of his poems in the last number of *Hora d'España*.

All the way from Barcelona there was that sharp blue crystalline light in the air, quick and fresh, and no sign of the war except for the occasional farm boys who sprang out of the shadows armed to the teeth, and the moment they appeared the truck would come to a lurching, grinding halt. Then there were shouts, greetings, clenched fists, embraces for Vicente Campos when he jumped down from the truck, advancing on them with a swinging stride, for usually the truck shot past them and he would have to walk back, and we would see the farm boys laughing and crowding round him. Then they would wave us on, and the poet would climb back into the truck, a little shame-faced, his cheeks flushed, conscious of his celebrity. We would learn later that everywhere he went in Republican Spain he would be greeted in the same way: these soldiers had a particular fondness for the poets who wrote their songs.

The strange thing was that there were no trucks, no cars, no horsemen, no columns of soldiers along the empty road. The Republicans had achieved a stunning victory, and you expected to see reinforcements streaming along the road to the south, but there was not even a staff car. From Barcelona to the Ebro all of Catalonia seemed to be given over to emptiness and solitude.

"But you ought to see this road at night," Vicente Campos said. "There are columns of trucks a mile long, bumper to bumper in the dark. Heavy trucks, armored trucks, every kind of truck—"

"Are you sure?"

"Why, of course. How do you think we keep supplying the Army of the Ebro? Everything comes to life at night."

Perhaps it did, but we were never completely convinced. Those columns of trucks a mile long seemed to exist in an agreeable limbo of the imagination, for we saw none of the telltale signs which would inevitably be left behind by huge convoys of trucks. The road was unspotted, and for twenty miles the only sign of the war was a two-seater airplane standing incongruously in the shade of some olive trees on the edge of an open field.

We told ourselves we were the first correspondents about to visit the victorious Army of the Ebro, but the war had vanished. From time to time Vicente Campos pointed out the sights—high up on those craggy hills was the Monastery of Montserrat where the monks guarded the golden chalice of the Last Supper. Or was it a silver chalice? It was a long time since he had been there, and he had long ago lost any interest in religion. "If you want to see it," he said, "we can stop on the way back. It's a terrible climb. Four thousand steps to the top of the mountain. People faint on the way up, and they have to be carried to the top by stretcher-bearers. They say that if you have made the journey to Montserrat, a thousand years in Purgatory is remitted to you."

"What happens if you make two journeys?" I asked, but Vicente Campos was already talking about the war—that war which was so vast, so distant, and so invisible.

We came to see the war much sooner than we expected. We were coming out on the plains when someone shouted "*Bombardeos!*" and pointed to two little silver specks streaking above the horizon. The truck lurched to a halt, and we all spilled out of it, for the horizon was uncomfortably close and it was inconceivable that the airplanes had not seen the truck with its huge squirrel's tail of yellow dust. The truck was the only moving thing in all that summer landscape, and the airplanes were coming straight toward us. We ran into a vineyard which must have been a mile long and threw ourselves down in the purple shade of the vines, untended for many months, the grapes black and small and wrinkled under the coating of dust. The stunted vines offered little shade, and we all tried to squeeze our bodies into the smallest possible shape, curling ourselves round the vines, until the brittle leaves and the sharp knotted branches bit into our skins. Some yards away Vicente Campos was making urgent, graceful movements with his hands, no doubt ordering me to keep my head down, but my head was caught in the branches, I was stuffing grapes into my mouth until the juice ran down my chin and over my shirt, and all the time I was looking at the airplanes. They were silvery Savoia-Marchettis, the same airplanes that had bombed Barcelona the previous night. We heard the drumming sound of machine guns, branches crackling, someone was shouting, the whole dusty expanse of the vineyard seemed to be tilting in the air, and we were no more than little rags of flesh knotted around the vines, scraping up earth with our fingernails. The shadows of the airplanes flew over us, and what struck me most was the sheer beauty of those airplanes with their slender fuselages and the glinting wings. They dived low, and seemed to be coming down into the vineyard, where they would certainly explode. A bomb fell about fifty yards away, obviously aimed at the truck, but it fell short. There was a dazzling black and brown explosion, more branches snapping, the truck vanishing from sight. Then the airplanes soared away, climbing rapidly, and we waited for a while, expecting them to return, but there was only the sky and the empty field.

Vicente Campos was contemptuous of the marksmanship of the Italian airmen.

"They could have got the truck!" he exclaimed. "Bombs and machine guns, and they missed every damned thing!"

He seemed annoyed that so much beautiful machinery had proved to be so ineffective.

We climbed back into the truck, well satisfied with our first strafing from the air. Half an hour later, when we were on our way to Mora de Ebro, I realized that I was stuck to the bench in the back of the truck. A bomb splinter had caught me in the buttock and the blood acted as a glue. There was also a trickle of blood from my right ear, and I was to learn later that the explosion of the bomb had cracked the eardrum. There was no pain, and I had not the slightest memory of being struck by the splinter.

When we reached the Ebro, the war still seemed far away. The brown and oily river flowed through deserted fields, calm in the afternoon sun. Suddenly the road turned, and in front of us was the small village of Mora de Ebro bombed into rubble, all black and green, with not a single house standing.

Vicente Campos had known Mora de Ebro before the war— one of those neat, composed, quiet villages clustered around a small church. Now there was no church, and you could not tell where the streets had been. Twisted iron bedsteads hung over heaps of charred brick, a woman's dress lay against a blackened chimney and part of the woman seemed to be in it. There was the sweet-sour smell of explosives. The village had been bombed the previous day and again during the morning. The Italians seem to have thought that it was strategically well-placed because it guarded the approaches to the old concrete bridge over the Ebro, but in fact it had no strategic importance whatsoever. The old concrete bridge was nothing but a tangled mass of wreckage which seemed to be lurching up from the river bed. Two hundred yards upstream the Republicans had built a wooden pontoon bridge, and though the enemy airplanes had attempted to bomb it out of existence, they had always missed it.

We stayed for a while in Mora de Ebro, trying to find out from the farm boys guarding the bridge where Juan Modesto, the commander of the Army of the Ebro, had set up his headquarters. There were anti-aircraft guns hidden in the ruins, and telephone wires crawled all over the rubble. The soldiers gave us red wine from their pigskins and showed us how to drink it, holding the pigskin high above the head and aiming the sprit of wine into the open gullet. After drinking, we gathered the small dusty grapes from the vineyards and sat in the rubble, waiting for Vicente Campos and the truck driver. I was wearing shorts, half red, half khaki, and there was some bawdy discussion about my blood-caked buttocks with the appropriate remarks about certain kinds of monkeys. I washed the blood away in the river, and as I came up the sun-warmed bank Vicente Campos was hurrying along the road.

"I have news for you," he said, "and I think you will like it."

"Have you found Modesto's headquarters?"

"Not that. I have started a poem. It's about you, or rather about *el parajito*." This was the name I had acquired because my hair stuck up on end, resembling a coxcomb. "It begins: 'The little bird has come to Spain, and is completely drunk with everything he sees.'"

I suggested that the next lines would be improved with some reference to *el parajito's* baboonlike tail.

"We may get to that later," he said, but he never did. In the course of time he completed five verses of the poem, it was set to music, and perhaps a few people sang it. Suddenly a young lieutenant emerged from nowhere to announce that they had finally succeeded in getting Modesto on the telephone.

"The road is clear," he said. "Clear all the way to Modesto." He spoke the name with obvious affection.

"Where is he?"

"Straight down. Just follow the road."

We crossed the long pontoon bridge, the wooden planks clanking, the landscape opening out on an immense valley stretching to the sierras. The sun shone hot on our faces and the valley smoldered in the heat. We drove along a dusty road, wondering at the emptiness and loneliness of the place where there had been fierce battles only a few days before, and there was no sign of battle. Here were the same dark withered vines, and the world was reduced to an emptiness of abandoned farmhouses under the shining sun.

The truck was chugging up a slope when we saw a red bluff with a man in an open neck shirt standing on it, silhouetted against the skyline. He stood there like a young landowner surveying his estates, and he looked so completely out of place that we had not the least doubt that this was Modesto or one of his lieutenants. Behind him stood a farmhouse and there were some farm workers digging in the red soil. When we saw these farm workers we realized that we had come to the headquarters of the Army of the Ebro, precisely because it was inconceivable that there would be any farm workers within twenty miles of the place. In that terrible summer all the farms of the Ebro valley were going to ruin.

The truck came to a halt, Vicente Campos tumbled out of it and went running up the red bluff, shouting: "Juanito! Juanito!" The words took our breath away. For us, Modesto was a legend, and beyond all familiarity. They were embracing and clapping each other on the back. Then we were all solemnly introduced to Modesto, who looked even less like a general when we were close to him. He wore a white shirt, khaki trousers, sandals, with no badges of rank. He was tall and well built with black hair streaming back from his forehead, his face deeply tanned. It was a powerful face, beautifully modeled, with a square jaw and high cheekbones; and there were powerful muscles around the mouth, and his eyes were very dark. But what was most noticeable about him was his air of casual authority. He smiled easily and well, and walked with a springlike motion, like a bullfighter. Three years ago he was a journeyman carpenter. Now at the age of thirty-two he was in command of an army of perhaps two hundred thousand men.

We assumed that the farmhouse was his headquarters and we were walking toward it when he said: "Here we are!" We were standing in the middle of a vineyard and we saw the entrance to the underground bunker, climbed down the steps, and found ourselves in a room perhaps ten feet long and six feet wide, most of the space being taken up by a plank table littered with maps and telephones. Very little light came into the bunker. There were candles stuck in bottles, and the grease from the candles had spread over the maps. Someone struck a match, lit the candles, and then we were blinded.

Modesto leaned over the table, pointing out one by one all the places captured from the enemy, the thrust of his forces, his fingers splaying out. On the night of July 24 the whole Army of the Ebro had swum across the Ebro or paddled across in fishing boats, taking the enemy by surprise, and within three days they captured eleven towns and some thirty villages and took six thousand prisoners. Over a sixty-mile front, from Mequinenza to Cherta, they captured all the heights, including the Sierra de Pandols. The booty in guns and ammunition was enormous, but

what seemed to please him most was that they had punished the
hated Moors, throwing them back in hopeless confusion. "They
were all crying: 'Allah! Allah!' and charging into one another,"
he said. "We thought they would be the toughest fighters of all,
but on a dark night they were all running away. We had sent
some agents behind their lines to scatter *chevaux-de-frise*—iron
balls with sharp spikes—and so they lost many of their horses.
On horseback a Moor believes he is invulnerable, but this time
he learned he was not invulnerable."

Modesto went on: "For weeks we had been bringing up Catalan fishing boats to the shores of the river. They came in carts
and trucks, until we had over two hundred of them hidden
away in the farmhouses and under canvas and under the trees.
We know they have spies on our side, and you cannot hide a
fishing boat easily, so we thought they must know what we were
up to. We have found their intelligence reports—they knew
nothing at all."

Surprise had been the main factor in the advance: surprise,
and the reckless courage of the attackers. Here and there the
Republican Army had been checked, but never for long. The
great bend of the Ebro had been cleared of Franco's troops.
It was like a battle in the textbooks, with the river bent like a
bow and the furthest advance of the Republican Army forming
a roughly straight straggling line. As he traced these battle
lines on the map, using the wine bottles to show where the
worst fighting had been, he resembled a young professor describing a battle which had taken place long ago.

Afterward we left the bunker and came up into the vineyard,
where the men we had thought were farm workers were really
unwinders of telegraph wire. Modesto sat down on the ground,
and we sat around him. He kept asking questions about Barcelona. What was it like there? What were people eating? What
was the bombing like? He talked about General Rojo, the chief
of staff, the man most responsible for the successful crossing of
the Ebro. "They don't make men like that any more," he said.
"What a man! He knows everything!"

Someone asked whether General Rojo had come to visit the
Army of the Ebro.

"No, he stays in Barcelona. At a time like this, you understand,
to stay at Barcelona is the real heroism. He has to depend on

reports. Here we can see what is happening with our own eyes. It is much easier at the front. The food is better. The atmosphere is better. You are not so easily frightened. I pity a man who has to stay at his desk in Barcelona."

I thought of General Rojo in his eighteenth-century office among the mirrors and the candelabras: so weary that he could scarcely keep his eyes open, and so courteous that he seemed to belong to an earlier age. Modesto belonged to the present: youthful and heroic, always underplaying his role, seemingly unconscious that he was already a legend. There must have been a lull in the fighting, for the whole countryside was quiet under the afternoon sun.

What was astonishing was the peace that had settled upon us. The war was over, or had never begun. There was only a small group of people sitting in a vineyard. The shuttered farmhouse was deserted, the soldiers unwinding the telegraph wires were silent, and the only sound came from the cooing of the doves or from a solitary dust-colored car going into high gear as it came up the slope past the red bluff. Sometimes in the distant hills there was the bright silver glint of a heliograph, as one company of troops signaled to another. The heat came beating up from the earth, the mountains trembled in the heat haze, and far off, skimming over the vines, making for the Sierra de Pandols were the little snub-nosed yellow fighter planes called *chatos*. When I said something about the quietness of the place, Modesto laughed and said: "We have to have time for sleep. We fight at night." Then for the first time I saw that his eyes were bloodshot.

Actually the silence was deceptive. Behind the green shutters of the farmhouse, behind the coils of barbed wire and the camouflage netting, behind the vineyards eternally stretching sunward, there was ceaseless activity. Sappers were burrowing into the earth, soldiers were cleaning guns, telegraph wires were humming, spies were sleeping but would soon make their way through the enemy lines, and their sleep was a form of violent activity, just as the recharging of batteries is a violent activity; and along the red roads of Catalonia the peasants were carrying their pots and pans to Barcelona, shuffling through the heavy dust, very slowly but with the power of pistons.

We were walking across the bluff looking at the *chatos* vanishing in the perfectly blue sky when a boy came up to Modesto, saluted and presented a report. The boy looked about fourteen, with a humorous mouth and a dark, sunburned face. Modesto said the boy had made a long journey through enemy lines and his report was full of information about enemy guns and airfields. The boy blushed fiercely as Modesto recited his feats of bravery and then went off in the direction of the farmhouse.

The shadows were falling, and we were all conscious, I think, that the day was already passing into history. This lull was only temporary; and the boy's happiness was only temporary. There was something insufferably oppressive in the harsh sunlight, in the absence of any traffic along the road, in the decaying vineyards, in the flashing river winding below, and in the burned green and black village of Mora de Ebro. The air was somehow exhilarating and oppressive at the same time; and the sun's heat struck through our flesh and bones.

Once Modesto had pointed to a burned-out farmhouse in the distance, saying the enemy had bombed it a week ago, diving again and again until they were satisfied that everything in it had been destroyed. Then from time to time they had bombed other farmhouses at random on the off chance that Modesto might be in one of them.

"We don't mind them bombing farmhouses," Modesto said. "There are no farmers. They have all been evacuated. We don't mind them bombing the pontoon bridge, because we can always repair it in seven or eight hours."

We were standing on the red bluff when we saw the three Savoia-Marchettis again. They came out of the sun and bombed the pontoon bridge from a height of four or five thousand feet, not daring to come lower because the anti-aircraft guns immediately opened fire. The strange screaming sound of the bombs falling on the river, like millions of strips of silk being torn to shreds, startled us, for we were accustomed to the low, grinding roar of bombs falling on the earth or on cities. Then, having unsuccessfully bombed the pontoon bridge for five minutes, they veered round and came straight toward us. We flung ourselves under the vines, Modesto vanished quick as lightning into his bunker. I had been talking with Vicente Campos about Rim-

baud, and while the bombs fell round us we shouted lines from
Rimbaud above the uproar:

> Oisive jeunesse
> A tout asservie,
> Par delicatesse
> J'ai perdu ma vie.

These and many more lines we shouted at one another, while
Georges Soria, the correspondent of *L'Humanité*, took photographs of us, saying afterward that we looked exalted, terrified,
and very happy, and all these simultaneously. He had a passion
for taking photographs during air raids and seemed to regard all
other photographs as scarcely worth taking.

Then the airplanes streaked away, vanishing over the hills,
having caused no damage to the pontoon bridge or to the farmhouse, but leaving small smoking craters in the vineyard, while
the darkening sky was smeared with hundreds of gray smudges
of smoke from the anti-aircraft shells. The high winds tore these
puffs of smoke apart, turning them into wings and horses' heads
and strange scribblings like the letters of an unknown alphabet.
Afterward—and this was a sound I never heard during the bombings in Barcelona—there came a beautiful rustling or a long-
drawn sighing, like the sound of the wind springing up in a
forest, and this came, I think, from the millions of little crumbs
of earth as they settled back again after being dislodged during
the explosions. It lasted for about half a minute, and then there
was silence again.

Just before sunset the whole Sierra de Pandols erupted into
flame.

This sharp-toothed mountain rose far away across the valley,
bleak and ominous at all hours of the day. By day the mountain
seemed to be made of burnished copper; in the evening light it
glowed with a rich purple color. As far as I could see during
the afternoon, there had been no movement on the mountain,
and indeed there were only the thin scorings of donkey paths
winding up the steep slopes. Suddenly the flames rose from the
crest, as though there was a volcanic explosion, and the whole
mountain turned reddish gold. We all wheeled round and
stared open-mouthed at this apparition which had appeared

so unexpectedly and so silently. The light of the flames stretched across miles of space and lit our faces, as we stood on the red bluff facing the dark valley already sinking deep into the night.

I could not imagine what could burn on the mountain, what the flames could feed on. About twenty seconds passed before we heard the heavy rumbling of the artillery barrage, and by this time the bright flashing of the flames was already darkening into smoke. Gleams of fire continued to erupt along the crest, but they died quickly. Yet the mountain seemed to be alive, shaking and crumbling before our eyes, and the pounding went on. It was growing darker, there was no moon, but the first stars were coming out. The thin flames scrawled across the mountain top were like the fringes of an immense black curtain which rose slowly until it filled half the sky. All round us the pigeons wheeled and moaned, confused in the shivering air.

Modesto vanished into the bunker. At the moment when he heard the distant detonations, he made a single leap down the eight steps. By the light of a candle stuck in a wine bottle, he studied the maps while the telephones rang, and sometimes they were answered by the staff officers by his side, and sometimes by Modesto. I was standing on the third stair. I heard Modesto's crisp, sharp voice: *"Bueno, camarada, bueno.* Hold on, hold on." His left hand held the telephone, his right moved across the map, pausing to pencil in a gun position, a redoubt, a defense-post high up near the top of the mountain. He was giving orders, but all the orders were the same. "Hold on a little longer, hold on through the night. Supplies will be coming up. Hold on."

There must have been six or seven telephones, and now they were all ringing at once, and he would pass from one to another lightly and easily, like a man long accustomed to listening to desperate cries for help, knowing that he could offer no alleviation of suffering to the men who were crouching in dugouts on the mountain, while the flames roared out of the sky and the red-hot shells exploded all round them. His face in the candlelight was like a mask.

I went out on the red bluff again and watched the mountain boiling with smoke, and now there were only a few startling gleams of fire, but the ragged ends of the smoke cloud were black arms stretching across the sky. The stars were brighter now, and the rumbling of each exploding shell seemed to grow more distinct as the night wore on.

And then suddenly, inexplicably, there was silence. After eighteen or nineteen minutes the barrage ceased as shockingly as it began. There were no more flames. The smoke cloud lifted itself off the mountain, the violet sky poured through, and the hidden stars came out again. Far away to the east a small fighter plane shot across the sky and made its way toward the mountains.

About five minutes later Modesto sent a message, inviting all of us down into the command post.

With the map in front of him he pointed out the positions of the German guns and the line across the Sierra de Pandols held by the Republican troops. There had been some losses during the barrage, but the lines were holding. "They have tried hitting us there for a week, but our lines have been maintained," he said. A young Spanish correspondent said: "How many heavy guns have they got?"

"Eighty-four," Modesto answered.

"How many have we got?"

"Three."

The three guns came from warships which had proclaimed their loyalty to the Republic.

"Is that bad?"

"Yes, it's bad. They're bringing up more and more guns, and more bombers. More and more."

His voice trailed away. The telephone rang again. This time it was Barcelona with some question about supplies, and when this was over someone asked what would be the official communiqué for the day. He grinned and said: "Along the Ebro front all quiet." High up on the Sierra de Pandols the Moors and Foreign Legionaries were being fought back by the weary and battered Republicans.

It was dark now, and there was some talk of where we should eat and where we should put up for the night. There were more telephone calls, this time to the headquarters of Enrique Lister, who shared with Modesto the command of the Army of the Ebro. We heard that we had been invited to dine with Lister, then that the invitation had been rescinded, and then again that there would be a banquet to celebrate that we were the first correspondents to have crossed the Ebro. Then we heard that there would be no banquet, and that there would only be a brief interview. All these bits of information and rumor came to us as we stood round Modesto's dugout in the middle of the vineyard. Finally, we clambered onto the truck and made for Lister's headquarters, inching along a dark road with headlights no more than faint blue slits. We were climbing toward the Sierra de Pandols. In the faint starlight we could make out the flickering blue roofs of the trucks crossing the pontoon bridge in the distance.

We crawled along the road for about three miles and then turned down a narrow path leading to a large farmhouse sheltered by a spur of the hills. The farmhouse gleamed in the starlight. Cedar trees stood in front, and there were guards everywhere. Here every approach was guarded, booby-trapped and defended, unlike the red bluff where Modesto had his headquarters. It was a large, well-built farmhouse, built around a courtyard. For us, it was a fantastic courtyard because against all the rules of probability it was brightly lit with kerosene lamps, and was open to the sky. Along one side of the courtyard there was a long table covered with a snow-white tablecloth.

We were blinded when we entered the courtyard after an hour of peering cautiously into the thick murkiness of a sunken road. Lister was there, his back turned toward us: a huge, heavy, fleshy back. He was in shirtsleeves, and he must have heard the sound of the truck, and he knew we were coming, but he was quite properly paying no attention to us, immersed in some problem of his own. Then, very slowly, one hand on his knee, the other on his revolver holster, he turned around, and there was something so deliberate and studied in the gesture that we felt like applauding.

Lister belonged to legend and to history. Men spoke of his cruelty and his friendliness, his absolute contempt for danger and his incredible daring. They said that when the Montaña barracks in Madrid was attacked in July 1936, Lister was among the first to reach the balcony around the inner courtyard and from there he threw at least four Fascist officers into the courtyard so forcefully that their skulls cracked open and their brains splashed on the cobblestones. He was half-lion, half-bear, and I pitied anyone who quarreled with him.

You could feel the electricity in the air, the electricity he generated. Pock-marked, deeply sunburned, with thick black hair brushed back from a broad forehead, a pug nose, a heavy mouth, boxer's shoulders, he looked very dangerous. Modesto was pure Castilian and resembled an aristocrat; Lister, an Asturian miner and dinamitero, resembled a peasant. They were like people from different worlds.

There was something grotesque about this courtyard open to the sky, filled with so many lamps, with the white tablecloth and the gleaming cutlery. There were rifles stacked in the corners, and soon the guards seemed to be everywhere, with hand grenades hanging from their uniforms like buttons. In the light of the kerosene lamps the shadows jumped over the courtyard, and somewhere a dog howled.

Lister was enjoying the impression he made. He was the perfect host. He introduced his staff: they were all very young, none of them more than thirty, and most of them were Asturians. He had a habit of leaning back in his chair and sticking his fingers in his belt: his fingers were the size of sausages. I kept watching him warily, but Vicente Campos pushed me forward and I felt myself being crushed in a bear hug, and thereafter kept as far away from him as possible. This amused him, and he would call for me, and there would be another bear hug. The sounds of battle had long ago died down. Soldiers were preparing the table for a feast.

I was awed by Lister, and so were the Spanish correspondents, who remembered how often he had prevented a retreat by shooting his own men out of hand as a warning to others. He was completely and perfectly ruthless, but as he moved around the courtyard he was like one of those very strong men who behave with exaggerated gentleness for fear of destroying everything in their path.

We sat on benches round the table, while Lister sat at the head of the table on a plump, gilded chair which must have been taken from the manor of a rich landowner. It was the kind of chair that Cardinal de Richelieu would have sat on, but now it was Lister's throne. For some reason he had decided that Boleslavskaya, the correspondent of *Pravda,* and I should sit by his side. Since we both spoke excruciating Spanish, Vicente

Campos was provided with another chair and sat kitty-cornered at the table.

The meal was enormous. There was duck soup followed by fish and lamb and an incredible *bombe* of ice cream. There were four different kinds of wine, "all," Lister said, "captured from the enemy." I suspect that the *chef* was also captured from the enemy, for at our request he appeared at the end of the meal, and he looked a timid, frightened creature, as much in awe of Lister as we were ourselves. But with this awe went our immeasurable gratitude, for we had gone hungry in Barcelona.

"If I had known you were coming, there would have been time to prepare a good meal for you," Lister said, grinning.

It was a pleasant grin, and he talked well. There were people who said he was illiterate and had been given a high position in the army only because he had a great following among the troops, but he was well-read and superbly intelligent on the one subject which interested him above all others—revolution. He talked of revolutions like a professor, analyzing them, always seeking the main thrust of power. In his view Europe was in the throes of a violent revolution which would not end until power finally came into the hands of the people. The Terror, as in the days of the French Revolution, was the weapon of the people against their oppressors.

I objected that the Terror was terribly wasteful, that it killed too many people who were good and useful to the state, and that in any case it always failed in its purpose. The French revolutionaries had killed Lavoisier, the physicist, and gained nothing by it. I said that nothing would convince me that the problem would be solved by guillotining the best men in the country.

Suddenly Lister was boiling with rage. He pounded the table with his enormous fists, the blood rushed to his cheeks and his small eyes seemed to explode.

"Then you are a Fascist!" he shouted. "Anyone who thinks like that must be a Fascist! My God, do I have to shoot you— to put some sense in your head!"

His hand went to his holster and he pulled out his revolver and slapped it on the table. There was a terrible silence, broken by Boleslavskaya, who said: "Put it away, put it away—" Vicente Campos swung himself between Lister and me. Boleslavskaya asked him about the attack on the Sierra de Pandols earlier in the evening, and then his rage against me gave way to a greater rage against the enemy massed behind the sierras. He shook his fists at the enemy. "Why do they come here?" he shouted. "Moors, Italians, Germans, what are they doing here? We don't want their dung here! Let them go! Let them go!"

A surprising thing was happening. The heavy face softened and all the roughness of his voice disappeared as he spoke about the Spanish earth he was fighting for. He even scooped up some earth from the courtyard and let it pour through his fingers onto the table, and all the time he was speaking about the young recruits he had molded into shape until they were able to form great armies.

"Who are they to come and take this earth away from us?" he said. "Who says we shouldn't kill all these people? We have suffered enough from them—families, villages, whole towns wiped out." Then he added: "I don't hate them any more—it is an emotion too deep for hate!"

After dinner he spread the maps on the table and traced the enemy lines with his heavy fingers, and once more he showed us how the Fifth Army had made its way across the river deep into enemy territory.

Moths flung themselves against the whistling kerosene lamps, and all the time the heat seemed to be growing greater, the air windless and still, while Lister described those miraculous days when the Army of the Ebro went over to the offensive, telling us about these things so well that we could see the troops going over in the fishing boats and fanning out across the countryside. It was about one o'clock when we left. We were taken to a neighboring farmhouse, where mattresses had been thrown down on the floor, and we slept soundly. In the morning a messenger came from Lister, inviting us for breakfast. In the fresh morning air he looked less dangerous. Once he called me to him, shouted: "Lavoisier!" at the top of his voice, and there was another terrifying bear hug.

According to the plan, we were to drive up to the front lines beyond Corbera. The journey would take two or three hours, and we would return that night to Mora de Ebro. We were told that everything had been prepared. Suddenly we saw Lister and Vicente Campos, surrounded by reporters and soldiers, standing in a corner of the courtyard in heated argument. Everyone was talking at once. There was a pause, and then Lister's voice rose like the bellowing of a bull. "You are not going!" he shouted. "No one is going! Not one of you is going up to the front!"

In this way we learned that there had been reverses during the night.

We went out into the open fields beyond the farmhouse. The dew was on the grass, the long shadows moved across the red and golden fields, and there were no peasants, no soldiers: only the birds rushing across the sky. The Sierra de Pandols was copper-colored in the early morning light, and there was not the least sign of fire on its sharp and barren crests. We listened and heard nothing. All around us there was only the interminable silence of war.

JOURNEY INTO THE DARK

When we returned to Barcelona, we learned that all our dispatches would receive the "scissors treatment." We were, after all, the first reporters to cross the Ebro and to see with our own eyes that the Republicans were in command of large areas south of the river, and we half-expected to be allowed to send long and enthusiastic reports. We had met the two commanding generals at their headquarters, had observed the Sierra de Pandols in flames, and had many stories to tell about the course of the battle, for we had interviewed many soldiers who had crossed the river and routed the Moors. We had forgotten that censors existed.

The chief censor was the poet Quiroga y Pla, one of the editors of *Hora d'España* and a close friend of Antonio Machado. He sat in his darkened office, lit by three candles, frowning lugubriously. He was a man of about fifty, with one of those round, heavy, and deeply creased faces which belonged properly to a monk of the Middle Ages, and since he was a man of extraordinary gentleness and sweetness, the frown told us all we needed to know. He seemed to believe that anything we could possibly write about the journey across the Ebro would offer information to the enemy, and it was his duty to prevent us from saying anything at all. He wore thick horn-rimmed glasses, which magnified his eyes and gave them a mildly inquisitorial look.

"The scissors," he said, and pointed to the shears lying on the table.

Forewarned, we wrote our dispatches in such a way that they would be wholly innocuous. I wrote three pages in longhand, carefully reread it, concluded that there was nothing that could possibly arouse the interest of General Franco, and offered it to Quiroga, who was ill with diabetes and perhaps for this reason incapable of hiding his emotions. Sighing, he snipped out with his scissors two thirds of my dispatch until the three pages on yellow paper resembled ribbons festooned over his desk. It was permissible to say that there had been an attack on the Sierra de Pandols, because presumably this was known to the enemy, but it was not permissible to say that the headquarters of the two generals were on the south side of the Ebro. It was not permissible to say there was no traffic on the road, that Lister had provided us with a feast, and that Modesto had worn an open sports shirt without any sign of rank. I rewrote the dispatch in two pages, and Quiroga pored over the new version with the expression of a man who fears the worst and is accustomed to seeing it taking place before his eyes.

"Scissors, scissors," he said, and went snipping away busily until no more than a page remained.

Though he spoke English with a heavy accent, he possessed a phenomenal knowledge of all the nuances of the language and he was a past master of the game of reading implications in a text which looked harmless. He read and spoke five or six languages equally well and he knew most of Shakespeare by heart. He was the most improbable of censors, for he was gentle, courteous and long-suffering.

I worked on my dispatch for another half-hour, and there was some consolation in the fact that Boleslavskaya, the correspondent of *Pravda,* and Georges Soria, the correspondent of *L'Humanité,* suffered the same fate. Finally, the mangled remnants of my dispatch, revised six or seven times, was delivered by telephone to the office of the *News Chronicle* in London. It took another twenty minutes to dictate this solitary page on a spluttering telegraph wire. There were three telephone booths in the censor's office, and everyone who used them suffered from migraine headaches.

Quiroga, of course, suffered more than anyone else. I imagine that he was elevated to the post of chief censor for the same reason that it sometimes happened in mediaeval Spain that a saintly monk was elevated to the rank of Grand Inquisitor. He was not by nature a practical man, and he detested being in a position of authority. He could easily have left Spain for a teaching post abroad but he had long ago elected to serve the Republic. Nearly all his relatives were fighting on the other side.

Later that night, returning to the Hotel Majestic, I learned that Theodore Dreiser was occupying the presidential suite on the first floor. As far as I knew, no presidents had ever occupied the suite. They said that Dreiser had been unusually cantankerous, made advances to every woman he saw, and finally gone to bed with a chambermaid. Vicente Campos had had a long talk with Dreiser and wondered whether he was not an impostor traveling under a famous name.

"Tomorrow they are giving a farewell party for him," Vicente Campos announced, adding meaningfully: "Then we shall see whether he is an impostor or not."

"If he acts like an impostor," I said, "then you may be sure it is Dreiser himself."

There was no sign of Dreiser the next morning. He remained in his suite, and from time to time government officials arrived at the hotel to confer with him and to bring him expensive presents. Ernst Toller went to see him and said later that it was like being granted an audience by a king. Unshaven, wearing pajamas and a dressing gown, Dreiser growled at him, cursed Franco, the Pope, the Masons, and the English government, and held onto the hand of the chambermaid, saying: "Don't leave me, honey," whenever she attempted to take her hand away. He was drinking royally and was already in a stupor.

By evening Dreiser had recovered sufficiently to attend the farewell party in his honor. It was not, as I feared, an official party offered by the government, but a small party given by writers and journalists. André Malraux was there, pale and serene, his face convulsed in dreadful tics, his handshake limp, his damp hair matted across his forehead, every wild gesture asserting in some mysterious manner the power of the human intelligence. Ernst Toller smiled his sad refugee smile, said very little and brooded compassionately. Herbert Matthews sat bolt upright, thin as a rake, with one of those long faces which always reminded me of the Easter Island stone gods, forbiddingly austere, or so it seemed, until he began talking about his travels and then the wintry face gave way to spring. Louis Fischer, dark and saturnine, pondered the extraordinary events taking place around the table with brisk composure, while Boleslavskaya regally translated for Malraux's benefit some of the more outrageous statements of the guest of honor. Malraux was accompanied by Josette Clotis, a woman of such astonishing beauty that we scarcely dared to look at her. She wore a white clinging gown and her long auburn hair streamed down her back. Happily for our comfort she nestled so close to Malraux that she was sometimes very nearly invisible.

Dreiser can rarely have enjoyed a more distinguished and respectful audience, and though he pretended to be put out by Malraux's late arrival and even for a few moments succeeded in confusing Malraux with Maurois, he was in characteristic form, truculent and opinionated as ever. He announced that all the troubles of Europe were due to Masons and Catholics acting in unison, and it was this unholy alliance which was responsible for the war in Spain. Hitler and Stalin were Catholics. Franco was a Mason. Together the Masons and the Catholics were about to plunge the world into another and more terrible war, of which the Spanish Civil War was merely the prelude. His voice quavering with passion, he called upon the democracies to thwart the evil designs of their enemies even though he was quite sure it was too late. "I tell you there is going to be a war more terrible than any war that has ever been visited on man," he declared. "There's no hope for Europe. The whole continent is riddled with the disease of war. I may not live to see it, but by God I know it is coming!"

All the guests were sitting around a large black circular table lit by candles stuck in bottles. The waiters, impeccably dressed, served a pale watery vegetable soup followed by black leathery squid floating in remnants of their own juices. It was said that real food was available at the Ritz Hotel, where Malraux was staying, but at the Majestic it was regarded as a point of honor that the guests should follow the example of the people of Barcelona. But if there was little food, there were plentiful supplies of wine, and Dreiser was drinking copiously, becoming more and more vehement as he attacked the conspirators who already had the world in their power. The chief conspirator was an institution called the Grand Orient, a Masonic order with headquarters in Paris.

Louis Fischer would sometimes interject a cutting phrase in an attempt to change the subject, but Dreiser could not be stopped. Herbert Matthews listened with appalled politeness, and Toller sometimes gave way to deep sighs of incomprehension. Malraux, who had some difficulty following Dreiser's argument, asked

Boleslavskaya for a translation of the main points and then, speaking very rapidly, shaking a long finger in Dreiser's face, with something of the appearance of a judge condemning a particularly unruly prisoner, he explained that a war was perhaps inevitable, but its inevitability was in no way due to the causes advanced by Dreiser. The Catholics and the Masons were guiltless; vast historical forces were at work; the seeds of the war were planted long ago by men who were completely incapable of understanding the folly of their actions. If the war was inevitable, it was perhaps because people had abandoned the hope of directing their own affairs and saw war as the only possible way of removing the dictators from power; and in this they were wrong, for the war would only reinforce the power of the dictators, leaving the people in a worse plight than before. All this and much more was translated for Dreiser's benefit. He looked startled, attempted to interrupt, and was silenced by Louis Fischer who bristled with impatience at the thought that anyone should interrupt a discourse by Malraux even in translation. Finally Dreiser subsided, toying with a bread cob. He was evidently not listening to Boleslavskaya's brilliant exposition of Malraux's ideas. She spoke English perfectly, knew Malraux well, and moved easily among his ideas. She was the perfect translator, but it was all wasted on Dreiser, who was beginning to show interest in Josette Clotis, insisting that she sit beside him and becoming grotesquely ill-tempered when she refused. Not long afterward he rose, announced that he was going to bed, embraced Malraux, and climbed the marble stairs to the presidential suite.

In Barcelona in those days nothing happened according to rule and one strange and unexpected event would usually be followed by others in quick succession. The incredible and the improbable were commonplace, and what we thought would happen never happened.

Since Toller was about to make a secret journey to Madrid, flying at night over enemy-occupied territory, it occurred to him that the time had come to pack his possessions, and I was invited to help him. I thought it would be an uneventful evening, listening to him and drawing him out. As we walked up the stairs I was thinking about his secret store of chocolate, cigarettes and excellent sherry.

On each landing of the marble staircase a solitary candle gleamed, and by this light we made our way up to Toller's room, which was somewhere near the top of the building. We were halfway up the stairs when we saw a powerfully built Negro leaning against the wall on a landing. He was evidently an American Negro from the International Brigade. He was leaning there out of weariness, and we heard the slow steady rise and fall of his breathing. He had huge black hands and a fine gleaming black face, and there was a submachine gun under his arm. As we passed he must have heard our footsteps, for he was instantly awake, and he began waving his machine gun at Toller. It had recently been oiled, and glinted in the light of the leaping candle flame.

"You don't have to wave that thing at me," Toller said, as one might speak to a child. "I'm Ernst Toller."

"Hah, Ernst Toller, pleased to meet you, sah!"

The Negro, who wore a khaki shirt with the sleeves rolled up, put out one enormous and thickly veined black arm. Toller shook the hand firmly. The Negro's eyeballs were pure white. A look of suspicion crossed his face; his smile hardened; and perhaps he had forgotten where he was and thought he was back again on the Ebro front. The black hand went slowly back to the oiled gun.

"You're a fuckin' liar!" the Negro said, dead beat, leaning against the wall, the black fingers fumbling for the trigger as he waved the gun at Toller. He said in a tone of triumph: "Ernst Toller, sah, I've read about you! There's a feller called Ernst Toller who writes poetry! How do I know you're the same guy?" He dug the machine gun into the pit of Toller's stomach. I think Toller expected to be killed. There was an extraordinary look of compassion on his face, as though he was already forgiving the man about to murder him. The wind came down the stairwell, and sometimes the candle on the landing faded away, only to spurt up again. It was the strangest place to die, there on the third or fourth floor of the Hotel Majestic, with a solitary candle spitting and the tallest Negro I ever saw jabbing at him with his machine gun, and what made it all the more horrible was that the Negro was incredibly drunk with weariness, could scarcely stand and had evidently returned from the Ebro front only a few minutes before. He was so powerfully built that he resembled an enormous black statue with huge muscles rippling over his skin.

He gave another ferocious jab at Toller's stomach and said: "How do I know you are Ernst Toller, sah? How do I know? Let's hear your fuckin' poems!"

So Toller began to recite from the book of poems he wrote in prison, *The Book of Swallows*. He recited them in German, speaking very softly, as though to himself, his eyes closed, swaying a little. The Negro listened with his huge bony head held a little to one side, then he let the machine gun clatter to the floor, and said: "Ernst Toller, sah, pass on!"

Toller however continued to recite his poems. The Negro gazed at him as though fascinated. From downstairs there came Malraux's high-pitched voice as he ordered a car to take him to the Ritz Hotel, and somewhere on one of the distant landings a chambermaid was walking stealthily on slippered feet, keys ringing from her belt. And then at last, while Toller was still reciting his poems, the Negro slumped to the marble floor.

I thought there would be no more excitement that evening, but there was more—much more—to come. When Toller opened the door to his room, we saw an enormous hairy man with muscles nearly as powerful as those of the Negro we met on the stairs. He was stark naked, jumping up and down in one of those small hand baths that were common in Victorian times and very rare in our own. He was pouring water over himself, and his whole body was glistening and shining in the light of the candles he had stuck along the dresser.

Toller's room was already in a state of wild disorder. There were piles of books on the bed, papers everywhere, clothes over the floor, for he had no particular gift for packing. Toller's visitor was General Hans, late of the German Army, now one of the commanders on the Tortosa front on leave in Barcelona. He was almost as legendary as Lister, and in a rather brutal Prussian way almost as handsome as Modesto. He was a magnificent physical specimen, and since we were obviously startled by him and at the same time impressed by his physique, he began to adopt various classical poses—Discobolus, Apollo, Zeus the Thunder-bearer, and a coy Venus rising from the waves, and all this was accompanied by raucous laughter, leers, and splutterings. Toller applauded gravely, like a child at a pantomime.

It turned out that General Hans had arrived at the hotel, learned that no rooms were vacant, examined the list of guests, and decided that Toller was his most likely victim. He had forty-eight hours in Barcelona, and what he wanted most was a bath, a bottle of whisky and a good night's rest. He had very little sleep that night because Toller found an unopened bottle of whisky, plied him with it and made him talk about the Tortosa front. He told stories for hours, while we listened like children at his feet.

He looked like a storyteller from somewhere in eastern Mongolia as he sat there wrapped in Toller's dressing-gown. He had heavy features, high cheekbones, a close-cropped skull, and looked more like a Tartar than a German. In addition, he was nearly seven feet tall. He had been a colonel in a famous German mountain brigade, and had remained in Germany for many years after Hitler seized power, secretly directing Communist propaganda among the soldiers. At last he escaped to Switzerland, and so made his way to Spain.

He said: "I can't shoot fear-crazed men. I don't have Lister's ability to shoot in cold blood, but sometimes I have had to do it. One day on the Tortosa front my soldiers absolutely refused to fight. They were retreating in disorder, panic-stricken. I had to stop them, and I was sure there must be a better way. I told my orderly to bring me a large basin of water and a kitchen chair and to put them down in the middle of the road. And then slowly and leisurely I took off my socks and boots and let my feet soak in the water. My men were retreating because they were worn out, desperate, without sleep for seven days. But when they saw me sitting there, they laughed and the message went round that General Hans had taken off his stinking socks and had no intention of retreating. And they were ashamed and went back into line . . ."

There were many other stories, and he told them well. He had a special dislike for Dr. Goebbels, and one day when he was a guest at a party in Berlin there was a competition in weight-lifting. Everyone had been drinking, and the atmosphere was rowdy. General Hans seized Dr. Goebbels by the scruff of the neck with one hand, and one of the propaganda minister's assistants with the other hand, and lifted them off the ground. "The awful thing was that I found my fingers tightening round

Dr. Goebbels' neck," General Hans said. "I fought against it, but I couldn't prevent it. My fingers held a life of their own independent of my will. Dr. Goebbels had a very thin neck, and I could have snapped it with the greatest ease. Finally, I let them both down, and Dr. Goebbels ran his fingers along his neck and said: 'If I had not known you so well, Hans, I could have sworn you wanted to murder me.' Then we went on drinking."

As he told these stories, General Hans acted out all the parts. He stretched out his arms, and we could almost see the diminutive Dr. Goebbels hanging in mid-air. He had the gift of painting in the background. While he was talking there came the dull roar of the bombing planes from Majorca, as they dropped bombs on the harbor of Barcelona.

The next morning Dreiser set off for the French frontier by car. He was in a lordly mood, resembling a *grand seigneur* who had been visiting one of his outlying properties and was now at last returning to the comfort and security of his town house. There were tearful partings with the chambermaids, and he gave them small gifts: a bar of chocolate, a packet of cigarettes. To a correspondent of *Vanguardia* he said that his mission to Republican Spain had been accomplished successfully and within a few days he would be sitting in the White House with President Roosevelt. The correspondent smiled politely, but he was under no illusions about the extent of Dreiser's influence.

Just as Dreiser was leaving, all his bags packed, everyone standing around the car in respectful silence, he shouted to me to come along with him for the ride. I thought it would be a good opportunity to see northern Catalonia, and it might be possible to learn a bit more about Dreiser. I had met him in Paris a few weeks earlier, and from the very beginning I had wondered at the strange dichotomy between the man and his writings. With his heavy dewlaps and thick lips, he looked like the down-at-heel owner of a general store in Germany. He was slovenly, incoherent, lecherous, without a trace of nobility. He had written abysmally silly books, but he had also written *Sister Carrie* and *An American Tragedy*, which were minor masterpieces. He had once possessed a great talent, but he had allowed it to slip through his fingers. Why?

He settled back in the automobile with the air of a man who had forgiven all his enemies and was content with the world.

He was obviously glad to be leaving Spain, and at the same time he was profoundly grateful for the experience of seeing Spain at war. "Wonderful people," he said. "Of course they are all doomed —caught in a trap, poor fellows. They don't know what they are up against."

"You mean the Catholics and the Masons?"

"That's right."

"What about Hitler and Stalin?"

"They are tools of forces greater than themselves," Dreiser said with an air of finality. "They are really working together. They have the same aims, the same purposes. When you see Hitler, you see Stalin."

He talked for a long time about the interchangeability of the Communists and the National Socialists. The serious drinking of the day had not yet begun, and he made a good deal of sense, but quite suddenly there would come incoherent rumblings about the Masons and the Catholics, who were the real rulers of the world. He never looked at the Catalonian countryside flashing past, with its white villages, red roads and groves of olive trees. For twenty miles we drove along the coast, and he never once looked at the calm sea and the gray warships anchored on the horizon. He was lost in some interior world of his own, nursing his wounds.

Wherever he went, he carried a hip flask of whisky, and now at increasingly short intervals he went through the ritual of slowly unscrewing the cap and pulling out the cork, and after drinking and then rubbing the neck of the bottle with his thumb and forefinger he would hand it to me with the warning that I should not take too much, because I was obviously not an experienced drinker. Once he said: "I heard the bombs last night. My God, I've never been so terrified in all my life. It's so goddam tragic, you have to drink yourself to death to understand it."

But what he talked about most during the journey to the frontier was women, the innumerable women he had encountered during his long life. There were so many of them, and in his imagination they had all become one woman. "There is only one thing in life," he announced. "Go after women! Remember that. There's nothing else—there never will be anything else until the end of the world. That is what the Bible is trying to say when it talks about Jesus and Mary Magdalene. I've had more women than anyone else in the United States, and I'll tell you this—they are the balm of Gilead."

He was writing some articles about Spain. I asked him whether he had taken any notes. "No, it's all in my head," he said. When I tried to get him to talk about *Sister Carrie* and *An American Tragedy*, he said: "I don't care a shit about my books. I think about what is going to happen to the world—the whole bloody mess—I just don't see where literature comes in. Books never helped a man to get a woman or buy a loaf of bread or prevent a war from breaking out!" The dewlaps were sagging, and he suddenly looked very old, very vulnerable, and very tired. He revived when we came to the frontier with the French police standing on the other side of the road. He shook hands with our driver, gave him a bar of chocolate, and surveyed his mountain of calfskin luggage which looked so completely out of place, so deliriously expensive, in this small town of Republican Spain.

"Let's get the stuff into France," he said, and he began to make clicking noises with his fingers at the people who gathered around him.

They watched him silently, not knowing who he was, and not caring—a heavy-set man with a face like a gray jelly, wearing his expensive overcoat in the French manner, falling from his shoulders. None of them offered to carry his luggage the ten yards to the frontier, and finally the driver and I carried it. As he marched those ten yards, he muttered: "God bless Spain . . . poor fellows . . . caught in a trap."

We were just about to drive back to Barcelona when the frontier police sprang into activity. They crowded round the car, demanded to see our papers, examined the trunk to make sure we were not carrying any contraband, and finally declared that I was under arrest because I had no passport and indeed no papers at all except a poem I had written about Mora de Ebro and Quiroga's translation of it, which was unsigned and therefore of no use even as a certificate of good poetic behavior. My passport was lying in a drawer in the hotel. I behaved stupidly, said they were fools and worse, and found myself looking down the barrel of a gun. This was the second time within a few days that I had looked down that little black hole, and I did not like it. A moment later I was being marched off to the local jail and locked in a cell that smelled of straw, urine and excrement, with the driver, an excitable Asturian, standing outside as though on guard and shouting far worse things at the frontier police. Then quite suddenly the driver vanished, and there were no more voices. I could hear a telephone ringing at the end of a corridor, and then a long silence, for a door had been closed.

There was a small wooden stool in the cell and I found that by piling straw on the stool it was possible to climb up and look through the small barred window. Outside, children were playing among apple trees and the sky had never looked brighter. The experience of being in a cell was not particularly distressing, perhaps because there had not been time enough to realize that it had really happened. I supposed there would be a brief and perfunctory trial, and at the very least there would be a term of imprisonment for insulting the frontier police. Enrique Lister had taught me some good Spanish swear words, and the one he liked best was *puta de setenta leches.* No doubt this was the one which so severely annoyed the frontier police.

After about five minutes I heard a door slamming, footsteps, someone shouting into a telephone, and then silence again. Once again a door opened, and this time there was such an uproar that it seemed that everyone in the neighborhood was engaged in a shouting match. Finally the uproar came to an end, the door of the cell was flung open, and the driver and the chief of the frontier police were standing outside. The driver was smiling from ear to ear and the chief of the frontier police looked as though he had been sentenced to death.

What had happened was very simple—they had finally got through to Barcelona on the telephone and Constancia de la Mora, in charge of the ministry of information, had said that all foreign correspondents were mad anyway and it must be expected of them that they would sometimes leave their passports behind. The chief of the frontier police was instructed to make amends by serving us with a feast. For weeks afterward I lived on the memory of that feast presided over by the chief of police, and we were both bloated when we drove back to Barcelona.

Toller's journey to Madrid continued to be delayed. Every night he expected to be flown out of Barcelona, and at the last moment there would come a message saying that the plane was delayed, or being repaired, or needed by the military. His room at the top of the Hotel Majestic was in a state of permanent upheaval. He wanted to go to Madrid to make a speech which would be beamed to the United States, but he also wanted to go to Madrid for its own sake, since Madrid stood at the center of his hopes and Barcelona was merely on the circumference.

Meanwhile he packed and unpacked his luggage in a kind of fury, unable to concentrate on his own work—he was completing his play *Pastor Hall*—or to settle down to a sensible program of interviews because the airplane might be taking him to Madrid tonight or tomorrow night. Piles of books and manuscripts appeared and reappeared on the bed and the tables, while he paced restlessly along the narrow corridors between the bed and the piled up luggage. One evening he showed me a copy of the *Völkischer Beobachter*, the Nazi newspaper. There were screaming headlines announcing that Toller was working for the Spanish Republic and there was a large photograph showing him resembling an anthropoid ape. In fact, the *Völkischer Beobachter* was continually coming out with news about Toller's journeys, his speeches, his books and plays, which were always unmercifully derided. The Nazi newspaper could be bought on the kiosks in Paris, and I would occasionally buy a copy. Invariably there would be the same picture of Toller and an article about him. I asked him why he carried this absurd newspaper around with him.

"To remind me to be careful," he said, sitting on the edge of the bed. "I sometimes forget that Hitler exists. I suppose I carry this newspaper around with me to remind me that I am always in danger. Four times they have tried to assassinate me— once in Paris, once in Switzerland, once in Stockholm, once here. They have received orders to kill me, and I am quite certain they will succeed in the end, because I am totally defenseless. But what puzzles me is why they should be so determined to do away with me. They describe me as the leader of the great Jewish-Communist conspiracy, the chief Communist representative in western Europe, the man responsible for the calamities that have been inflicted on Europe, and they forget that I am no longer important, I have no official position, I am not a

Communist or even a fellow-traveler. I am a playwright who makes a living by writing plays."

It was one of those August nights when you could feel the presence of the enemy airplanes even though they were still far out to sea. There was a strange quivering in the air, a strange quietness. It was as though an invisible wave were about to fall on us and blot us out. Toller was in a mood to speak about ultimate things. He went on:

"Everything depends on the war in Spain. If the Fascists win, then of course there will be a world war of colossal proportions, and this should be obvious to the meanest intelligence. For a hundred years, maybe, the world will lie under a Fascist dictatorship, but the grass will grow, children will be born, and sometimes but very rarely there will appear men who are merciful, who understand mercy. What we must work for now is the day when the quality of mercy will revive in the world; and I am sure of only one thing—only mercy can save the world.

"What is happening now is something so terrible that the mind can scarcely dwell on it. We have entered the age of terror. Naked terror is being fought by naked terror, and we are becoming as hard as our enemies. The Moors who crucify the Republican soldiers, the Fascists who drop the bodies of our comrades from airplanes, the hostages who are slaughtered, the girls who are violated, demand vengeance. It is as simple as that. And yet it is not so simple, because there are always a few people with mercy, who refuse to take vengeance. Blessed are the merciful, for they shall lead the way to the promised land.

"Europe will vanish, Europe will die, and all the rivers will run with blood, but in the end Europe will be reborn. We shall have to live for this day.

"I belong to a generation which has outlived its usefulness. I was twenty-six when I became President of the Bavarian Soviet Republic, and I really believed that it would be possible to bring about a decent society in which all men would be equals. I thought it was in our grasp. I know now that a century will pass before we can even begin to build up a decent society.

"When I was in prison in Bavaria, some swallows built a nest in my cell. The prison governor ordered that the nest be destroyed. The swallows built another nest, and then another. Time after time they rebuilt their nest until the governor gave up in despair. In the end we shall be able to build our nests in quietness and peace."

He spoke about many things that night, always in a mood of detachment, as though the world and the bombing planes were far away, as though he was looking down at the earth from a distant planet. He had an idea that this was the night when the airplane would take him to Madrid, and so once more the books were carefully packed. I was entrusted with his will, his private papers, and the silver-framed photograph of his wife Christine, from whom he had long been separated. He was still desperately in love with her, and it was not difficult to understand why. She was a ravishing creature with blond silky hair and an expression of bemused absorption in her own beauty. She was fourteen when she attended one of his lectures, and at the end of the lecture she came up to the podium and announced with total conviction: "I shall marry you." They were married three years later, and during the following years Toller had many reasons to regret the marriage, for she broke his heart. He said: "You know, of course, that some of these planes going to Madrid have been shot down. If I am killed, I want you to tell Christine that I loved her always in spite of everything."

He was talking gravely and simply, without drama. This is what he wanted done, and it would be done. His plan was to spend a week in Madrid, then return to Barcelona and take the first available ship to New York. Like Dreiser he believed he would be granted an interview with President Roosevelt.

The Savoia-Marchettis came from Majorca and bombed the harbor around midnight. The candle on the table jerked; and with every grinding bomb the flame changed shape and color, resembling a seismograph that accurately reported every wound suffered by the city. At such times Toller gazed straight in front of him, expressionless, his deep brown eyes filling with slow tears. There were depths upon depths in his eyes, and sometimes it was possible to guess the extent of his suffering by the way his eyes quivered. Tomorrow morning we would know how many working-class dwellings had been shattered and how many families of dockworkers had been killed.

Usually the raids followed the established pattern: having

dropped their bombs over the harbor area the Italian planes would turn tail and flee to the safety of Majorca. They were hit-and-run raids, with little danger to the airplanes, for the anti-aircraft guns were notoriously ineffective. But tonight the sound of bombing came from another direction altogether.

"They are bombing the airfield," Toller murmured. "I might as well unpack the books."

Half an hour later there was a knock on the door. He was wanted on the telephone downstairs; we both knew what it meant. We ran down the stairs, and this time there was no American Negro to bar the way. The candlelit lobby was deserted; there was only the night clerk on duty, an old man with swollen eyelids wearing a white tie and a faded frock coat. "The airplane leaves tonight . . . The bus will pick you up at the airport terminal . . ." It was as though flying to Madrid at night was the most natural thing in the world.

The night was dark and silent, for there was no moon and no street lights shone. We groped our way to the airport terminal, Toller carrying an umbrella over his arm. In the bus taking us to the airfield Toller talked about the play he wanted to write for radio: a play of the Spanish war constructed out of the authentic sounds of war. A baby's cry, the explosion of a bomb, the rumble of airplanes, the clatter of machine guns, men and women talking in the underground shelters. "It should be possible to compose a play out of the sounds of war, and it could be made in such a way that people would never dare to go to war again."

A shadowy single-engined plane stood on the empty airfield. There were no formalities. Toller simply climbed into the plane, waved with his umbrella, and then the cowling closed over him. A moment later the plane was taxiing along the runway, and less than a minute later it had vanished into the night.

THE EXILES

When Toller left for Madrid, life in Barcelona seemed to lose its flavor. Suddenly I realized how much I had depended on him, how much I admired him. All his treasures, everything he had accumulated during his travels in Europe and Spain, were now piled high in my small room, and I sometimes found myself wondering what on earth I would do with them if he was killed in Madrid. Paintings, books, letters, even furniture, were piled in more or less orderly heaps against the wall, and surmounting them all was the silver-framed portrait of Christine with the yellow hair cascading down to her shoulders, a mysterious half-smile playing on her lips.

It was a time of frustration, of shattered hopes, of rumors and worse than rumors. The bombing went on, the front was stationary, the sun shone. One by one the correspondents were going home, for there was little to report. Day after day the official bulletins announced only minor engagements, while we knew obscurely that far-reaching changes were taking place as though underground, and we felt like men standing within a fortress that is being mined. There were rumors of an organized Fifth Column only waiting for the signal to come out into the open. There were more rumors of people being shot at Montjuich "for crimes against the Republic." Consciously or unconsciously everyone seemed to know we were entering the most dangerous stage of the war.

Modesto had spoken of the vast quantities of armaments being assembled by the enemy on the Ebro front, and only a trickle of armaments was reaching his own troops. The frontier with France was still closed; no supplies were coming in; the Republic was living on its own flesh. Constancia de la Mora, the acting minister of information, was saying openly that only a favorable change in the political situation could save the Republic. By this she meant that Britain and America might suddenly have a change of heart and send in the needed supplies, and there was not the least sign of a change of heart.

Barcelona was starving. The little brown bread cobs, the little pieces of fish, and the little pieces of squid floating in the soup became smaller. But strangely the people walking in the streets held their heads high, and if you walked along the Ramblas you could imagine you were in some Mediterranean town untouched by war. The bookshops were crowded, the flower-sellers smiled behind their heaped-up baskets, the girls swung their skirts, and the men greeted them with the one word, *guapa,* they wanted to hear. The bombings went on, the airplanes coming over in daylight, for they had nothing to fear; and one bomb fell near the Ritz, seemingly a punishment for too much high living. But in fact those fifty-pound bombs, though they could slice through a house, were far less terrible than the knowledge that the Republic was doomed. In those days one could live on sunlight, the excitement in the air.

It annoyed me that I could not speak Spanish fluently, and so I decided to take lessons at the Berlitz School. The teacher was a gentle, scholarly man with an ample paunch and a smile of great sweetness. His eyelids drooped, his clothes were threadbare, his boots were scuffed, and he held himself with a kind of casual dignity. Because he was immensely likable I looked forward to spending an hour a day with him for a month, and settled down to learning Spanish in the Berlitz way, the old man pointing at an object and saying the word in Spanish. Here is pen, pencil, paper, desk, carpet. Here is a fly walking on the wall. This is a photograph of a young man. It was dull work, but somehow he made it amusing and he liked to make little jokes in English or German.

He said his name was Pablo Iglesias, which must be one of the most common names in Spain. Most of his life he had been a professor of languages, not a particularly rewarding occupation. Once he said he had known Picasso; my ears pricked up, but he said no more, hinting that later on, when I could talk more Spanish, he would tell me about his meetings with Picasso. So day after day I climbed the rickety stairs to the Berlitz School just off the Plaza de Catalunya, always looking forward to those meetings with Professor Iglesias in a small barren room. One day I arrived, but he was not there. I waited for about half

an hour, and then went in search of him. There was no one in
the office that morning except a small mousy girl, whose face
was dead white.

"Where is Professor Iglesias?" I asked, and she only shook her
head dumbly from side to side.

Her whole body was shivering.

"Where is he?" I insisted, for something had obviously gone
wrong.

"He is in prison," she said at last. "They took him away last
night."

She was weeping uncontrollably, her small shoulders shaking,
her hands clenching and unclenching. I went to see Constancia
de la Mora and asked her why an obscure professor of languages
should be arrested and she promised to make inquiries. Some
days later she called me into her office and said that a certain
Dr. Pablo Iglesias, engineer, had indeed been arrested that night.
He had been caught red-handed on the roof of his house signaling
with a flashlight to the airplanes. There had been a military
court martial and he was shot in the early hours of the morning.

I found it difficult to believe that Pablo Iglesias belonged
to the Fifth Column. I could not imagine that slow-moving,
paunchy man climbing to the roof of his house. But the correspondents sitting round the empty tables at the hotel were not
surprised. "The Fifth Column is everywhere," they said. "Didn't
you know?" I did not know. When I went back to the Berlitz
School, there was no one there.

August was coming to an end, and we wondered whether we
would ever be able to report anything the world wanted to know.
We visited schools and hospitals, boat-building yards and engineering shops, and yearned to go to the front, where as Modesto
had said, "life is more beautiful and so much simpler." In the
engineering shops we saw trucks being converted into armored
cars, the workmen slicing the ships' plates and riveting them to
the trucks. When we saw the armored cars again they were
rolling up the Paseo de Gracia to take the salute from the
President of the Republic. It was early in the morning, the
dawn breaking, and in this light the long line of armored cars,
dappled in the misty sunlight, looked curiously festive with
their black-red anarchist pennons. There were speeches, a trum-
peter played a dirge, and a band played the Catalan national

anthem, a jaunty dance tune, surely the most gentle and charming of all national anthems. We heard a few days later that the armored cars were thrown into battle on the Ebro. They advanced in a long column in a cloud of dust, and no one ever saw them again.

The desire to reach the front or at least to see Modesto and Lister had become an obsession with us. We told ourselves we knew every street and stone of Barcelona, all its obscure and secret corners. We knew the mortuary where the bodies were laid out after every bombardment. We knew the hospitals where the patients suffering from gas gangrene were encased in plaster. We knew the inside of too many government offices, and we knew that neither the government nor the people of Barcelona were decisive factors in the war. The only decisive factors were the two armies facing one another on the Ebro.

We made the lives of Constancia de la Mora and Quiroga very nearly unendurable by our constant pleading. "No transport, no gasoline," we were told, though we needed no telling. When we threatened to leave *en masse* unless we were allowed to go to the front, Constancia de la Mora, who looked like a queen and was never more regal than at this moment, said: "Do you think it makes any difference whether you stay or go? We shall keep on fighting even if there are no correspondents in Spain." Our rebellion quickly came to an end.

By some mysterious means Boleslavskaya, the correspondent for *Pravda,* acquired some gasoline for the journey to the Ebro. She had a small Citroën and an Asturian driver, with a revolver strapped to his side, another on his lap, and a third in the glove compartment; and just as Quiroga with his dewlaps resembled to perfection a prince of the church, so the Asturian driver with his thin dark face, tight lips and burning eyes, resembled a Jesuit priest who would stop at nothing to preserve the faith. If by some misfortune we fell into the hands of the enemy, the Asturian driver was determined that we would give a good account of ourselves. Boleslavskaya also had a small Beretta pistol in her handbag.

This day was even more breathtaking than the day we drove to Lister's headquarters. The sky was a silvery blue, the hawks hung on the summer clouds, autumn was beginning to creep over the red fields, but where previously the landscape seemed strangely deserted, as though it was beyond belief that anyone had ever lived there, now with the hint of autumn in the air it had the look of abandonment, as though no one would ever live there again. The acres of vines would wither away, the farm-houses would gradually disintegrate, the hawks would fall out of the sky, the earth itself would vanish. Perhaps it was the very clarity of the air, or perhaps it was the sight of so many vineyards going to seed, which gave us the feeling that all these fields were melting into nothingness. Boleslavskaya was chanting the poems of Pasternak, the driver was singing Asturian love songs, the little Citroën hummed along the lonely road, and nothing could have been more beautiful than these blue mountains and red fields, yet everywhere there was deadness, silence, emptiness. There was no traffic on the road, no sign that any traffic had passed during the night. Once we stopped the car because we thought we had seen the marks of a truck in the dust, but when we examined them we concluded that they were not truck marks at all. A few soldiers were loitering near the pontoon bridge at Mora de Ebro, they recognized the Asturian driver and waved us on, and five minutes later we saw Modesto standing on the red bluff, looking out toward the Sierra de Pandols. Arms akimbo, head held back, shirt open at the neck, he seemed to have been standing in the same attitude and in exactly the same place for more than a month.

We climbed the red bluff. Nothing had changed—the same slit trench, the same coils of wire, the same farmhouse. Modesto looked neither older nor younger, and once more he was the young farm owner looking out over his farm.

Boleslavskaya asked him how things were going. He smiled, shrugged his shoulders, and said: "*Plokho!*" which means "badly" in Russian. She asked him how he was, and he said "*Khorosho!*" which means "well." Then having exhausted his entire Russian vocabulary, he settled for Spanish, saying "no" in a variety of ways, but always kindly. No, we could not go up the road. No, we could not see the maps. No, there had been no fighting in the Sierra de Pandols and in fact there had been no fighting for a week except for some small skirmishes. Boleslavskaya said: "Is there anything I can write?" Modesto replied: "Say we are well, and we hope the democracies will send us guns." "I have written that before," Boleslavskaya said. "Yes, but this time we need them more urgently," Modesto said. "Write it in larger letters."

On the way back to Barcelona Boleslavskaya did not chant the poems of Pasternak and the Asturian driver did not sing love songs.

In September 1938 the people of Barcelona already knew they were doomed. It was only a matter of time. Franco could break across the Ebro whenever he wanted to, for his guns were massed wheel to wheel and the Republican forces were lacking in artillery, airplanes, tanks, everything that goes to make a modern army. There remained human courage, and it was not enough.

The girls in the Ramblas still swung their skirts, the old women still sat over their baskets of flowers, the city looked calm and beautiful under the yellow sun, but the Republic had only a few more months to live. Jaume Miravitlles, the youthful minister of information, held nothing back. "Of course we are in a perilous situation," he said. "We have no illusions. We have told the truth in our newspapers, and we shall go on telling it to the end. We shall not surrender!" He hoped for a miracle, remembering that miracles had happened before. In May 1937 Barcelona had erupted in a private civil war of its own, with the anarchists fighting against the Catalan government forces, the police and the civil guard and everyone else. Jaume Miravitlles was one of the very few who dared to walk the streets when every window was filled with men with revolvers and rifles. He made the journey from the Generalitat, the government headquarters, to the anarchist headquarters, expecting every moment to be shot. "But they did not shoot me, and that was a miracle, and there were many other miracles."

For a few days I stayed with a working-class family and learned only what I knew before: that these handsome, bronze-skinned Catalans were impervious to fear. An old Catalan worker reminded me that Catalan ships had once ruled the Mediterranean and would do so again. I had tea with Federica Monseny, the anarchist minister of education. Plump, energetic, grandmotherly, dressed in black, she fussed around her small apartment with the air of a woman devoted to domesticity, while talking about murders and assassinations. "If you like milk in your tea, I have a little powdered milk," she said. "I am afraid there is no sugar."

In September I flew to Paris, envying the Catalans for their gaiety in the face of disaster. The Parisians looked more morose than ever: fear was creeping across Paris, but no one yet knew the name of the fear. My letters at this time are full of plans for voyages to South America, Mongolia, Finland, Central Africa. One week I am about to sail for Dakar, the next week I am on my way to China. I was suffering from a serious and painful ear infection apparently brought on by the bombing on the road to Mora de Ebro. The eardrum was cracked, there were streptococcal blisters in the passage of the outer ear, and the doctor believed that the infection had already reached the inner ear. Accordingly, he cut the drum away and packed the inner ear, as far as he could go, with whatever drugs were available at the time. He was quite pleased with himself. He had never, he said, enjoyed such a good look at the inner ear. "You will be permanently deaf in your right ear," he said, "but you may find some compensations when you are sitting next to someone you don't want to talk to at parties."

He was a charming and garrulous man, who had a habit of taking a sabbatical every two or three years and traveling in the Far East. While prodding my ear, he talked about the cities of French Indo-China, China, and Japan, painting them in such bright colors that they came floating into his surgery on the Boulevard Malesherbes. He had written three or four books about his travels, but they were merely intellectual exercises written without any real passion. When he spoke about the Far East in his surgery, he was all passionate intensity. "Go there, my dear fellow, and then you will forget that like Van Gogh you have only one ear," he said. I told myself I would go to the Far East in my own time, but the time had not yet come. For some reason I was dreaming more and more of voyages in Central Africa.

This was the September when Neville Chamberlain and Edouard Daladier flew to Munich and signed the treaty which was to bring "peace in our time." The French military authorities knew better, for they placed the French army on the alert. Chamberlain announced somberly but without conviction that he had plucked safety from the nettle danger, while Daladier with more conviction said: "They are all fools," when the people cheered him at the airport after he signed a totally meaningless document at Munich, for he knew better than anyone that there was nothing to cheer about.

From my windows on the Avenue de l'Observatoire I looked down over the Luxembourg Gardens, where the children played and the fountains threw their rainbow-colored spray into the cloudless sky. I had been reading *Les Thibaults,* the great prose epic written by Roger Martin du Gard about a French family on the eve of the First World War, and some of the color of his story seemed to stain the air of Paris. Indeed, many of the events of *Les Thibaults* took place in the Avenue de l'Observatoire, and the same characters could be recognized in the streets. One day, looking out of the window, I saw some soldiers digging zigzag trenches in the Luxembourg Gardens.

I went to see my cousin, the mayor of Paris. My ear was bandaged.

"*Grand mutilé de la guerre!*" he exclaimed, when I entered his golden office. "So you were wounded in Spain! I told you it was stupid of you to go there!"

I talked about the slit trenches in the Luxembourg Gardens.

"Are you sure they were being dug by soldiers? Nonsense, they were just workmen. They are probably putting a sewer through the gardens!"

"Yes, they were soldiers."

"Well, I have much more important things than to worry about whether a couple of soldiers are digging trenches near your apartment. I assure you we are not expecting German bombs. We have our own sources of information, and we know for absolute certainty that Germany will not attack. Germany is secure behind her new frontiers and wants nothing more!"

"And Spain?" I asked.

"Ah, Spain," he said, "who cares about Spain?"

He waved Spain across the table, as though it was an offending fly, then he made a little bow and said: "When you are in a mood to discuss intelligent matters, come and see me, but not now." He looked at his watch. "I have an appointment in five minutes with Monsieur Laval, and I must prepare my documents."

I telephoned my cousin at various times during the following months, but never saw him again. Predictably, since he belonged to the small and powerful group around Pierre Laval, he became a traitor working with Pétain and the Germans. At the end of the war he was an old and broken man under arrest for crimes against the state, and he would have been shot like Laval but for the fact that his son was a resistance hero. He was allowed to go free, to live out the few remaining years of his life in obscurity.

As autumn came on, it seemed to me that everyone in Paris took on the aspect of dancers at a masked ball waiting for midnight to strike. I spent a few days in England. Herbert Read was living in Berkhampstead in a house crammed to the ceiling with books, all the world's art at his fingertips. The lean Yorkshire face was deeply lined, his youngest child was crawling across the carpet, the books gleamed in the firelight. When I talked about Spain, he said: "When things go wrong, I always take a walk in the woods." Things had gone terribly wrong, for the child of his closest friend had died and her body lay in a small coffin strapped to the car. They would bury her later in the afternoon. It was one of those cold, raw days with a whistling wind, and the woods looked stark and bare. "I suppose," he said, "we are the sport of forces we shall never understand, but even if this is true I shall never permit my intelligence to believe it. I think the philosophers have failed—only the artists, and perhaps women, know what it is all about."

Epstein was more fearful, for he stood in the middle of his studio at Hyde Park Gate surrounded by the towering figures he had carved out of marble, and said: "It would take only a small bomb to destroy every trace of my work." He had a small house in Epping Forest, and we drove there in a taxi with his two-year-old grandson. In the course of an hour he drew seven or eight sketches of the child with a scratching pen. "Have you noticed," he said, "that artists are always at their best when they portray the people they love? That is why the artist is the enemy of war." One evening at the Café Royale we met Robert Flaherty, the maker of documentary films. Epstein and Flaherty had not seen each other for many years and now they fell into each other's arms, laughing like schoolboys. They had grown old with their art, but their art had kept them young. An Italian countess wearing a red wig, her face ravaged by disease, suddenly caught sight of them and threw her arms round them, murmuring endearments, and when they tried to shake her off, she screamed abuse at them. They waited patiently until the screaming came to an end. "We must be kind to her," Epstein said, "for she once posed for Modigliani."

When I returned to Paris early in November, Spain was already crumbling and my French relatives still believed that war with Germany was impossible. Only two people I knew really seemed to have taken the measure of the enemy. They were Max Raphael and Maria Osten, who were both German exiles and therefore in a position to understand the workings of the German mind. Max Raphael, working in a bare room off the Boulevard Montparnasse, surrounded by the collected works of Flaubert which he was now studying with the fervor of a recent convert, spoke with the gravity of an Old Testament prophet, saying that he was as certain as a man could be that Hitler within a year or two would bring about the destruction of European civilization, but nevertheless he saw no reason to abandon his study of Flaubert. An artist had a duty to go on creating, whatever the hazards. Even if he was sure that a final cataclysm was about to destroy the work of centuries, he must continue. An artist is "appointed"; he cannot appeal to the rulers of this earth, for he has nothing to say to them. He has no business fighting or dying, for his task is to create at all costs.

Max Raphael talked in these absolute terms because they were the only ones he knew. For him, art had a primacy above all other things. In his eyes the architect of a Doric temple or the creator of a great painting gave humanity its reason for existence. A world without art would be tasteless, valueless, and absurd. When he thought of Hitler, he thought of the museums going up in flames.

Maria Osten was the daughter of an East Prussian Junker, and she visualized Hitler in more practical terms. Through her apartment in the Rue Racine there passed the gramophone records made by Thomas Mann and others, which would be broadcast from secret transmitters just inside the French frontier or within Germany itself. She knew the world of conspiracy and had no enthusiasm for absolutes. She enjoyed working on proclamations denouncing Hitler and arranging for them to be sent through the underground to Germany, where they were mysteriously scattered at Nazi meetings. Denunciations of Hitler were printed on the covers of Swedish matchboxes and sent to Germany in hundreds of thousands. In Berlin copies of *Mein Kampf* appeared with strange alterations: the opening pages had been removed, and in their place were long lists of Hitler's crimes. Soapboxes, the slip-cases of gramophone records, Bibles, dictionaries, and magazines were all used in a similar way.

Maria Osten had very round dark eyes, a slightly tiptilted nose, a wide mouth which curled with laughter at the edges, and a delicate firm chin. Her temper was sardonic, and among her writings was a short novel called *Baghdad*, about the collapse of an imaginary Nazi uprising in the capital of Iraq, which ended with the Nazis goose-stepping into a desert sandstorm. She had also written a long account of her childhood and youth on her father's estate on the borders of Poland, where every year the Polish women came to do the harvesting. They were treated like slaves, raped and sometimes murdered by the Prussians, and when they returned to Poland they had little to show for their months of work. "So I became a Communist," she said simply. "What else could I become?" For a while she worked in a bookshop in Berlin, and when Hitler came to power in 1933 she escaped to Moscow, where she became the mistress of Mikhail Koltzov, the editor-in-chief of *Pravda*. Koltzov took her to Madrid when he was appointed chief Russian correspondent. He also took his wife. According to Maria Osten, Stalin was mildly amused by the *ménage à trois*, saying that if it helped Koltzov to be a good reporter or a good editor, he saw no reason to interfere.

I fell into the habit of going to see her every day, at first because I was fascinated by her conspiratorial work and also because she had more accurate information about Spain and Germany than anyone else I knew, and later because I became fascinated by the woman who was pert and high-spirited. She spoke with a slight lisp, which somehow gave weight to her words, and her rippling laughter rang like a bell. But as the weeks passed there was less laughter, for the news from Spain was becoming progressively worse, the hoped-for miracle was nowhere in sight, and there was also a private grief which she rarely spoke about—Koltzov had vanished. There were rumors that he was in prison or that he had been shot. She knew enough about the ways of the Communist world to take these rumors seriously, and she grew quieter, more reserved, as though the effort to nourish her hopes demanded the gift of silence.

Sometimes, but very rarely, she spoke of the years she spent in Moscow in a small gaily decorated apartment overlooking the river. She had known nearly all the Russian writers of the thirties. Once at a party she had fallen asleep with her head on Pasternak's knee, and for an hour he had recited poetry while she slept, and when she awoke at last he said: "Go to sleep, little one, your dreams are your poetry." One day in the Kremlin she was walking up some stairs when to her astonishment she saw Stalin coming down alone, one hand behind his back, his heavy face glowing in a shaft of sunlight. "It was like an apparition," she said. "I flattened myself against the wall, but he stopped, asked me who I was, talked about the work of the German committee, and then patted me on the head as though I were a child. Of course, I saw him often afterwards."

Her "of courses" were sometimes bewildering, for she disliked talking about herself and there were many gaps in her story. From others I learned that she had known Stalin quite well, for she sometimes accompanied Koltzov to parties in the Kremlin, where she sang German songs and amused the commissars by talking in her heavily accented Russian, which was sometimes incomprehensible. Many years later André Malraux told me that on one famous occasion Koltzov and Maria Osten received a sudden invitation to the Kremlin. She changed into a dress cut low at the back, threw on a fur coat, and hurried into the waiting automobile, pleased with herself because she had changed so quickly. When they reached Stalin's apartment, she removed the fur coat and realized to her horror that she was wearing her dress back to front. She was about to run off into another room when Stalin caught sight of her, raised his glass, and drank a toast to her. She was rooted to the ground, blushing crimson, her arms flung across her breasts, and then Stalin went up to her, lifted her hands, and commanded that they all drink another toast to her beautiful breasts. Thereafter she was known as the woman with the beautiful breasts.

Late in October Maria Osten received a welcome visitor from Russia. He was Hidalgo de Cisneros, the commander-in-chief of the Spanish Republican air force, who had fallen ill in Spain and had spent a few months recovering in Russia. Tall, elegant, very much the aristocratic descendant of generations of mediaeval princes in the Spanish courts, he had arrived on a Soviet ship which had docked at Le Havre that morning. He brought news from Koltzov, who was alive and well somewhere in the outskirts of Moscow, but apparently in disfavor and living apart from his wife. It was sketchy news, and she kept asking him for more information, but there was little he could tell her. But what especially pleased her was that he had brought with him the three-year-old Spanish boy she had adopted in Madrid, having found him alone in the rubble after a particularly heavy bombardment. All round him were the dead and the dying. He was then about a year old, very beautiful, with enormous dark eyes and a sturdy well-formed body, and she had swept him up in her shawl and carried him to the house where she was living with Koltzov. She called him Juanito. Some months later, because there were terrible food shortages in Madrid, she had arranged for the boy to live with some friends in Moscow.

Now at last he was back in her arms and she was overjoyed. When I first saw him, he lay in the center of the enormous bed, looking very weak and small, like a featherless chicken, worn out by the long journey and weeping uncontrollably. Long after midnight he was still weeping and shivering, while she bent over him, gazing at him helplessly. But the next morning, after a fitful sleep, he revived, and during the following days we took him out for walks in the Luxembourg Gardens, while he jabbered in a strange mixture of Spanish and Russian. He was as brown as a berry, full of gay impudent life, and there were incredible depths in his eyes. He wore on the lapel of his coat the badge of an officer of the Spanish Republican air force given to him by Hidalgo de Cisneros.

Maria's life now revolved around the boy with the little winged blue badge, which he proudly displayed to everyone he met. The small round face, the smell of bath water, soap, milk and woolens, the way he scampered about the apartment and hurled himself on his wooden horse or his toy bicycle, and the way he would immediately make friends with the children he encountered in the Luxembourg Gardens, talking with them at length across unfathomable barriers of language, all these things delighted her and raised her spirits. Only his happy impudence sometimes troubled her. One day he slipped into the kitchen, closed the door, and turned on all the knobs of the gas oven, and when she found him a few minutes later she promptly fainted. Juanito went on laughing. He was her life, and she could not live without him.

Into this haunted apartment—for in some mysterious way nearly everyone who entered it was aware of the ghostly presence of Koltzov—there came an unending stream of German refugees, many of them working on the secret radio, to be greeted by a radiant Maria with the boy in her arms. Many of them had been in Hitler's prisons and most of them were dedicated Communists. Hermann Kesten, the novelist, pink and fat, came and told stories by the hour. Willi Bredel, short and muscular, talked with the accents of a dock worker. He was famous for having led the dock workers against the Stormtroopers in one of the most bloody battles fought in the streets of Hamburg. Ernst Toller came—he had flown safely out of Madrid, found his possessions intact in Barcelona, and had been making speeches for the Spanish Republic in Sweden until his throat was hoarse and his eyes were bloodshot. He, too, had fallen in love with Juanito and sometimes engaged in long whispered conversations with the boy on matters that were obviously of extraordinary importance. Sometimes I placed a copy of his play *Masses and Men* in front of him and asked him to read from it, and then he would read a few lines and toss the book aside and invent new scenes until an entirely new play with the same characters emerged. I regarded him as among the greatest playwrights of our time and wanted him to write more plays. Surely he could write a play about Spain! "In five years time," he said, "but not now! All I can do now is to shout at the top of my lungs that Spain must be saved or we shall have a European conflagration unlike any we have seen up to this time!" I asked him what he would do when all the wars were over. "I'll go to a small fishing village in the south of France, and sit in the sun, and do nothing." Thereafter, whenever we met, we talked about the fishing village in the south of France, an entirely imaginary village consisting of a single street on the waterfront, houses with red and green shutters, gardens, two excellent restaurants, and a well-run post office. There came a time when we were able to walk through the imaginary village blindfold. We knew the names of everyone on the street and sometimes we spoke of going there, completely forgetting that it had no existence outside our imaginations.

The pitiless cold winter came down, a fierce wind blew along the Boulevard Montparnasse, the trees in the Luxembourg Gardens were bare, and the zigzag trenches dug by the French soldiers in the autumn were filled with rainwater and green scum. It was the last Christmas of peace, and the shops were brightly lit. We took a wide-eyed Juanito to the Galeries Lafayette and he returned home laden with a Teddy bear as large as himself, a zebra on wheels, a monkey that squeaked and dog that barked when you pulled its tail. In that melancholy winter the sight of Juanito in a fur cap, clasping his small menagerie to himself, is the only pleasant memory.

Barcelona fell at the end of January and the refugees came streaming across the frontier. I went to Perpignan and saw the French Zouaves prodding them with bayonets, cursing them, and treating them like cattle. They poured into France with their few possessions tied up in string, with cardboard boxes and cloth bundles, and they came with a peculiarly Spanish nobility. They were very quiet even when they were prodded with bayonets; they held their heads high; and they were gravely courteous even to the French police. "Pray ye," said Jesus, "that your flight be not in the winter."

I returned to Paris, having accomplished precisely nothing on the frontier. One day in February I found myself sitting next to Alvarez del Vayo, the foreign minister of Republican Spain, as he drank an anisette at the Deux Magots. A French reporter was needling him because he was sitting in a cafe while Spaniards were dying. "I am here for a very serious purpose," Del Vayo said. "I am watching the French, to see how they behave. Very soon they will have to endure what we endured, and the British, too. Soon the bombs will be falling on London and Paris." Del Vayo's lean face had grown heavy with sleeplessness and he had a three-day growth of beard. The French reporter laughed in his face. "*Monsieur le ministre*," he said, "you once prophesied that the Spanish Republicans would win the war. We do not listen seriously any longer to your prophecies."

Among the refugees from Spain was a man who at all times looked least like a refugee—Hidalgo de Cisneros. He was as calm, as elegant, as sweet-tempered as ever. He said: "In the end we had exactly one airplane on the Barcelona front." There was still some fighting on the Madrid front, but the war was lost. "The democracies, if they are sensible, will use our trained men in the coming war, they will study our documents, and they will learn from us," he said. "But I doubt whether they will take a single Spanish Republican soldier into their armies." By some mysterious means he had brought with him a large japanned box crammed with information about German and Italian air bases in the Balearic Islands, the capabilities of the enemy airplanes, the information gleaned from captured pilots. It seemed to me that the box, which was hidden under Maria's bed, for he was hiding in her apartment from the French police, was immensely valuable. What should be done with it? He thought it unlikely that the Russians would have any use for it, for they were not likely to be attacked from bases in western Europe. He distrusted the French air ministry, because it had sabotaged his efforts to buy airplanes in France. There remained the British, who were pragmatical and sensible, and could be expected to examine the documents seriously and to learn from them. Three or four days passed while he pondered the problem. He was in no hurry. He was meeting Spanish Republican officials, walking around Paris openly. "At least you should take taxis," Maria laughed, pointing at his shoes, which were elegant and two-toned and shone with a peculiarly Spanish luster. "All the French police have to do is to look at your shoes, and they will pick you up at once." At night a strange, bearded man kept watch under the lamppost near her apartment, and she was sure she was being followed whenever she went out in the street. I telephoned to a friend in London who knew the minister of air, asking for an airplane to be sent to Le Bourget to take Cisneros and the box to London. The friend said it would take a day or two to make the arrangements. That night the same strange bearded man was standing under a lamppost outside my apartment.

"He hasn't made up his mind," Maria said of Cisneros, when I told her the news from London. "He is staying at the Spanish Embassy tonight."

The next day at lunch he sauntered into Maria's apartment, sat Juanito on his knee, talked about the latest news from Spain, stroked his mustache, and said in the most casual way: "What did you hear from London?"

"Everything is all right. I am sure they will send an airplane."

"When will you know?"

"Tomorrow."

"When will the airplane come?"

"Probably the day after tomorrow."

He asked about places to stay in London, and seemed relieved at the prospect of leaving France. He thought he would spend the next two or three months in England and then go to Mexico. The important thing was that the airplane should come as soon as possible.

The British bureaucratic mind moves in mysterious ways. It likes to contemplate a problem at length and to postpone decisions until every aspect of the problem has been examined in a leisurely fashion. Four days later a message came from the British air attaché in Paris, saying that an airplane would be waiting for Cisneros at Le Bourget at eight o'clock that evening. The message came early in the afternoon. I hurried to Maria's apartment. She was looking pale and strangely dispirited. For many months she had half-known, half-guessed that Koltzov was in prison: all the scraps of information she had received could lead only to this conclusion. Yet quite deliberately she had thrust this knowledge to the back of her mind, preferring to believe that he was living incommunicado just outside of Moscow, as Cisneros had told her. Now someone from Moscow, someone who could speak with unimpeachable authority, someone apparently from the Soviet embassy, had told her that Koltzov had been arrested in August and there was no question that he was in great danger. She had decided to return to Moscow to do everything in her power to help him, and nothing anyone could say could dissuade her.

In this way she talked for some time, clutching Juanito to her breast, tears streaming down her cheeks. I said it would be much wiser if she delayed her decision. Koltzov had been editor-in-chief of Pravda, a reporter and political commissar in Spain, with direct access to Stalin. If he was under arrest, then it was probably as the result of a long series of errors, misunderstandings and compromises—no one could possibly discover any single cause, and therefore there was nothing that could be done. Stalin was totally unpredictable, and it would be much more sensible if she went to Scandinavia or Mexico. So we argued, and it was an hour later before I remembered the airplane and asked her where I could find Cisneros.

"He left for Moscow yesterday," she said. "After all, the Russians helped the Spanish Republican Air Force and sent them airplanes, and the British didn't."

"The black box?"

"The black box went with him."

I took a taxi to the British embassy, and learned that the airplane had already left England.

In the following days I saw Maria three or four times. She was almost unrecognizable, very tired, her eyes red with weeping, the mouth forming a hard line. She who had been so gay became strangely mute, saying that it was her duty as a Communist to return to Moscow, but she had never spoken about duty before. She would appeal to Stalin, and perhaps everything would be cleared up or perhaps nothing would be cleared up. She was sick with terror, and I had the feeling that nothing anyone said to her penetrated the frozen, unyielding mask.

One rainy evening, at the corner of the Rue Racine and the Boulevard St. Michel, I met Ernst Toller. I asked him about Maria, and he said: "It is no use. We have all spoken to her, but she is determined to go back. She thinks she will be safe in Moscow, but no one is safe anywhere in the world."

We walked in the rain down to the Seine. We talked about our imaginary village in the south of France, and then, standing under a gas lamp while the rain poured over his bare head, he said he was leaving for America. "Maria is going to Moscow, and I am going to New York, but what we are really doing is going as far away as possible from Spain. We are haunted by Spain, and we shall be haunted by it for the rest of our lives. And you—I suppose you will go back to England and forget that you were ever in Barcelona. *Prosit!* The charade is over, and soon the real wars will begin! As for me, I have no hope whatsoever. Believe me, I have studied Hitler, and he will not be satisfied until he has drowned the earth with blood—that is his only wish, his only desire."

As we walked, the rain increased in fury and we took shelter in a bistro. Leaning over the zinc bar, we talked lightheartedly of suicide, especially of Hitler's suicide, for I had long ago advanced the erroneous theory that Hitler would kill himself when he lost his first battle. Many of Toller's friends had committed suicide, and his face darkened. "They have ways of killing you that look like suicide," he said. "Promise me that if you ever read that I have committed suicide, you will not believe it."

Suddenly out of the steaming rain a procession of gypsies came running into the bar. They wore brightly colored rags, their faces were painted, they wore bells in their high caps, and they carried drums and castanettes. They were students from the École des Beaux Arts, and for a few moments, while they cavorted around the bar, it was as though sanity had descended on the world again. Far in the distance, floodlit in the rain, we could see the towers of Notre Dame turning into a bright silvery mist.

The next day I left Paris for Singapore, where my father was manager of the Naval Base. A few days later Maria went to Moscow, where she vanished from sight. Many years later Leon Feuchtwanger, the author of a once popular novel called *Jew Süss*, told me that when he visited Moscow shortly after the war he had inquired about her. He learned that she was arrested when she landed on Russian soil and died of typhus in 1942 while awaiting trial in the Lubyanka Prison in Moscow. It is much more likely that she was shot in the back of the neck, like all the others who returned to Moscow from Spain.

THE NAVAL BASE

I sailed from Marseilles third-class on a ship of the Messageries Maritimes line, and sometimes dreamed I was on a German prison ship. There were Indochinese students on board, thin-boned and beautiful, and the French officers took a special delight in maltreating and humiliating them. There seemed no reason for it. Quiet, unobtrusive, speaking French with an enviable grace and facility, these students simply accepted their fate and tried to pay as little attention as possible to the officers. It puzzled me that they did not revolt, and I would not have been in the least surprised to wake up one morning to find the officers lying in neat rows on the deck, each with a knife in his back.

From the beginning the third-class passengers were in a state of near revolt. The food was unpalatable, the stewards were rude, the paint was peeling, the cabins were unventilated, the smells were appalling. For me the journey was made endurable by the presence of the young Indochinese students, those friendly ghosts who glided across the decks without touching them, talking in musical whispers, their enormous eyes radiating a quiet confidence. Asked why the officers behaved so drastically toward them, they answered that it was customary to recruit the officers of a merchant ship from "a low class."

Sometimes we caught glimpses of the first-class passengers parading decorously in the upper regions of the ship and smiling down at us. Music from the first-class ballroom was wafted into our desolate cabins through the open portholes. I had not thought a passenger ship to the Far East would be a breeding ground for revolution, but so it was. The ports of call were Port Said, Djibuti, Colombo, Singapore, Saigon and Haiphong, and most of the Indochinese were bound for Haiphong.

I came to know a young Annamite, Le Duc Trong, who had been a student of mathematics at Montpellier University. His attitude to France and to French culture was one of amazed delight at all the richness displayed before him. In his rhetorical way, he liked to say: "When I die, Montpellier will be found engraved upon my heart." He made a distinction between the Frenchmen of France and the Frenchmen who went to the colonies. "We get the very worst—the very dregs! You will never understand how much we hate them in Annam and how much we love them in France. What a strange country, which exports only its worst." Speaking in a soft low musical voice, inaudible to any ship's officer, he spoke of the day when the colonial government would be destroyed root and branch, and on that day the governors' palaces would be transformed into schools staffed with French professors. Almost he adored the schools of France, and he uttered the names of Descartes, Pascal, Racine, Baudelaire and Rimbaud with reverence.

"But I suppose," he said sadly, "that if Pascal or Racine had stepped ashore on Annam, they would be inoculated with the same poison. They all get it. That is why we must get rid of them."

He asked about the war in Spain—why had the Republic lost? Did they lose heart? He said: "They lost the first round, but there will always be another. In Indochina we may lose twenty rounds, but we will keep on fighting until no Frenchman stands on our soil except by our permission. We shall have guns and airplanes, and we shall never lose heart."

Many years before, André Malraux had made the same journey on the same ship with a proper loathing for its vulgarity and ugliness, and also with a glow of gratitude. A young's man's first sea voyage to the Orient can be unbearably exciting. Every port of call wears the colors of a revelation, every landfall is a promise of majestic departures, every sunset introduces us to new colors. A journey to the Orient is always mysterious and improbable; everything we have learned in the West becomes forfeit; there are no standards for measuring the East. Day by day we were sated with new colors, new shapes, new tastes, new smells, new dawns, new sunsets. We charted our progress by the intensity of the sunsets, and forgot the syphilitic stewards and pock-marked officers in the contemplation of skies, seas and coasts of astonishing ripeness.

We stopped to coal for a night in Port Said. The ship was dark with coal dust, and the port was no more than a white glare in the darkness. From the ship's railings we looked out at an Egypt smelling of coal, coffee, and decaying fruit, and wondered what lay beyond the steel derricks and the brilliant arc lamps and the bedlam of the port. Most of the Indochinese had been rounded up and locked in their cabins, presumably because it was felt that they might get in touch with Egyptian revolutionaries if they went ashore. Because the ship had become intolerable, I slipped down the gangway.

Beyond the port lay a village of small whitewashed houses with date palms curling over them. Each house resembled a small box, scarcely more than the height of a man, with a single window and a single door. It was past midnight, very quiet, some dogs were barking in the distance and the palm trees were waving listlessly. The village was ghostly-white, the houses shuttered and silent. Suddenly out of nowhere there came a boy in a long gown, who took my hand and said: "My sister, very cheap." Happily, his sister was on the other side of the village, which consisted of seven or eight streets, and it was easy, by the tug of his hand, to know which direction he wanted to go and therefore which direction to avoid. In this way, hand in hand, we wandered through the sleeping village, while the boy jabbered about the beauty of his sister and how, out of love for me, he would see that I would have her at a good price. He smiled engagingly, and kept tripping over the long cotton gown, his only covering. Ten pounds, eight pounds, seven pounds. "For you, Effendi, she will do everything for three pounds." "What is everything?" I asked, and he answered at great length, in hoarse whispers, for he seemed not to want to awaken the villagers. With thirty words of English he could say anything that needed to be said. His name was Ahmed, and he had a round innocent face.

Ahmed amused and terrified me. I had supposed that something of the sort would happen, but had not counted on such a mingling of innocence and depravity. His sister was twelve years old, and had been born in Alexandria. Ahmed was nine years old, and had lived in this village all his life.

It occurred to me that this was the first time I had set foot in the Orient, and this small, sheltered, silent village was as good a place as any to find oneself. There was the advantage of simplicity, for the square houses were like houses seen in a dream, with the date palms soaring over them. There was no danger of losing oneself, for the port was brightly lit, less than a mile away. Also, the boy babbled away pleasantly about his sister and his life in the village. Once, when I told him finally that I had no intention of seeing his sister, he grew angry, and he suddenly pulled out the long curving knife he had had hidden in his sleeve. The knife flashed, but fell to the ground when I struck his arm. Then he stood there for a long time gazing at the knife, whimpering, the hot tears forming on his eyelashes, while I read him a sermon on the disadvantages of murder at so young an age and that as a punishment I proposed to cut him up and eat him, adding that I supposed that if I had gone to his house I would have met the same fate. He said nothing, but threw himself on the ground, pleading for forgiveness. I gave him back the knife, which vanished in his long sleeve, and we walked back to the ship across the fields.

I saw him last from the top of the gangway. He was jumping up and down, smiling from ear to ear, and waving the knife above his head.

I had learned that the East was dangerous, innocent and depraved, sweet-smelling, with square houses admirably designed to show up the splendor of the date palms. I had learned, too, that you could move from murderous rage to smiling affability in an instant, if you were a nine-year-old Egyptian boy.

The ship weighed anchor in the early morning: then it was Suez, with the statue of De Lesseps standing on the breakwater in the attitude of a Roman conqueror, and the long journey in the drenching heat down the Red Sea, which was the deepest, most royal blue, with camels loping along the sandy shore, their long necks gliding with the grace of serpents. I thought the squalid ship would melt in the heat, and was pleased that the officers looked as faint as I was, while the Indochinese, accustomed to the heat, merely smiled and waved their paper fans. March was a bad month for going through the Red Sea, and April, May and June would be worse.

We reached Djibuti late at night, the town hidden in a sulphurous haze of coal dust, smoke and darkness. Here when we anchored the ship's officers went mad, screaming at the top of their lungs and running about the deck like scalded ants.

What terrified them beyond measure was an invasion of young Somalis, so dark that they melted into the night, so lithe and agile and slender that they were able to climb up the ship's side and slide through portholes with ease. Long-legged, naked except for dark loincloths, they swarmed over the ship. Coarse netting was hurriedly hung between the decks, the portholes were closed, armed guards were posted at the top of the gangway and wherever it was thought the Somalis might congregate. They came singly, gliding like apparitions along the corridors or suddenly appearing in the rigging to distract the attention of the officers, who climbed after them. The Somalis had the ship at their mercy.

It was a lesson in guerrilla warfare, for they were well organized, knew exactly what they were doing, and had nothing to lose. No doubt the ship's officers could have shot them down and pitched their bodies into the sea, but there were good reasons for treating the marauders gently. If a single Somali had been shot, ten thousand of them would have come marching out of Somaliland and torn the ship's plates apart with their bare hands.

To escape the bedlam on the ship, I went ashore and found Djibuti given over to a bedlam even more disturbing. There were brothels within twenty yards of the dock, the girls standing in front of the dusty curtains naked to the waist, so much smaller than their agile brothers that at first I took them for another race, until I realized that these girls were eight or nine years old. The town reeked of stale alcohol, sweat, and all the fermenting juices of Africa. Djibuti was a hellhole.

When I returned to the ship two hours later, it was past midnight. By this time most of the Somalis had vanished, but the officers said they were fearful of a second invasion. The netting was drawn more tightly between the decks, and raking searchlights picked up the last survivors scrambling in the rigging. "I think the war is over," one of the officers said, and even as he spoke he was looking over his shoulder. Then we heard a splash and rushed to the railings. A Somali, who had dived off the ship, was swimming with strong strokes, while from his shoulder there trailed behind him a fleet of women's dresses knotted together.

We reached Colombo early in the morning a few days later. The city, all white and gold and green, dazzled in the heat.

The open harbor was crowded with motor launches, while more and more ocean-going ships dropped anchor. There was such a bustle in the harbor, so many pennons were waving, so much brightness came out of the sky and the sea that I felt that I was entering Paradise. The smell of spices came over the sea, heady as new wine. Here was the Orient at last in all its splendor, and I would not have been in the least surprised to see dragons and unicorns appearing at my side.

Colombo had none of the hellish fascination of Djibuti: it was Paradise laid out in orderly rows in the English fashion, white-washed among the Flame of the Forest trees, the graceful Singhalese moving about with extraordinary quietness, the women floating in clouds of brilliantly embroidered saris. As a child I had dreamed of journeying from Ceylon to the Himalayas, and it was wonderful to see the beginning of a dream coming to abundant life.

There remained only a few days before Singapore appeared on the horizon, a green island on a green sea. The slovenly ship with its peeling paint floated past the small islands, each as large as a garden and each with a single palm tree, on the high seas off Malaya. The sky, which had opened wide at Colombo, opened still wider, and I was as delirious as the gulls and the flying fish when we berthed at Singapore, the ancient Singapura, the City of the Lions.

My father was waiting for me, his face an incongruous tomato-red, his blue eyes glittering under eyebrows surprisingly touched with gray, his uniform a white shirt, white shorts, white socks, and white shoes. He was the manager of the Naval Base, lord and master of a vast estate, but wore no badges of rank. He carried himself with a very English jauntiness and was like a stranger to me, so long immersed among Austrians, Frenchmen, Spaniards and Indochinese. With an effort I realized that I had lost in Vienna and Barcelona whatever jauntiness I once possessed, while he had changed very little. He said: "You look thin. Your mother will feed you up. Jump into the car." He drove quickly through the city of Singapore across the island to the Naval Base, carved out of the low hills and swamps facing the Straits of Johore. On a hill overlooking blue waters and the primeval forest stood a house like a white bird that has only just alighted and is still folding its wings.

I lived in this house for nearly three years, never quite accustoming myself to its beauty. Like nearly all houses in Malaya, it was built on stilts and had a lightness and airiness beyond belief. Huge windows let the sun in, and when necessary bamboo blinds kept it out. One wing of the house was mine, the other belonged to my parents, and between them were the dining room and drawing room that looked out on the Straits of Johore. A covered passage in the back led to the kitchen compound where the Chinese cook and his assistants lived, worked and slept. At the gate stood a frangipani tree, whose white buds possessed an overpowering fragrance.

The house on King's Avenue was for me a revelation of simplicity and perfection, as though finally someone had achieved an architecture superbly appropriate for a superb setting. Below, through a mirage of heat, lay acres of curling grass, white engine shops, a graving dock a thousand feet long, the guarded headquarters of the Far Eastern Command, long wharves like slots cut into the landscape, and ships at anchor, while the huge floating dock, like a high-walled fortress, was moored in the shadow of the ancient forests of Johore. Hawks flew lazily overhead, and Flame of the Forest trees scattered their blood-red blossoms. The Naval Base looked more like a college campus than a powerful military installation, and everything about it was quiet, clearly defined and orderly. Chinese and Malay mechanics, Tamil laborers, Sikh guards, and English workmen were employed; nearly all the nations of the East were gathered there. Simply to stand beside the frangipani tree and watch the ships gliding up the Straits was to know a quiet contentment.

Most of the Naval Base came under my father's control, for the base was essentially a dockyard and he was in charge of all the docks and repair shops. Every ship that came to be repaired or refitted fell under his command. In theory the base was commanded by the Admiral Superintendent and the Captain of the Dockyard, but in peacetime they had very little to do, their functions being largely decorative. Most of the radio messages received from the Admiralty in London concerned him, and it amused him that though the Admiral Superintendent and the Captain of the Dockyard saw them first, and carefully initialed them, they knew scarcely anything about the repair and refitting of ships.

My father was not an office man and he had a peculiar horror of paper work. He liked to see things done and spent most of the day out of doors. There were naval architects who had spent their whole lives on design boards in the Admiralty, but he felt that he had done his proper share of designing. He took a sensuous pleasure in the shapes of things, delighting in the powerful curve of a cruiser's bow and the curving lines engraved on the mold-loft floor showing cross sections of a ship in patterns of great abstract beauty. When a ship entered dock, when all the water was finally pumped out and the keel rested securely on the blocks, then the ship was fully in his possession and he made decisions on the spot, gave orders and saw that they were carried out. At such times his face lit up with fierce enjoyment and his blue eyes sparkled.

One day, when he was studying at Keyham Naval College, he was playing cricket when a cricket-ball came out of the sun and smashed into his spectacles. His left eye was torn by fifty splinters of glass, and for a while it was thought that he would lose the sight of both eyes. For weeks his eyes were bandaged, while he continued his studies with the help of an older brother who pricked out on his hands the complicated shapes of spherical geometry and electrical circuits. He passed the examinations for entering Greenwich Naval Academy by a prolonged act of will: he could scarcely see the paper he was writing on. In Singapore he was still half blind, and sometimes when driving his car along the winding road from the Naval Base to Singapore, he found himself plowing across a rice field, roaring: "What in hell has happened to the bloody car?" Then somehow the car would be on the road again, and he was muttering: "Well, we gave the car a good shaking."

For me, Singapore, the island, the city and the Naval Base, were the purest benediction, for all the East was congregated here. There were Buddhist temples with butterlamps twinkling beneath gleaming porcelain Buddhas garlanded with jasmine. Indian firewalkers marched nonchalantly over flaming coals outside Hindu temples ornamented with fiery Indian gods. A kindly voice announced from the minarets that God alone was great and Mohammed was his prophet, while the dark-eyed Malays, in brilliantly patterned sarongs, bowed in worship under the cavernous domes of the mosques where ostrich eggs hung suspended at the end of long threads. And everywhere there were Chinese, nearly all from South China, going about their affairs with an air of quiet enjoyment, not in the least inscrutable. Chinese junks and sampans sailed up the Singapore River, which was perhaps two hundred yards long, all that remained of an ancient river that once flowed down the entire length of Malaya.

I had the feeling that Europe was so far away, so unreachable, that its decisions could not possibly affect the fortunes of Singapore, which had been created for my special delectation. Storms came, and suddenly the perfect blue skies were filled with roaring clouds lit by lightning, but the storms rarely lasted more than an hour, and afterward there were blue skies again. These brief storms only underscored the calm and effortless beauty of the days.

One evening, at the Great World, the fun fair on the outskirts of Singapore, I was turning over the pages of a book in a Chinese bookshop, when suddenly a young Chinese came up and said: "So you read Chinese?"

I said I could not read a single word, but liked the shapes of the characters.

"If you would like to read Chinese, I will teach you," he said quietly, and from that day I became his pupil.

His name was Wang Chieh, and he worked in a bank. It appeared that he also had obscure political connections, and when he walked down a street in the Chinese district he was usually greeted with ceremonial bows, as befitted a man of some eminence in the community. He was older than he looked, and was perhaps thirty-five. Handsome, broad-shouldered, with a full round face and a sturdy body, tending toward portliness, he carried himself with an air of authority. He knew everyone in Singapore, and seemed to have read everything in Chinese literature. When I went to see him in his small house with the red pillars, or when he came to visit me at the Naval Base, I was aware chiefly of his enchanting smile and of his exemplary patience as he discussed the intricate workings of the Chinese language.

I studied with him without ever learning Chinese well, perhaps because we met only once a week and Chinese deserves a more demanding schedule.

"You should study a bit harder," he said. "At this rate it will take you about twenty years to learn Chinese properly."

"How long does it take a Chinese to learn Chinese?"

"About twenty years."

I was enjoying the leisurely pace: to learn a few characters each week and make sentences out of them was pleasurable, while a concentrated regimen of Chinese would have been back-breaking work. Also, I was lazy. I was spending my days wandering around the Naval Base and the streets of Singapore, writing a novel, or gazing out of the window at the Malayan sunsets with their daily explosions of emerald and gold. Baudelaire speaks somewhere of the enviable existence of a man who simply watches the comings and goings of a great seaport while having no attachment to anything in the world. He watches others exerting their wills, obsessed with the desire to grow rich or to travel abroad, while he enjoys the shapes of the ships and the waves and the multitudinous activity of the port for their own sake. Such a man, says Baudelaire, enjoys "a mysterious and aristocratic pleasure." There was nothing mysterious or aristocratic in the pleasure of being in Singapore. The mystery was that there were not more Singapores, so beautiful and so tranquil under the sun.

Even then I think we knew the tranquillity would come to an end. We spoke half unbelievingly about the possibilities of a Japanese invasion and we were certain there would be war with Germany, while the very beauty of the island made it impossible to believe that these things could happen. We studied the maps and saw how the Japanese threatened all of the mainland of Southeast Asia. We thought that even if the Japanese came, the great power of the Naval Base would keep them at bay.

THE GHOSTLY DANCERS OF BALI

That summer, while Hitler was ranting and all Europe was on the verge of catastrophe, my father decided on the spur of the moment to take my mother and me to Java and Bali. He argued sensibly that time was running short and that there might never be another opportunity to see them. We sailed from Singapore to Batavia on a Dutch ship filled with portly Dutchmen and their even more portly wives, who resembled queen bees. Never before or since have I seen so much white blubbery flesh, so many trembling chins, such rotund buttocks, and I came reluctantly to the conclusion that such mountains of flesh were native to the Dutch East Indies.

Between Singapore and Batavia there are a thousand islands, and a man standing on deck, watching the islands emerging and then vanishing again in the sea mist, has the illusion of entering a world of enchantment where all the ordinary laws of nature are held in abeyance. There are only islands. Sometimes these islands were only large enough to support a single palm tree reigning majestically in perfect isolation. Sometimes, too, you would come upon an island with a few huts and beached fishing-boats, where the Malay fishermen live exactly like their pirate ancestors. The sea was an intense tropical blue, almost purple, the waves so gentle that there was scarcely any breaking of the crests, only a ghostly whiteness where the crests had been. At night the sea gleamed with a fiery phosphorescence and strange shadows lurked in its depths. Though day followed night, there was the sensation of floating in a shimmering world where time hung suspended.

One morning time came to a halt. I was idly reading the news bulletin, which seemed to have nothing whatsoever to do with the world around me. Some flying fish had just fallen on deck; a whole cluster of islands floated past. The bulletin announced that Hitler had delivered one more of his threatening speeches, Chamberlain had spoken in the House of Commons, and there had been a fire in Chicago. Then, at the bottom, like an afterthought, there came a single sentence. *Ernst Toller, German poet, committed suicide in the Mayflower Hotel in New York.* Suddenly the clouds came racing over the ocean, and the sea turned milky white.

When I last saw Toller at the corner of the Boulevard St. Michel and the Rue Racine, it was a damp winter evening with a mist coming up from the Seine and he was huddled in a long greatcoat. I had seen him nearly every day during the winter, and we had no secrets from each other. I knew he had been murdered, and I knew that on this ship coasting along the shores of Java, half a world away from New York, there was nothing I could do about it.

The memory of Toller haunted me throughout the journey. He was always present, the wonderful smile lighting his face, the brown eyes gleaming with every new thought and melting as each thought came to an end. You could almost read his thoughts by watching his eyes. He seemed to walk beside me in the streets of Batavia and he came gliding among the columns of the sultan's palace at Djogjacarta. He was present when we came to the beehive temple at Chandi Mendoet, where a youthful honey-colored Buddha ten feet high reposed on a majestic throne, and there was about this youthful Buddha a sense of quiet holiness, and such compassion and grace, that he seemed living. The Buddha of Chandi Mendoet is one of the supreme works of Buddhist art, but at the time I knew little enough about Buddhism or its art, and this statue of a naked sleeping youth came to me with the force of a revelation. Here was majestic beauty enshrined in a small beehive, the feet smooth and gleaming because they had been kissed by Buddhist pilgrims throughout the centuries. "Look, Ernst, the eyes are closed, he blesses, and he lives."

A few miles beyond Chandi Mendoet there was another Buddhist monument incalculably larger and more intricate, yet lacking the simple majesty of the enthroned Buddha in the beehive. This was the enormous *stupa* called Borobudur with its hundreds of relief carvings along the narrow roads winding up to the summit of the artificial mountain. These reliefs carved in soft sandstone were wonderfully vivid, but so numerous that we soon wearied of their magnificence. Later we would study photographs of the reliefs and wonder how we could have torn ourselves away from those galleries which possess some of the greatest sculptures in the world.

From Soerabaya we flew to Bali, skirting the land and looking down on calm green lakes high up in the mountains and smoldering yellow volcanoes lost among tropical forests; and sometimes we saw the mountain eagles. I had not enjoyed Java except for the honey-colored Buddha of Chandi Mendoet and the interminable carvings of Borobudur. There were too many preposterously fat Dutchmen wandering through the streets and too many small-boned Javanese hurrying out of their way. The arrogance of the conquerors was unendurable, and the island seemed ripe for rebellion.

Bali seen from the air resembled an immense emerald dipped in purest water, quivering and shimmering in the sun. The air was luxuriously blue, the palm trees luxuriously green. We tumbled out of the airplane into another earth, outside time and space, a remote and perfect corner of Paradise.

A long winding palm-shaded road, the girls at the wells, the men looking up from the rice lakes with their hoes in their hands, and then we were in Den Pasar. In those days Den Pasar was a very small town with only a few hotels and government offices, a few mud houses, a museum, a large temple and a football field, and the fact that the town scarcely existed at all was very much in its favor. We found a small hotel opposite the large temple, and every morning and evening we watched the worshipers coming with their offerings of flowers and fruit. Beyond the temple lay the terraced rice fields and the hills. The sun shone strong, and the early morning mists were soon burned away.

The women and the men walked with uncommon grace, as though they owned the earth. There was no trace of servility in them, and I never saw one who was not handsome. They were bare to the waist, golden-colored, with flashing eyes and brilliant red lips from chewing betel, larger-boned than the Javanese, and much fairer, and the young children four or five years old walked with the same dignity as their elders. The girls and the women wore small clumps of leaves or large yellow earplugs of bone in their earlobes, and for some mysterious reason these yellow and green decorations seemed wonderfully appropriate. Their sarongs were more gaily colored than the ubiquitous dark brown patterned sarongs in Java. They walked with the dignity of princes, but they had paid dearly for the dignity they retained in spite of being conquered by the Dutch.

I knew the story well, and was haunted by it throughout my stay in Bali. On May 27, 1904, a Chinese steamer was shipwrecked on the beach of Sanur about four miles from Den Pasar. The Dutch government, which held only a light suzerainty over the island, learned that the steamer had been looted and destroyed at the orders of the Prince of Badung and immediately claimed an indemnity of 7500 florins from the Prince, who refused to pay, preferring war to total submission. The Dutch therefore decided to send an expeditionary force to Bali. They took their own time, and it was not until September 20, 1906, that a Dutch force armed with cannon and machine guns appeared at Den Pasar and surrounded the Prince's palace. They appealed to the Prince to surrender, but he refused. During the night they heard chanting and in the early hours of the morning the entire palace went up in flames, though the heavily guarded palace walls remained unharmed. The Dutch were aware of confused movements behind the walls but no sounds reached them. Whatever the Balinese were doing in the courtyard, they were absolutely silent.

At the first dawnlight the great gates of the palace opened wide and the Balinese poured out with the Prince of Badung at their head. He wore a gold turban and a sarong of gold thread and wielded a gold-handled kris; and all the rest of them, young and old, were in their finery. The men wore red, black and gold sarongs, and the women and girls wore white sarongs, and their bodies were covered with jewels and pearls. The women carried their children in their arms. More than a thousand Balinese marched out of the palace courtyard straight toward the Dutch guns. Fifty yards from the guns the Prince drew his kris from its scabbard and gave the signal for the assault. The Dutch opened fire, and when the smoke cleared there was a heap of bodies lying close to them, but the Balinese were still advancing. Children armed with knives flung themselves against the cannon; warriors hurled their spears; the only Dutch casualty was a Dutch sergeant stabbed to death by a girl wielding a kris, and the only survivors among the Balinese were some babies who had fallen from their mothers' arms. The Dutch tore down the palace walls and plowed up the palace courtyard, so that no trace of the massacre remained. Where the palace had been they made a football field and where the bodies had fallen they built a hotel.

In 1939 there were so few Dutchmen in Den Pasar that their presence could easily be forgotten. The land seemed to belong to the Balinese, and especially to the women, who resembled bronze statues. Even when they were laughing, they had about them the reserve and dignity of statues, not that they were unapproachable, but they moved in a world that possessed the grace of the highest art. Something very similar must have happened among the ancient Greeks, who also lived in the open air, regarding their houses simply as places to sleep in. There was something manifestly self-conscious in the way the Balinese invariably assumed the exactly right posture or made the exactly right gesture. A girl bathing in one of the streams outside Den Pasar would enter the water as though she were conferring an honor on it, and if she carried a basket of fruit on her head, she carried it in such a way that it might have been a crown. It was as though they all regarded themselves as empresses.

The villages began at the outskirts of Den Pasar, and each village had its temple of red sandstone, courtyard after courtyard, one opening out into another, the gateways magnificently carved with stone flowers and fruit and the figures of the gods. These villages were no more than thatched huts, which could be swept away in a high wind, and even the temples lacked permanence, for the Balinese were continually reworking them, tearing down the carved gates and putting them up again. There was nothing old in Bali except the ancient traditions, deriving from the time when the Hindu conquerors first settled on the island. The dances, too, were continually being renewed, but always within the traditional forms. The ancient past weighed very lightly on them, but was always present.

One evening the great dancer Mario performed in the courtyard of the Bali hotel. He was then about forty, long past his prime, but he looked about twenty-five with his thin, sensitive face and slender body which seemed to have been carved out of golden wood. He sat cross-legged on a platform with a bank of musicians playing on gamelans behind him, and when the music began there was a strange alteration in him, as though a new kind of life, more subtle and delicate and at the same time more fiery than the ordinary everyday life of the senses, had entered into him. From being carved wood his body became molten. His long arms shot out, his fingers fluttered, danced, became wings and trumpets, faces and desires, ghosts and premonitions. Only the hands danced, and only the hands seemed to possess life, for his body had become merely the support for those incredible hands which described the creation of whole universes and their passing away in flames. For half an hour he danced without pause, and then abruptly the music ceased and the hands that had held our attention for so long, because they were capable of inventing whatever they wanted to invent, dropped to his lap. He rose and vanished into the darkness. There was no applause, for we were too stunned by that hallucinatory dance to realize that he was no longer there.

The Balinese dances are now well-known, but in those days they came to us with the force of revelations. The lion-masks, the towering crowns, the richly embroidered costumes of the girls, and their dazzling command of sudden, furious gestures, so that half a dozen girls acting the roles of ancient Hindu princes suggested an entire army on the march and the intoxication of battle, all these things filled us with astonishment. These highly wrought, artificial dances performed in the shadow of the temples descended from ceremonial dances in ancient Indian courts, but they possessed an extraordinary directness and relevance. Even if you did not know the legends on which they were based, you were aware of the passion, the violence and the tenderness. There were sudden changes of mood, silences, interludes of incredible ferocity, the patterns continually changing. There seemed to be no end to the subtleties of this aristocratic art performed by peasants.

I came to know a young Balinese who proclaimed that he was a *gusti* or prince, and was remarkable chiefly because he was without any illusions whatsoever. When he was younger, he suffered from epilepsy, a not uncommon disease in Bali, but he had recovered and there had been no further attacks for many years. Yet the memory of the attacks remained with him, and there were moments when he vanished within himself, completely lost to the world. He was well-built, very sturdy, and did not in the least look like someone who was haunted by the vanity of everything under the sun. His eyes were very large, golden brown and liquid, and sometimes the light would go out of them.

I suppose it was the remembered epileptic attacks which made him so indifferent to everything that happened, as though nothing in the world interested him. At one time he had wanted to go to America; later he wanted to go to Holland; the Dutch colonial officials refused to let him leave Bali. One day he said: "Bali is a prison—they arrest everyone who tries to go out."

"Can you go to Java?"

"Not without special permission, and they rarely give it."

"So you remain in Bali, and there are people who would give their right arms to be in Paradise with you."

He laughed, but there was sadness in his laughter.

"If you think this is Paradise," he went on, "then at least you should see the real Bali—not just the dancers who perform outside the Bali Hotel."

So he took us under his wing, and showed us what he called "the real Bali of the villages and the hamlets," which was sometimes terrifying, because the people were caught up in taboos and superstititions and lived in dreadful fear of the spirits. One night, long after dark, he drove us to a small hamlet on the Tabanan coast. I remember huge moths, brilliantly colored, dashing themselves against the headlights and soon there was such a thick crust of flaming red and purple moths on the headlights that we could scarcely see where we were going. Here and there we came upon small thatch-roofed houses on stilts set back from the road, and sometimes there would be a dead cock nailed to a tree as a warning to the evil spirits not to come near the place. There was no one else on the road, for the Balinese dislike traveling at night and have no love for darkness. The young Balinese was taking us to a small hamlet where five- or six-year-old girls danced the *sanghyang*, the most eerie of their dances, for it was performed in a trance, as though by puppets, and yet, so he informed us, with extraordinary technical skill. "The gods speak in the *sanghyang*," he said, "and you will hear them."

The hamlet we were coming to was not marked on any map. There were four or five thatched huts reached by a winding road through the palms. In the faint light from the headlights the hamlet looked poor and woebegone. One of the thatched roofs had fallen in, and no one had troubled to restore it. Some benches had been arranged haphazardly around a beaten-earth floor, and some old men were squatting around a brazier, chewing betel nuts. They looked up quietly when we appeared, and then resumed their conversations. There was a heavy scent about the place, of chicken droppings and sickly sweet frangipani flowers and decaying foodstuffs and hot peppers. When I think of Bali now, I remember the smoke of the cooking fires, the girls bathing in the streams with their long black hair floating on the surface of the water and many dances, but most of all I remember this small forgotten hamlet seen in the light of our colored headlights, so empty and purposeless a place that it might have been at the bottom of an abandoned quarry lost to the world. The car lights went out, and there were only the old men squatting over the brazier.

We must have come early, because half an hour passed before people from the neighboring hamlets came wandering onto the beaten-earth floor. The night was hot and still, and the lights in the small compound were very dim. A gamelan was playing; someone was practicing on the drums; suddenly the girls appeared, as though they had drifted out of the night, wearing high headdresses and brilliant costumes of gold thread. Someone poured some herbs into the brazier, and the smell hanging over the hamlet became even more sickly sweet than before, while they knelt over the brazier, absorbing the scented smoke in their lungs. There were four girls, and not one of them could have been more than seven years old and the youngest may have been five. Yet they were dressed like the most splendid princesses, with gold sashes round their waists, their costumes as ornate as the costumes worn by the girls who performed at Den Pasar, and even their fans were made of some intricate cloth veined with gold threads. They looked as though they had just woken up and were still drowsy, and were all the more drowsy because they were inhaling the fumes from the brazier. They were so small, so thin-boned, that we felt pity for them, forgetting that they were perfectly happy and sometimes even now they would look up mischievously and smile at us, like actors who peer through the curtains at the audience before the play begins.

The music began playing and the children shuffled away from the brazier, their eyes closed. Gamelans, gongs and drums could be heard, but the musicians were somewhere in the darkness. The summer lightning played above the palms, while the four dancers, knees slightly bent, continued to shuffle through the dust. Then the music grew louder and they began to sway, while at the same time their long slender fingers jerked upward like flowers suddenly unfolding, and from that moment the real dance began, with its fierce alterations of tempo, its strange passages of barbaric splendor, so that the little patch of dusty ground seemed to be inhabited by a whole army of dancers clashing their shields; but there were no shields, only the little gold-veined fans.

There was nothing in the least improvised in the dance: it was as though they had studied the steps and the gestures as a musician studies a score and learns it by heart. They knew, or rather some part of their brains, knew precisely what they were doing. They danced at a dizzy pace, with sudden leaps and gyrations, their thin arms rippling and undulating like the necks of intoxicated swans. Strength poured into them from the music. They assumed grandeur and power, and it was perfectly possible to imagine that they were possessed by the gods. They were not simply dancing: they were saying things for which there were no words. Some mysterious power worked on them as they celebrated the rites of some unknown goddess, now approaching her throne reverently, now retreating, now hurling themselves upon her and driving her from her throne. There were terrible silences when nothing seemed to be happening except the fluttering of their fingers, and then the music seemed to take them by the throat and hurl them across the stage, which seemed immense, though it was perhaps only ten feet square.

There came a time when the sweat flew from their faces, and still they danced, their naked feet pattering on the dusty floor. They were in a trance—this much was certain, but could the trance be maintained? What depths of unconsciousness had they reached? Had they gone beyond unconsciousness into another world altogether, where all was violence and the flashing of gold? Instantaneously obedient to the music, they danced like sleepwalkers caught up in a strange passionless adventure, for their painted faces were totally impassive and only their bodies expressed the yearnings of their souls. What was extraordinary above everything else was the violence of the dance, which drained them of energy, yet they continued dancing. If the music had stopped suddenly, they would have fallen like matchwood to the ground and crumpled up.

I had the feeling that someone in the audience, perhaps the old man sitting by the brazier, was ordering this performance, commanding it by his mere presence, like a puppet-master pulling on the strings. Strange forces were at work on the dancers, whose faces were devoid of expression, like masks. There were brief moments when they looked exactly like puppets: if their richly embroidered garments were removed, we would find sticks of wood bolted and jointed together. The young Balinese was saying: "Now they are offering flowers to the goddess." At that moment they were raising their arms in what appeared to be a solemn gesture of supplication.

It was all mystery and hallucination, for they had the power to convince us that they were in some extraordinary way mediators between heaven and earth. What they held in their frail hands was nothing less than destiny. All the other dances we had seen were performances, but these children were acting out a truly religious rite, with a grace and energy which could have come only from some divine source. Now, as I recall these times, I see the blue smoke rising from the braziers and the crowded faces forming a circle around the dancers, and I seem to be moving away from them, seeing them as though from the reversed end of a telescope, until they become no more than specks of light in a distant and untraveled sky, shining like the fixed stars. In my mind they have an unchanging beauty, and they were the most beautiful children I had ever seen.

The end came, as it comes in all Balinese dances, suddenly and without warning. There had been an unusually furious dance, an approach to the very throne of the goddess, followed by a tumultuous retreat, and then the music of the gamelan and gongs had fallen away only to revive again slowly with a sound like the wind playing among leaves. This music continued for a little while longer, but the urgency had gone from it. The music stopped. At that very moment the young men from the hamlet ran toward the dancers to catch them before they fell. They were wrapped in coarse blankets and carried to their homes, but for a long time afterward the air was still flashing where they had danced.

On the following day the young Balinese drove us to the cremation grounds not far from Kerimun, saying that we were doubly fortunate because the body of a local rajah who had died six or seven years before was being cremated that afternoon. There were not many rajahs and they did not die often. In fact, there had been no similar cremation for at least two years, and very probably it would be one of the most splendid cremations of all time.

We drove along a sunken road with the rice fields rising in terraces on either side, and there was the pleasant sound of water trickling down the slopes. The countryside was deserted, for no one works in the fields on the day of a cremation and people gather from miles around to take part in the festivities. For a long time before we reached the cremation ground we heard shouting and the booming of drums.

Then at a turning in the road we saw a crowd of men carrying what seemed to be an immense tree with brilliantly colored leaves, green and scarlet and silver, with ribbons hanging down. It was nearly fifty feet high, swaying dangerously. The artificial tree was a hearse, for on one of the lower stages we could see a body wrapped in a white shroud, and above this rose the shafts of bamboo branching out, pagoda-like, with such a wild display of tinsel and bits of colored paper that it seemed to be covered with jewels. An army of half-naked men, jostling and shouting, was carrying the great tree to the cremation ground on a steep rise above the sunken road. Four or five immense banyan trees stood on the rise, and already there was a pile of logs as high as a house stacked beneath one of the banyans. In the shade some girls had already set up their stalls, selling lumps of sweet rice, sugar cane and pink lemonade.

Suddenly the great tree came lurching up the rise, and the shouting grew louder. So large, so heavy a tree, demanded the utmost effort, and so they came grunting and jostling, to the clanging of bells and the beating of drums, halfway up the rise and then back again to the sunken road, while the tree swayed so dangerously that it seemed to be in danger of crashing down onto the road. And behind the tree came another procession, equally disorderly, of younger men pulling an enormous wooden bull, rough-hewn, with black eyes, flaming nostrils and curving horns, and this procession suddenly catapulted into the procession carrying the tree, which began to wave and jerk crazily, so that it appeared to be jumping around like a puppet on an invisible string. Firecrackers were exploding, clouds of blue smoke swept through the crowds, and suddenly the scarlet bull was lifted high above their heads and began to pitch backward and forward like a ship in a stormy sea. A priest was sprinkling holy water from a bamboo tube over the mourners who were laughing uproariously because the crowd carrying the tree was now inextricably intermingled with the crowd carrying the bull. Finally the tree was hauled up the slope, and the relatives of the dead rajah climbed up a bamboo ladder and carried the body down to the ground. There were prayers and incantations, and more holy water was sprinkled. No one except the priests and the relatives paid much attention to these rites. The men who had been carrying the tree and the bull now congregated around the girls selling pink lemonade.

These girls were quite astonishingly beautiful, and that day they all made small fortunes. Bare-breasted, with bright green tubes of leaves in their ears, wearing brilliant sarongs, they seemed to be playing an essential role in the drama as they dispensed their cakes of sweet rice bound up in banana leaves and ladled out the lemonade that tasted like water. There was a good deal of banter and innuendo; they were joking and laughing; and the flashing of their eyes and the quickness of their smiles suggested vivandières accompanying an army on the march. The priests spent a great deal of time praying over the corpse, and long before it was lifted into the wooden bull the girls had sold out their wares.

A Balinese cremation is a complicated affair. The corpse has to be placed in the right position, the priests have to perform very complex ceremonies, and every possible entreaty has to be made to the innumerable gods of the Balinese heaven. But no one except the relatives paid the slightest attention to the priests. Everyone was enjoying himself. The young men were dancing and shouting, working off their animal spirits, while the girls looked on shyly. An hour passed, and then the priests gave the signal to place the corpse in the bull, which was then carried onto the funeral pyre. Once again there was a great deal of jostling and shouting, while oil was thrown on the logs and more offerings were placed on the bull and between its feet. A boy climbed up the pyre and manipulated the bright red genitalia of the bull, to the screaming of the girls and the happy guffaws of the men. At the same time, at the other end of the bull, a priest poured more holy water from a bamboo tube and a live cock was tied to the enormous coffin, which could have contained at least twenty corpses.

By this time nearly everyone was exhausted, and a curiously solemn mood descended on the onlookers, who no longer had any role to play. Someone set light to the pyre and for a few moments a glorious sheet of golden flame rose and seemed about to consume the bull in a single instant; but in fact the wood was damp, and the flame soon died out, leaving only clouds of angry smoke. More oil was poured on the wood, and fifteen minutes passed before the pyre was properly ignited. Through the smoke we could see the flames licking the bull, and soon there came the smell of burning varnish and long-decayed flesh. All the time a priest was chanting from a high ladder leaning against a nearby banyan, which was in danger of being burned down. The cock tied to the coffin escaped with a broken neck. The coffin split apart in the flames and the corpse turned into a flaming golden cocoon, writhing in the fierce heat. The flames reached the corpse only just in time, for at that moment a small rain began to fall. It was time, then, to set fire to the many-colored tree which had served as a hearse, and now there were two fires blazing on the mound above the rice fields.

Later, when the body was completely consumed, the ashes were gathered together and carried in procession to the seacoast, where they were thrown to the waves. Only the relatives and the priests took part in this rite. For everyone else the ceremony was now over, and they began to drift away in the direction of the girls selling lemonade. New supplies had been brought in from the neighboring villages. Even though the rain was falling, the paper and bamboo tree burned merrily, and in the light of the fires the girls' bodies turned to molten gold.

One afternoon, toward the end of our stay in Bali, we drove to Tampaksiring to see the tombs of the ancient kings carved out of the rock face. These tombs were said to date from the time of the Madjapahit empire, and we were told that sculptors from India had portrayed the features of the kings. No one seemed to know much about the tombs, and this was all the more reason for examining them. We drove to Tampaksiring on a clear hot day, the rice terraces steaming and reflecting the intense blue of the sky. Wild duck flew overhead, and crested woodpeckers were hammering at the trees. The road wound among avenues of palms, and all the time there was the musical sound of trickling water from the sluice-gates, the water flowing from one terraced rice field to another. Small boys with silver anklets were waving the birds away or lying stretched out in the sun on the backs of water buffaloes. In the fields the dark-skinned peasants stood knee-deep in water, their sarongs tucked tight between their thighs.

When we came to Tampaksiring it was no longer possible to go by car. The approach to the tombs could be made only on foot along the raised edge of the rice fields, and so we followed these paths in the direction of a rock cliff about half a mile away where we could see very faintly some carvings which did not in the least resemble the faces of kings, and indeed the rock was so overcovered with moss and creepers and there were so many pepper trees that we came to the conclusion that there was scarcely anything to be seen. The rock was sandstone, bright yellow, the same color as the temples in the valley.

Gusts of heat came from the soft, crumbling rock, immense white butterflies went in and out of the caves, while the blue jays darted in the pepper trees. It was one of those calm afternoons when the visible world seemed astonished by its own beauty, and in the mirrored pools the small clouds sailed effortlessly across serene skies. We decided not to explore the tombs, but to return along the raised paths between the rice fields. Suddenly, as though they had sprung out of the ground, we saw three old men approaching along the path. They wore the customary brown sarongs and carried knives at their belts, and no doubt they were the elders of one of the neighboring villages. Only their faces were old and deeply lined, but like many old men in Bali they possessed sleek glowing bodies and their movements were vigorous. To us they seemed more like apparitions than men, so suddenly had they appeared in an empty landscape, and we stepped aside to let them pass. Today, when I remember this valley, I see these three old men coming toward us in the heat of the afternoon, grave and solemn in their walk, with smiling faces and clear eyes, wearing long stiff sarongs, dark against the sun, and they have about them the majesty of ancient kings.

Always, wherever we traveled in Bali, there were these strange moments when perfectly normal things acquired the appearance of apparitions. These three old men seemed to belong to the landscape, to have been there from everlasting, and almost they were angelic presences. The legendary past obtruded continually upon the present, and while walking through a kampong or along a country lane we would find ourselves wondering why the sights were so familiar. The explanation came on the night when we attended the shadow play. There was a great crowd of Balinese watching the shadows of the puppets on the screen, a bedsheet spread between two poles. The leather puppets were beautifully made, the movements of their heads and arms being controlled by long slender strips of wood. The shadow plays described the adventures of heroes from the Indian epics, the *Ramayana* and the *Mahabharata*. Huge armies moved across the screen, heroes stood knee-deep among the corpses of their enemies, the gods descended to earth and assumed the disguise of princes or poor beggars, and were never happier than when they were consorting with earthly women. The storyteller, a thin intense man with a priestly topknot, mimicked the voices of the gods and heroes while the gamelans played softly in the darkness. What the Balinese were seeing was a kind of cinema, yet totally unlike the cinema we know: for these puppets cut out of buffalo hide, pierced with hundreds of little holes to give an impression of dazzling light and energy pouring through them, permitted their imaginations full rein. They would spend an evening and a whole night listening to the storyteller; their lives, their thoughts and their dreams were impregnated with the ancient epics, which they knew by heart. These shadow plays were their education, and instinctively they saw themselves as heroes like the figures on the screen.

It was this, I think, that gave them their superb poise, their human elegance. The least of these peasants was profoundly cultured, and was perfectly at ease in the world of the gods. They enjoyed making extravagant gestures. So, at a cockfight, a man would lift up a winning cock with a gesture of triumph so naked that he might have been David exhibiting the head of Goliath. He would throw his head back, while his arms swept up in quivering exaltation to show the unwounded cock with a curving five-inch-long razor attached to the spur. So, too, you would come across a girl combing her hair in the sunlight, the long blue-black hair reaching to her waist, while the old men of the village looked at her wistfully, and it might have been Susanna watched by the Elders. The gestures were always bold and inviting, and wonderfully elegant.

There were some young Germans living at Sanur on the sea-coast. They made a living by catching exotic fish and exhibiting them in an aquarium. There were small tusked sharks about three feet long, but there were also delicate spidery starfish, vermilion flame fish, and yellow angel fish. The Germans had asked themselves where in all the world they could find a civilization which was the exact opposite of German civilization. They said they had walked from Weimar to Bangkok by way of Turkey, Persia and India, and never for a moment had they forgotten that Bali was their destination. From Bangkok they took a coastal steamer to Batavia, and then another to Bali. On the second day they came to Sanur, and there they remained. When they spoke about the Balinese they resembled mediaeval monks discoursing about paradise, with paradise all round them.

"The trouble is that we don't quite believe it," said Helmut, the tall, bronzed German with the fiery Viking beard. "We came out of the misery of Germany into the health of Bali, and we carry our sickness with us. The sign of our sickness is that we are continually astonished by everything the Balinese take for granted."

We strode along the shore under the palm trees, the surf breaking, the fishing boats far out to sea.

"This is the only community I have ever come across where the people are at peace with the world, without guilt, and this is because they regard every person, every tree, every leaf, every grain of rice as holy," Helmut went on. "Thank God they have been isolated from machines and modern industrialism. For a few more years—"

For a few more years! For, quite obviously, paradise would soon be corroded by our polluted world, soldiers and mechanics would come, the industrialists would open up the mines, and huge hotels would arise where now there were only palm trees. I thought of Ernst Toller and the little fishing village in the south of France, which existed only in our imaginations. We had seen an island when the people were still innocent, and we did not envy those who would come after us.

THE OTHER PARADISE

When we returned from Bali, the spell was still on us. There existed a civilization in full flower, so perfect, so wonderfully fashioned to answer the needs of the people that we wondered why the rulers of the world did not go there on pilgrimage to discover how people could live in harmony with one another. It was as close to paradise as we ever hoped to reach.

Singapore was another paradise, even though in many ways it was the exact opposite of Bali, which possessed a homogeneous culture and ancient traditions. In Singapore there were so many cultures that they were beyond counting and there were no ancient traditions. You could stand on Raffles Square and in twenty minutes you would have seen people of twenty different races. You saw Filipino girls in flowered dresses with leg of mutton sleeves, Malay girls in sarongs, Chinese girls in tight-fitting gowns with slit skirts, Indian girls in saris, and sometimes there would be Arab women in purdah, their faces concealed by veils, and Japanese women in embroidered kimonos bobbing along like painted dolls. All the East poured into Singapore, and there was no other place in the world where so many races congregated.

In Singapore all traditions were in the melting pot, and all religions were practiced. A man could practice Buddhism or Zoroastrianism, and no one would ever dream of preventing him. The Hindus and Muslims were at each other's throats in India, but here they lived peacefully together. The Chinese and Japanese were at war, but here they lived in peace. You came upon Armenians, Parsees, Papuans, Melanesians and tribal chieftains from Borneo, and none of them were making war on each other. A fantastic diversity was the rule; tolerance was the cement which bound people together. Singapore under the British seemed to be a foretaste of the future, when there would be no more war and no more animosity between nations.

I reveled in the diversity of Singapore, and shared my enjoyment with my friend Karl Duldig, the sculptor, who was continually plucking people off the street in order to model them in clay. "What skins! What cheekbones! What eyes! What noses!" he said, grumbling to himself because the delicate texture of an oriental skin was so difficult to render. I would watch his strong hands molding the clay into shape and marvel at his assurance, his dexterity. He was a small thin nervous man whose eyes glowed with fire while he was working, but seemed to cloud over with smoke when he remembered that he was in exile, and sometimes he would fall into long silent meditations. By origin a Polish Jew, he had settled in Austria long enough to develop a consuming passion for his adopted country. Hitler came, and he escaped just in time. In Singapore he lived in poverty, his studio being the veranda of a rickety house in the suburbs. Giant palms shaded the veranda, and chickens scurried about in the dust. Whenever I came to his house, there was usually a Malay boy or a Chinese coolie being modeled. "I'd never get a European to sit so still," he said. "I give them a few pennies and they sit for hours! Miraculous!"

Indeed in Karl Duldig's eyes everything was miraculous, his escape from Vienna was miraculous, his shabby house with scarcely any furniture was miraculous, and most miraculous of all were his young wife and baby daughter. He received very few commissions and seemed perfectly content to live in poverty. When Britain declared war against Germany in September 1939, the Singapore government decided that he was an enemy alien and sent him to an internment camp in Australia, but not before he had landed the only lucrative commission in his career: a bronze bust of Aw Boon Haw, a local millionaire who had made his fortune with a sweet-smelling ointment called Tiger Balm. He was said to be the richest man in Malaya and he paid well for the privilege of being immortalized.

The Naval Base was now on a war footing. A War Room was established; more ships came to be refitted; a torpedo net was stretched across the mouth of the straits; French and Dutch ships paid visits which were no longer ceremonial. But no German raiders invaded the Indian Ocean, and Singapore was half a world away from the battle front. With every news bulletin broadcast by the B.B.C. we were reminded of the war, but no one walking the streets of Singapore would have guessed that a war was going on. The same colorful crowds marched through the streets, the same Chinese sampans jostled together in the wide creek known as the Singapore River, and the same Governor General in a white uniform and plumed hat inspected the same guards at Government House. There was no blackout: life went on in Singapore exactly as before.

My own leisurely life came to an end, for I went to work in the drawing office at the Naval Base. I had spent two years as a draftsman in a shipyard in the north of England, but had no particular liking for a draftsman's work and no particular ability, and sometimes wondered what I was doing there. I was bored to death in the office and happy the moment I stepped out of it. The Naval Base was the source of endless fascination and the drawing office was the only dull place in it.

Since my father commanded most of the resources of the Naval Base, he was in his element. The great ocean-going liners sailed secretly into port, vanished into the huge graving dock, and emerged as troopships. In this way the *Queen Mary*, the *Normandie*, and the *Nieuw Amsterdam* came into his possession, and he alone bore the responsibility of converting them from luxury liners into instruments of war. The ships were gutted, and sometimes the sides of the graving dock were piled high with Venetian mirrors, Aubusson carpets, Gobelin tapestries, and the most expensive furnishings that men have ever made. It was a little like watching the sack of a mediaeval city, while the plunderers piled great heaps of treasure outside the city walls.

I usually found an excuse to accompany my father when he made his first tour of inspection of a doomed ship. As he strode through the great pillared dining rooms and chandeliered ballrooms of the *Queen Mary*, he was Nemesis disguised as a ruddy-faced Englishman with bushy eyebrows and intense blue eyes, humorous and merciless. The soft carpets, the engraved mirrors, the chandeliers, the sofas and the staterooms all vanished; the interior of the ship became a labyrinth of bunks so coarse and utilitarian that it would have given pleasure to a Puritan. Down came the mirrors! Down came the chandeliers! Down came stairways and bandstands and cocktail bars! The carpets were rolled up, the paintings were torn out of their frames, and all the ornamental scrolls became matchwood. Nemesis devoured everything he touched until there was nothing left but plain unornamented wood. If an extra fifty men could be squeezed in anywhere, he knew where to find a place for them.

The Admiralty had ordered that the luxury liners should be gutted in the shortest possible time. My father regarded the shortest possible time as far too long; he favored instantaneous miracles. Because he was likely to turn up in any part of the ship or the graving dock, there was no slacking. Hundreds of men worked in the knowledge that Nemesis was only too likely to appear, having mysteriously plummeted down into the bowels of the ship or even more mysteriously emerged through an armored bulkhead. He had spent nearly all his life in ships and shipyards, and he knew all the hiding places.

It is the nature of Nemesis to be terrifying, and he could inspire a proper terror. If anything went wrong, if the workmen botched their work, if faulty materials were being used, he was instantly on the spot, roaring with the loudest voice in Christendom, blue flames shooting out of his eyes. There was something about him that resembled a hurricane. Whatever was wrong would speedily be put right, but no one who ever faced him in his rage was quite the same again.

He had a wonderful impatience with protocol, broke all the rules, and terrified the Admiral and the Captain of the Dockyard as much as he terrified his workmen. The Admiralty sometimes sent signals from London which showed a demonstrable ignorance of the real conditions in the Naval Base, and my father would reply with a signal addressed to a Sea Lord which read: "Don't be daft." One day he returned to lunch, looking unusually calm and meditative. Then the calm gave way to a quiet shuddering, which reminded me of the slow spitting of the flame of a lit fuse, and a moment later he was convulsed with silent laughter. "I barged into the Admiral today," he said, "and gave him a piece of my mind." What had happened was comparable to a sudden volcanic explosion, an outpouring of fiery lava. Once again something had gone wrong, and he had found the shortest and simplest way to put it right. Since the Naval Base was essentially a dockyard, and he was the manager of the dockyard, he was not expendable. He did as he pleased, and his greatest pleasure was to see that the Naval Base was in full working order and humming with activity.

For me the Naval Base was an intricate and beautiful machine to be observed and studied at a distance, while I studied Chinese, wrote novels and poems, gathered notes for a history of Europe, and contemplated a life of Sir Stamford Raffles, who founded Singapore for the express purpose of bringing into existence the kind of civilization that had finally emerged. I worked obediently in the drawing office, but the real work went on elsewhere—in Raffles Library in Singapore, in my book-cluttered study, and in the houses of a few Chinese friends. For many years I had been translating Boris Pasternak's short stories. Since he was then totally unknown to English readers, and no publisher could be found to show the slightest interest in them, I decided to publish them myself, and the longest of the short stories was printed on the presses of the *Straits Times* in an edition of two hundred copies, bound in green boards with a cloth spine. To protect the copyright, and to ensure that it survived the war, I sent copies to the British Museum, the Library of Congress, the Bibliothèque Nationale, and a few friends. Altogether only about seven or eight copies survived the war.

There were passages in Pasternak's long story which were all the more pleasurable because I was living on an island where no snow had ever fallen. He gloried in the Russian winter, and wrote passionately about it, so passionately indeed that he was able in some mysterious way to suggest the fullness and immensity of a winter storm:

> The snowstorm was increasing. The sky quivered, and white kingdoms and nations toppled from the sky, impossible to keep score of them, mysterious and terrible. It was obvious that these territories, falling from no one knew where, had never heard about life and earth. Arctic and blind, they smothered the earth, neither seeing it nor knowing anything about it.
>
> They were exquisitely terrifying, these kingdoms, ravishingly satanic. Zhenya reveled as she gazed at them. The air reeled, grasping at this falling universe, and far, far away the countryside howled with pain as though struck with whips. Everything became confused. Night rushed upon them, maddened by those grey thongs falling on the earth, cutting it and blinding it. Everything was screaming

and scattering, and it was impossible to see any roads. Shouts and echoes vanished altogether, having never met: a confusion of sounds borne upward over many rooftops. Snowstorm.

Pasternak's prose resembled his poetry: it was virtually untranslatable, rich with meanings and music, fully orchestrated, full of assonances, superbly controlled. He would take an idea or an image to the very limit of comprehension, and somehow it remained vividly comprehensible. Something of the same quality could be seen in Chinese poetry of the T'ang Dynasty, which possessed an abundance of strange and beautiful images; and the more I studied Chinese poetry, the more I became aware that it was magnificently endowed with a strangeness and beauty foreign to English poetry. It could say things we could not say, invoke landscapes we had never dreamed of, and describe emotions we had never experienced. The very first Chinese poem I ever learned seemed to open up an entirely new world of images. Wang Chieh found the poem in a well-known collection of T'ang poets and then copied it out in his handsome calligraphy, each character standing up sharply, and then very patiently he would explain all the possible meanings of the characters:

The arrows of Chimpoko are tipped with hawks' feathers,
Our pennons gleam with swallow-tails.
They wave alone, proclaiming the new order.
A thousand companies raise a single shout.

In the dark forest the grass is frightened by the wind.
At night the general stretches his bow.
In the morning he finds the white feather
Hidden amid white stones.

Dark night; the wild geese fly high.
The Shanyu are fleeing, fleeing.
We pray for daylight and a cavalry charge:
A great snowfall conceals our bows and knives.

In the desert our broad tents filled with food:
The western tribesmen praise the victory.
We drink and dance together in iron mail;
The thunder of drums moves the mountain rivers.

This poem written by the soldier-poet Lu Lun in the eighth century A.D. was my introduction to Chinese poetry. I had read and admired Arthur Waley's translations of the Chinese poets, but he had chosen for the most part quietly meditative poems written by men of exquisite refinement, and I had long suspected that there was a Chinese poetry of more robust quality. As Wang Chieh discussed the characters, the poem came vibrantly to life. Thereafter, once or twice a week, he presented me with new poems, and we carefully went over them, gradually forming a small anthology of translations. This was the beginning of the anthology known as *The White Pony*.

Meanwhile the war was coming closer to Singapore, for the Japanese made no secret of their intentions. By the spring of 1941 we knew they were merely waiting for an opportunity to attack Indochina and Thailand, and then it would be the turn of Burma and India. We never expected them to attack Pearl Harbor, and we assumed that they would avoid any entanglement with the United States. The East was ripe for the plucking, and sometimes we wondered whether anything except a miracle would stop them.

In April 1941 my father was recalled to take charge of Devonport dockyard, the largest naval base in England. The ship taking him to England zigzagged for six weeks across the Indian Ocean and the Atlantic. His successor at the Singapore Naval Base was Tony Jackman, a man of an entirely different character. He had a long face, a quiet manner, an athletic temper. Engagingly boyish, he enjoyed sports of all kinds and could never understand why everyone did not share his enthusiasm for yachting, swimming, fishing and playing tennis. He thought I was the worst yachtsman he had ever known, and the worst fisherman. He had only to throw a line into the water and immediately the succulent red fish known as *ikan merah* were swarming toward his bait, while the same fish deliberately avoided my bait as though they knew it was poisoned. Similarly, in his small yacht, it was clear that the wind obeyed him and resolutely refused to fill any sails I had touched. But what was chiefly notable about him was the smile that played constantly on the corners of his lips as though he was continually expecting something pleasurable to happen, and in fact pleasurable things were always happening simply because he wanted them to happen. He could not bellow and roar across the whole length of the Naval Base like my father, but he could exert his authority in other ways.

I remained in the house, occupying one wing, while Jackman occupied the other. I saw him at meals and in the evenings, and marveled at his quietness under pressure, his tolerance, and his good humor. We explored Singapore together, and every weekend there was a pilgrimage to Johore Bahru and the Malay kampongs where the Malays lived exactly as they had lived centuries before the British occupation. He was learning Malay much faster than I was learning Chinese.

One day in July, while working in the drawing office, I received a summons to go immediately to the office of the Captain of the Dockyard. I had not the faintest idea what he could possibly want of me. He was one of those rather abrupt and hot-tempered naval officers whose mere presence inspires fear, and as I drove to his office I remembered that a few days earlier at a dinner party he had announced that the most exciting period of his life was when he was in command of a Yangtze gunboat "shooting up the damned Chinese Communists on the banks of the river." Whereupon I had delivered the inevitable speech about the enduring greatness of Chinese civilization and the absurdity of all our efforts to colonize China and the still greater absurdity of shooting up unarmed villagers from the safety of an armored gunboat. The hostess had quickly changed the subject to the cultivation of roses, and the Captain of the Dockyard gave me a withering glance which resembled a bolt of blue lightning. Long before I reached his office I came to the conclusion that he had thought of some way of punishing my notorious insolence.

There were red leather armchairs and blue curtains in his office, and he seemed to be in a relaxed mood. He smiled pleasantly. There was a wonderful wide-sweeping view of the Naval Base through the open windows. He asked whether I was enjoying my work in the drawing office, and I said I was bored to death by it. He took a book out of a drawer and laid it on the table. The book had a blue dust jacket with a picture of Russian soldiers on horseback. I knew the book well, because I had written it. It was *The Mountain and the Stars,* a long novel about fighting in Mongolia at the end of the First World War.

"I have been reading your book all through the week," he said. "I didn't know you have been in Mongolia."

"I haven't."

There was a long pause.

"Well, you write about it as though you knew the damned place. How did you get all your information?"

"From books—other books, mostly in Russian."

"So you read Russian?"

"Yes."

"And Chinese?"

"The Russian is fair, but the Chinese is slow going."

"Why?"

"Because it is impossibly difficult. You have to learn six or seven thousand characters."

It turned out that the Captain of the Dockyard had taken Chinese lessons in Shanghai and given up in despair. He went on talking about the novel and about the chief character, Baron Ungern-Sternberg, an exemplary sadist, and the two boys, Mitka and Petka, whose adventures in the Far Eastern Division were described at vast length. I had enjoyed writing about the boys and some of the enjoyment, I hoped, was communicated to the reader. There were descriptions of the ferocious tortures invented by Baron Ungern-Sternberg and of battles fought in snowstorms, of long marches across Mongolian deserts and of sudden improbable massacres. The Captain of the Dockyard wanted to know how much of it was true, and the answer was very simple: all of it was true, for only the two boys had been invented. A survivor of the Far Eastern Division had written a brief account of the campaign and published it in Harbin, and I had simply fleshed out his description of that strange and terrible adventure.

I was beginning to wonder where the conversation was leading, for it was beyond belief that the Captain of the Dockyard had summoned me for the purpose of discussing a novel about a forgotten war in Mongolia. What on earth had Mongolia to do with the Singapore Naval Base? He went on to talk about Spain. Had I been there? Yes. On what side? The Republican side. Had I fought there? No, I had been a correspondent. All the time he seemed to be weighing something in his mind, but exactly what he was weighing was unclear. There were occasional moments when he seemed to be about to inflict the coup de grâce, but these moments would pass. The green scrambler telephone on his desk rang. It was Jackman's voice, and the Captain of the Dockyard said: "No, I haven't told him yet." Obviously the coup de grâce could not be long delayed, but I was still completely mystified about the form it would take.

As he placed the telephone back on the cradle, the Captain of the Dockyard said: "The papers have been drawn up. As of this moment, you have been appointed an Assistant Armament Officer. Do you know anything about explosives?"

"Nothing at all."

"You'll learn quickly. You are also in charge of camouflage, and you can call yourself Chief Camouflage Officer. I don't believe the Base can be camouflaged, but the Admiralty has sent a signal saying they want someone to examine the problem and you're the most likely candidate."

"Why?"

"Because you write novels, I suppose."

It was not a very satisfactory reply, but it was the best he could offer.

"We'll get the air force to lend you a plane and you can take as many photographs as you like and study the problem. As Camouflage Officer you report back to me. As Assistant Armaments Officer you report to the Chief Armament Officer. Is that clear?"

"Yes, but I don't know why I have been chosen to do the two jobs I would most like to do. How do you know whether I am going to be any good?"

"We don't know," he said, and waved me out of the office.

I went back to the drawing office and announced that I was finished forever with drawing boards, and then returned to the house on King's Avenue. Jackman was pouring himself a drink of curaçao and pineapple. I asked him whether he was responsible for these two appointments, but he only smiled his enchanted smile.

"I hear," he said solemnly, "they are going to give you an airplane. My advice to you is not to fly too low."

As it happened, the air force had no small plane available and a Piper Cub was rented from the Singapore Flying Club. During the following week I flew over the Base several times a day, making the same runs at different heights and accumulating a vast number of photographs. Flying over the Base was the purest pleasure, especially in the early morning, when the long shadows swept across acres of emerald green grass and the ships and machine shops seemed to be made of cut glass. There were far more Flame of the Forest trees than I had ever suspected, and there were whole regions of the Base which I had never explored. I would leave the Base long before dawn, drive to the Flying Club, climb into the plane, and take off as soon as the first light broke. Dawns in Singapore are nearly as beautiful as the sunsets, with banks of rainbow-colored clouds melting into one another. Sometimes, on the excuse that it was necessary to study Johore and the straits, I would cruise over the mainland and look down at immense forests and the small clearings where the Malays had built their kampongs and the smoke of their cooking fires rose straight into the windless air.

Camouflage, I learned, was an art which had reached perfection in the First World War and had then been relegated to a proper obscurity. There were no available textbooks, and certainly there was nothing to explain how an entire Naval Base with its hundreds of white buildings could be made to vanish into the surrounding landscape. The photographs showed only that the problem was very nearly insoluble. The buildings could be painted in green camouflage patterns, a false causeway could be built comparatively cheaply, a painted cloth could be rolled across a graving dock, and the immense petroleum tanks could be covered with green netting in such a way that they would come to resemble the neighboring hills, but none of these things could be done without armies of workmen. I compiled a large book of photographs and thirty pages of recommendations, and a copy of the book went off to the Admiralty, where no doubt it was treated as one of the minor lunacies of the war. If there had been time and money and a large work force, something could have been done to camouflage the Naval Base, but in fact nothing was done. During the following months there were occasional conferences on the pressing need to introduce at least some experimental "camouflage units" and an order of priorities was established. Officers in gold braid listened patiently to the Chief Camouflage Officer, admired his photographs, deliberated on the millions of gallons of green paint which would have to be imported from Australia, and offered tentative estimates of the costs. By the end of October nothing more was being heard about camouflaging the Base.

All this time I was working in the Armament Depot, relishing the knowledge that I could go off at any moment on important business connected with camouflage and was therefore not entirely at the disposition of the Chief Armament Officer, a kindly gray-haired man who was a little bemused by the antics of his newly appointed assistant.

The Armament Depot was one of the most beautiful places in the Naval Base, very lush and green, with its low hills overlooking the Straits of Johore. These hills, however, were lethal, for they contained enough high explosives to blow Singapore off the map. They were honeycombed with tunnels and galleries kept at a constant temperature and filled with shells, magnetic mines, depth charges, detonators, and every conceivable kind of destructive agent; and in these long, winding, dimly lit corridors faced with concrete there was an atmosphere of quietness and peace, as of a well-kept and scrupulously clean wine cellar. In the midday heat I would usually find an excuse to visit one of these hills, kicking off my shoes at the entrance and putting on cloth slippers. There was always a sharp turn at the entrance, so that if there was an explosion inside, the full force of it would not blast out of the mouth of the tunnel. This at least was the prevailing theory. In fact no one knew what would happen if there was an explosion inside one of those gentle hills.

Outwardly there was very little to suggest that the Armament Depot contained the largest concentration of high explosives in the Far East. Sikh guards, wearing flaming red and green turbans, patrolled the barbed wire fence surrounding the depot, but they always looked as though they would be more useful at a ceremonial Trooping of the Colors than at guard duty. They were magnificently built, with flashing eyes and fierce beards; when they saluted, they stiffened until their whole bodies shook with the violence of the gesture, knees braced, arms snapping out like whips, faces rigid as though transformed into stone. They were the exotic accomplices of our daily work, and I could never quite believe in their existence.

The English workmen in the tunnels had spent most of their

lives among high explosives, which they regarded with casual affection and a certain indifference. All of them had tales to tell about the strange and unpredictable habits of cordite, which resembled cheese in color and consistency. They said it would explode in your face if you gave it too penetrating a look, but it could be cut, rolled up, molded into any shape you pleased and otherwise mishandled in comparative safety; it could be dropped and nothing would happen; people had been known to eat it, apparently with no ill effects; it was tasteless, odorless and good for the digestion. People who spend their lives among high explosives are said to develop a yellow complexion, but these ruddy-faced workmen had not a trace of it. They were remarkable only for being unremarkable and might have been carpenters, joiners or machinists: they were skilled craftsmen of explosives.

My special delight was in making bonfires of over-age cordite. Great bundles of it would be carried out of the tunnels and piled up in the thick grass overlooking the straits and then detonated from a respectful distance. The delight lay in the triumphant *whoosh* followed by a shimmering golden blaze twenty feet high which hung in the air for a few seconds, turning everything to gold. Afterward there was only a small circle of scorched grass, and the trembling of the air.

Altogether there were no more than twenty people working in the Armament Depot, and since warships came rarely there was not very much work to do. When warships came to the Naval Base, we worked round the clock; at other times we did very much as we pleased. I was still seeing Wang Chieh, for there were ample opportunities to visit Singapore, spending evenings at the Great World or in his house which was crowded with babies and children of all ages. Wang Chieh himself was beginning to emerge as one of the leaders of the Kuomintang in Singapore, and one evening I asked him point-blank whether he was directing the activities of the Kuomintang on the island, and he smiled and said nothing. Chinese dignitaries from Chungking were continually appearing in his house, or he would take me along to see them. At the same time he was helping me to buy Chinese paintings, which had become a passion even greater than playing Beethoven's symphonies on the gramophone against Malayan sunsets.

Singapore was essentially a Chinese city with most of its wealth already in the hands of Chinese bankers, property owners and entrepreneurs. The Kuomintang, which the Singapore police regarded as a conspiratorial movement, was already acting as a shadow government, giving its own orders, raising its own taxes, and arming its own armies. They were at the moment very small armies, but the Chinese were well aware that the Japanese might attack Singapore and the Chinese inhabitants of the island would be in the front lines. In those days the Kuomintang was still a powerful and active party, defiantly anti-Japanese, and not yet blighted by a reputation for corruption. There were old men in Singapore who had known Dr. Sun Yat-sen and spoke about him with bated breath.

"We want to organize a Chinese militia," Wang Chieh said one day. "The government should arm the Chinese. We have a long experience of fighting the Japanese and we would give a good account of ourselves."

I asked him whether the governor had been approached, and he seemed surprised at the question.

"What good would it do?" he said. "We are trying to reach the military. The governor would be the last person to see."

This was probably true, for Sir Shenton Thomas was notoriously inaccessible to new ideas. He was a plump, well-meaning man who enjoyed his occasional appearances in full uniform with feathers springing up from his sun helmet and broad ribbons across his chest, and he was inclined to regard the Chinese as necessary nuisances, loyal to China, without any real roots in Singapore. The last thing that could have occurred to him was that they had a stake in the future of Singapore. Meanwhile the police were busily arresting obscure Chinese on the grounds that they were dangerous revolutionaries, and usually they were kept in prison for a few days and then released for lack of evidence.

Wang Chieh was deeply puzzled, for there was simply no way for him to communicate with the British authorities as a representative of the Kuomintang. Only the Kuomintang could throw the whole weight of the Singapore Chinese into the fighting, and the British could not bring themselves to admit that the Kuomintang existed as anything but a conspiratorial organization owing allegiance to a foreign power. Above all, the Kuomintang was never to be permitted to exercise authority in a British colony. It was a maddening dilemma, and there was no solution in sight.

In October the Chinese government sent to Singapore a man who had far greater authority than Wang Chieh. This was George Yeh, who many years later became Foreign Minister in the Kuomintang government on Taiwan. He was then about thirty, with a daredevil look about him when he was excited, so that one could easily imagine him leading revolutionary armies. When his features were in repose, they appeared to be carved out of marble, the skin very white, almost transparent. He reminded me of General Modesto; unlike the Spanish general, he spoke English impeccably and had in fact taught English at Tsinghua University in Peking. He was the most handsome Chinese I had ever seen. According to Wang Chieh, he was one of those Kuomintang officials who had remained behind in Shanghai after it was captured by the Japanese, his task being to organize resistance in the city. Arrested by the Japanese, he was thrown into jail and savagely tortured. Day after day he was carried out of his cell, interrogated and beaten until his back was a bloody pulp. Finally he had escaped and made his way to Chungking.

George Yeh had come to Singapore to discuss the arming of the Chinese workers, and he was no more successful in convincing the British authorities than Wang Chieh. Since he had diplomatic status, he had access to high officials in the government, and where Wang Chieh spoke diffidently, George Yeh spoke boldly. He was on good terms with Robert Scott, the head of the British Ministry of Information, who knew China well and was sympathetic to the idea of training a Chinese militia.

The war was coming closer. Since July the Japanese had been established in French Indochina, and there was only Thailand between Malaya and the Japanese. Thousands of Australian troops arrived in Singapore, where they stayed for a few days before taking train to encampments in the forests of northern Malaya. Within a few weeks Singapore had altered its appearance and even its language, for everywhere you went you heard the Australian broad vowels and saw the brawny muscular Australians in slouch hats, khaki shirts and khaki shorts. The city was changing its character, and for the first time there could be detected a note of apprehension. With the coming of the Australians, so many of them young and obviously untrained, there came the realization that a Japanese attack was almost imminent.

Compared with crowded, bustling Singapore the Naval Base resembled a green oasis, calm and orderly and very beautiful, seemingly untouched by the war. There were no warships anchored in the straits, but this did not alarm us, for we knew that many were on their way. A munitions ship had arrived and was anchored off a pier near the Armament Depot, and for three or four days there was intense activity; then once again quietness descended on our green hills.

There was a long-standing tradition that the army and the navy existed independently of one another. I never saw any soldiers at the Naval Base except once when General Percival, commanding all the troops in Malaya, was taken on a guided tour of the Base. One of the consequences of the tour was that naval officers were invited to attend lectures on military strategy. The inaugural lecture was given by the general himself, standing on a platform with a blackboard behind him. He was tall and impeccably dressed, but in spite of his red tabs and commanding manner it was impossible to take him seriously. He looked like an elongated rabbit with his small mouth and two prominent teeth, a long fleshy nose, and lackluster eyes, and he spoke in a high fluted voice. He made some weak jokes about the navy's inexperience in hand-to-hand fighting, and these jokes were greeted by a withering silence. He had begun badly, and went on to try the navy's patience even more by drawing on the blackboard a purely imaginary landscape and then showing how a Japanese attack could be broken by a proper use of tanktraps and by sniper fire from well-concealed positions. He drew a bridge on the blackboard and explained the three or four different ways in which a bridge could be blown up. He did not seem to know very much about high explosives. He dwelt lovingly on the bridge and expanded on the difficulties of transport across a bridge destroyed by dynamite. "Usually," he added, "you will find a culvert near a bridge, and this culvert will provide you with an excellent observation post." As far as we knew there were no bridges on Singapore island except for the bridge across the Singapore River. He went on to explain that all approach roads would be mined by sappers and that personnel mines were destructive to personnel. At the end of the lecture he asked for questions. I rose and asked whether there was any plan for arming the Chinese in Singapore. Amused, he stroked his mustache, smiled with his two enormous teeth, and said: "What Chinese?" Then he went on to the next question. Five minutes later the naval officers walked out of the lecture hall, cursing under their breaths. They had never had any great respect for the army, and they were now convinced that the commanding general in Malaya was totally incompetent.

My own confidence in the army was reduced a day or two later when I was arrested by Military Intelligence. I was working in the Armament Depot when the bell rang from the Chief Armament Officer's office. I had just stepped into the office when a heavy hand fell on my shoulder, and a Cockney voice said: "You're under arrest." The Chief Armament Officer was sitting at his desk, looking gray and worried. He was one of those exceedingly gentle and self-effacing men who go to great pains to avoid trouble but face it squarely when it comes. He said quickly: "Military Intelligence wants to talk with you. It's something about communicating with enemy aliens. You had better go and talk with them."

His voice sounded small and thin, unlike his usual voice, which had a hard cutting edge. He had obviously come to the conclusion that Military Intelligence would not act unless it had received some reliable information.

"Does this man have the right to arrest me?"

"I'm afraid so."

"Then for heaven's sake tell Jackman."

"Of course."

A moment later I was being driven out of the Base in a staff car. The Cockney was saying: "If you don't make trouble for me, I won't make trouble for you." He had been a London policeman and no doubt he had said the same thing to the jewel thieves and pickpockets he had arrested. He leaned back and puffed quietly on a pipe. A soldier drove the car. It was a wonderfully calm day with small white clouds drifting across an intensely blue sky, and Singapore had never looked lovelier.

It occurred to me that communicating with enemy aliens in wartime was a serious crime, punishable at the very least by a long term of imprisonment. What was an enemy alien? Wang Chieh and George Yeh could not conceivably be described in this way. We were at war with Germany, and I knew no Germans in Singapore and those I had known in Germany had long since vanished into the anonymity of exile or had become faceless figures in the German army. "Something about communicating with enemy aliens." That meant at least two, and perhaps more. I knew a Eurasian taxi-dancer who had once been the mistress of the Sultan of Johore, and I remembered she had German, Javanese and Chinese blood. She was the most expensive taxi-dancer I had ever known although she accepted no money: she demanded bolts of silk for her favors and had already acquired a fabulous storeroom of silk which she intended to unload on the market in due course. By the time we reached Singapore I had convinced myself that she was an enemy alien and a spy, and would be shot at dawn. This seemed a pity, because she was very beautiful.

The staff car stopped outside a two-storied bow-windowed house in the outskirts of Singapore. It was wholly unpretentious and did not look like the headquarters of Military Intelligence. There was a small front garden surrounded by a cast-iron fence and three steps led up to a door paneled with colored glass. It was so absurdly unlike anything I had expected that I burst out laughing. "It's not a laughing matter," the Cockney policeman said, and half carried me up the steps.

Inside, the house was even more improbable, for it had obviously belonged until quite recently to an Anglican clergyman, whose photograph hung in the narrow hallway beside the hatstand, where four or five military caps were hanging. A barometer hung on the wall, umbrellas and walking sticks were in their proper places, and there were framed photographs of the clergyman's wife wearing a long white dress and playing croquet. If this was really the headquarters of Military Intelligence, then they deserved credit for camouflaging it so well.

The Cockney led me into the clergyman's library, said: "The major will see you in a few minutes," and then went out, locking the door after him.

I have a passion for libraries, especially theological libraries, and was perfectly content to spend a few minutes there. I pulled down a commentary on Hosea and began reading it for no

better reason than that it was a book I knew nothing about.
It is a short and dull work in spite of vehement diatribes against
whoring priests, and the commentary was even duller. It was
soon replaced on the shelves. A Dictionary of Christianity proved
to be more exciting fare even though it was published in 1860
and from the appearance of the faded steel engravings it was
obviously a reprint of a book published much earlier. I could
hear footsteps in the corridor outside and someone was continually walking up and down a creaking staircase. The few minutes
became half an hour, then an hour, then two hours. By this
time I had come to the conclusion that it was all an elaborate
and perhaps dangerous charade, for this was certainly not the
headquarters of Military Intelligence, the Cockney policeman
was not a policeman at all, and something completely incomprehensible was taking place.

I wondered what Jackman was doing, for he was one of those
men who acted quickly and enjoyed cutting through red tape.
At any moment I expected to hear the scream of brakes as a
naval car came to a stop outside the house, then there would
be the sound of shattered glass as the sailors broke in and rescued
me. These pleasant dreams were occasionally interrupted by
memories of General Percival in the lecture hall. *Usually you
will find a culvert near a bridge, and this culvert will provide
you with an excellent observation post.*

About three hours passed, and then the door was unlocked.
"The major will see you now," the Cockney said, and led me to
a small room fitted with a desk near the front door. No doubt
this was the room where the Anglican clergyman interviewed his
parishioners. The major sitting behind the desk had a clipped
gray mustache and his lean face with the high cheekbones inspired confidence. He was studying a thick yellow folder. There
must have been fifty pages in the folder, and this bewildered
me, for it seemed inconceivable that there should be so much
information on my short and unnecessarily virtuous life in the
official files. Unless someone had been trailing me all over Europe
for two or three years and had followed me every time I left
the Naval Base, it would have been impossible to compile a
dossier of more than two or three pages. Something was very
wrong about the yellow folder.

According to the major, I would be well advised to make a

clean breast of things and throw myself on his mercy. I had been in communication with an enemy alien and it was his task to ascertain why I had done so and all the circumstances surrounding my correspondence with him. This statement immediately changed the picture: the taxi-dancer would not be shot at dawn, and instead of enemy aliens there was one single masculine enemy alien, unnamed.

The major would have saved a lot of time if he had named the enemy alien, but he wanted me to supply the information, and I could not. "We have evidence that you were continually seeing him," he said. "There is not the least possibility that we have made an error." Grimly he demanded the name, and just as grimly I pronounced that the name simply did not exist or existed only as a fiction of the major's imagination. He lost his temper, subsided, turned to a page in the dossier, studied it carefully, and then ordered me to recount all the events of my life from the beginning to the present day. This was a fishing expedition, which did no good to him and only reminded me of a misspent youth. From time to time he would consult the yellow folder and nod approvingly, as though it was all there in those massive reports compiled by secret service agents in all the countries of Europe, but when he asked questions they were curiously tame and he had very little more information than I had supplied.

So the game went through the morning and the afternoon, and by about 3:30 P.M. he had had enough of it. He summoned the Cockney policeman and said: "You can bring the evidence in now." I expected to see the enemy alien pushed into the small room in handcuffs. Instead he brought in something that appeared to be a book wrapped up in wrapping paper. The major pounced on it, unwrapped it, and displayed it triumphantly. It was the Phaidon book of Cézanne's paintings, full of magnificent reproductions, and as it lay on the table it seemed to have as much to do with the interminable interrogation as the moon.

"Look inside!" the major shouted.

I looked. On the flyleaf there was written: *Karl Duldig. With warmest admiration. Robert Payne.*

"Do you deny that you tried to send this book to a prisoner of war camp in Australia?"

"Of course not."

"Do you deny that Karl Duldig is an enemy alien?"

"No."

"Then you realize this is a serious matter."

"I realize nothing of the kind. Only a drunken fool would think that 'With warmest admiration' is a communication which endangers the British Empire."

It became a shouting match the major growing increasingly apoplectic, while I was moved to pent-up fury by the interminable suspense of a wasted day. Finally, when we had both simmered down, I reached for the telephone on his desk, called the Naval Base, got Jackman, and told him the story. What saved the day was his bright crackling laughter which filled the small room. Confronted by this laughter the major's defenses went down, and he was almost apologetic. "You must admit we had cause for complaint," he said; and these words, like General Percival's thoughts on bridges and culverts, acquired during the following days the luster which comes from affectionate repetition.

When I returned to the Naval Base, Jackman was pouring a drink. He said he had spent most of the day trying to find out what had happened to me. It appeared that Military Intelligence had taken over a number of obscure houses in Singapore and regularly interrogated its prisoners in them, acting in absolute secrecy. They refused to give out any information whatsoever.

"If you had really been in communication with an enemy alien," Jackman said pleasantly, "you would probably by now be in a sack at the bottom of Singapore Harbor. From the moment you left the Naval Base, you simply vanished into thin air."

"What happens now?"

"The Captain of the Dockyard now insists that the authority of Military Intelligence stops at the gates of the Naval Base. It will never happen again."

A day or two later Jackman said casually over lunch: "We received the signal this morning. Force Z is on its way to Singapore."

THE BATTLESHIPS

All through November we were aware of a quickening in the air. The Naval Base lay calm and quiet under the sun, glowing in its beauty, so remote from the war that it seemed to have acquired the special quality of remoteness. In the early mornings there was always a misty haze on the green hills of Johore, but within an hour the sun burned through it. There were no seasons, each day was like every other day, and when the Flame of the Forest trees shed their brilliant petals, there were always more the next day. But though the Base remained changeless, the men who worked in it were changing in many subtle ways. Although the existence of Force Z was a closely guarded secret, everyone seemed to know that it was on its way and eagerly looked forward to it. The Base, after all, was no more than an eagle's nest, and the eagles were coming back to roost.

Altogether about twenty people knew which ships were coming, and among them were the officers of the Armament Depot, which would inevitably supply them with munitions. Once more there was a burst of activity at the depot. Happily we found a good deal of over-age cordite and there were more opportunities to burn it. Happily, too, there were long hours when we could wander round the Base at our leisure, explaining afterward, if any explanations were needed, that we were making tours of inspection. In fact, it was the dazzling beauty of the Base that provided the real excuse for these wanderings. All the eastern part of the Base with its inlets and mangrove swamps and nests of wildfowl remained to be explored. Occasionally we saw crocodiles and once we saw a brown and gold cobra at least ten feet long streaking through the grass. Another Assistant Armament Officer had been appointed. His name was Sorenson, and he had the fair hair, bright blue eyes and fine features of his Scandinavian ancestors. He worked quickly and well, and had led a happy-go-lucky wandering life all over the Far East, never resting in any job for any length of time. He joined the Armament Depot because he liked explosives.

"I'll be off on another job within six months," he said, "unless the war interferes."

"Where will you go?"

"Java, I think. I know a small island off the south coast where a white man could live like an emperor. I could make a fortune from the teak growing on the island, but there would be no need to make a fortune. I would have people waiting on me from morning to night."

"Is that what you want to do with your life?"

"Yes, and that's what I am going to get."

He said this quietly and with complete assurance, and for all I know he is living on his island today.

Although the threat of a Japanese invasion was growing greater each day, the knowledge that Force Z would soon be steaming along the Straits of Johore gave us a feeling of security. We were devotees of the Royal Navy, which could do no wrong. It had destroyed the Spanish Armada and no doubt it would destroy the Japanese Armada, and there would be little left for the army to do. This was a fortunate circumstance, since we regarded the incompetence of the army as an article of faith: General Percival had merely reaffirmed our long-standing distrust of the military. When we looked at the calm blue waters of the straits, we saw the dark ships with their fifteen-inch guns which would soon be anchored there, and it was inconceivable that any power on earth could triumph over them.

We had a fair idea of what the Japanese would do if they decided to attack. They would land troops from transports along the coast of Malaya, and the Navy's task would be to blow the transports out of the water. In the Armament Depot I was working on a design for a depth charge which would explode when it was ten feet under the water. The idea was to send a high speed motorboat filled with these depth charges against enemy transports and when they were very close to the enemy the motorboats would simply toss the depth charges overboard and then swing away. Fitted with a small compressed gas engine, the depth charges would have the same effect as torpedoes, while being much easier to manufacture. Jackman liked the idea and we drew up detailed plans for depth-charge torpedoes, but the Chief Armament Officer, who knew a good deal more about high explosives than either of us, thought they were unwieldy, and asked what was wrong with torpedoes? There were long discussions and sometimes he seemed to waver; for a while there was talk of a pilot project, more plans were drawn up, and we labored to make them look attractive in red and green ink. We were still discussing them when the Japanese invaded Malaya.

In Singapore Wang Chieh and George Yeh were still discussing the Chinese militia. They had acquired a useful ally in Robert Scott, who ruled over the Ministry of Information in the Cathay Hotel, and it was becoming clear that the Ministry of Information was very much more than it seemed to be. Exactly what it was, and what powers it possessed, were unknown, for like the Naval Base it seemed to exist in its own right, independent of all outside authority. According to George Yeh, who had a conspiratorial turn of mind, Robert Scott was the most powerful figure in Malaya, the one man who could be counted on to act decisively and with full authority, having been specially appointed by Churchill to cut through the tangled web of Malayan politics.

For two or three weeks I had been seeing very little of the Chinese in Singapore, and there came, as so often before, a longing to be among them. I called George Yeh and arranged to have dinner with him. Since I had an automobile and he had none, it was decided that I should pick him up at his apartment, and we would then go to the restaurant together. I arrived early, a Chinese maid opened the door and said he was having a bath, and a cheerful voice came from the bathroom: "Come in. We can talk in here." The bathroom was full of steam, through which I saw the white glistening face of the envoy from Chungking. While scrubbing himself, he talked about English poetry, which he recited with a faint singsong intonation. Then he stepped out of the bath, disappeared for a moment behind a frosted glass screen, and emerged looking as youthful and graceful as a boy of sixteen. He was talking about Sidney Keyes, a young English poet whose work he admired. He looked dazed and happy from the bath, but there was something faintly disturbing in that white body glowing in the incandescent heat of the bathroom.

At first I could not think what was disturbing about him:

certainly it was not that look, which the Chinese have, of being completely clothed when they are naked. Then I remembered Wang Chieh saying his back had been torn to ribbons by the Japanese in Shanghai. But there were no marks on his body, all ivory and rippling muscle. There was no trace of a bruise or scratch, and there was not the slightest possibility that any whip had touched his back. The legend outran the man, who was now reduced to a more human shape.

Later in the darkened restaurant he talked not about Shanghai but about the bombing of Chungking during the summer. Like everyone else I had seen the film of the bombing taken from the south bank of the Yangtze River, the black smoke exploding over the screen while the city was being pounded into rubble and flame. He had been there during the raids. He talked about Peking, where he had lived for years, and in the darkened restaurant the unimaginable city with the yellow roofs came to life. At last he said: "Why don't you come to China?"

I said the idea was preposterous, I was working in the Naval Base, there was no earthly reason for me to go to China. I had always dreamed of going to China and eventually I would go there, but not now, not in the middle of a war.

"It is all one war," he said. "Whether you are in China or here—"

This was true, but it was not an argument which had any relevance. It was simply beyond belief that I could go up to Jackman or the Captain of the Dockyard and say, "Goodby, thank you for everything, I am leaving tomorrow for Chungking." If I said this, they would shake their heads and suggest it was high time I saw a doctor.

"I shall be seeing Robert Scott tomorrow," he said, and I knew they would be discussing the perennial question of the Chinese militia.

We went out into the darkened street, and I observed for the first time that some of the shop windows were plastered with crisscrosses of white paper against Japanese air raids. Much had changed during the last two or three weeks: Singapore had finally become conscious of the war. It was strange to see the city dark, full of ghostly Australians walking arm in arm and singing drunkenly. I wore white socks, white shorts, white shirt, tin helmet, with a pistol strapped to my side, and was sure I looked ridiculous, and then it occurred to me that the Chinese envoy looked equally ridiculous in his white seersucker suit, as though he alone, among all the ghostly shapes of Singapore, was dressed for a time of peace. We picked up the car in Raffles Square and I drove him back to the apartment.

"You're sure you don't want to go to China?" he asked at the doorway.

"No, not now. Anyway, there is not the ghost of a chance."

Some days later—the exact date was November 21, 1941— there came a brief note from Robert Scott, saying he would like to see me on some urgent business. Could I come down that afternoon? The letter had come by messenger and I wondered why he had not troubled to use the telephone. He proved to be a tall, ruggedly built Scotsman with a broad freckled face, and a heavy brown mustache. Mild-mannered, imperturbable, he quietly got down to business. The Ministry of Information desperately needed someone in Chungking, and would I go? I said I had other fish to fry and there was not a ghost of a chance that I would be released by the Naval Base. What was I supposed to do in Chungking? On this subject he was exceedingly vague. He would soon be flying to Chungking, and when he got there he would be able to tell me. Plans were being drawn up: plans of vast scope which vitally affected the conduct of the war. It was necessary to send to China someone who was persona grata to the Kuomintang government. I hotly denied that I was persona grata to any government, adding that it was quite useless to send me to China because I had only a fragmentary knowledge of Chinese. It took me half an hour, aided by a well-thumbed dictionary, to read a column in a Chinese newspaper which any coolie could read in three minutes. I liked the Armament Depot, was very good at burning cordite and designing depth-charge torpedoes, and did not see any reason to be uprooted. Finally, the only Chinese I had ever known well was Wang Chieh, and we spoke in English.

Robert Scott took the pipe out of his mouth long enough to say: "Precisely."

"Why precisely?"

"Because Wang Chieh is the Kuomintang man in Singapore, as I suppose you know, and if you didn't know you know it now."

There was a long silence. I had known, and not known. It

had always seemed the least important thing about him, and it was absurd to send me to China on his recommendation as an agent of the Kuomintang government. The argument was getting nowhere. Why not send someone else? Robert Scott was puffing quietly on his pipe. At last he said: "According to our information you know a good many more Chinese than you take credit for. How many do you know?"

"About twenty, all of them casually. A few generals living in Singapore for their health and a few people who sell Chinese paintings."

"How many Chinese paintings have you got?"

"About ten."

"Has it occurred to you that in China you will be able to buy them every day of the week?"

"Yes."

"Also, for someone living on the Naval Base you have been living pretty deeply among Chinese?"

"Yes."

"So you have been spending every available minute with the Chinese, and now we offer you the opportunity to spend all your time with them, and you refuse."

"I am not refusing. It is simply that it can't be done. The Naval Base does not permit armament officers to go off and take a holiday in China."

I thought that was the end of it, and was about to go when he said: "Will you agree to go if I can get authorization for your release from the Naval Base?"

"Yes, but they won't grant it."

"We'll see about that," he said grimly.

As I left his office he was standing by the window and puffing at his pipe, while he gazed down at Singapore all green and white below him, and he had the look of a man who knew how to deal with civilians and would make them jump to his orders, but he did not know the clannishness of the Navy. The silent service worked in mysterious silent ways and pursued mysterious silent purposes. Many months would pass before the Navy would give its verdict and by that time the war would probably be over and I would be able to travel under my own steam.

I never saw Robert Scott again. He vanished into the limbo of half-forgotten things, to be remembered at long intervals for his memorable burr and his rugged handsomeness. It never occurred to me that my destiny for the next five years was already in his hands.

On the afternoon of December 2, 1941, the battleship *Prince of Wales* and the battle-cruiser *Repulse* steamed into the blue Straits of Johore with their flags flying. Four destroyers accompanied them. The long-awaited Force Z had at last arrived, and in the afternoon light the dark ships seemed to fill the straits with their power. They looked, and were, superb engines of destruction, massive and murderous, bristling with guns. The *Prince of Wales* had ten fourteen-inch guns, the *Repulse* had six fifteen-inch guns, and they had a combined complement of three thousand men. At anchor in the deep straits they swung with the tides and seemed strangely restless.

That afternoon there had been an unusually prolonged downpour, and when I first saw the ships there were still patches of cloud over the Johore hills and the sky was still gray. Then the sun came out clear and strong, the ships sparkled with thousands of points of light, and the damp flags stiffened and fluttered briskly in the wind. From the mast of the *Prince of Wales* the heliograph flashed signals to shore, and that evening the lights came up on the ships, long chains of light from stem to stern reflected in the calm waters of the strait. It was like a gala or a fairground, a dream of lights.

There was something dreamlike in the appearance of these ships at night, so huge, so menacing, so palpably present, yet dissolved into shapes of light. They were there, and not there. In the morning mist they loomed up like gray towers and at noon in the desolate heat they assumed the hard angry shapes of power. They were streamlined, slender like knives, carrying their weight of armor plating lightly.

For us, of course, their presence was the purest intoxication. For too long we had been living in the quiet backwaters of the war, ill-at-ease and conscience-stricken by our leisurely lives. Now at last we had a purpose and a claim on the world's attention. The sight of hundreds of naval ratings and officers walking around the base or crowding into buses which would take them to Singapore was proof that we were wide awake after months of sleeping. Suddenly the Naval Base became alive and we were dazzled by our good fortune.

Parties were given for the newly arrived officers and there was a good deal of talk about the *Prince of Wales*'s battle with the *Bismarck* when she was so new from Cammell Laird's shipyard that she had about a hundred shipbuilders' men on board, and about the journey to Newfoundland for the meeting between Mr. Churchill and President Roosevelt. They were hot nights and our starched shirts wilted. Dressed in white coats, dark trousers and cummerbunds, we were tongue-tied in the presence of these men who carried themselves like conquerors. The women wore their finery, and the gold braid gleamed. When Admiral Sir Tom Phillips appeared, we instinctively made a path for him as though he was an emissary from another world possessing powers not granted to ordinary mortals.

I was fascinated by him and watched him closely, for he resembled no naval commander I had ever seen. Ruddy-faced, with a bulldog expression, clear blue eyes and bushy eyebrows, he looked like a middle-weight boxer and he had a boxer's habit of rolling on the balls of his feet. He had been Vice-Chief of the Naval Staff, and carried himself with an air of authority. But the most noticeable thing about him was that he was very small, about five feet five inches, and sometimes when talking to a much taller man he would stand on tiptoes, so that he gave the appearance of being able to change his height at will. In a crowd of naval officers he would sometimes vanish completely.

Jackman, who had known him in England, thought he looked tougher and keener than before, but was more burdened by the weight of responsibility. "He snaps more," Jackman said, meaning not that he snapped at people during an argument, but that he was like a whippet which snaps cleanly on a running rabbit. "You should look at his mouth. It snaps open and snaps shut, and that's a dangerous mouth."

I suggested he was bellicose because he was unusually short.

"No, he is bellicose by nature. If he was six feet tall, he would snap just as much."

He was commander-in-chief of Force Z, and if you saw only his face you would say he looked the part to perfection, but I was haunted by his shortness until Jackman reminded me that

Nelson was two or three inches shorter. The sailors adored him and called him Admiral Tom Thumb.

On the evening after the arrival of the ships, a gala reception was given by the *Prince of Wales,* now tied up at the wharf. There were Sikhs in flaming turbans standing like carved statues at the foot of the gangway. Searchlights played on the ship's flags and an especially powerful beam of light was directed on the Union Jack, which whipped and curled in the wind coming up the straits. The fo'c'sle deck was almost unrecognizable, for carpets had been spread out and there were upholstered chairs under a striped awning, where the Admiral greeted his visitors, his sleeves a solid sheet of gold braid up to the elbows. Somewhere a band played and somewhere else a news film was being shown, while young sailors carried trays of drinks as though they had performed this office every day of their lives.

Distinguished visitors were piped on board with a bosun's whistle, a thin and reedy whistle which could rarely be heard above the uproar of the naval band. The Sultan of Johore came, wearing a voluminous cloak of cloth of gold, his turban tied in a way permitted only to the Sultan, one flap of the turban raised high to represent a lion's claw. Nearly seventy, fat and jowly, he was accompanied by his nineteen-year-old Rumanian bride of only a few weeks. Malay princes in glowing sarongs, Chinese businessmen in seersucker suits and old school ties, Englishmen in evening dress, Indians in turbans—they were all there, together with generals and air vice-marshals gaudy with medals. The fo'c'sle deck was like a dance floor with people milling about in closed circles. A Sikh officer, who must have been six feet five inches tall, was bowing over the hand of the Admiral. I found myself with a thin nervous man in evening dress who talked with a pronounced lisp, and when I asked him who he was, he said: "I am the Japanese consul general."

The lights of Johore shone in the distance, and the green hills were black against a sky crowded with stars; and there came the smell of the mangrove swamps and the sharper smell of well-oiled machinery, like acid. The *Repulse* lay at anchor in the straits, outlined by ribbons of light. She was the forgotten ship, silent and anonymous, or so we hoped, for the Admiralty had announced only the arrival of the *Prince of Wales* "and other heavy units." The Japanese consul general spent a long time gazing at this ship and presumably he was memorizing the shape of her gun-turrets and counting her guns.

This day was the eve of my thirtieth birthday, and it seemed to me it was being celebrated with appropriate fanfare. There was no place in the world where I wanted to be more than on the deck of the *Prince of Wales*, in the shadow of her guns. It was not, I think, that I possessed any deep faith in Britain's imperial destiny in the Far East, but I was excited beyond measure by the knowledge that the presence of British ships brought peace to these waters. For more than a hundred years our warships had patrolled the coasts of Malaya, bringing peace to a land which would otherwise have been the prey of warring kingdoms. Where else in the world could Malays, Chinese and Indians work together in harmony? The *Pax Britannica* had given the world a breathing space, and the *Prince of Wales* with her powerful guns was an instrument of peace in the threatening East.

The Union Jack whipped in the wind, and never had it appeared more beautiful or more glorious. It was an immense flag, perhaps fifteen feet long, the rainbow colors running into one another, the blue so intensely blue, the red so red, the white so luminous. The streaming colors flashed and sparkled against the starlight, as restless as the waves.

The naval band was playing "Roll out the Barrel," a film was being shown and Churchill must have appeared on the screen, for there was another burst of applause. The Admiral was still receiving visitors, his gold-embroidered cap at a rakish angle, his gold sleeves flaming like cordite bonfires. Since he was so busy I simply touched his hand for luck and went in search of Jackman, who commented that he now knew what it was like to attend a *durbar* when all the reigning princes of India offer homage to the sovereign's majesty.

"Sultans galore!" he said. "Half close your eyes, and there's the King-Emperor himself!"

We thought we were seeing the British Empire at high noon, and did not know we were looking at the sunset.

On the night of December 7, I was duty officer in the Naval Base. This meant that I was under orders to stay awake through the night and watch over the Naval Base, taking appropriate action in the event of an air raid. It was a task eminently suited to a very junior officer, for no one even remotely expected a Japanese air attack at this time and in this place. If Japanese airplanes were on their way or were sighted, I was to telephone the Chief Engineer's office, where someone was standing by to throw the switch which would put the Naval Base into darkness and then telephone all the senior officers in turn.

From the wide windows of the house on King's Avenue I could see two thirds of the Base: the ships, the straits, the hills of Johore, the graving dock, the machine shops were all clearly visible in the brilliant moonlight. So was the floating dock, moored in the middle of the straits and festooned with lights. The moon was full, with blue shimmering rings, and the sky was the deep purple color which usually presaged a day of great heat.

Jackman had gone to sleep in the west wing of the house and the Chinese servants were asleep in their own small white-washed house in the compound behind the house. Except for the throbbing of electric generators there was no sound, and over large spaces of the Naval Base there was no sign of life. Red lamps shone from the radio towers. Starlight and moonlight were so bright that roofs shone like ice. It occurred to me that even if there was an air raid, no purpose would be served by throwing the switch and putting out the lights because every detail of the Naval Base was only too visible: the enormous moon threw everything into high relief.

So the hours passed while I stood by the window without any sense of waiting or expectation. On that night the Naval Base was mine, and mine alone. Once or twice a car moved along one of the winding roads, but otherwise the entire Base seemed to be frozen into immobility in the silence and beauty of a summer night. The blue moon-rings pulsated, and as the night advanced the moon grew smaller. At 4:15 A.M. the windows rattled and the house shook as though there had been a distant earthquake, and this inexplicable shaking—for Singapore is not in the earthquake belt—was our first intimation that something unusual was happening. A few moments later searchlights sprang up from the ships, wavering in all directions across the sky, and then I went to the telephone, gave the order, and all the lights went out. With the searchlights probing the sky, the Naval Base was even brighter than before.

I had just called the Captain of the Dockyard to tell him that the *Prince of Wales* and the *Repulse* had turned on their searchlights when there came a thundering roar of anti-aircraft guns. Like a chain of fireworks the tracer shells curled slowly to the sky, but the Japanese airplanes, keeping perfect formation, flew serenely above the range of the guns. There was now no need to wake anyone, for the noise of the guns echoing and re-echoing across the straits must have thrown everyone out of bed. Salvo after salvo was fired, and all the time the little silver planes caught in the searchlights continued to move slowly across the sky. There were seventeen airplanes and each one of them had just sent a bomb hurtling down on Singapore.

The crack and roar of the anti-aircraft shells, the silver flashes in the sky as they exploded, the earth shuddering and the smoke lit with a red glare streaming over the decks of the battleships, all these were satisfying and beautiful, but it would have been more beautiful if the airplanes had fallen in flames out of the sky. It was intolerably frustrating that they should be flying about a thousand feet above the range of our guns, and there was something else which seemed at that moment to be intolerable: the great floating dock, moored in the straits, was lit up like a Christmas tree. I kept calling frantically to the floating dock, but there was no answer. At last I got the head of the night crew and cursed him. "I know all about that," he said, "but I can't find the bloody switch!" By this time the Japanese airplanes were out of sight, flying northward to their bases in Indochina.

Jackman, awakened by the shattering noise of the anti-aircraft fire, was now gazing gloomily out of the windows and saying over and over again: "Where in hell were our airplanes?"

An hour later the sky cleared and the dawn came up with flaming clouds shot through with emerald green and chrome yellow bars of light, as calm and sumptuous a dawn as any I had ever seen. In the early morning light the Naval Base glistened as though there had been a soft fall of rain. The great battleships were at anchor, flags and pennants flying. Nothing had changed, but everything had changed. Simply by flying high above our heads, the Japanese had shown us how vulnerable we were.

At six o'clock the Singapore radio came on, and then we learned how vulnerable were all the countries of the Far East.

Hongkong, Thailand, Java and Hawaii had all been attacked during the night by Japanese airplanes. Later we learned that we had the dubious honor of being the first to be struck, for the bombs fell on Singapore an hour and ten minutes before they fell on Pearl Harbor. About the damage on Singapore the radio was exceedingly vague: a few buildings had been destroyed and a few lives had been lost. During the afternoon we learned that Chinatown had been heavily hit, and "a few buildings" could be counted in their hundreds. We learned there had been a Japanese landing at Khota Bahru on the northwest coast of Malaya, and our troops were pulling back. Worse still, eighty-four airplanes, mostly on the airfields of northern Malaya, had been destroyed by Japanese bombers, and in a single night we had lost half our air force.

We thought we had one supreme consolation: we still had a small but powerful fleet. It was not the fleet we had hoped for, since the original plan involved sending the aircraft carrier *Indomitable* as well as the *Prince of Wales* and the *Repulse,* but the *Indomitable* ran aground a day or two before being posted for sailing to Singapore. We were left with the two great capital ships, four destroyers and the cruiser *Exeter.* Two other cruisers were in the neighborhood. With the Australian and Indian troops in the Malayan jungles and with our ships patrolling the coasts we thought we had a good chance of holding off the Japanese. Very soon we expected the battleships to sail out against the invaders.

They sailed out of the straits on December 8, just after sunset. I was standing with Jackman at the gate of the house. The air was sweet-smelling, for the frangipani tree nestling against the gate was in full bloom, the white waxen flowers pouring their scent on the air. A hush always descended on the Naval Base after sunset. Suddenly there was a confused sound coming from the ships below: voices, music, machinery combining to form a sound which was strangely unlike any of them, and then the wind changed and we heard the grinding of the anchor chains. A moment later the gray hulks were gliding away. Only a few lights were showing, and when we last saw them there were no lights at all. Without the ships the Naval Base seemed strangely empty.

For a while in the darkness we talked about the events of the day, most of them disturbing and some of them catastrophic. Above all, there was the loss of so many airplanes and the knowledge that we were very nearly defenseless. The Japanese aim was to take possession of all the Far East, and there was very little to prevent them. No doubt Hongkong would fall, Thailand would be conquered, Java and the Philippines would be plundered, and what was there to prevent the Japanese from landing in India? As though mocking us, the moon came out with its full regalia of shimmering blue rings and the frangipani flowers endlessly poured out their intoxicating scent.

What we feared above all was a parachute descent by Japanese troops. A hundred well-trained and well-equipped men could have captured the Base without too much difficulty. In the Armament Depot we were quite seriously discussing erecting poisoned stakes, having heard that they were being used to protect airfields in Java. On the following day my chief occupation was the study of poisons, and that meant a hurried expedition to Raffles Library in Singapore and some curious conversations with local druggists. The forest of poisoned stakes was never planted, for there was simply not enough poison available. Booby traps and mines to be touched off by the parachuters were also abandoned as impractical. We learned that no one had contemplated the possibility of a parachute descent on the Naval Base, no plans had been prepared, and the only anti-aircraft guns belonged to the destroyer *Tenedos*, which was left behind when the three other destroyers accompanied the *Prince of Wales* and the *Repulse* into the South China Sea.

It was a time of rumors. We expected victories, and rumor supplied them. We feared defeats, and rumor supplied them with the same largesse. We heard that the Singapore Harbor Board with its extensive dockyards had been totally destroyed, but a quick telephone call told us that it was still in existence. But further afield, in places out of reach of our telephones, imaginary defeats and victories were taking place at an extraordinary pace. We studied the maps, drew lines across them, calculated the positions of the Japanese forces and our own, and when we looked at the maps again they had all dissolved into the misty colors of rumor.

At a little after four o'clock on the afternoon of December 10, fifty-six hours after the beginning of the war, the Chief Armament Officer called us into his office. During the afternoon we had all been to see him on various errands, and he had been good-humored and kindly, with a red glow on his cheeks. Now, suddenly, as we gathered in his office, he looked strangely old and white, as though in the space of a few minutes he had been attacked by a withering disease. He said: "I have called you in to tell you that the *Prince of Wales* and the *Repulse* were sunk early this afternoon by Japanese torpedo-carrying airplanes. This is not a rumor."

He did not seem to be speaking with his own voice: it was the voice of another man, unknown to us. He did not look at us, but stared at a piece of paper on his desk, as though if he stared at it long enough it would say something else. We asked questions, but he answered wearily that he knew no more than he had told us. An hour passed, and we were called in again, to learn that Admiral Sir Tom Phillips had gone down with the *Prince of Wales* and that the three destroyers were speeding back to the Naval Base with the survivors.

At midnight we received a signal that the destroyers were in urgent need of anti-aircraft shells, for on this night of all nights we expected an air raid or a parachute descent. In normal times it would have been a simple matter to transport the shells across the Naval Base, but these were not normal times. Everything was going wrong. The two trucks belonging to the Armament Depot were out of order: one had suffered a broken axle during the morning, the other had been in a collision during the afternoon. The only large car available in the depot was a blue Rolls-Royce, the most magnificent automobile I had ever seen, the gift of a Singapore Chinese millionaire to the war effort. We had possessed it for all of twenty-four hours. We filled it with shells until it seemed to sink up to the wheel hubs. There was no time to treat the shells respectfully: we simply stuffed them in the back of the Rolls-Royce and hoped they would behave kindly to one another. At the last moment we remembered that all cars moving in the Naval Base had to be provided with blue lights, otherwise they would be shot at. No one had bothered to paint over the enormous headlights of the Rolls-Royce, and nowhere in the Armament Depot was there any blue paint. We searched for blue paper, but found none.

Finally I remembered that matchboxes had half an inch of blue lining, and this was peeled off and gummed to the headlights. Then with a Sikh driver I drove across the Naval Base, the Rolls-Royce lurching heavily, the shells slithering over one another like fish, the springs creaking, the sweat pouring down the face of the Sikh, as he leaned forward with his head against the windshield, for on this night of all nights the moon was hidden by clouds and we could scarcely see where we were going. The blue lining of the matchboxes had proved to be only too effective. Twice we lost ourselves, and once we nearly drove into the sea. The familiar shapes of derricks and machine-shops appeared and vanished; the Naval Base, which we knew so well, had become totally unfamiliar. Finally we reached the quayside only to discover that the road was under repair and the whole length of the quay was covered with clinkers. The tires could not grip them, and the wheels were spinning. Once again the Rolls-Royce was careening from side to side and lurching.

"It doesn't work, sahib, it doesn't work," the Sikh kept saying, but all the time he was making it work.

Finally the Rolls-Royce came to a halt at the gangway of the destroyer *Vampire*, which had arrived in port only a few minutes before. Clutching two anti-aircraft shells, like bottles, I went on deck and asked for the officer of the watch, who could not be found, or the chief gunner, who had gone ashore. Frustrated, I asked for the captain, but they said he was busy looking after the survivors. Someone was distributing blankets, and little huddled groups of blanketed men were making their way slowly down the gangway, leaning heavily on the rails. One single powerful electric light on the dockside illuminated the ghostly scene.

There were naked sailors on deck, and some of them were dead. For about an hour the three destroyers had been picking up men from the sea. When the *Prince of Wales* and the *Repulse* sank, there was such a thick film of oil on the sea that men drowned in oil or choked to death in it. Those who had been hauled out of the sea were hosed down with fresh water and left to lie on the deck, for there were not enough hands to attend to them and the captain's orders were to return to the Naval Base as quickly as possible. So now, long past midnight, the survivors waited patiently until they were given blankets and half carried off the destroyer. I heard no one complaining, and there was scarcely any talking. Indeed, all through that dreadful night I cannot remember a voice raised above a hoarse whisper.

It took half an hour to find a first lieutenant who would send a party down to remove the anti-aircraft shells from the back of the Rolls-Royce. By this time, tables had been erected on the quayside and behind them women were serving coffee and tots of rum to the men as they came off the destroyers. Most of the men were barefoot and they hopped painfully when their feet touched the clinkers. The first lieutenant was saying: "We picked up five hundred men! Jesus Christ, have you ever been in a destroyer with five hundred drowned men!"

I watched the men from the destroyers walking along the quayside in a deathly silence broken only by the crunch of bare feet on the clinkers, their backs bent, their faces as ashen as the road, their hair glistening with oil. Buses were waiting for them, and they would soon be taken to the barracks where they would spend the night. An English sailor will burst out singing in defeat, but this was not defeat. This was something else, something that had never happened to the English before, and they had no name for it.

For a while I stayed on the deck of the *Vampire*, while the anti-aircraft shells were parceled out between the destroyers and chits were signed, for the purposes of bureaucracy must be preserved even in the midst of total disaster. In this way I acquired proof that the shells had been safely delivered to the appropriate authorities.

On the way back to the Armament Depot, while the Rolls-Royce was still moving erratically along the clinker road, the pale blue light of the headlights picked up a man leaning against a wall, his arms above his head, and he seemed to be trying to claw his way up the wall. We stopped the car and asked him if there was anything we could do. He said: "I want to see the Admiral." He was dressed in civilian clothes, and said he was an American correspondent who had gone down with the *Prince of Wales*. He looked gaunt and ill, swaying in the darkness, and all the time he was saying: "I want to see the Admiral," as though he had no other thought on his mind. He was an unlikely apparition on a night of unlikely apparitions, but we dragged him into the car and drove him to the War Room, which was guarded by a single sailor with a fixed bayonet. I showed my pass and slipped into the War Room, which I had never entered before.

What was chiefly remarkable about the room was its total silence. Just as none of the men leaving the destroyers seemed capable of speech, so here, at the nerve center of the Naval Base, there was a strange flow of silence, an unbroken stillness. Heads were bent, hands moved across the maps on the table, and sometimes a map was rolled up and another replaced it. The admirals and the captains seemed made of stone which had weathered and left strange hollows and folds in their features. I knew them all by sight, and one or two I knew well, but they were all nearly unrecognizable.

A lieutenant went up to Admiral Sir Geoffrey Layton, the commander-in-chief, who sat at the head of the table, and whispered to him that an American correspondent was waiting outside for a message to his newspaper. The Admiral nodded, rose heavily from his chair and walked the whole length of the room with his eyes closed, like a sleepwalker. The American correspondent was standing by the sailor with the fixed bayonet in darkness outside the War Room. Tears were streaming down the Admiral's cheeks. "We have taken hard knocks before, and we shall take them again, and—" He paused, because the tears were choking him. "—we shall win in the end." Then he turned abruptly on his heels, having delivered the only message he intended to give, and then he marched back into the War Room and the silence of the long night.

I should have been among those who spent their last hours in Singapore blowing up every mortal thing we possessed. Instead I was sent to China at the orders of Robert Scott, who plucked me out of the Naval Base and threw me like a stone into a country I had never known. A week after the sinking of the ships I was flown to Rangoon by way of Semarang in Sumatra and the Andaman Islands, and the only other passenger in the small seaplane was Evert Barger, a young archaeologist. We were the advance staff of Robert Scott, with letters of appointment addressed to Sir Archibald Clark Kerr, the British ambassador in Chungking. We did not know and could not guess what was expected of us. All we knew for certain was that we would spend the rest of the war in China.

THE CLIFFS OF CHUNGKING

As the airplane came down on the sandspit in the Yangtze River, we saw white mists breaking against the cliffs of Chungking and the waves were white with fury. Sampans floated through the mist, sails flapping. High above us the cliffs glowed in the sultry yellowish light of winter. Higher still hung the heavy gray clouds which hide all this region of Szechuan from the sun for six months of the year.

I came to know Chungking well during the following years, but the first view of it was the one that left the deepest impression. Seen from the sandspit in mid-river, the city possessed the grandeur of a petrified nightmare. It was inconceivable that anyone should want to live on that appalling rock hung in mid-air under those lowering clouds. Quite suddenly the city began to vanish as a rain squall swept across the river, and then there was only the black oily water, the sampans sliding steeply away, the bitter cold in the air. We climbed into a motorboat, hauled our luggage onto it, and soon we were chugging across the Yangtze with the river roaring in our ears, all the world blotted out. By the time we reached the shore the rain had cleared a little, and we could make out the Wang Lung Men steps carved out of the rock face, a stairway rising through the mist and the rain to the city on the cliffs.

Wang Lung Men means "Emperor Dragon Gate." The Emperor Dragon was the Yangtze River, crackling with a life of its own, more tumultuous than any river I had ever known. Long ago the carved ornamental gateway at the head of the steps had been blown to smithereens by Japanese bombs. There was no gate: only the naked steps.

As we looked up, we wondered how on earth we were going to carry our luggage to the top of the cliff. The problem was soon solved. Half-naked coolies, with white turbans wrapped round their heads, those turbans which are worn by all Szechuanese peasants as though they were badges of honor, stood around us, clamoring for permission to carry us up the cliff wall in chairs fashioned out of two lengths of bamboo with a precarious perch lashed between them. We would be sitting in the little perches, while they climbed the steps with the bamboos resting on their shoulders. Their ancestors had been climbing these steps for two thousand years and they were as sure-footed as mountain lions.

In this way we had our first chair ride up the Wang Lung Men steps, finding ourselves tiptilted crazily, unable to see anything except the clouds and the mist, while the coolies grunted in unison and the bamboos creaked and swung under our weight. Because there were so many people being carried up the cliff, the rhythmic grunting of the coolies and the creaking of the bamboos formed, with the roaring of the river, a symphonic overture to our arrival in Chungking.

But of course it was not Chungking, but some other city —nameless, unreachable, unknowable. I think nearly everyone who lived in Chungking during the war had the feeling that it was totally unreal. In Singapore you could expect things to happen in an orderly fashion, the houses would be built in a predictable way, there was some residual logic in people's actions. Here, in Chungking, nothing was what it seemed to be, and the people who lived on that cliff edge jutting out over the Yangtze River had about them a strange air of unreality, as if they believed neither in their own existence nor in the existence of their city. Like the haunted crossroads in the Forest of Broceliande, the city was inhabited by ghosts and goblins.

When we reached the top of the cliff, there was no sign of Chungking: it had vanished in a rain squall. Gradually little pieces of it began to reappear: a telegraph pole festooned with wires, the burned stump of a house, a completely naked man wandering about with a look of bemusement as though searching for something, a ricksha boy wearing a cloak of rice straw, two coolies carrying a dead pig between sagging bamboo poles, the blood dripping from the gashed throat with the sound of rain falling. There were no colors, only a smoky gray or grayish yellow. The body of the naked man, wet from the rain, looked perfectly appropriate in this setting. A ricksha pulled up, and with our luggage piled on our knees we were bowled along in the direction of the British embassy at the other end of the city.

We had known that Chungking had been bombed, but no one had told us that it had been leveled to the ground. Scarcely a building had survived the bombing. Whole streets were made up of plaster-and-lath shop fronts, which a high wind would have no difficulty in tossing to the ground. The roads were muddy pot holes strung together, and everywhere there were huge piles of debris from the bombing in the autumn. Behind the shop fronts stood the jagged, smoke-blackened walls of shops and houses which had long ago ceased to exist. An occasional bus lurched along the broken roads, trailing a huge black exhaust like a fox's tail. Bomb craters were filled with water and a grayish scum, where women washed clothes, rocking on their heels. There was more than the predictable number of dead rats, and indeed the only specks of color came from their split bellies. Looking at Chungking from the air, I had thought it was flat with perhaps a few gentle inclines. In fact, half the roads were steep, and the ricksha puller would climb them at a snail's pace and then go slithering down the other side, hanging for dear life between the shafts of the ricksha, his feet scarcely touching the ground. On that winter day, with the fog and mist swirling along the streets and with a sulphurous cloud overhead, Chungking was a city of utter desolation, weirdly beautiful, like the ruined castle in a fairy tale.

The British embassy lay in a sunken garden and consisted of seven or eight bungalows surrounding a withered peach tree. The mist swirled over it, the paint was peeling, and there were bomb craters nearby. Predictably, the first person we met was a gnomelike man whose body was bent double, so that his chin came very nearly on a level with his knees. He wore a bright red woolen scarf and a porkpie hat, and he was shuffling along the circular stone-flagged path around the peach tree, his hands clasped behind his back. Though we had half expected to see such a man, we could make nothing of him. He was the lord of the ruined castle, or—and this was more likely—he was a janitor attached to the embassy. He was muttering to himself, stealing glances at us, and was probably annoyed by the way we stood with our small piles of luggage at our feet, spellbound by the sunken garden where nothing whatsoever was happening except that an old bent gnome was walking round a peach tree.

Suddenly the gnome paused in his shuffling to dart an inquiring glance at us from under thick sandy-colored eyebrows. "What are you fellows doing here?" he asked in a penetrating voice. "Don't stand there! Are you coming or going?"

This was not a question we could answer. At the top of the steps leading down to the sunken garden there was an enamel plaque with a lion and a unicorn and the words BRITISH EMBASSY, but obviously we had taken the wrong path. The real British embassy was probably in the next garden, or somewhere else entirely.

"Oh, make up your minds!" the gnome said impatiently, shuffling right up to us. "If you want the American embassy, it's on the other side of the river."

Then he left us and vanished into one of the bungalows. We climbed up the steps, made sure there was only one path leading to the embassy, and found ourselves in the sunken garden again. A Chinese girl came out of one of the bungalows and asked whether there was anything she could do for us. We told her we would like to see the ambassador.

"You can't, because he is having lunch with the Generalissimo," she said. "You can see Sir Eric Teichman, if you like."

Everything was happening in slow motion, as in a dream. In the garden all the sounds of Chungking were blotted out. If this was the British embassy, then it was the strangest embassy on earth. Even before the Chinese girl led us to the bungalow, we knew we would encounter the gnome again. He was sitting on the edge of a sofa, reading a Chinese newspaper.

"Ah, there you are!" he exclaimed. "So you have finally decided to enter the lion's den. I think I know who you are, because we received a cable about you from Singapore! All right, sit down and make yourselves comfortable! I suppose you would like some tea, eh?"

Sir Eric Teichman was the Chinese Secretary of the Embassy, and therefore he ranked above the first, second and third secretaries, and in power and influence was almost equal to the ambassador. Chinese Secretary meant that he was knowledgeable in the Chinese language and in Chinese affairs, and in the old days he would have drawn up the official pronouncements of the ambassador in the proper language of the court, with all the interminable flowery circumlocutions. The British Foreign Office had chosen well, for Sir Eric Teichman was a considerable scholar of Chinese, Tibetan and Mongolian, and he had once played an important and little-known role in history when he acted as mediator between China and Tibet during the troubles at the end of the First World War. He had written books about his travels through Tartary and Tibet, which have become classics. Sitting on the edge of the sofa in the small shadowy bungalow, his body so bent and twisted that it bore only a faint resemblance to a human body, he talked about the political situation in China now that the Pacific War had broken out, and he found no comfort in it. He had spent forty years of his life in the Far East, and he had never known the Chinese so demoralized, so exhausted.

"They're going to let us do the fighting, and take a rest— a long rest," he said. "They have reached the stage when they are simply fighting for survival, and they have no understanding of what is happening around them."

He seemed to be sighing for the years of the warlords, when the Chinese at least knew what they were doing. He had known China when it was ruled by the Manchu emperors, and he talked about Peking as though it were the only city in the world worth living in. The Japanese invasion of China had the effect of splintering China into fragments, and he seemed to despair that the fragments would ever be put together again.

There were Chinese scrolls on the wall, porcelain vases, a desk looking out on the sunken garden, Chinese books everywhere. His eyes, under the bushy brows, were startlingly blue and childlike, and although he was obviously in pain his narrow face was curiously youthful and unlined. He had traveled in the most desolate regions of the earth, he suffered terribly from arthritis and a strange disease of the spine, but neither his travels nor his sufferings had left any mark. He asked us what we expected to do in Chungking, but when we told him we would know when Robert Scott arrived, and not until then, he seemed to be content. "A lot of strays are wandering into Chungking," he said, and the words were not spoken unkindly.

I think he was half-amused by our presence in the embassy compound. We were so raw, so inexperienced, so baffled, so useless, and so dirty. We had not eaten since Rangoon, we had not shaved or washed, our clothes were crumpled, and we looked like beggars. Sometimes he stroked his chin and he would look at us with the same air of disbelief with which we looked at him.

By this time it was about three o'clock in the afternoon and we were ravenously hungry. We went off to a restaurant for lunch, and when we returned to the embassy we found the ambassador waiting for us in his bungalow at the bottom of the sunken garden.

If Sir Eric Teichman resembled a gnome in a magic cave, the ambassador, Sir Archibald Clark Kerr, resembled the king of the mountain. Six feet tall, heavily built, red-faced, hook-nosed, his enormous brown eyes flecked with gold, he looked like a Roman Emperor, so certain of his massive authority that he never needed to raise his voice or make a demonstrative gesture. Indeed his voice was very quiet and gentle, with a beautiful Scotch burr. He was sitting at his desk facing the window with an immense white goose quill pen in his hand. He looked us up and down, said a few words, and went on writing, the pen making a squeaking sound. Darkness was coming down, and we heard the ticking of a clock.

At last, when he turned round, we were aware of the extraordinary toughness in him, for the fading light had turned his face into a bronze mask. He said he had received the signal from Robert Scott, knew all about us, was happy we had arrived safely, and had not the faintest idea why we had come. Then he launched into a long carefully reasoned account of the current political situation in China, not so pessimistic as Sir Eric Teichman's but nevertheless without the slightest optimism. It was going to be very rough, and would be much worse before it got better. The Chinese were very nearly at the end of their resources, and while the opening of the Pacific War had given them a great boost in morale, it had simultaneously deprived them of any reason to fight the Japanese, since the Allies would do the fighting for them. Their resources—nil, except for their courage. Worst of all, they had lost hope.

So he talked, while a pale fluttering light came on in all the bungalows, making the garden look as though it was fathoms deep under water. Electricity in Chungking was never dependable, and there was something eerie in this constantly flickering light, which made everything appear impermanent. He was saying: "Do be careful. Don't ever get it into your head that you understand the Chinese, because you never will! The only rule is to study them unrelentingly without any pre-conceptions at all. In the end you will grow so fond of them that you will never want to leave them."

He spoke simply and courteously, but we would learn later that he was far more complex than he appeared. His reactions were always immediate and subtle, but sometimes in the follow-ing days we would see the flame-lit depths behind the bronze mask. Finally he waved us away and went back to the letter and the goose quill pen.

Our destination was the Chungking Club on the south bank of the river. So we rode in rickshas across Chungking, where the street stalls were lit by flickering tung oil lamps, to the Wang Lung Men steps, now dark and slippery and more menacing than ever in the frail moonlight shining through the clouds. We saw now that the cliff was a rabbit warren of tunnels and caves, with bamboo huts perched precariously on the ledges; and all day long and half the night coolies went down to the Yangtze to fill their buckets with water and then climbed the steps again. Here the river was nearly a mile wide, roaring in the darkness with the fury of an enraged beast. Standing at the bottom of the steps, the wind in our faces, we became aware for the first time of the appalling violence of the river. If Chungking was hard and implacable, a place designed for the sole purpose of breaking men's hearts, so was the river. Far away, on the south bank, we saw the ghostly shapes of hills like endless waves.

The ramshackle ferry boat once carried passengers across the Clyde. Now, in old age, it creaked and wheezed across the Yangtze with such a rattle of chains and machinery that it seemed to be simultaneously coughing up its life and clamoring for atten-tion. It smelled of tung oil, rust and rotting timbers; lurched violently with every wind and wave; and had such a tendency to drift downstream that we sometimes thought we would reach the Ichang gorges before we reached the south bank. The first thudding of the paddle wheels sent such a shock through the poor ship that it seemed about to disintegrate into its separate parts; then, recovering, moving half sideways, ungainly always,

Rangoon, December 1941

Correspondents with General Lister near Mora de Ebro, July 1938. Author on extreme right.

The author with General Lister

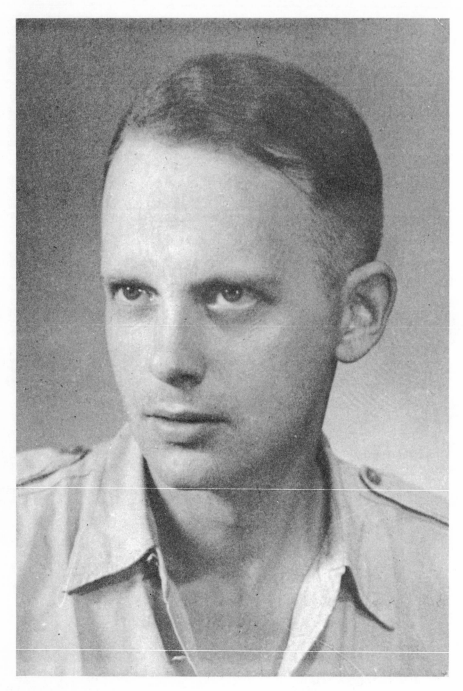

Chungking, March 1942

The Japanese prisoner at Changsha, January 1942

The Chialing River near Peipei

OPPOSITE: A gateway in Kunming (*Sydney Greenberg*)

Wen Yi-tuo

it nosed out into the dark spaces of the river, a mysterious landscape where the only certain thing was the white foam caught in the gleam of the bow lights. You could feel the tug of the river trying to pull the ship down to the bottom.

The shores of Chinese rivers are littered with shipwrecks: if we had known this, we might have been more frightened. Inevitably the fierce current drew the ferry boat along a zigzag path: drifting downstream, wheeling helplessly in the whirlpools and somehow climbing out of them, veering back to shore and then suddenly swinging into midstream. When the long journey came to an end, we had the feeling that an impossible task had been accomplished. We had crossed the river of Lethe and returned to life again.

Best of all was our welcome on the south bank, for the night of murk and mist, when we reached the landing stage, suddenly exploded in brilliant colors as small boys came running down to the water's edge with bamboo flares dipped in vegetable oil to light our way. Their shadows were leaping crazily on the rocks, and the faces of the boys glowed with the colors of the red bulls in Spanish caves. There were no cliffs on the south bank, only a wild tumble of rocks and stones. The boys looked wonderfully handsome and healthy with their red cheeks and dark gleaming eyes, shouting to us good-humoredly that they were the world's most perfect guides and would take us anywhere. Some came riding on small Tibetan ponies with purple saddlecloths, and their coming was always joyful. After the grayness of Chungking and the blackness of the river, this sudden explosion of color was the purest benediction.

So for a while we watched the passengers disembark, to vanish in the darkness amid bobbing lanterns and smoking flares, and sometimes there would be the immense shadow of a pony on a white and flickering rock. Then the rock would vanish, and there was only a shadowy elemental landscape where there were no pathways. Many of the passengers lived in remote farmhouses set among rice fields, and they would journey for about an hour before they reached their homes.

We hired a boy to light the way to the Chungking Club, which perched on a rocky outcrop not five hundred yards away from the landing stage, and we might have guessed that the club was a place of desolation. We had not expected to spend our nights in a drab Victorian lodging house with a crumbling tennis court, scuffed billiard tables, a library full of decaying year-old magazines. We were lodged in what was euphemistically called the ballroom, and since Christmas was coming, we were greeted with the sight of a Christmas tree festooned with paper ribbons; the needles lay in a pile at the foot of the tree, and the ribbons were thick with last year's dust. I thought the club was the most miserable place I had ever lived in, and it was endurable only because the unwashed windows looked out on the vast reaches of the Yangtze and the white cliffs of Chungking.

Winter had come down, there was a cold tang in the air, and sometimes Chungking vanished in the clouds and the mist. All day and all night there was the roar of the river, and when the mist came down there came the booming of iron drums. High up, ghostly in the mist, the pepperpot hills of the south bank looked down on us. They seemed to have been shaped by hand, and I never saw a mountain in China which did not look man-made, so artfully were they constructed. Even Chungking looked as though its bombed and broken walls had been carved by a genius.

The days passed, and there was no news from Robert Scott. The Japanese were pouring across Southeast Asia, Penang had fallen, Kuala Lumpur was about to fall, and already there was talk of mopping-up actions in the Dutch East Indies. Thailand surrendered, Rangoon was bombed, the Philippines were crumbling. People were talking about the grand alliance of the A.B.C.D. powers—America, Britain, China, the Dutch—but this alphabetical alliance seemed strangely incapable of stopping the Japanese. The whole of the East was going up in flames.

The Chinese viewed the conflagration without any outward alarm. In the offices of the government officials you were greeted with impeccable politeness, given glasses of hot tea, and asked for your opinions on a variety of subjects which had no connection with the war. They had known that the Japanese would attempt to conquer all of Asia, they had uttered innumerable warnings, and no one had paid the slightest attention to them. They were prophets happy that their prophecies had come true, and without much bitterness.

Higher up, among the rarely seen demi-gods of the ruling

Kuomintang Party, a corrosive bitterness was at work, but the full extent of the corrosion was rarely perceived, though it could sometimes be felt as one can feel the approach of a storm on a calm winter's day. Sometimes, but very rarely, we saw it in all its unadorned fury. Ho Ying-chin, the minister of war, gave a banquet to honor the ambassadors of the A.B.C.D. powers. He was a short, solidly built man with a brutal pock-marked face and a piping voice, an impatient manner, and a habit of making chopping gestures with his hands. He was the principal speaker, and he made a completely innocuous speech, evidently written by a secretary, welcoming us into the brotherhood of the great alliance, in which the Republic of China would always play a prominent part, and he reminded us that China had been fighting the Japanese since 1931. The Republic of China would place all its resources unreservedly at the service of the alliance. The speech went on and on, and at long intervals there would be a pause for the benefit of the pale and rather frightened translator. Then came speeches from the American, British and Dutch ambassadors. Ho Ying-chin was having difficulty containing himself. In the middle of an ambassador's speech he would offer a toast, insist that the ambassador come forward and drink with him, and afterward he would sit down with a look of amazed contentment. Finally, just as the banquet was coming to an end, he offered the toast that was to make the evening memorable. He raised his small cup of rice wine to his lips and said: "Let us drink to the day when every damned foreigner has been run out of China!" In the stunned silence that followed, the interpreter said: "The minister is drinking to the defeat of the Japanese."

Clark Kerr shot a glance at the drunken minister of war and carefully wrote out the words on a place card. He knew Ho Ying-chin well, and had no high opinion of him. Indeed, he had no high opinion of any of the leaders of the Kuomintang Party and only a kind of pity for Chiang Kai-shek, who was continually giving orders without knowing what the problem was. Chiang Kai-shek was living in a house called the Eagle's Nest, far away from the center of Chungking. No one could reach him without first going through a battery of aides who saw to it that he was never asked any awkward questions. "At least Ho Ying-chin is honest," the ambassador said, as he left the banquet.

"Those words were not written for him. They were his own personal contribution to the alliance."

Two or three days later, we were summoned to lunch with the ambassador in his house perched high up on the cliffs. It was a small house, and he had somehow made it over until it looked a little like a country house in Scotland. A great log fire was blazing in the hearth, there were photographs, an enormous bookcase, comfortable sofas and armchairs. In Singapore George Yeh had told me: "Be careful of him. He comes into your room, rolls up his sleeves, takes out his pipe, says quietly, 'Let's get down to the root of the matter,' and before you know where you are, you find yourself agreeing upon everything." It was a good description, although it omitted many of the complexities of his character. The man we saw at lunch did not in the least resemble an ambassador. He resembled a Scottish laird who enjoyed walking across his estates, books, good food, fine wines, and the companionship of scholars. There were three or four young Chinese professors waiting in the small pavilionlike anteroom for lunch. The ambassador came in late. He had been walking for miles with his collie in the mist, and the fumes of the mist still clung to his tweed coat.

I suppose he must have possessed some books and papers relating to diplomacy, but I never saw any of them in this house. There were at least a thousand books, and he especially enjoyed eighteenth-century memoirs. He had all of Jane Austen, most of Smollett, and there was a shelf of Virginia Woolf, whom he knew well. There was Peter Fleming's *News from Tartary* and James Bertram's recent book on his Chinese travels. He liked leather bindings, first editions, and well-designed bookjackets. One can often tell a man's character from his library, but this was not the library of a bookish man. I suspect that he enjoyed books in exactly the same way that he enjoyed wines: they were to be tasted and savored, relished for their excellence and rejected if they did not come up to his high standards. Cocktails were served, and the small group of professors broke up into smaller groups, the ambassador passing from one to the other, furiously inquisitive, wanting to know everything that was being said.

Just before lunch he brought out his great prize, a copy of James Joyce's *Finnegans Wake,* a huge book in a brilliant blue jacket, smelling of printer's ink. In that atmosphere, among Chinese professors who rarely saw newly minted English books and who had learnedly discussed this book without ever having set eyes on more than a few fragments which had appeared in magazines, *Finnegans Wake* came as a revelation, as though a little-known bird with majestic plumage had suddenly taken up residence in the room. The book was passed from hand to hand, the ambassador hovering over it protectively. "Arrived yesterday in the diplomatic bag," he said, and at that moment he resembled a conjuror telling us how he performed his tricks.

At lunch James Joyce was the chief subject of conversation, and by the time the ice cream was being served the ambassador was reading passages aloud, his spectacles on the end of his nose. He told a story about Joyce's funeral in Zurich—heaven knows where he had heard it, but it may have been in a letter from Virginia Woolf. A little man came up to the grave, unknown to any of the mourners, saying over and over again: "Who is he? Who is he? Why are they burying him? What is he doing here?" It was almost a Chinese ghost story. Many Joyces were present in the room. There was the spectral Joyce, the Scottish Joyce, the Chinese Joyce, the Joyce who had wandered over Europe out of hatred for Ireland and England, and the Joyce who had come to rest in Chungking.

Sometimes, of course, the talk verged away from Joyce. One of the professors was saying that during the May bombing the previous year, he had stood with the ambassador on a hilltop overlooking the embassy. "The Japanese airplanes made their runs over the city and then calmly wheeled round and did it all over again. It got so hot that I raced for the shelter, but the ambassador simply stood there, looking up at the airplanes. He wanted to see what was happening, and everyone else wanted to bury their faces in the ground."

I left the ambassador's house late in the afternoon. A smoky, greasy mist was pouring over the Chialing River, which meets the Yangtze not far from the house. It was growing dark, and the stark shapes of the bombed and shattered city stood out against the sultry sky. A cold wind was blowing. There was always a strange silence in the outskirts of Chungking, but the highways of the sprawling city were filled with people in violent activity. The orange sellers were shouting, the kettle boys in the teahouses were racing about, pouring long fountains of boiling water into the waiting glasses, the ricksha pullers were bowling along the street, the market places were crowded, everyone was in a hurry. A girl with a white powdered face and a rich brocaded gown was being carried on a palanquin through the market place, and the bearers shouted at the top of their voices: "Make way! Make way!" but no one paid the slightest attention to her, though she had stepped out of a fairy tale.

Ducks and geese hung on strings in the market place, and in the light of the kerosene lamps they glowed bright yellow. Five-year-old girls carried their four-year-old brothers on their hips, and moved about the market as though they were the equals of the elderly peasants who stroked their beards and the old women with bound feet who moved surprisingly fast, though their toes were deformed and their soles were bent double. In a corner of the market place a scribe was painting an inscription on an immense sheet of crimson paper, smiling as he admired his own dexterity, his small wizened head bobbing up and down. For an illiterate peasant who had paid him a small fortune the scribe was writing a scroll which read: "Happiness and good fortune for ten thousand years." The peasant was smiling from ear to ear.

There was so much vitality, so much roaring and bargaining and trumpeting, and everyone was moving so fast, that the market place took on the aspect of a brightly lit stage filled with dancers in brilliantly colored costumes. Elizabethan England must have been like this, with the water-boys running up and down the streets, the carriages jostling together, and everyone wearing flamboyant costumes. A youth with a red cape rode past on a donkey, his white Szechuanese turban giving him the appearance of a wounded warrior out of the ancient wars. Another palanquin was borne through the crowd, but this time there was a dead man propped up in it. Peasant women carried bundles of hens by their legs, so that their heads bounced against the cobblestones and left trails of blood. The air was sweet with the smell of crimson oranges, and the market was humming and throbbing like a hive.

I walked down the Wang Lung Men steps, thinking that it was good to be in China, and good to have an ambassador who enjoyed *Finnegans Wake*. Down below, at the foot of the cliff, the Yangtze roared ominously and the mists swirled across the river, blotting out the opposite shore. A crowd of people waited at the landing stage, but there was no ferryboat in sight, only a shadowy darkness, and sometimes a pale ghostly shape sped past—a seagull, or a wrecked sampan, or simply the reflection of a light from the shore. The Yangtze roared like a high wind, waves crashed against the rocks, the landing stage creaked and smelled of old river slime. China had vanished, and there was only the dark river.

THE BATTLE OF CHANGSHA

The British military attaché in Chungking was a gentle, kindly, pipe-smoking man with a nut-brown face and deep wrinkles around his eyes, and I suspect that the wrinkles came from the habit of being quietly amused by nearly everything he saw. He liked to puff silently on his pipe, with long meditative pauses in the conversation. Slightly built, quick and nervous in his movements, he was one of those men who could lose themselves very easily in a crowd. He was so quiet, so withdrawn from the world, that you could have taken him for a professor of one of the more obscure branches of knowledge, like Babylonian cuneiform inscriptions.

That first impression however would have been deadly wrong, for he was made of steel. He was a dedicated soldier whose only concern was to destroy and obliterate the enemy. He had been wounded many times, his body being a patchwork knitted together by armies of surgeons. We did not have men like this in the Navy. For me, he was a new breed, and I liked to slip into his office and watch him at work over his maps, puffing furiously on his pipe while he kept scratching out wavering lines and replacing them with new wavering lines. In his view there was nothing to prevent the Japanese from marching into Chungking.

"Is it as bad as that?" I asked.

"Much worse, if you only knew," he answered, and sighed contentedly.

"There is nothing to prevent them from taking over India, either," he said a little later.

"So it's very bad indeed?"

"Oh, it could not possibly be worse, thank God!"

"Why do you thank God?"

"Because when you have reached the very worst, you know exactly where you are. Malaya, Java, the Philippines are all going down the drain. The Japanese have got most of their Co-

Prosperity sphere already, and they have won the war. All that remains now is a mopping-up campaign."

"So the war is over?"

"No, but the Japanese think it is. It is an extremely dangerous moment when you think you have won the war."

The colonel enjoyed talking in the authentic accents of doom, but the ultimate doom was always reserved for the Japanese. The formula had long ago been established: the more victories they won, the worse it would be for them. Observing the Japanese victories at the beginning of January, he was the only person in the embassy who seemed to be elated by disaster. "Wonderful!" he would say, as another city fell to the Japanese. "Now they are really asking for trouble!"

Since he was one of the few people who possessed a staff car, and since he lived on the south bank, I sometimes succeeded in stealing a ride with him. While the Chinese driver drove us to the head of the Wang Lung Men steps, he would relate with gusto the latest blessed defeat of the Allied forces. Another city in Burma had fallen! Hongkong was under the Japanese heel! Twenty ships had been lost in the Indian Ocean! But according to his unchanging philosophy our final victory was certain, for victory belonged only to the defeated.

"You should read Hardy's *The Dynasts*," he said. "The gods are having sport with us, and especially with the Japanese!"

I borrowed his copy of *The Dynasts* and many other books, and came to know him reasonably well. I learned among other things that he was abnormally accident prone, for he usually succeeded in falling down some of the four hundred steps leading to the river. Most people walked down the steps with the utmost caution. The colonel, incapable of caution, seemed to enjoy going down head first. A severe fall was regarded as part of the day's work. It became one of my duties to pick him up and put a handkerchief to his wounds.

"There is nothing inherently wrong in falling down steps," he explained, "and you must admit that one saves a lot of time. Falling is an art, and after a good deal of experience one becomes quite proficient at it!"

He knew many other arts, adored literature, collected the works of T. E. Lawrence, and half worshiped the Chinese. He had a theory that the Chinese face was one of God's most perfect creations, while a Western face could be appropriately compared to two potatoes stuck together.

One evening, while we were tentatively climbing down the Wang Lung Men steps, he paused and said: "There's a battle shaping up in Changsha, and the ambassador said that since you are not doing anything in particular, we might as well send you as an observer."

I denied that I was doing nothing in particular. I was writing speeches, helping to edit the *British Bulletin*, and had just been appointed cultural liaison officer, a post with large undefined duties. I knew nothing, or very little, about battles. The ambassador had been misinformed.

"Nonsense!" he said. "We are understaffed, and you will have to go!"

Two days later I was on the gray sandspit in the middle of the Yangtze. A small crowd of military observers and newspaper correspondents were huddled together like prisoners in the cold dawn. Only one of them was recognizable. That was Major David Barrett, the American military attaché, round-faced and paunchy, with a wonderful smile and extraordinarily penetrating eyes, his cap askew, his fur collar pulled up against the cold. He looked no more like a military attaché than did the British colonel. Chewing on an unlit cigar, he announced that the battle of Changsha was over.

"Then why the devil are we going there?"

"To count the bodies, I suppose," he answered. "It's the first victory won by the Allies since the Pacific War broke out, and therefore you should treat it with the proper respect."

The small C.I.N.A. passenger plane flew off just after the dawn broke. I thought we were flying straight to Changsha, and settled down to study a book of reproductions of Chinese paintings, filled with fantastic landscapes. There were mountains like twisted candy, cliffs bellying out over peaceful fields, huge outcrops of gnarled rock arranged as they were arranged nowhere else in the world, one outcrop balanced precariously on another, and I marveled at the imaginations of the Chinese painters. I marveled a little less when we came out of the clouds and saw the same mountains through the airplane window—mountains that shot straight out of the earth, each one looking as though it had been deliberately shaped for the maximum effect. The earth was flat as a chessboard, and the mountains rose up like sculptured chessmen, separated from one another by five or six hundred feet of intervening fields; and as the airplane banked and flew among them, there was the sensation of entering a perilous fairyland. Clouds floated across the peaks of the mountains, and blue-sailed sampans floated along green rivers below.

The captain announced that we had reached Kweilin, and that the rest of the journey would be made by train.

At first we were disbelieving, for it seemed impossible to believe that trains were still running in China. Similarly, when we walked through Kweilin, it seemed impossible to believe that we were in war-torn China. There had been a light rain, the city was fresh and gleaming and sweet-smelling with its flower beds and avenues of lime trees. The shops were full, people were walking about at a leisurely pace, there were no bombed buildings, and the atmosphere of the place was as much French as Chinese. From the bakeries there came the unmistakable smell of French bread; there were French automobiles; and there was French elegance. All this came about because the French had penetrated deeply into southwest China, regarding the provinces of Yunnan and Kwangsi as their special sphere of influence. They established schools and colleges, bookshops and dispensaries, churches and missions, and they hoped that one day southwestern China would be added to French Indochina. After the rock-hewn majesty of Chungking it was strange to come to a small elegant provincial city untouched by the war, dreaming in the shadow of bewildering mountains.

The train was even more improbable than this small city smelling of French bread. It was the Blue Express, which formerly traveled between Peking and Shanghai, and was fitted out with the utmost luxury, with sleeping berths and silk cushions and bouquets of flowers in every compartment. There were servants in white uniforms, soft carpets lay on the floor, and there was even a dining car. So much luxury went to our heads, and we gazed out of the wide windows with expressions of disbelief. The Blue Express, in our eyes, was not so much a train as a luxury hotel on wheels.

The train traveled at twenty-five miles an hour, the idea being that if the Japanese airplanes strafed it, we would be able to jump out and hide in the ditches. Major Barrett, having a healthy respect for Chinese train engineers and Japanese airmen, thought we would be safer traveling at sixty miles an hour. It was absurd to be going to a battlefield in slow luxury.

Winter held China in its grip. The fields were Chinese paintings, the winter trees stark against the ice, only a few solitary peasants wandering across an empty landscape. Chungking, crumpled and bleeding on its rock, was no painting, but there were paintings everywhere else. In this eerie landscape, haunted by low-flying clouds, man had no place, and our Blue Express had all the appearance of an improvisation. Here and there small streams wandered among the icy fields, and sometimes smoke rose far away, curling up from the peasants' straw-thatched cottages.

We reached Hsiangtan late at night, for the Japanese had cut the railroad to the north. A few miles from Hsiangtan lay the village where Mao Tse-tung was born, but on this subject we kept discreetly silent, for there were four or five Kuomintang officers in charge of us. Hsiangtan was a small bustling town, all darkness and noise, huge shadows moving across the walls of narrow cobbled streets. This was Hunan, the land of black turbans and red peppers, the faces livelier than the faces of Szechuan, the eyes more piercing. Through those dark streets, still crowded though it was near midnight, we came to an inn which promised to be considerably less luxurious than the Blue Express. This vast sprawling inn, built around a courtyard, was not unlike an Elizabethan tavern, heavy with the smell of animal dung and human sweat. We climbed up rickety stairs to a loft where straw beds were laid out for us, and slept fitfully, for we were the guests of the gray rats creeping in the straw. All night men clambered up the stairs to peer at us, the first foreigners they had seen, while we lay there in our separate stupors, and the lanterns flared up or faded away on these strange spectators of our misery.

Happily, we were awakened before dawn to stumble half blindly down the stairway. A black-turbaned giant, naked to the waist, was ladling out steaming noodles in the courtyard by the light of a kerosene lamp. Before dawn we made our way to the river, picking the straw out of our clothes, stepping lightly around the beached fishing boats by the gray flicker of flashlights. We had come to Hsiangtan in the dark and we left in the dark, and we were glad we saw no more of it.

The motor launch shot out into the dark river, and the cold spray shook us into wakefulness. Then the sun came up over the low reddish hills where bamboos were waving on the crests, and there was no more Hsiangtan, only the wide swift-flowing river turning from misty black to pearly gray to the dark green of the open sea. The sea was a thousand miles away, but this river seemed as wide as the sea. I wore an oilskin coat and fur cap, but the cold crept under them, and soon my fingers were numb from the wind and the icy spray. The Hsiang River was in spate, beautiful in its swiftness, and the gulls hovering over the bow of the motor launch alone were motionless. All the time we were gazing at the sky, for Japanese airplanes were believed to be nearby.

White-sailed sampans flowed down-river like immense swans, and sometimes we swept past black fishing boats, each boat with its flock of cormorants, their long necks ringed so that they could not swallow the fish they caught. The cormorants were as ugly as vultures, and they hopped on the decks of the fishing boats with ungainly wings. Meanwhile we chugged along the river at a preposterously slow speed, and came at last to Changsha, "the city of the sands," flanked by white sampans, looking clean and fresh in the rain-washed air, sparkling like dew. We waded knee-deep through the sands, and when a Japanese airplane flew overhead we were already wandering down a country lane toward a large green-tiled house, which would be our home. The fields were white with broken ice, and the magpies cawed in the branches.

Here we learned that the last Japanese had been pushed out of Changsha forty-eight hours before. There was still some skirmishing outside the city, but the Japanese, according to a young Chinese major, had been severely punished and were not likely to return. A great, a very great victory had been achieved.

About that victory we were to learn many things during the following days, as we studied maps, rode across battlefields, talked with Chinese officers and questioned the solitary Japanese soldier who had been captured. From the maps we learned precisely where the Japanese had attacked and where they had been routed. We were presented with impressive lists of the numbers of dead Japanese and the amounts of captured supplies, to the last canister of poison gas; we dined with Hsueh Yueh, the commanding general, one of the very few Kuomintang generals who possessed any military ability, and the more we pondered the victory, the more mysterious it became. Perhaps all victories are mysterious, and the traveler who comes forty-eight hours late to a battlefield will rarely know what happened.

The Chinese claimed that 57,000 Japanese were killed in the battle of Changsha. In his book *China's Destiny* Chiang Kai-shek wrote that the battle was the turning point of the Pacific War: "The Japanese received a fatal blow, and afterward it was inconceivable that they would ever recover their strength on the mainland of China." According to the Generalissimo, the Chinese victory at Changsha so weakened the Japanese forces that they were compelled to abandon their carefully planned invasions of India and Australia.

But for us, tramping over the battlefield and the bleak, burned-out city of Changsha, there were no easy solutions. There had been no pitched battle. Instead, there were a series of hard-fought skirmishes inside and outside the city, and the evidence lay in the Japanese bodies we saw in the open fields, at the city gates and in obscure side streets under the city walls. When we tried to reconstruct the fighting, essential elements were always missing. When we asked the young Hunanese soldiers, with faces like ripe apples, what they had seen, they said the Japanese had broken through the city gate and been mowed down. They did not know what happened elsewhere. The colonel in charge of defending Changsha produced maps in thirteen colored inks, showing where the Japanese penetrated into the city and where his own troops made sorties, and the maps looked wonderful, but we were never able to follow the course of the battle. The colonel was a small pudgy man who spoke slowly, with immense authority, and yet never convincingly. Quite obviously, there had been minor engagements all round the city and at one point a Japanese column had penetrated within a hundred yards of the heavily fortified house which served as the colonel's headquarters. We asked whether there were any other deep penetrations. "A few," he answered, and we wondered why they were not shown on the maps.

Gradually some of the larger pieces of the jigsaw puzzle fell into place. We learned, for example, that though the Japanese had continually bombed the city, there were never more than two or three airplanes in the sky. The Chinese had no airplanes and no anti-aircraft guns. A battery of howitzers on a nearby hill was never brought into action. Did the Japanese have field guns? None at all. According to the colonel the fighting was mostly hand to hand and a great deal of it took place at night. Once the Japanese cavalry rode up to the East Gate, but fled in disorder, leaving behind a beautiful white stallion as a prize for the Chinese commander. Someone, remembering that the colonel had spoken of a battery of howitzers on the hill called Yulosan, asked who was manning the guns. "Of course we were manning the guns ourselves," the colonel said, and then added: "We had some Russian advisers." This was news to us. Also, the fact that the guns had never fired meant that the Chinese were never able to spot large formations of the enemy and most of the Japanese attacks took place at night. The silence of the guns on Yulosan haunted us. The Chinese had an air force, but not a single airplane had come to the assistance of the beleaguered city. We were learning to ask about the things that did not happen, and in this way we sometimes came closer to what really happened than by asking direct questions.

We asked how many prisoners had been taken, and the colonel replied that it is not the custom to take prisoners.

"On both sides?"

"Neither side takes prisoners," the colonel said, as though it was a matter so well known that it was scarcely worth mentioning.

One of the apple-faced Hunanese soldiers led us through the streets of Changsha. Here and there we came upon small clumps of Japanese dead, the flesh already turning green. They always lay close together, and there were never more than four or five. A few were bearded, and about half of them were burned black, so that there came to us the strange feeling that they had been placed on a funeral pyre and then someone had given orders that the fire should be extinguished and that the bodies should be scattered along the road for our benefit. Sometimes the bright yellow entrails had broken through the blackened flesh. These bodies puzzled us. It was becoming impossibly difficult to re-create the course of the battle.

The cheerful apple-faced Hunanese led us to a courtyard where the booty was laid out for our inspection. Blood-soaked Japanese flags, rifles, bullets, helmets, uniforms and blankets were spread out as though in a market place. Machine guns on tripods were arranged at elegant intervals. The sun shone on the thick dried blood, on bullet-punctured helmets, on green tent-cloths, and on little heaps of photographs and letters. The photographs of Japanese girls were often hand-tinted, the photographs of mothers and fathers were in black and white. The white stallion captured at the East Gate was brought to the courtyard. It was the most beautiful stallion we had ever seen, so white, so silvery, so ghostly in its beauty, that it seemed to have stepped out of a mediaeval romance. It whinnied terribly, pawed the earth, shook its head wildly, ran round the courtyard and stopped dead, and there was something about all its movements that suggested that it was mad.

Changsha had been attacked; the Japanese had penetrated deeply, but apparently in very small numbers. Japanese planes had bombed large areas of Changsha, but whether the bombing had taken place during the attack or many months before was unknown, for the Chinese rarely answered our questions. We had the odd feeling that we were looking at a film that was being run backward.

Later we were given small donkeys, round-bellied, well-fed, very sleek. They frisked their long silken ears and pretended to be the most docile donkeys in the world, but as soon as we mounted them they showed a determined desire to unseat us. They were accustomed to having Chinese soldiers on their backs and they did not like foreigners.

We rode north through quiet villages and the small hamlets where perhaps twenty people had lived, most of them deserted now. In their retreat the Japanese had been absolutely merciless. They killed every Chinese peasant they could find, and the dead peasants lay where they had fallen in the village streets. No ammunition had been wasted on them, they had been slashed to death with sabers, and they lay in small companionable heaps, like lovers. But the Chinese army had followed close on the heels of the Japanese, and here and there we came upon the bodies of the Japanese, shining white in the winter sunshine, for they had been stripped of their clothes.

Toward evening we came to the Liuyang River, where an immense waterwheel, some thirty feet high, turned silently. Nearby there was a walled village rather larger than most of the Hunanese villages, and here the Chinese had caught up with the main body of the Japanese. A young Chinese sergeant in a sky-blue uniform said that most of the fighting had taken place at night, with the Japanese attempting to battle their way into the village. The Chinese had taken cover in some rice fields, and a thick mist had fallen over the whole region. Although it was dark and misty, a pitched battle was fought on the banks of the river. When the dawn came, the Japanese were in full flight, and on the grassy slopes beneath the waterwheel perhaps a hundred Japanese lay dead.

They lay there in the dusk, very white in their nakedness, looking like bathers who have climbed out of the river and thrown themselves down to sleep. The waterwheel was turning silently, and the dead were very beautiful. Farther up the bank some old peasants were digging a shallow grave, and the tock-tock of their mattocks was the only sound in all that stillness. The Chinese sergeant in the sky-blue uniform pointed to the body of a Japanese officer sprawled face upward in the grass with five bullets still clenched between his teeth—those bullets which he was storing against the time when he had exhausted the bullets in his revolver. Soon a gust of wind sprang up, and the waterwheel began to turn more swiftly, creaking a little.

We rode back to Changsha in the moonlight, scarcely understanding what we had seen, remembering the black crows hopping heavily across the small battlefield, because they were gorged with blood, and the Chinese sergeant who walked so proudly among the dead. Clouds covered the moon, and sometimes we rode in darkness, while the wind rose and the clouds raced more furiously across the sky.

To our surprise a banquet had been arranged for us in the courtyard of the house where we were staying. General Hsueh Yueh heaped delicacies into our bowls, offered us silk banners embroidered with storks and dragons, symbols of longevity and good fortune, and explained the course of the battle in a way which would have surprised the Chinese sergeant on the Liuyang River. According to the general, the Japanese had fallen into a carefully contrived trap. Chinese intelligence agents had sent information about all the enemy movements, and it was therefore easy to deal with them. The Chinese army pursued the Japanese to the shores of the Milo River, and then lost contact with them. Where were the Japanese now? He did not know, and smiled indulgently, as though this was a question that should not have been asked and only our inexcusable ignorance led us to ask it. He seemed to be saying: "The Japanese have vanished like the morning mist, and we shall not hear of them again."

We drank solemnly to his victory with little cups of brown rice wine, a wine so sweet, so delicate and so lethal that we were soon tipsy. Even General Hsueh Yueh was a little drunk, his eyes bloodshot and the veins standing out on his forehead; his voice was louder, more commanding, more self-assured, as he announced that if the Allies would only follow his example the Japanese would soon be driven back to their wretched little islands. So we drank to the day when the Japanese were no longer bent on conquest, and the general beamed at us and we beamed back at him.

I was sitting opposite the general and watched him closely, the small brown eyes, the quick and lazy smile, the tongue slipping in and out between the teeth, the way he held his head a little to one side, like an alert bird. The skin was drawn tight over the cheekbones. His uniform, too, seemed to cling tightly to his body and had evidently been made by an accomplished tailor. Ho Ying-chin, the minister of war, wore expensive uniforms, but always managed to look slovenly in them. General Hsueh Yueh, on the contrary, looked impeccably dressed, neat and elegant, with no fat on him. He looked as a general should look, and was so precisely a general that he was almost a parody.

Yet the more one looked at him, the more mysterious he became. There was something almost boyish in him, and there were moments when he looked fifteen or sixteen. The Chinese sometimes age in a very strange manner: that is, they do not age at all until they are well into their fifties. A man of fifty will sometimes resemble himself at eighteen: the same eyes, the same hair, the same features, even the same voice. General Hsueh Yueh was forty-eight, and he had been winning victories for twenty years, but none had left its mark on his face, which was as smooth and gleaming as polished leather.

The general was saying that three months before the Pacific War broke out his soldiers found on the body of a certain Colonel Kato documents indicating that the Japanese High Command had already decided to attack American and British possessions in the Pacific and in Southeast Asia. These documents were turned over to the American and British governments, which had not paid the slightest attention to them.

Suddenly a telephone bell rang and the general excused himself. We knew even before he rose from the table what was happening. The air became electric, the Chinese officers stiffened, the soldiers who were acting as waiters held themselves ramrod straight, and very faintly in the distance we heard General Hsueh Yueh saying those completely empty things which are always said when one is addressing Generalissimo Chiang Kai-shek. Two minutes later he returned, walking very solemnly and apparently deep in thought. For a few moments he faced us silently, savoring the importance of the message he was about to deliver.

"The Generalissimo has just called me," he said, "to ask how you are faring. I told him you were all in good health and were being kept very busy. He especially asked me to be sure you saw everything you wanted to see. If there is anything you need, you have only to ask for it. If there is anything you want to know, I am always at your service."

We had expected as much, or as little. We were not unduly grateful, knowing that it was inconceivable that he would ever answer the one question we wanted to ask: What happened at Changsha? We had seen the maps in many colored inks and listened to many lectures, including one delivered by the general himself, and we were still hopelessly at a loss to understand the course of the battle.

The next morning broke fresh and clear after a night of incessant rain. The skies were a perfect blue, the red cliffs on the further bank of the Hsiang River looked as though they had been painted, the river was the deep blue of inland seas, and all the trees were glowing in the sun. It was one of those wonderfully crisp winter mornings which are common in Hunan and unknown in Chungking.

We had just finished breakfast when a staff captain announced that we would be permitted to interview the young Japanese captured near the East Gate of Changsha. He was the only prisoner the Chinese had taken, and this had come about almost by accident. Cut off from the rest of his platoon and surrounded by Chinese troops, he had attempted to blow himself up with a hand grenade, but the grenade failed to explode. The Chinese sent him back to headquarters and interrogated him in the hope of finding out the Japanese plan of operations.

He came walking toward us out of nowhere, wearing a brown coat many sizes too large for him, his face gray and tired, and there was about him an extraordinary look of sorrow, as though he no longer cared to live. He said his name was Kyoshi Kowahara, he was twenty-five, the son of a small mill owner, and he had been an insurance agent in Nagoya with a wife and three children. He sat among the correspondents with his head bowed, his black hair shaven to the skull, his hands folded between his knees, rarely looking up. A Chinese colonel acted as interpreter. The prisoner answered each question quietly, matter-of-factly, but without really caring. The world of the correspondents was so remote from him, and so meaningless. He said he received twelve yen a month basic pay, and this was enough to provide him with a woman each week and a few necessities since the Japanese army provided him with food, shelter and clothing. A cold wind sprang up, and he shivered a little. He had a round, handsome face, and in his quietness and gentleness he might have been taken for a young Buddhist monk.

Once he said: "Will you shoot me?"

He said this with no more excitement than if he was asking someone the time of day. There was no answer to his question.

He went on talking about life in the Japanese army, where the soldiers ate three full meals a day. His food in the Japanese army consisted of rice, corned beef, a kind of powdered sauce. He had lost his greatcoat during the fighting at the East Gate of Changsha. One of the correspondents asked him when he thought he would see his wife and children again, and he said nothing.

Finally the Chinese colonel told him he could have the freedom of the garden, and he walked away in the direction of a low wall. He sat there cross-legged, facing the river and the red cliffs, looking more than ever like a young Buddhist monk, lost in meditation, remote from the world as in a grave.

That evening we were invited to attend a dinner given by the army newspaper. The printing press was in a villa about a quarter of a mile away. During the afternoon it rained, and now in the evening with the storm clouds racing across the sky the garden where we had interviewed the Japanese prisoner looked dark and menacing. The others had gone on ahead, but I heard them talking in the distance. I jumped over the low wall and ran after them, taking a short cut through a copse of birch trees. On the edge of the copse my feet sank up to the ankles in a freshly dug grave.

When I returned to Chungking, the ambassador wanted to know all about the battle of Changsha, which had filled the headlines of the newspapers for so many days. I drew maps in many different colored inks, and described the lay of the land, and where the Japanese attacked and where they were repulsed.

The ambassador listened politely, and at last he said: "You are not describing a battle. I don't know what it is, but it is not a battle."

Many years later I learned that the battle of Changsha had a respectable place in the official histories of the war. A few days ago I discovered that it was mentioned in the Encyclopaedia Britannica, that infallible guide to all the world's histories. It described how the Chinese armies at Changsha repulsed 100,000 Japanese, who suffered 57,000 casualties.

THE CATTLE SHEDS

On the afternoon of February 15, 1942, a small group of British officers under General Percival drove halfway across the island of Singapore to the village of Bukit Timah, carrying a white flag. At the Ford Motor Works they surrendered to the Japanese. At that moment the British Empire in the Far East came to an end.

In Chungking we had known for days that Singapore was about to fall, and could have calculated almost to the exact minute when the surrender would take place, but the shock waves came hurtling across the embassy compound and left us stunned. The ambassador heard the news while writing a letter: the goose quill pen hung above the page and remained suspended in mid-air. I thought it would hang there forever, and that his face had turned to stone. A week later he said: "There is no news about Robert Scott. We lost a good many ships off Singapore. He may have been on one of them, or he may not. The last cable arrived a week before the fall of Singapore, and it said nothing except that he was all right and very busy."

Many years later I learned what happened to him. He left Singapore just before the end in a small coastal steamer. Everything went wrong. The ship was overcrowded, there was little food, Japanese airplanes bombed it, and somewhere off the coast of Sumatra a Japanese destroyer sank it. Robert Scott was among the survivors who rowed ashore in the ship's dinghy and found refuge with some friendly villagers. A few weeks later the villagers betrayed the handful of survivors and they were sent in chains to Singapore. The Japanese did not know the real identities of their new captives, and it was some time before they realized that Robert Scott was among them. Rightly or wrongly, they had long considered him their most dangerous single enemy in the Far East, the mastermind of British imperial power, and accordingly they tortured him in the hope of making him reveal all the British secrets even though there were no secrets worth knowing. They beat him nearly to death and kept him in solitary confinement. He was a tall, heavily built man, but at the end of the war he was little more than a malaria-ridden skeleton weighing less than a hundred pounds. On the day the Japanese surrendered he discovered the door of his cell was open and the guard had vanished. He had just enough strength to crawl away on hands and knees, and some hours later a Chinese workman found him lying motionless by the side of the road. There was still a little life in him, and the Chinese carried him in a wheelbarrow to the nearest hospital. When he recovered he was knighted, and Sir Robert Scott became the first British High Commissioner for Southeast Asia.

Meanwhile there was scarcely a day when the ambassador did not talk about him as though by repeating his name it would be possible to conjure up his presence. It was not only that Robert Scott was one of those men who possess a towering strength and an ability to solve complex problems, but according to the ambassador he inspired everyone around him with the same strength and the same ability. When, as sometimes happened, a third or fourth or fifth secretary at the embassy would ask what on earth I was doing there, with no defined duties and unrestricted entry into the ambassador's study, he would say: "Oh, he was sent by Robert Scott," as though "Robert Scott" was a badge of honor which explained everything. Meanwhile I sharpened the ambassador's goose quill pens, wrote speeches, visited the universities, quarreled with most of the Old China hands, and did very much as I pleased.

Although at various times a search was made to discover whether Robert Scott had sent any documents about us, none was ever discovered. Evert Barger, the young lecturer from Bristol University, quickly attached himself to the Chinese Red Cross. I suspect that Robert Scott was grooming him for a high political office, and that I was to be sent out to blow up railroads. Neither of us spoke or wrote Chinese well, and our chief merit was that we were passionately in love with China.

As I came to know the ambassador better, I realized that there were storms beneath the calm patrician surface. Intelligence streamed from his heavily lidded eyes, he always moved lightly and easily in total command of any situation, and he feared no one on earth. Yet deep down he was troubled with nightmares. His wife had left him, he was beginning to drink heavily, age was creeping over him. He had taken a lover, who was very young, very handsome, and stateless, having been born in one of the countries occupied by the Germans. The whole embassy knew about the affair with the boy even though it was conducted with the utmost secrecy. Worse still, the embassy was gradually being invaded by missionaries who were recruited because they had a long experience of Chinese affairs, and they visibly disapproved of the ambassador's affair with the boy, started rumors, and prayed for the day when they would have a more compliant ambassador.

My own feeling was that the ambassador was entitled to his pleasure and that the embassy did not deserve the missionaries who flocked into the embassy compound like black crows. None of them had the faintest realization that British influence in China had plummeted to zero after the fall of Singapore, and they paraded as though they were lords of the earth by divine right. The ambassador found them insufferable but was under the impression that the embassy was understaffed. Therefore they were hired, given offices and titles, tolerated, pampered and placated, while they declared an unrelenting war against the ambassador.

That war was never fought to a conclusion, because Churchill suddenly needed a strong ambassador in Moscow. Sir Archibald Clark Kerr was asked to fill the gap and immediately refused on the grounds that he had no experience of Russia. Churchill sent another telegram, saying that he was not making a request but giving an order, and the ambassador was to proceed to Moscow within three weeks. There was a good deal more in the telegram, for Churchill had an unbounded respect and affection for the ambassador.

By the purest accident I was among the first to know that the ambassador was leaving China, and argued against it, saying that the embassy would become meaningless without him, and that the ambassador alone, simply by his presence in Chungking, was necessary for the survival of British influence. We had no influence now, and we would have influence again in the future only if he remained. He laughed, and said the decision was out of his hands. Then for a long time he gazed out of the window

Marshal Feng Yu-hsiang

Rose Hsiung,
circa 1938

OPPOSITE: Hsiung Hsi-ling
and Madame Hsiung
Hsi-ling

Rose Hsiung, 1942, at Peipei

Jacqueline, 1946

The Valley of Yenan. Woodcut by a Chinese Communist artist.

A dinner at Yenan, July 1946. Mao Tse-tung and Madame Mao Tse-tung at left. The American colonel and Chu Teh at center. Author at right foreground.

人生不朽鬚眉健似如春壽健康
只是其我日憶裏公園看生好春光。
六三年冬 十月劉珙兄寫
葉戊 [印]

Author
disguised as
Ming Dynasty
scholar.
Scroll painting
by Rose Hsiung.

at the desolate compound of the embassy, where the black crows were milling around, as yet unaware of their good fortune. "I love China," he said. "I think I understood the Chinese. What in God's name am I going to do in Russia?"

On the night before his departure I was summoned for the last time to the small study with the large desk set against the window. All the other offices were empty, for everyone had gone home and the compound was a pool of darkness. He talked somberly about the journey to Russia and about his successor, who had no experience of China. He thought he could understand the workings of Chiang Kai-shek's mind, but how many years would it take before he understood Stalin? He talked about Robert Scott, the familiar presence, and about the unwieldy mushrooming embassy. At last he said: "What about you? Do you want to stay on? If you have any sense you will leave the embassy and go into the Chinese universities." I said I wanted it more than anything else, and he wrote two letters, one to his successor confirming the appointment and the other to the Chinese ministry of education. Then he gave me his collection of goose quill pens. I never saw him again.

A week later I was teaching English literature at Fuhtan University.

Fuhtan, which means "the rising sun," had several advantages over the other colleges and universities around Chungking. It was poor, ill-equipped, and totally unpretentious, consisting of six or seven large cattle sheds on the banks of the Chialing River. To the north was Splendid Cloud Mountain. A narrow gorge had cut through one of the shoulders of the mountain, and the Chialing River raced through it. The landscape was wildly romantic, the blue-gray mountain looking as though it had been painted on the sky by a Sung Dynasty artist. Most of the mountain was covered with pine forests, and when the wind was in the right direction we heard the distant soughing of the pines like the subdued roar of a thousand waterfalls. Down below, in the valley, there were fields of Indian corn and long stretches of rice fields, with here and there a few white farmhouses with straw-thatched roofs. The village of Peipei was on the other side of the river, and nearer the gorge were the mineral springs bubbling out of the earth at the foot of Splendid Cloud Mountain.

I had visited Fuhtan twice while touring the universities around Chungking. I liked the students and professors, and I especially liked its remoteness and silence. Chungking was thirty-five miles down the Chialing River, a day's journey by steamer or half a day's journey by bus. Officialdom rarely penetrated the university, which was too obscure and unimportant to warrant the attention of officials. China's parliament, the Legislative Yuan, met in a great mansion four or five miles from Peipei, but since the Generalissimo no longer listened to the legislators, it had long ago lost whatever influence it once possessed. Yet the mere presence of the Legislative Yuan, headed by Dr. Sun Fo, the son of Dr. Sun Yat-sen, afforded a measure of protection to the university. If we were ever raided by the Kuomintang secret police, we had only to run up the road and report to parliament. It might not do any good, but it could do no harm.

In Singapore, Wang Chieh had told me that Chinese students regarded their professors with profound respect amounting almost to worship, and no doubt this was true in an earlier age. It was not true at Fuhtan. The students were respectful, but they had no illusions about the wisdom of their professors. Many of them had walked across the whole length of China, most of them were very poor, living, as we all lived, on the wretched food provided by the government, and they sometimes asked hard questions and received scant answers. They were bright-faced and courteous, and very direct. At the same time they were shamelessly capable of assuming expressions quite contrary to their real feelings. When I delivered my first lecture, they craned forward, nodded at the appropriate places, smiled when I hoped they would smile, and appeared to be passionately interested in the subject. Afterward a student said: "You must speak more slowly. None of the students understood a word you said."

The professors were equally courteous and equally direct. Fat Professor Lo Chung-pei, who liked to support his stomach in his clasped hands, said in his piping voice: "Please wear Chinese gown. Coat and trousers are out of the question." So I learned to wear a Chinese gown and to bow deeply and to handle chopsticks with ease. One day the heavy clouds rolled away, the sun shone, Splendid Cloud Mountain tossed off its gray mane, the Chialing River turned from muddy gray to the brightest blue, and almost simultaneously the Indian corn threw out silky orange and yellow tassels. Spring came to Szechuan in rainbow colors.

The professors lived mostly in the neighboring farmhouses, whitewashed and thatched with rice straw, with paper windows, mud floors and little furniture. They were abysmally poor, spent most of their money on their children, and suffered horribly from malaria, which was inevitable, since they were surrounded by rice fields under water. Clouds of mosquitoes roamed the countryside, and no one discovered a remedy against them.

To reach these farmhouses you walked along the raised edges of the rice fields past the wayside shrines with their little clay earth gods, and usually there were flowers and offerings of food in the shrines. You had the feeling that for thousands of years the landscape had remained unaltered—the same shrines, the same houses, the same rice fields had been there since the Han Dynasty. The rice fields were usually under water, and as you walked along the raised boundaries, you had the illusion of walking in the sky, for the clouds were brilliantly reflected in the silver pools.

For about a month I wandered blissfully from farmhouse to farmhouse, enjoying the hospitality of the professors. Rare bottles of wine were broken open, small feasts were served, and they showed me their few treasures—scroll paintings, carvings, old books, which they had carried halfway across China. They had all come from Shanghai and told hair-raising stories about the Japanese attack on the city. Then quite suddenly it dawned on me that I was beggaring one farmhouse after another, that none of them could afford to give these feasts, and that there were ways of accepting their invitations while at the same time indicating that I would accept nothing more than a glass of tea. The poorer the professor, the more overwhelming was the hospitality.

With the students the question of hospitality scarcely arose, for very few of them had any money at all. They ate in the communal dining rooms, sometimes breaking their teeth on the lead pellets which mysteriously found their way into the rice. With the rice came tiny slivers of meat and a small side dish of vegetables, bean curd and bread cobs. For dessert there was sometimes a kind of jelly made from powdered lotus root. I was fascinated by the making of the jelly, for the white powder turned purple when boiling water was poured over it. The jelly was very sweet and tasted like cream.

During this time I was staying in the little inn in Peipei, across the river from the university. For some reason the inn was painted black, and looked dreadfully ominous. The manager smoked opium, the servants were surly, the smell of decay hung over the courtyard, which served as an echo chamber magnifying all sounds. Occasionally there were pistol shots, which echoed and re-echoed across the courtyard. One got used to them, as one got used to the sudden screams and the wild creaking of the bamboo beds. But worse than these were the rats, which infested the place as though it belonged to them, as though the guests were merely temporary usurpers. Sometimes while correcting students' papers late at night by the light of a rapeseed-oil lamp, I would look up to see a brown rat, as large as a full-grown cat, gazing at me from the bed, its mouth wide open so that I could see the sharpness of its teeth. When I looked again the rat was three inches nearer. Half an hour later, made drunk by the smell of the rapeseed oil, the rat would be on my table. When I banged the table with my fist, it leaped away into the shadows and vanished through mysterious tunnels. Though I sealed every crack in the wall, rats came every night.

I did not like the inn, and the more I heard about it, the more I hated it. One of the students told me that two or three years before, a local warlord had discovered his concubine in bed with one of the inn servants. The warlord cut them to pieces with a meat ax and scattered the remnants over the courtyard, then rounded up all the village dogs, and all the cats, so that they could enjoy the feast. I did not believe the story. Long before the dogs and cats reached the courtyard, the rats would have been there.

Sometimes, too, the night was disturbed by the roaring of tigers and the terrible barking of peacocks, but these sounds came from the zoo half a mile away. It was a pathetically small zoo, and all the animals in it had come down the Yangtze River from Nanking, where they were once housed in splendor. Now they were housed in rather crude cages on a hillside covered with cedars and bamboos. There, after climbing a winding stone-flagged path, you found yourself confronting a beautiful white snow leopard and a golden tiger. Their coats were glossy, and they were well cared for. The peacocks were especially beautiful, the blue and green of their feathers possessing a depth and intensity of color I had seen nowhere else. They strutted among the green hills superbly aware of their magnificence.

Quite obviously the time had come for me to leave the inn, but it was not so obvious how this would be accomplished. An abandoned temple near the river was considered until an architect decided that the roof was about to fall in. A farmhouse two miles from the university seemed the best solution until it was discovered that its ownership was disputed. Then the university remembered that it owned a small brick cottage on a hill overlooking the river. The cottage had a hole in the roof because at one time it was hoped to transform it into an observatory; the astronomer died, the telescope was believed to be in a warehouse in Chungking, or perhaps it had been destroyed during the bombings, or perhaps it had never existed. Roofers were sent to the cottage, and a week later I had a cottage of my own shaded by a vast banyan tree, with the river below and the mountains beyond. To reach the university there was a winding path down the hillside, then a walk across three rice fields and an immense field of Indian corn. The view from the window looked too much like a Chinese painting.

There came a time when I felt I had spent many years in this remote corner of a remote province of China. Europe and Singapore faded away, and there was only the Chialing River and Splendid Cloud Mountain. In those white cattle sheds, weathered to the color of old bone, I imagined I had been teaching since the beginning of time, though I had been there for only four or five weeks. I wore a Chinese gown as though I had never worn anything else, and sometimes I jabbered in a language which I fondly believed to be Chinese.

I thought, in my ignorance, that I knew a good deal about China, and learned that I knew nothing at all, and it did not matter. China was shaping me, the very landscape was pouring through me, and the intricate ceremonies of Chinese life were becoming natural to me by a process of osmosis. I had a Chinese name, Pai-ying, which means "white hero," and I was aware that the name involved an absurd irony. No one could have been less heroic than the blue-gowned scholar who walked along the banks of the Chialing River as though in a trance. Part of this happiness came from an unsuspected quarter—I was suffering from tuberculosis. Nearly all the ricksha pullers suffered from it, and so did many of the students, who spat blood into their handkerchiefs and thought nothing of it. China had evolved a particularly benign form of tuberculosis which permits you to go on living for a dozen years with no more discomfort than afternoon fevers and an occasional painless welling of blood in the throat. The lesions heal, or do not heal, and no one seemed to know why some people went on living quite normally while others died. The patient suffering from tuberculosis is granted strange compensations: his senses and his enjoyment of life are quickened, and at the same time he feels a certain detachment from life, a withdrawal from the world, as though the world were too precious to be touched. The body becomes pure sensation, the nerves sing, colors shine with unaccustomed brilliance. There is no pain, no languor: only the telltale spots on the handkerchief. Life goes on, but at a more quickening pace in a world bathed in rainbow colors.

At the hospital in Peipei I looked at the X rays of ricksha pullers. Their lungs were riddled with lesions, but they went on living. I looked at my own X rays with their small scars and thought I would live at least as long as the ricksha pullers.

"It's fantastic," the doctor said, holding up an X ray white with scars. "This man is sixty years old. His wife died, and he has married again and has three children. He is probably infecting all of them, but what can we do? We can't stop him from marrying. Opium helps, of course."

He suggested that I should go and stay in the monastery high up on Splendid Cloud Mountain and rest for three months. If I wanted opium "for medicinal purposes," it could easily be supplied. I had been to the monastery, and the black-robed monks with their shaven heads looked miserably unhappy. For nothing in the world would I leave the enchanted valley.

About once a month, on weekends, I journeyed to Chungking by riverboat. It was a pleasant journey, for the river wandered between strange rocks and under shadowy cliffs and was continually changing its color. During the T'ang Dynasty artists painted the river on long scrolls, delighting in the abrupt hills and the soft valleys, decorating every mountain with the flaring roofs of a monastery. The official purpose of these journeys was to obtain books for the university library by raiding the book stores, the embassy, and the British Council. The unofficial purpose was to see Rose Hsiung, who resembled to perfection the Chinese princess of my childhood dreams.

She had slanting eyes, full red lips, high cheekbones and a skin of ivory. When she smiled, a radiance poured from her face. They said of Yang Kuei-fei, the consort of the Emperor Ming Huang, that her smile was so ravishing that it led to the destruction of the kingdom, and Rose's "kill-kingdom" smile was of the same order of things. Small and slender, silky black hair streaming to her shoulders, she was quite simply the most beautiful woman I had ever encountered, but this was the least important fact about her. The most important fact was that she was living with extraordinary intensity, so vividly alive that I wondered why the air around her did not catch fire.

Much later I learned that her father had been prime minister of China and that as a child she had played with the boy-Emperor Pu Yi. When Yuan Shih-kai became dictator of China and planned to make himself the first emperor of a new dynasty, he arranged that Rose should marry his eldest son. The prime minister was a sensible man who objected to having a future empress for a daughter, and smuggled her out of the country. Yet even now there was a hint of imperial magnificence in her smile.

She was perfectly aware of her beauty, and I suspect that she was equally aware that her smile was dangerous. Her ancestors were Miao tribesmen from the province of Hunan who had never been completely assimilated by their Chinese conquerors. They were a rebellious people, hot-tempered, with a liking for highly seasoned food and red peppers, physically robust, impatient of the usual Chinese circumlocutions, and it is perhaps significant that many of the Chinese Communist leaders, including Mao Tse-tung, are descended from Miao tribesmen. Rose reveled in being a Miao, and she reveled even more in being a citizen of Peking, where she had spent most of her life.

If her beauty was disturbing, so was her knowledge of languages. She had learned English while a student at Mount Holyoke in America, and she had picked up Italian, French and

German during her wanderings in Europe. She had learned Russian in order to read Chekhov in the original, looking up each word in a dictionary. "Learning languages is easy," she said, "but writing poems in them is very difficult." In this way I learned that she had written poems in English, French and Italian. Her English poems were not very good, being formed from her reading of T. S. Eliot, and after reading them I was less intimidated. But what delighted, and at the same time horrified me, was the easy grace with which she would swing from English into German or Italian or French without the trace of an accent. "You ought to have been a professor," I suggested. "What, and correct all those dreary term papers?" she replied. Her favorite book, which she seemed to know by heart, was the four-thousand-page classic called *The Dream of the Red Chamber* which relates the adventures of a young aristocrat who fell hopelessly in love with all the women in the innumerable courtyards of his palace.

This, I thought, was the clue, for she was more vulnerable than she seemed to be. I had decided to marry her the moment I first set eyes on her four days after arriving in Chungking, but I soon learned that she was obstinately opposed to marriage, having been married twice, once to a Chinese official, who died, and then to a French diplomat, whom she divorced. Marriage in her view was the purest tyranny, not to be thought of. I thought about it most of the time.

One day in May, after I had left her early in the evening, I wandered about Chungking in a daze, dazzled by her smile and perturbed because the prospect of marrying her was as remote as ever. The day had been oppressively hot, the sky a deep indigo blue, the sun pouring down relentlessly. There had been rumors of an imminent air raid, but no one had taken them too seriously, for it was common knowledge that this year the Japanese would not enjoy undisputed control of the skies. In previous years they had bombed Chungking to rubble; this year it was expected that they might make a few sneak attacks. Yet all day there had been a strange fever in the air, many of the shops had closed early, and some officials at the foreign office had wondered aloud whether there were enough American airplanes to keep the Japanese away from the city. Someone said that when the alert sounded the streets would be cleared and anyone found walking in them would be shot dead.

The sun set in a ball of fire, but even when it grew dark the streets were still steaming with the day's heat. Usually in the evening the wind raced along the two rivers, but there was no wind that day, nor would there be any wind for many days. The air was heavy and damp, and the dust hung in the air. There were only a few people in the streets, and sometimes a ricksha came bowling along the dusty roads. I walked slowly, enjoying the quietness that had descended on the city. Old temples and quiet courtyards and deserted market places, all framed by the bomb-blasted walls of another year, gleamed in the darkness, and soon the moon came out from its hiding place and rose high over the city. It was a "bombers' moon," filled with light, surrounded by pulsating purple rings, and I imagined that my students at Fuhtan were all lying on the grass and gazing at the moon, for moon-watching is one of the pleasantest of Chinese occupations. In the moonlight all the broken walls turned white and the shadows formed pools of impenetrable darkness. Chungking was very beautiful.

I realized dimly that something very strange had happened, for never at any previous time had I seen the city so quiet, so deserted, so motionless. A cat, wandering down the road, sniffed at a dead rat and then leaped into a patch of shadow. I was alone again, not quite sure where I was, and not in the least disturbed, because if you walk long enough in Chungking you come either to the rivers or to open fields, and it is easy enough to find the Wang Lung Men steps or the center of the city.

Suddenly at the end of the street drenched in moonlight I saw a soldier squatting over a machine gun. The barrel of the gun glinted blue in the moonlight. In his drab uniform, half sprawling, half kneeling over the gun, the soldier looked comic. Obviously he had no business being there, it was a very quiet night, and it was absurd that he should be slowly moving the gun round, following me. I went up to him, waved, and watched him freeze with terror. Then I walked on, dreaming about Rose, and only in some deep recess of my mind wondering at the strange behavior of the soldier. I was walking toward the center of the city and passed two more soldiers squatting over machine guns and each time the guns moved slowly, following me. I seemed to be in a dream, and as in dreams one sometimes finds oneself reasoning about the probability or improbability of what one sees, so now I concluded that the soldiers with the machine guns were highly improbable and perhaps insubstantial, and I went on walking through the deserted city.

About half an hour later, when I was near the top of the Wang Lung Men steps, there came the long drawn wavering wail of the siren, and for the first time I realized fully that I had been walking through Chungking during an air raid alert. Suddenly the electric lights came on, people began to stream out of their hovels near the steps, and the city began to roar like a lion awakening in the night.

I went back to see Rose and told her about the machine guns. She looked puzzled and a little frightened.

"Didn't you know they have orders to shoot everyone walking in the streets during an alert?" she said, and then more softly: "You must be very lucky."

The next day I returned to Fuhtan, and it seemed to me that the Green Dragon was walking by my side.

Over the weekend a new professor had arrived. His name was Liang Tsong-t'ai, and he did not resemble any of the other professors. He liked to wear shorts and to go about shirtless; he liked to swim, and he enjoyed walking fifty miles a day. He was self-consciously athletic to a degree unusual in any country and simply astonishing in China, where professors are expected to walk sedately and slowly with their hands folded in their sleeves. He was head of the French department, spoke French perfectly and English with some pleasant imperfections. He had translated the great Chinese poet Tao Yuan-ming into French, Paul Valéry had written the introduction, and he had never quite recovered from the days when he sat at the feet of Valéry, Gide and Cocteau. He had known them well and remembered every conversation he had with them. In Paris he was fêted as a brilliant translator and as an impeccable stylist. Valéry had once called him a genius, and the fatal accolade effectively prevented him from doing any more serious work. He was doomed by his early success.

In the eyes of Liang Tsong-t'ai English literature was the poor stepsister of French literature, with the result that we debated furiously and got nowhere. When the debates were over, I tried to make him talk about Taoism, a subject he had studied deeply. He could talk equally well about philosophical Taoism and about the magic spells of the Taoist priests, and hinted that he had once studied under a master who taught him spells to raise the wind and shake mountains to their foundations. During the day it was easy enough to disbelieve him, but at night, with so many ghosts lurking in the rice fields, it was much more difficult.

One day toward the end of the summer semester Liang Tsong-t'ai announced that a strange visitor had arrived on Splendid Cloud Mountain: no less a person than Feng Yu-hsiang, the "Christian general," who held the rank of Vice-Generalissimo. A small party of professors had been invited to have tea with him, and Liang Tsong-t'ai proposed to lead the expedition. It appeared that Marshal Feng was living either in the monastery or very close to it, and there was some mystery about why he was living there, for he was still very powerful, his pronouncements were printed in the newspapers, and he was serving as acting president of the Supreme Military Council. It was assumed that he had come to spend a few days on the mountain to avoid the heat of a Chungking summer, or perhaps he was secretly visiting a concubine, or perhaps he was in disgrace. For a few days the presence of Marshal Feng on the mountain was the main subject of conversation in the university.

Although Marshal Feng was chiefly remembered in the West as an old warlord who baptized his troops with a fire hose, and had once ruled over North China, the professors had other reasons for remembering him. They admired him for his calligraphy, his poetry and his prose style. It had never occurred to me that the "Christian general" was anything but a general. They said he had written an autobiography which was a minor classic, and he had recently published a volume of speeches which had given no pleasure to the Kuomintang, because he attacked the feudal landlords and demanded a new deal for the peasants. "Of course, his calligraphy is not perfect," Liang Tsong-t'ai said. "It is rough and heavy, but undeniably powerful. His poems are not the kind of poems that Valéry would admire, but they are original and memorable. He is a man of many talents."

It was a good day for walking up the mountain, the hawks wheeling in the blue sky, and sometimes a white heron tumbled out of nowhere to hover over our heads. The river sparkled, the straw roofs of the peasants' huts shone silver, and even the shadowy gorges seemed to be filled with light. We puffed and wheezed as we climbed the mountain, with Liang Tsong-t'ai leading the way. To say that he led the way is an understatement. He leaped ahead, ran up to a shoulder of the mountain, hallooed to us, swung from the trees and perched like a mountain goat on the crags, and then came charging down on us, displaying a robust sunburned chest and well-shaped legs, for he had stripped to a pair of shorts and wore his shirt like a handkerchief knotted round his neck. Then when he was among us, he threw back his head, strutted, and declared that we were all weaklings unworthy of the new China which was certainly about to come into existence, and would come into existence all the sooner if we would only do deep-breathing exercises and run twenty miles a day. He exhausted us, and in self-defense we jeered at him, examined his muscles, and asked him what tribe of monkeys he belonged to. Then he was off again, running up the mountainside with easy strides, superbly indifferent to our slow laborious progress.

The monastery stood among cryptomerias and ginkgo trees, in a deep shade. Stone lions guarded the gates, and the flaring roofs could be seen above the walls. All round us were the pines, forest upon forest of pines drowning us in their scent. Even fat Professor Lo Chung-pei, whose face became as white as chalk when we were climbing the most difficult paths, seemed to revive when we came in sight of the monastery. But long before we reached the monastery gate we saw the Marshal's encampment in a little clearing of the forest. There were four or five simple bamboo huts, a table and some chairs, and the Marshal was performing a kind of slow dance among the chairs. He was about six feet three inches tall, with massive shoulders and a powerful round head shaven so close to the skin that he appeared to be bald. He wore a light summer uniform, baggy and comfortable. He was practicing the slow dance often performed by elderly gentlemen in the early morning, a kind of solitary shadow-boxing, with graceful lunging movements of the arms and legs. Seeing us, he paused on one leg, one arm outflung and the other bent to his chest, and continued the motions of the dance only when he saw that we were amused and delighted by the spectacle.

Tea was served in delicate china cups by soldiers with Mausers at their hips, while black-robed monks walked along the road just outside the clearing. The soldiers were brisk, watchful, intensely alive, while the monks resembled dark ghosts, their heads sunk on their chests, deep in meditation. Soon the huge fish-shaped wooden drum would call them back to the monastery. Meanwhile the Marshal entertained the professors, being very gentle with them, asking the proper questions, not yet at ease with them, curiously distant, as though his mind was elsewhere. The professors obviously admired him, and were in awe of him, for not only was he the Vice-Generalissimo, possessing vast powers in the present day, but they could not forget the vast powers he had wielded in the past, for he was the last survivor of the age of the warlords and therefore he was part of their history. Once his will was law all over North China; he had fought all the other armies of China to a standstill; he had made an alliance with Chiang Kai-shek which profoundly changed the direction of Chinese history. No one forgot that in any history of modern China he would have a whole page or a whole chapter to himself.

So he smiled, and told stories, and looked down at us from a great height, for even when he sat at table, he resembled a mountain. A soldier stood behind his chair, delicately waving a long horse-tail fly-whisk above his head, and all the time he looked like a Tartar chieftain who has ridden across the deserts of Asia, coming to rest in the mountains of Szechuan. We were almost choked by the sweet smell of the pines. I could make very little of him. There was something grotesque in his bulk, his fleshiness, the face round as the moon, the hands so powerful that they could have torn a man in two. He was saying: "I have called this place the Hall of the Empty Heart," and was pleased when the professors nodded, for they knew that the empty heart, in Buddhist and Taoist tradition, meant a heart devoid of all human attachments. The empty heart was the full heart, open to all the winds of Heaven. "I am an old man, I am in retirement," he went on, and the professors laughed. They did not believe him, but if he chose to pretend that he had retired from the scene, they were prepared to accommodate him.

I could make out some of his characteristics—his intelligence was all in his eyes and he had the disarming smile of a child. His face was a mask, he could paint whatever expression he chose on

it, while the hooded eyes looked out, probing relentlessly. He
was cunning as a wolf, and so accustomed to command that he
would be ill-at-ease among people who could not be commanded.
Hence his diffidence with the professors. I suspected that he
was as awed by them as they were awed by him. When he talked
about scholars, the voice became reverent. When they complimented him on his poems and calligraphy, he looked at them
searchingly, as though he half suspected they were playing a
trick on him.

Later, when it grew darker, he began to chant poems, throwing his head back and filling the whole clearing with a strange,
high-falsetto warbling. Lamps were placed on the table. The
tea was prolonged into supper, and we noted that the food was
of the highest quality, and the sweet rice was the most expensive on the market. From far away there came the chanting
of the monks in the temple.

Sometimes, for my benefit, he spoke in English, a wonderfully
ungrammatical English he had invented with the help of Baptist
missionaries. It seemed incredible that such a vast frame should
produce such a soft, tinkling, English sound. He told stories
about his first battles fought with bows and arrows on the
borders of Annam, and of the days when he was the dictator
of North China, ruling out of a small room where there was
scarcely a stick of furniture. "Well, why not?" he exclaimed. "If
I had lived in the Forbidden City, they would have thought
I was the emperor. I didn't want to be emperor. Me—an emperor!"
He roared with laughter, but I never saw anyone who looked
more like an emperor than this heavy man sitting at a table
in a pine forest, his face lit by the smoking rapeseed-oil lamps.

When we left two hours later he accompanied us a little
way up the road to the monastery, where a room and some
straw mattresses had been set aside for us. We slept badly, for
the monks chanted all night, and so did the mosquitoes. But
the morning had the pale blue color of a perfect day, and
from the monastery we could see the river winding far below,
valley opening on valley, and here and there the mist glinting
silver in the sun. We hurried down the mountain early to avoid
the sun's heat, passing the Hall of the Empty Heart, the small
clearing with the bamboo huts, but there was no sign of the
Marshal or his soldiers. In the early morning light, in the shadow

of the pine trees, the encampment was deserted. There were no tables, no chairs. The huts might have belonged to poor woodcutters.

"It looks as though the Marshal left for Chungking during the night," Liang Tsong-t'ai said, and I wondered whether I would ever see him again.

A SUMMONS FROM
THE MOUNTAIN

The longer I lived in it, the more I enjoyed the small house on the hill overlooking the Chialing River. The warm red brick, the gray tiles, the arrangement of the two small rooms upstairs and the storeroom downstairs, the huge barn which lay a little way down the hill and the orange grove nearby, all these things enchanted me. A stone's throw away from the house stood the monumental grave of a Chinese admiral of the early years of the Ch'ing Dynasty. The grave was guarded by stone animals and looked down on the gorges. His titles and great appointments were ceremonially listed on the grave stone. He had died in Tientsin, far in the north, and he had come to his resting place on one of the great river-barges belonging to the emperor. Now he rested in an orange grove, and the white blossoms fell on his grave.

Sometimes students came up the winding path, and there were lessons under the banyan tree. Sometimes, too, there were "moon-regarding" evenings, with blankets spread over the damp grass, while the students dreamily contemplated the passage of the enormous moon across the skies. There was no hand holding, the girls keeping apart from the boys. Yet they were friendly toward one another, and most of them seemed to go through adolescence without too much strain. What was most admirable in them was a kind of inner quietness, a certainty that came from a calm sense of responsibility. They were polite, modest, very gentle with one another, and curiously innocent. Those moon-watching children had a maturity far beyond their years.

One afternoon, walking back to the house with one of my students, I noticed that the door and the windows were wide open. We were walking through the fields of Indian corn, but the house was clearly visible on the hill. I kept thinking there must be some perfectly good explanation for the strange appearance of the house: the windows might have become unlatched, and perhaps I had forgotten to close the door. But when we reached the house, we were dumfounded. Everything had been taken away—clothes, books, mattresses, pillows, even the yellow flower vase I had bought in the market place at Peipei the day before. It was as though a swarm of locusts had invaded the house and eaten everything except the bamboo bed, the desk and some papers. We came out of the house in a daze. Down below, the lazy fields were smoking in the summer heat, the white cattle sheds were glistening, and the ferryboat was making its way upstream.

The student was white-faced with anger, and I was saying: "There wasn't very much in the house, anyway—"

"We have to report this at once," the student said.

He was broad-shouldered and powerfully built, with a formidable knowledge of English, quite easily the best of my students.

"Who do we report to?"

"First to the president of the university, and then to the chief of the village police. With luck, we'll have everything back before sunset. Let's hurry!"

We took one more look at the empty house and then hurried down the hill. The president was in his office. He was tall, dark-faced, with a brooding gentleness of expression. "Terrible! Terrible!" he kept saying. Afterward he alarmed me by saying that he had always known that the house on the hill was too far from the campus and could not be protected. We went to see the chief of the village police, who was plump, surly, and seemed to know all about the robbery. He said he would do what he could, barked a few orders to the men around him, and quietly resumed his interrupted game of Chinese chess.

"We'll have to do the work ourselves," the student said, while we raced back to the university, the white sheds, the blue-gowned students sauntering across the campus in the late afternoon sun.

He collected a group of students, told them what had happened, and divided them into two groups. Some were to accompany us to the house, others were to go to the village and make inquiries. When I remonstrated, saying that I had lost so little that it was scarcely worth the trouble of mounting a full-scale detective operation, he said: "It is a question of face! We cannot let them do this to you, and get away with it! Also, you must have all your things back by tonight!"

We went back to the house and searched for clues, but there were none. I made a list of the missing objects, and the student announced triumphantly that there must have been at least three thieves, for the sheer volume of the stolen goods was against a single thief carrying them away. I was not convinced: a man with a donkey could have carried everything away without too much difficulty. The more I thought about it, the more I was sure that nothing would be recovered. The wonderful house was still there with four walls, a roof, a desk, a bed. I reflected that in summer in Szechuan possessions are a positive nuisance.

The house was now a command post. Night came down, but there was a full moon and the whole valley shone with a ghostly blue light. It was another "moon-regarding night" with my students lying about in the grass. Sometimes shadowy figures could be seen moving up and down the hill. Two professors came with presents. One brought a lamp, another brought a mattress and a blanket. They, too, discussed the strategies to be employed in recovering stolen property and examined the house with expressions of wonder and alarm. Finally, at two o'clock in the morning, I fell asleep on the bamboo bed. Two or three students dozed in the doorway, keeping guard.

On the following day the examinations began. For a few hours the robbery was forgotten in the excitement of handing out examination papers. The president came to my cattle shed to say that the police in all the villages around were busily searching for the culprit. He smiled and said: "One must hope. Is it true that an English poet says: 'Hope springs eternal in our human breast'?" He beamed at the class and wandered away, the students bent over their papers, yellow butterflies were swarming across the campus, and the summer heat made us all drowsy.

When evening came, there was still no sign of the stolen property, but there was a curious excitement in the air. The command post was shifted to the large barn near the house, while more and more students came up the hill. They had discovered something, but exactly what they had discovered was still a mystery. I remained in the house, correcting papers. From time to time the student in charge of the investigations dropped in to see me. He looked like a young hero in a mediaeval Chinese drama, with a handsome clear-cut profile and a debonair manner which suggested that all things were possible to those who were bold, determined and blessed by fortune. I asked him whether there was any news, and he said he expected there would be some developments later in the evening.

"Oh, there is no doubt about it! We are very close now!" he said. "I think you will have all your property back this evening."

I was not quite so sanguine. The student left, and I went back to work. Just before midnight I heard a loud scream coming from the direction of the barn. The scream ended abruptly, as though someone had suddenly clamped a hand over a man's mouth, or as though a man's life had ended in mid-scream. I ran out of the house to find a dozen students squatting in the barn around a kneeling peasant whose arms were bound behind his back. The peasant was about forty, small, thin, and sharp-featured. He was breathing heavily, the sweat pouring out of him. He was moaning softly. I looked up. There was a rope hanging from the rafters, and it was obvious that they were about to string him up when I entered the barn, or perhaps they had already strung him up. I untied the rope binding his arms, and then he began to sob and kiss my shoes. None of the students said anything. Someone helped the peasant to stumble to his feet. I could see no wounds except that the rope had bitten deep into the flesh of his arms. He shook himself like a dog coming out of water, staring round craftily at the students, unsure of himself, wondering whether it was all over. I told him to go, but instead, his whole body shaking, he threw himself down on the ground and began kissing my shoes again, and when I stepped back, he crawled after me, clutching at my legs, refusing to let go.

"If you had given us another five minutes," one of the students said bitterly, "we would have got the truth out of him. We know he did it, but we don't know where he hid the things or whom he sold them to."

It was like a nightmare. The students looking at me with resentment, the man crawling across the ground, the rapeseed-oil lamp flickering and throwing strange shadows on the walls of the huge barn. The students were tense, watchful, accusing. I suppose I should have spoken to them about democratic procedure and due process, but it would not have helped. They were doing what they believed they had to do, for there was no law in China and everyone took the law in his own hands. If a peasant was robbed, he did not go to the police: he went to his friends and tried to find the robber and punish him in his own way.

I disengaged my foot from the peasant, and was about to leave the barn when I observed that one of the students had a revolver. One can say many things by silences, and it was not necessary to tell him to put the revolver away. The man lunged for my legs again. His rumpled blue cotton coat was lying in the straw. I picked it up, gave it to him, and then walked slowly out of the barn. A few moments later the students trooped out, pushing the peasant in front of them. A moment later we were all standing under the banyan, in the blue light filtering through the heavy branches, and it was clear that nothing had been decided. The students were still looking at me accusingly, and the peasant was still gazing at us with a frightened expression, as though he expected to be taken back to the barn and strung up again.

Gradually, as we stood there, something very strange began to happen. Without any words at all, everyone knew what had to be done. The peasant was the first to move away, walking slowly to the edge of the hill. Suddenly he was gone, running down the path as though he had been shot from a cannon. Then three or four of the students began to drift away, and one by one the others went down the path. At last none of them was left, and I walked alone into the empty house.

A few days later, when the examinations were over, Liang Tsong-t'ai brought me a letter from the Marshal. The letter was about two feet wide and four feet long. In bold characters the Marshal asked, commanded, requested—the tone of the letter changing with every sentence—that I should spend part of the summer with him on the mountain. "You may stay as long as you like, and leave whenever you please. You will teach me English poetry for a few minutes every day. I am at your command."

When I reached the Hall of the Empty Heart it was midday, and the Marshal was sitting in the middle of the clearing with a book of Chinese poems on his lap. He looked even taller, ruddier, more imposing than when the professors visited him. In the sunlight, the wind roaring in the pines, he looked completely at ease, as though this clearing in the forest was his natural habitation. The flesh was laced with muscle, the small glinting dark eyes shone with amusement and intelligence, and there was nothing in the least forbidding about him. He bowed deeply. I bowed deeply. Then he said: "Let us begin the first lesson."

I spent three weeks on the mountain with the smiling giant who walked about in his underwear reciting English poetry at the top of his lungs. The world vanished: there was only the small clearing, the pine forest and the monastery. The summer mists drifted over the river, the white herons hovered in the dark blue sky, and sometimes there came the booming of the fish-shaped drum summoning the monks to prayer. Sometimes, very faintly, from thousands of feet below, there would come the sharp cries of the haulers pulling the ships upstream. It was the summer of 1942, the world at war, and for some unaccountable reason I was as far as it was humanly possible to be from the conflict.

I do not remember any feelings of guilt: only of surprise and wonder. The Green Dragon was a pine forest curling up the slopes of the craggy mountain, his horns were the curling roof of the monastery, his voice was the strangely musical soughing of the pines which continued all day and all night, even when there was no wind, and the summer lightning flickering off the top of the mountain was his breath. In this enchanted clearing everything was possible—even the presence of the Green Dragon.

"I am at the mercy of my guards," the Marshal complained one day, but it was the only complaint he ever made.

These guards were fresh-faced Honanese peasant boys, who spoke a language virtually incomprehensible to the Szechuanese. They had very little to do except to watch the winding road up the side of the mountain and to see that no one entered the encampment without the Marshal's permission. Altogether, with the aide-de-camp, the sergeant at arms, the cook and five or six guards, we were about a dozen people living in bamboo huts in a clearing in the pine forest. The Honanese peasant boys had faces like red apples and were always laughing; the black-robed monks, who sometimes wandered along the road with their heads bent and their hands hidden in their sleeves, were strangely pale, and they never laughed.

I suspect the Marshal chose the spot because it was virtually impregnable. Once, when I asked him why he had come there, he said he was seeking the protection of Buddha, but he was smiling wickedly. He had no feeling for Buddha, disliked the young monks for their pallor, and could barely tolerate the presence of the priests who occasionally came to him with some request or other or with an invitation to attend a service at the monastery. From time to time he liked to send them presents of food, saying that he had observed that many of the monks were starving.

Although the Marshal professed to dislike Buddhism, regarding himself as a Christian in good standing, he was on excellent terms with Abbot T'ai Hsu, the Supreme Abbot of China, who ruled over the monastery. The Abbot was kindly and tolerant, but he found Christianity totally incomprehensible. He was a very small man, coming up to the Marshal's waist, with a pug-dog face and a curiously gawky walk. He wore the same black gown as all the other monks. There was nothing in the least remarkable about him except his eyes, which were very dark and soft, the darkness and softness being magnified by the thick lenses of his spectacles. When you looked into his eyes, you saw the Buddhist saint, but if you came upon him walking around the monastery, you would have thought him the lowliest caretaker.

The Marshal and the Abbot ruled the mountain. They were in an uneasy alliance, fundamentally at odds with one another, for the Abbot genuinely detested soldiering and the Marshal was genuinely puzzled that anyone should spend his life in fruitless prayers.

"They were good farm boys," he would say, "and now look at them! Pale as fish! They are no use to the country, no use to themselves!"

Saying this, he would suck in his cheeks, lowering his eyes and hunching his shoulders, while he recited some mumbo-jumbo which sounded like Buddhist prayers, and then he would roar with laughter. If I went to the Buddhist monastery, he would say: "Don't stay there too long! You'll come back with a long face, mumbling prayers!"

The long summer days were filled with a blaze of excitement. In Szechuan, in that intense heat, you can hear the trees grow, the seeds sprouting and pushing up through the earth. A clump of green bamboos near the entrance to the encampment became a forest of bamboos, twice the height of a man, within a month. There were melons three feet long, brimming with rosy flesh, the sweetest I have ever tasted. Sometimes I would climb to the top of the mountain and throw myself down among the pine needles, and I was sure I could hear the flow of juices through the veins of the trees, and the smell of the pines was richer than the smell of the incense in the monastery. Down below, in the blue haze of summer, the hills rolled in endless green waves, and sometimes, far in the west, I thought I saw the white mountains of Tibet.

From time to time strange visitors climbed up the mountain road, to be ushered into the Marshal's bamboo hut, where they were given small cups of green tea. They were usually military men, uncomfortable in their patterned gowns, for it was generally understood that no one in uniform was permitted to appear on the Buddhist mountain. They always came rather surreptitiously, accompanied by their own guards, who looked equally shamefaced, the shapes of their heavy snub-nosed pistols clearly visible under their gowns. They brought with them an air of melodrama and conspiracy, and while they were present an electric tension could be felt in the encampment. They rarely stayed for more than an hour, and they vanished like a puff of smoke.

These interludes served to remind me that the Marshal was still a power to be reckoned with. As Vice-Generalissimo, in theory second only to the Generalissimo, his advice on military matters especially was continually being sought, and many of the officers who visited him had fought in his armies and were his devoted followers. Strangely, he seemed to derive no pleasure from these visits, and was happiest on the days when no one came to visit him. "Why do people come and bother me?" he complained. "I am in retirement, an old horse with nothing worth while to say to them!"

This, of course, was nonsense. He did not look or behave like an old horse. He was incredibly young in spirit, delighted in everything that happened around him, and was perfectly content to stay on the mountain in this cluster of bamboo huts overlooking the gorges.

The military officers who came were all generals, and all were members of the Supreme Military Council. Whenever the Generalissimo was absent from Chungking, the Marshal became president of the Council. It was not a position he ever wanted to abandon, and in fact he was more powerful on his mountain top than he would have been if he had stayed in Chungking.

Meanwhile, there were all the pleasures of the mountain to be explored. Moon-watching delighted him; so did solitary walks through the pine forest; and he especially enjoyed doing nothing and gazing at the river winding below.

In theory there were programs to be followed, and the round-faced aide-de-camp was kept busy drawing up programs, which were nearly always abandoned. The Marshal usually rose at dawn, when a milky-white mist filled the valley, and in the half-dark he liked to engage in the balletlike shadow-boxing with which Chinese gentlemen of the old school begin their mornings. When the first yellow light came shooting across the encampment, a breakfast of noodles and boiling hot tea was served under the pines. At breakfast he announced the plans of the day, which were faithfully recorded by the aide-de-camp. There would be a walk halfway down the mountain, followed by the writing of scrolls, and then he would learn an entire English poem by heart. Afterward one of the monks from the monastery would be invited to read to him. In the afternoon there might be the visit of some professors from Chungking, who would then go on to pay their respects to the Abbot T'ai Hsu. Later the Marshal would seclude himself in his bamboo hut and continue work on his autobiography. The days never followed the prescribed plan, because unforeseen events were always happening. A walk down the mountain would be abandoned because one of the guards had brought in a wounded sparrow, and he would spend the rest of the morning attending to the sparrow. Or else it occurred to him that it would be more pleasant writing scrolls, and there were days when he did nothing else. A narrow table was set up in the clearing, long sheets of rice paper were carefully laid on it, and all the rituals of scroll-writing would be followed with an almost mechanical precision. The ink must be exactly of the right consistency, the boy holding the horse-tail fly-whisk must be standing in exactly the right place. Then, for perhaps ten minutes, he stood there looking down at the paper, humming and crooning tunelessly, until the spirit moved him to attack the paper with huge brush strokes. Blue jays perched on the table, pine needles fell on the ink stone, drops of sweat fell on the characters he was writing, and all the time he was in ecstasy, his face glowing, his lips forming little tuneless songs. Once he had started he would go on writing scroll after scroll. Each scroll would be lifted carefully from the table and laid out to dry, until it became impossible to move about the courtyard for the scrolls lying there.

Most people in China have small seals carved out of ivory or stone, about an inch square. The Marshal's seal stone was ten times larger, a great block of green-veined marble with a lion carved on it, resembling in shape and size the Great Seal of an ancient imperial dynasty. When the time came to affix his seal on a scroll, the Marshal liked to meditate for a long time to discover the exact place where it should go. Then the seal was dipped into a cushion of scarlet ink, and it would come down with relentless force on the thin rice paper.

Just as he enjoyed writing scrolls and composing poems when the spirit moved him, so he enjoyed learning English poetry whenever the spirit decided that the propitious moment had come. One day he asked me who was the greatest English poet. "Shakespeare," I said. "So, Shakespeare," he said, and rolled the word around his tongue until it came out effortlessly. "And what is the very greatest poem written by Shakespeare?" This was an unfair question, until I remembered "Full fathom five." The rest of the morning was spent in elucidating a text which reduced him almost to a state of happy madness:

> Full fathom five thy father lies;
>   Of his bones are coral made;
> Those are pearls that were his eyes:
>   Nothing of him that doth fade
> But doth suffer a sea-change
> Into something rich and strange.
> Sea-nymphs hourly ring his knell.

I suppose it was the worst poem I could have chosen. Burial at sea was not a subject which had any appeal for a Chinese.

Why "full fathom?" Why not "five fathoms?" What was a fathom? About his own height, six feet. This pleased him, and he calculated that the body lay exactly thirty feet below the sea. He reminded me that no Chinese poet would be so definite, and it would have been much better if Shakespeare had written "a few fathom" or "many fathom." It occurred to him that the English with their navy were accustomed to burial at sea, and no doubt this was why the poem was so celebrated.

One by one the problems were solved. Sea-nymphs he understood well enough, and that the eyes should become pearls did not alarm him, for when great Chinese saints are cremated, pearls are usually to be found among the ashes. This was also true of people, not necessarily saints, who lived lives of perfect chastity, and he was of the opinion that a considerable number of pearls would be found among my ashes, since I lived chastely and modestly and to all appearances had no use for women. His ideas about the pearls to be found in my ashes changed a few days later when Rose unexpectedly climbed up the mountain and presented herself at the encampment.

We labored over the poem all morning until he had learned it by heart and knew exactly what it meant. The generals of the Supreme Military Council, none of whom spoke any English, were greeted the next day with a thunderous rendition of Ariel's song from *The Tempest,* which sounded like:

> Foy foythen fife thy foyther rice;
> Office burns are curry made;
> Thoice are purrs that war his ice:
> Nawthing off hymn thadoth fade
> But dawth soffer a sea-change
> Into sumting rich and strange.
> (*long pause, then triumphantly*)
> SEA-NYMPHS OWERLY RING HIS KNELL.

In this way, over many days, the Marshal acquired a working knowledge of Shakespeare's songs, roaring out the words with great gusto. One day he thought it unfair that he alone on the mountain should be permitted to enter the secret world of Shakespeare's poetry. He thought the Abbot T'ai Hsu should be invited to the poetry sessions. Accordingly I went to the monastery, bearing a scroll announcing that the Abbot was cordially invited to attend readings of Shakespeare. It was an unfortunate meeting. There were clouds of mosquitoes in the air, and I kept slapping them involuntarily. A pained expression crossed the Abbot's face. Did I realize that I was bringing death to the monastery? What right did I have to snuff out the lives of those beautiful winged creatures? He clasped his hands, bowed his head, prayed reverently for the souls of the dead mosquitoes, and announced that he was too old to listen to the words of Shakespeare.

The Marshal was proud of his command of English, which he spoke without any conventional accuracy, but with great energy. He had a passion for pointing at things and giving them their English names. "A lime tree," he would say very slowly, every syllable clearly pronounced. Whenever he made a mistake, he clapped his hands to his forehead, shouted: "I am a nincompoop!" and roared with laughter. He could say quite complicated things in an orderly way, and then get stuck with something very simple, seeking vainly for a word like "candle" or "flower," words which he knew well although he could not remember them when he needed them. He was infuriated when his memory failed him, and delighted like a child when the words fell in the proper order.

Sometimes I wondered what I was doing on this mountain top in the midst of a war. A year before I had been an armament officer in Singapore, in charge of God knows how many tons of high explosives, and now I was living with an old general in a small paradise high above the world and all its doings. My shapeless life was made up of fragments, but this particular fragment seemed to me the strangest of all, beyond all prophecy. I told myself that I had absolutely no right to all this happiness.

"You are a fool to think about such things," the Marshal said. "I assure you, in a country like China moments of real happiness are very rare and it is permissible to enjoy them."

This led to a long philosophical discussion on the nature of happiness, which became so intricate and so involved that we finally decided that happiness could not be defined either in English or in Chinese, and afterward there was a long silence of exhaustion. Then he burst out laughing and said: "Silence is happiness."

These long conversations usually took place in the evening

after a sparse supper while he sat in a wickerwork chair in the middle of the encampment. "Moon-watching" and "pine-listening" are familiar Chinese pleasures, and if the moon was particularly beautiful or if the pines were whispering musically, he raised a warning finger and all conversation abruptly ceased. Sometimes, when moon-watching, he went into a kind of trance, head thrown back, eyes half closed, while he hummed and sang poems invented on the spur of the moment, and when he was especially moved, the voice grew louder and more visceral, totally unmusical, so that it resembled a dog's baying at the moon.

From time to time professors from the university climbed up the mountain to pay their respects to the old Marshal. They were not too welcome. He gave them melons, asked them a few desultory questions, and then announced that he must return to the study of Shakespeare. The professors whispered among themselves that the real reason he was staying on the mountain was to continue his love affair with a famous Shanghai dancing girl reputed to be living with him. In fact there were no women in the encampment, and there was no love affair.

So the summer days passed under the indigo-blue skies of Szechuan. At night, by the light of a rapeseed-oil lamp, I read the whole of Proust's *Remembrance of Things Past,* and when I woke late in the morning the Marshal was already preparing for his daily lesson. Once he announced that he would like to begin his Shakespeare lessons at the crack of dawn, and I must therefore go to bed earlier. It was an unfair battle of wills, for I possessed one weapon denied to him: I was a professor, and therefore according to Chinese custom far above the ordinary laws of mortals. I continued to read and write far into the night. "Extraordinary!" the Marshal exclaimed. "He simply refuses to obey my orders! I have had soldiers shot for less!" Since he had rarely been disobeyed, the experience had a certain freshness, and once he had overcome the first shock he delighted in telling everyone who visited the encampment: "Come and meet the professor who refuses to obey any of my orders, sleeps when he likes, and does exactly as he pleases!"

Surprisingly, the result of the battle of wills was to make the Marshal more tolerant, more gentle, and more affectionate. One evening he announced that I was to be regarded as his adopted son. When in Chungking, I must stay in his house near the foreign office. If there was anything I needed, I must come to him, and if I was in trouble he was the first person I must consult. There was the inevitable long scroll with two-inch-high Chinese characters describing the new relationship and a feast to celebrate it. This was a sumptuous gift to be treasured through all the years I remained in China.

One day a letter came from Rose, saying that she intended to spend a few days at the Hot Springs at the foot of Splendid Cloud Mountain. The Hot Springs was once a rather select resort for elderly Chinese gentlemen suffering from rheumatism and arthritis, who drank the boiling waters welling out of the caves. There was a small park with lakes filled with pink lotuses, and wooden chalets were set back from the paved gardens where the gentlemen strolled after imbibing the waters. But that was in the old days. Now it had become a pleasure resort, empty on most days of the week, crowded on weekends with visitors from Chungking who played their gramophones and danced in the park. Rose had chosen to come on a Monday, when the place was usually deserted.

On Sunday I told the old Marshal that I would be going down the mountain to stay at the Hot Springs and would probably spend the night there.

The word "coincidence" had long fascinated him, and he shouted at the top of his lungs: "Co-in-ci-dence! Very strange co-in-ci-dence! I, too, have to spend Monday at the Hot Springs! We shall go down together!"

As we walked down, he seemed to be strangely preoccupied, and he talked very little. He wore his peasant costume, a white shirt, white trousers rolled up to his knees, and straw sandals. He carried a heavy walking stick, which could be transformed into a swordstick by pressing on a secret spring. Halfway down the mountain we encountered an old bent peasant woman carrying a heavy load of charcoal to the monastery. The Marshal gave out a roar and began to shout at her. Who made her carry such a heavy load? How much was she paid? How many children did she have? Terrified, she sank to the ground. "Look at her!" he shouted to his bodyguard. "Look what they have done to her! We let old women do the work, when they should be looking after their grandchildren! What a farce it is! All their lives these old people have served the nation, which has never once re-warded them! Respect this old woman, bow before her!" We all bowed, the Marshal bowed, while the old woman gazed at him in terror. Soon we were all marching up the mountain again, and the Marshal was carrying her load of charcoal, which he solemnly deposited on the steps of the monastery.

When we finally reached the Hot Springs, Rose was waiting just outside the ornamental gates. She wore a white cotton gown hemmed with a thin red ribbon. A light rain was falling on the weeping willows and the lotus pools. The Marshal bowed very low to her and she smiled her enchanting smile. Some officers in gleaming uniforms were waiting for him. Soon he vanished into one of the cabins and changed into full uniform, and when he emerged he waved his hand and said: "For you—pleasure! For me—conferences, conferences, conferences!"

For more than three weeks, day after day, I had lived high up on the mountain listening to the booming of the gongs and the soughing of the pines. Now in the valley, listening to the chatter of the expensively dressed visitors to the Hot Springs, I was like someone in a compression chamber, gasping for air. I wanted to take Rose up to the top of the mountain, above the clouds and the rain. She, just as avidly, wanted to enjoy the pleasures of the valley, the teahouses, the gramophone rec-ords, walks beside the lotus pools of the Hot Springs. She insisted that the Hot Springs was the only place for miles around which had any pretensions to being civilized, while I regarded it as a disgraceful eyesore, fit only for the rich young bloods of Chung-king who were doubly damned for being rich and for coming here. She looked across the river at the cattle sheds erected on the low cliffs. "Is that where you teach?" she asked, and she obviously disapproved. "Why, they are no more than peasants' huts!"

So they were, but I liked them. She seemed amused as we walked along the flagstone paths in the light rain by my insistence that the cattle sheds were just as good as stone buildings. You could put up chairs and a blackboard in a cattle shed, and that was all you needed. As often as not, I took my students to a small garden behind the university and we sat on the grass. What was the use of a building? She wrinkled her patrician nose and said she thought there was something to be said for well-designed buildings and precious little to be said for cattle sheds.

As we walked in the light rain up one flagstone path and down another, arguing interminably, I suggested we should take shelter in one of the teahouses. "The Chinese like walking in the rain," she said. "We absolutely adore the rain, and we have hundreds of poems about the sound of the rain falling on pools and in the garden and on the roof." The rain, of course, had the effect of making her white gown cling to her skin, and she was becoming even more beautiful and more desirable.

We argued passionately, and there was scarcely any subject we agreed upon. I was all for the Chinese universities, and she thought they were so mismanaged that they could be dispensed with. I admired the Generalissimo, and she said quietly that he had long ago become corrupted by power and the Kuomintang party was corrupt beyond redemption. I admired the Chinese soldiers, and she said they did not know how to fight. Before I knew what was happening we were fighting like young lovers.

When the rain cleared in mid-afternoon we hired a boat and sailed up the Chialing River until we were in the shadow of the gorges. White herons floated overhead, caught in the hovering wind between the cliffs. The cliffs, seven or eight hundred feet high, towered above us. Our voices sounded strange as they echoed between the cliffs, and in the green light of the gorges we could no longer recognize each other or ourselves. Nevertheless we were still arguing, and in the course of the arguments I was learning a good deal about her.

Her mind was like quicksilver, and I could never come to grips with it. Self-taught and undisciplined, she gave an impression of fantastic erudition, but it was not for her erudition that I had taken her out in the boat, beached it in a lonely place in the gorges, and refused to leave until she told me more about her life. So she talked about her children, her son Jon and the two daughters Mary and Jacqueline. All were of school age. Mary and Jon were studying in Chungking, and Jacqueline was in a convent in Peking. It was astonishing that she could have children in their teens, for she looked about twenty-five. In the shadow of the gorges she spoke in a soft whispering voice, for otherwise she was drowned in the echoes.

"Did I tell you that Mary has murdered a man?" she said quietly.

"No, you didn't—"

"Perhaps I should tell you that story at another time," she went on. "It is very grisly."

The story as it unfolded was long, complicated, and not in the least grisly. It involved a one-armed secret service agent who was hiding in her palace in Peking, secret codes, and a store of ammunition hidden under the floorboards of the family temple. But the essential part of the story concerned a small band of schoolchildren, none of them more than fifteen, who dedicated themselves to killing Chinese officials who went over to the Japanese. Mary was chosen to be the leader, because she was a beauty with long black pigtails, rosy cheeks, and such an appearance of innocence that no one thought she could possibly be dangerous. At the head of the death list was the Salt Commissioner of Tientsin, a man of considerable importance because vast amounts of tax money passed through his hands. The headquarters of the schoolchildren was an ice cream parlor in Tientsin. They followed the Salt Commissioner's movements, learning that he attended a local cinema one afternoon each week accompanied by two armed guards, who sat beside him. On the following week the children sat behind the Salt Commissioner. They had already seen the film several times, and knew there was a noisy gun battle at the end of the film. At the height of the battle Mary calmly shot the Salt Commissioner in the back of the head, and in the confusion all the children escaped. They met in the ice cream parlor and took the next train to Peking.

Rose told the story well, almost too well, for there was more than a suspicion that she knew a good deal more about the murder than she admitted.

"It was quite a famous affair, and filled the headlines for many days," Rose said. "The Japanese never discovered who killed him."

"What happened to Mary?"

"She went back to school as though nothing had happened, and a few weeks later we all went to Chungking except for Jacqueline, who was too young to make the journey."

She lay there on the cushions, curled up in the bottom of the boat, talking dreamily about murders. It appeared that many more murders had taken place in Peking, and the ammunition hidden in the family temple was constantly being distributed among mysterious assassins commanded by a one-armed agent from Chungking. She smiled dreamily at the memory of these adventures which took place, it seemed, on another planet and in another age.

At last I rowed her back to the Hot Springs, where we learned that a fleet of cars had suddenly arrived in Peipei, taking the Marshal, the generals, and the bodyguard to Chungking.

"You are very clever," Rose said. "You arranged everything perfectly. You even managed to get rid of Feng Yu-hsiang. Now I am at your mercy."

I had not thought of her as being at my mercy, or indeed at anyone's mercy, but the sudden and unexpected disappearance of the Marshal had altered the balance of forces. I no longer served two masters. I was no longer at the top of the mountain, in an eagle's nest remote from the world. There was time to study her more closely, to discover what lay behind the cool mask, the veiled eyes, and the sudden smile flashing like lightning. As for marriage, she was so vehemently opposed to it that I thought her vehemence exaggerated, just as her beauty was exaggerated. I had known long ago that we would marry; it was not necessary to summon the Green Dragon; it was necessary only to wait until she fell into the trap which had been prepared in my childhood, when the Green Dragon announced without any ceremony, as though it was the most natural thing in the world, that I would marry a Chinese princess.

"Of course we shall be very miserable," she said, as we walked up and down the flagged path between the lotuses.

"Yes, of course."

"I am terribly difficult to live with," she went on. "I have a bad temper. Sometimes I shut myself up for days and do nothing except write poems. Then there are the children—you will probably hate them, or fall in love with them, which will be worse. I am ferociously jealous, vindictive, and spiteful. You won't have a moment's peace if you marry me. If you have any sense, you will spend the rest of the summer with the Marshal—"

I spent the rest of the summer with Rose, for we were married three days later. A pink and blue Chinese wedding certificate, suitably engraved with cooing doves, was obtained from a local

stationery store, and this was solemnly signed by the president of
the university one evening while we were sitting over dinner. In
a civil marriage it is only necessary that the bride and groom
signify their assent in the presence of an elder, a man of authority. The president was a man of authority, and he lent dignity
to the occasion by a genial silence. There were toasts in little
cups of rice wine, but no speeches. Except for the signing of
the certificate there was nothing to distinguish this evening meal
from many others.

Rose had a small farmhouse on the south bank of the Yangtze
near Chungking, and there we spent the honeymoon. The rice
fields were under water, and the farmhouse seemed to rise out
of silver lakes, almost lost in that gleaming immensity. The
mornings were loud with the cries of ducks and geese, and at
night the house creaked in the mysterious winds flowing over the
plain. The small pepperpot mountains were far away, as though
painted on the horizon, shimmering in the distance. The scenery
in Szechuan changes abruptly, and you could not have guessed
that the white cliffs of Chungking were only a few miles away.

Rose had decorated the farmhouse with embroideries from
Peking, so many embroideries of Chinese Immortals and deer
wandering through enchanted forests that the rooms in the
light of the oil lamps looked like fairyland. There were books
everywhere, and at least half of them were English books. I
imagined the books had been piled into tea chests and carried
on the backs of coolies across the length of China. There was all
of Eliot, Yeats and Auden, all of Valéry and Guillaume Apollinaire, and heaven knows how many others. She was no blue-
stocking, but she thought a day well spent if she could read
Yeats from morning to night.

Sometimes we made the journey to Chungking, walking for
miles along the raised banks of the rice fields. She found her
way down to the ferry as though by instinct, treading delicately on those slippery muddy banks no more than a foot wide,
wearing a peasant's straw hat or twirling a pink sunshade. On
one of these journeys to Chungking, I learned that the embassy
violently disapproved of the marriage. "One should not marry the
natives," they said, "and besides, it sets a bad example."

When classes began again after the summer holidays, we
returned to Fuhtan, the Chialing River, the mountains and the

gorges. The farmhouse among the dreaming lakes was exchanged for another farmhouse set among low hills a mile behind the university. This farmhouse was walled around like a castle, virtually impregnable. The president of the university had examined it and thought it a proper place for a professor. Rose felt at ease in the large upper rooms overlooking a pine grove. We employed a maidservant, a local farm girl, who was good-humored, sensible and pretty. Three weeks later, returning from the village market, she was bludgeoned and left for dead by a drunken peasant. She recovered, but the president had second thoughts about a farmhouse a mile from the campus and suggested that we take refuge in the black-timbered inn in Peipei.

"Stay there for a few days while we find somewhere safer," he said.

We stayed in the inn through the winter, while the heavy gray clouds settled on Szechuan, and it was five months before we saw the sun again. The embroideries of the white-faced Immortals and the deer wandering through enchanted forests hung in the small bedroom in the inn. The rats came and sat on our pillows; the reek of opium filled the corridors, and there were screams in the night. For me, it was endurable, for I crossed the river every day and lived among the students, but for Rose it was the purest misery. She read her books, wandered round the small town, bought groceries, cooked in a corner of the room, and waited for the spring. Sometimes, unable to bear the inn any longer, she took the boat down the river and returned to her farmhouse near Chungking, where there were no rats, where the birds sang and the geese cackled and the air was fresh and pure, unlike the stagnant air around the inn. Then she would return a week later, buoyed up by the gossip she had heard in the French and American embassies. She had a special fondness for the French embassy, saying that they alone cultivated gossip as a fine art.

February is the month when you look up at the heavy gray clouds, hoping against hope that there will be a little ragged blue space in the heavens. Hopelessness becomes a habit of mind. The rain falls, the earth steams, the clouds gather. Under the dark protective clouds of winter you have the illusion that you are living in a terrible undersea plantation full of strange ghostly fish and waving ferns, with scaly monsters lying in wait for you behind the gray rocks. You have the fixed conviction that summer will never come and that the sun has gone from the sky.

One February evening, returning from classes, I found Rose lying unconscious on the bed, and there were clots of blood on the floor and on the bedspread. She had had a miscarriage.

Because she was strong, she recovered quickly. Spring came, the sky cleared, the ghostly fish and the scaly monsters vanished, and suddenly there were emerald green fields and Splendid Cloud Mountain rose clear against the indigo-blue sky. One day, shortly after the coming of spring, while walking among the lotuses at Hot Springs, Rose said very quietly and firmly: "I am not going to spend another winter in the inn at Peipei. I am going to Peking. I want to see Jacqueline, and be sure she is well cared for. I'll get my jewels out of the bank in Shanghai, and then come back, and we won't have to live in poverty any more."

I said she must be out of her mind. No one could travel across Japanese lines, and nothing was more likely than that she would end up in a Japanese prison. How did she expect to go from Chungking to Peking?

"By walking, by bus, by mule-cart, by train," she said. "The Chinese are doing it all the time. Of course, if the Japanese recognize me, then it will be serious, but they won't recognize me. I'll dress up like a peasant woman, and I'll carry a passport with your name. Mrs. Pai-ying is a good name. It's going to be very easy and I'll be back in a few months."

A few weeks later she left jauntily for Peking, and I never expected to see her again.

THE CAMPUS IN
A GRAVEYARD

Fuhtan University was not among the great universities of China and very few of the professors were distinguished for their brilliance. These professors were gentle, kindly, rather remote, happy in their isolation, for they were far enough away from Chungking to enjoy their independence and few government inspectors took the trouble to make the day-long journey up the Chialing River to inspect us. We were living in the backwaters, far from the places where important decisions were being made, and we rejoiced in our unimportance.

Dimly we realized that a social revolution was taking place in China and that the Kuomintang government was losing its hold on the people. By the summer of 1942 Chiang Kai-shek's stature was visibly diminishing. He continued to make speeches, but we read them with alarm and disbelief, for they described a China which had already ceased to exist. He spoke of victories which existed only in his imagination and of a new social system which had no relationship to the feudal China we were living in. He presented himself as the great war leader, but the wars were being fought elsewhere. No one any longer believed the government communiqués. Something very strange was happening: the ruler no longer ruled.

But all this came to us as though from a vast distance, for in the university we were scarcely concerned with what happened in Chungking, thirty miles away. We were more concerned with the behavior of a local landowner called Sheng Tse-pin, who had suddenly decided to impose extra taxes on the peasants. When the university protested, the landowner threatened to burn all our buildings to the ground. He was a very fat, very oily man with a thick reddish mole on his chin, and it was said of him that he had deflowered all the virgins in the village that lay a stone's throw from the university. When he walked slowly up and down the village street with his bodyguards around him, glancing imperiously at every house and making only the slightest nods at the people bowing low before him, we knew what was meant by feudal power. The professors were not particularly disturbed by his threat to burn the university to the ground. After all, the buildings were only cattle sheds, they could be rebuilt cheaply, and there was nothing of value in them. What disturbed them was the very existence of this cutthroat who ruled a large area on the left bank of the Chialing River as though he were a mediaeval monarch.

Other things disturbed them. From time to time there came rumors that professors at Chungking University had been arrested and that students in the same university had disappeared without a trace. Sometimes, too, when we were walking in the countryside, we came upon columns of farm boys roped together: they were recruits being inducted into the army, and they were roped together to prevent them from escaping. They were also being prodded with bayonets and they left a trail of blood behind them.

In those days Szechuan was a powder keg, and it would have taken very little to bring about a revolution. The revolution, of course, would have been put down with extraordinary ferocity by Chiang Kai-shek's army and secret police, and no doubt this was the reason it did not take place. When I visited Dr. Sun Fo, the head of the Legislative Yuan, I would find him nearly speechless with rage at what he called "the drift toward dictatorial rule," but in fact there was no drift, for the dictatorial rule was already established. Inflation was rampant; rich merchants were hoarding goods on an unprecedented scale; all over Szechuan there were farmhouses filled to the roof with bales of silk, cotton, rice, sewing machines and electric generators against the day when they would be thrown on the market for huge profits. Worst of all was the hoarding of rice.

In the British embassy at Chungking there was an air of quiet hopelessness. I was told that China was about to collapse, and there was the very gravest danger that Chiang Kai-shek would make a separate peace with the Japanese. Old China hands, former missionaries and compradores from Shanghai, bitterly complained that China was no longer pulling its full weight in the war and was lacking in the Churchillian spirit. There had been a time when the British ambassador exercised vast power in China, but now the Chinese government listened only to the Americans. In the sunken garden the secretaries moved about like ghosts, aimless and ineffective. British power in China vanished on the day that Sir Archibald Clark Kerr went to Moscow.

One day, shortly after Rose had left for Peking, I met Professor Ernest Hughes at the embassy. He was a small, wiry, peppery man, who would occasionally startle his friends with an unexpected display of mordant wit. His official title was Reader in Chinese Literature at the University of Oxford, and it was his fondest hope that he would one day be elevated to a professorship. He had once been a missionary in China, but he had too great a respect for the Chinese to attempt to convert them, and he had returned to China to continue his studies of Chinese poetry and philosophy. His deep affection for Chinese Taoism and Buddhism, and a special reverence for Confucius, had led him to Kunming to continue his studies at Lienta, the complex of Peking universities which had moved across the whole of China to settle in Kunming.

"I hear you are teaching in Fuhtan," he said in his peppery way. "Never heard of the place. Well, where is it? Some backwater, eh? What are you doing in a backwater? Well, answer me!"

So I launched into a long defense of backwaters as places to be honored and treasured, because they are quiet, inoffensive and quickly forgotten. Fuhtan, under the shadow of Splendid Cloud Mountain, was the most delectable of backwaters, and it was the purest pleasure to know that he had never heard of it. While I extolled the lost and forgotten places, he was preparing his counterattack based on the theory that there existed "centers of civilization and intellectual eminence." It appeared that there were a few such places scattered over the face of the earth—Oxford, Cambridge, Harvard, Princeton, the Sorbonne, Lienta. According to Professor Hughes, Lienta, comprising the three universities of Peking, Tsinghua and Nankai, could be measured by the same standards as Oxford and Harvard, the two universities which he regarded as unchallengeable centers of intellectual eminence. The question was whether I had any respect for intellectual eminence. In much the same way he spoke of "scholars" and "scholarship," as though nothing else possessed the slightest importance.

Professor Hughes rode his hobbyhorses to a purpose, and he was soon demanding that I should ride beside him and gallop into the magic world of the intellectually eminent. It was a disturbing prospect, and for a while I argued heatedly against being removed from my backwater. Also, I was lazy. "We'll soon cure you of that," he snapped. Also, I was ill with recurrent bouts of malaria and tuberculosis. "Kunming has the finest weather in the world, and you will be well again in no time." Also, I was very fond of the professors and students at Fuhtan. "That," he said in his Oxford way, "is a very commendable remark, but it avoids the main issue, which is whether one spends one's life usefully or to no purpose." It was obvious that "usefully" meant Kunming, and "to no purpose" meant Fuhtan. He was riding his hobbyhorse at full gallop.

In later years, when I came to know him well, Professor Hughes sometimes wondered aloud why I behaved with such "inexcusable levity" during our first meeting. The reason was a simple one, but it was not easy to tell him about it. He had invented a strange jargon of his own, full of circumlocutions and abstractions and invocations of the true, the good, and the beautiful, and it was quite impossible to understand the workings of his mind. When he spoke about "the scholar" and "intellectual eminence," he made these harmless words sound faintly sinister.

In all this Professor Hughes was the direct opposite of Dr. Joseph Needham, the scientific adviser to the embassy. Needham was a huge, gruff bear of a man, who suffered atrociously from migraine headaches, spat out ideas as though they were machine-gun bullets, and had no use for abstractions. He was a biologist with an international reputation, chiefly interested in studying the shadowy frontier where life emerges from something that resembles matter and is scarcely distinguishable from matter. He was already beginning to work on the history of Chinese science, which was to make him famous, and though he sometimes spoke learnedly about Communism he had not yet adopted a Communist faith. He worked in one of the small offices overlooking the sunken garden, and there I found him.

"Hughes says I must go off to Kunming," I said. "What is so wonderful about Kunming?"

"Its distance from Chungking," he replied. "Pure freedom, and the best university in all of China."

He went on to describe the university in the same terms as a man might describe paradise. The weather was perfect, there were no clouds in winter, the sun shone every day, the scholars were magnificently intelligent, and if the scientific equipment was poor, at least they made the very best use of it. Above all, there was freedom, because the students and faculty were under the protection of a local warlord, who had grown so rich from the sale of opium that he could afford to defy the Generalissimo and to pay for a large standing army of his own. The province of Yunnan, with its capital in Kunming, was virtually an independent country. In addition, Kunming had a large American air force base, and was therefore all the more protected from the interference of the central government.

Characteristically Dr. Needham kept insisting on the freedom of the university. Freedom was the generator of all the other virtues; nobility, honesty, scrupulous precision, good fellowship and the ardors of scholarship were merely the ornaments of freedom.

In this way I became convinced of the superiority of Lienta over all the other universities of China. In September 1943 I drove with a Chinese captain in an army truck from Chungking to Kunming—a strange journey, for there was a good road carved out of the mountains with no traffic on it. There was the illusion that China was frozen into immobility, with no one going anywhere. The skies were clear, the mountains sharply etched, the birds sang, and there were almost no people, no villages, no towns. We passed perhaps one small town a day, and saw two or three villages in the distance. We saw no soldiers; there were no check points; and no one ever examined the mountains of documents we had obtained in Chungking from the police, the garrison headquarters, the transport bureau, the foreign office, the ministry of war, and heaven knows how many other organizations. Bureaucracy ran rampant in Chungking, but once you were outside Chungking no one seemed to pay any attention to it. In this way I learned that Chinese bureaucracy was a fine art, which no longer possessed any practical application.

When we came to a town we usually called on the mayor, since he was always the best-informed person in the region and would know whether there were bandits on the road, and what state the road was in, and where we could find accommodation. We would find him sitting below portraits of Dr. Sun Yat-sen and the Generalissimo, and usually he was an old peasant wearing a patterned gown without any badges of rank. The mayor of An-ning was made of sterner stuff. He was a thin, tight-lipped, sunken-eyed, fanatical man, who spoke to us as though he were addressing a political meeting. We were told that An-ning was a town where all the old vices had been eradicated and the moral order was strictly upheld. There was no prostitution, no drunkenness, no opium smoking, the streets were clean, the children obedient to their parents, the women modest. He announced that we had come at the right time, for the next morning we would be privileged to see the execution of a notorious opium smoker. "I am a man of justice," the mayor told us. "I myself presided over the trial, but I could find no extenuating circumstances. You will see that justice is carried out ruthlessly in An-ning."

The mayor's grim speech left us gasping, and we went to a small flea-bitten hotel in a mood of profound melancholy. We had scarcely settled into the bedroom when we learned that one of the mayor's boasts was simply untrue. The door creaked open, and a girl entered followed by an old crone with a lamp. The girl was unbelievably beautiful, her face dead white like the face of the heroine in a Chinese opera, and she moved toward the beds with uncanny grace in a robe of scarlet and green silk. We told ourselves that we had never in our lives seen anyone so enchanting as this creature whose gown gleamed and glinted in the quivering light of an oil lamp, whose white face dazzled us with its absolute perfection. We waved her away, and slept miserably among fleas and bedbugs. In the morning we could still remember every detail of her face.

When we woke up late the next morning, the band was playing in the street outside the hotel, people were shouting, firecrackers were exploding, and the poor opium smoker was walking along the cobbled street, wearing a white dunce's cap and a white silk gown. He was not bound, but two soldiers with rifles walked in front of him and another behind him. He was quite young, with a small mustache, very pale and bewildered and perhaps drunk, for he weaved from one side of the narrow road to the other. Some children threw stones at him, and he turned his head sharply and looked at them in a surprised, bewildered way, as though he had thought better of them and wondered why they were so ill-behaved. Then he vanished down the road, and ten minutes later there came the crack of the rifle bullets.

A week after leaving Chungking we reached Kunming in the early evening when the sky was sunflower yellow and the reddish walls of the city were bathed in a yellow light. We asked for the university, but no one seemed to know where it was. I remembered that Professor Hughes had written that he was living in a converted theater near the North Gate, and so we drove slowly through the bright cobblestoned streets with their painted wooden archways, until we came to the huge mediaeval North Gate studded with iron nails, with a great drum tower above, from which in ancient and very recent times Chinese drummers had announced the coming of invading armies. In the shadow of the gate stood a huddle of dark wooden houses and shops left over from an earlier age. Nearby was a wooden theater, where a Yunnanese warlord had once entertained his friends and concubines with performances of Chinese opera. Professor Hughes was living in a small section of one of the balconies of the theater.

"You've come to the right place," he said, standing at the top of the narrow stairway. "I can offer you a corner of my balcony."

He waved his arms in a lordly way, like the owner of a vast estate demonstrating the extent of his property. Some boards had been erected across his portion of the balcony, dividing it into two separate rooms, a bedroom and an office. The bedroom was eight feet by twelve feet, the office was eight feet square, with a large desk occupying most of the space. With great difficulty he had found a second bed for the bedroom, and he was very proud of his accomplishment.

"What do you think of it?" he asked, his eyes gleaming. "Of course, there's no rent to pay, which is a great advantage. I think we can accommodate ourselves to one another. The beauty of it is that we are very close to the university, which is just outside the North Gate."

"It's very small," I commented.

"Of course it is, but there's nothing wrong in smallness. A blade of grass, says the Chinese philosopher, fills the whole universe."

At that moment there appeared on the stairs an apparition resembling an enormous Arab, with liquid black eyes and a thick tangled black beard. He was wearing a patched black gown covered with the dust of the street. The apparition was Dr. Feng Yu-lan, the author of a voluminous history of Chinese philosophy. He had the thickest, longest, and most intricate beard I have ever seen, and his long bony hands gesticulated with amazing speed, as though he were catching flies. He was explaining the meaning of an obscure Chinese philosophical term, and while he continued his explanations, I surveyed my new living quarters, the plank bed, the rickety chair, the dusty floor, the view from the balcony over the empty theater which had once been painted apple green, but now in the dusk looked gray and ominous. A servant was carrying a lamp to a table set in the middle of the theater, and his huge shadow stretched to the empty stage. The Chinese philosopher went clumping down the stairs, and in the near darkness I heard Professor Hughes saying: "You can have a good view of China from this box in the theater." The trouble was that it was so dark that I could see almost nothing at all.

I lived in this small corner of a theater balcony for over a year, happy in the professor's company and always surprised by his amused patience, tolerance and kindliness. At intervals I was properly lectured on the nature of the true, the good, and the beautiful. Sometimes he wondered aloud why I wore a shabby blue gown and scuffed shoes, and he was a little perplexed by my habit of working at night and sleeping late in the morning. "You should keep regular hours," he said. "You are giving a bad example to your students." But I continued to keep irregular hours, and since all of my lectures were scheduled for the afternoons, the students did not know that I was setting them a bad example.

Dr. Needham had said that Lienta was paradise, and so it was. Paradise consisted of about twelve large white cattle sheds built over an ancient cemetery about half a mile from the

North Gate. In the center of the campus stood the library, the only building with any pretension to permanence, filled with books which had been carried by donkey cart from Peking and Tientsin. The library was a shadowy place, ill-lit and ghostly, full of treasure. Altogether there were perhaps no more than twenty rows of books in English, but the essentials were there— all the English poets, nearly all the great English and American novels, and a surprisingly large number of books of modern criticism. Most of the library, of course, was devoted to works in Chinese, and there was a special locked cupboard for the rare books printed many centuries ago.

The cattle sheds were our lecture halls, and they were provided with wooden platforms from which the professors looked down on a sea of faces. Since I felt ridiculous on the platform, I usually gave my lectures sitting on the edge of the platform, or walking up and down among the students, or sitting outside the cattle shed in the grass with the students arranged in a half-moon. They were brighter, more inquisitive, and more demanding than the students of Fuhtan, and this was due perhaps to the fact that there was more competition to enter Lienta than to enter any other university in China. There was also a strange ceremoniousness combined with a grave gentleness, an exquisite tenderness, which was sometimes so naked that it became painful. Over half these boys and girls had served in the army.

Dr. Needham had spoken of the freedom of Lienta. Here freedom was almost palpable. No one was afraid to speak or write as he pleased. The economists studied the economy, found it in desperate straits, and said so. The social scientists found the society in a state of disintegration and sent urgent reports to the Legislative Yuan, which put them in pigeonholes and forgot them. The historians wrote about the epochs when China collapsed under the weight of foreign invasions or its own inner strains, and their histories were sometimes printed on frail, brown pages which had to be turned slowly for fear that they would crumble into powder. Except for blackboards, which were plentiful, and for the books in the library, the university had few of the normal resources of a university. The chemistry department was a shambles, for there were almost no chemicals or test tubes. The university had no printing press of its own, and no electric light except in the library, where the students worked in the evenings in a gray gloom which reminded me of a London fog.

There were no fogs in Kunming, no mists, no clouds hovering for half a year. There was no autumn, no winter, no summer. It was eternal spring, and there was never a time in the year when there were no flowers blooming. People spoke of Suchow with its lakes and marble bridges as the most delectable city in China, but Suchow was brutally cold in winter. Kunming, a mile high, was far more enviable, for though it rained nearly every day, the sun came out every day, and it was never cold. In the city the streets rambled around the lakes with their marble bridges. Outside the West Gate there was a jade-green lake stretching to the foot of the reddish mountains in the distance. American airmen regarded the lake as treacherous, for it had the special quality of resembling a green field; and many planes crashed into it. Since the university lay at the opposite side of the city from the huge American air base, we saw little of the American airmen.

My closest friends were Pien Chih-lin and Wen Yi-tuo, both of them poets of eminence. Pien Chih-lin was slight, owlish behind his thick spectacles, very fragile, even though he had fought with the guerrillas in the Haihang Mountains. He lived, like most of the professors, in a single monastic room, where the only decoration was a map of the world upside down. He had translated André Gide and Henry James into Chinese and produced two slim volumes of poetry, which some of my students knew by heart. What was especially attractive about him was an inner gaiety which came out in sudden, unexpected monologues spoken very quickly, as though he were ashamed of taking up anyone's attention for too long. Since he spoke so well, his modesty was infuriating.

We soon learned that American pocket books and magazines could be bought in the second-hand market places in Kunming, and we therefore haunted the market places, hoping to be the first to acquire treasures. In this way Pien Chih-lin acquired a stack of *New Yorkers* and Isherwood's *Prater Violet,* which he came to regard for the space of two or three weeks as the supreme masterpiece of English fiction. He enjoyed the conversational rhythms in the prose of Isherwood and Virginia Woolf, and in his own poetry he liked to imitate the conversational rhythms of Chinese. Here is part of his poem *Peking:*

Peking city: flying kites on a rubbish mound,
here a butterfly, there an eagle
painted on the blue canvas over Madrid.
Across the sea of sky, what a pity that no one can see you,
Kyoto!—

O trailing a trail of dust
and leaving all the passers-by in a showerbath,
flying wheels, you swim in so shallow waters,
yet in so high spirits?

Not so dusty indeed, even *they* are running away
from something hot at their heels, howling over their heads,
over everyone's head. Here it is again:
The yellow-haired wind makes a mess of the immense incense-pot,
stirring up the ashes of many centuries,
sending them flying, flying, flying,
driving them into frightened horses, fierce wolves, furious tigers,

rushing, rolling, roaring along the streets,
swooping over your windowpanes, giving you a puff,
swooping over your ears'-eaves, striking off an ear,
or a glazed tile?—

I am a kite already severed from the string,
having stumbled on you, how could I not cling
on your dear willow-branches? You'll be my home, you'll be my tomb;

just send your catkins on every bower, every tower,
never mind if my looks are day by day withering away.
Peking city: flying kites on a rubbish mound.

Pien Chih-lin translated the poem into his own characteristically fluent English. When I finally reached Peking, I realized its deadly accuracy.

Wen Yi-tuo* was already a legend, and he would become a greater legend. He had a lean, rather craggy face and wore a

---

* Wen Yi-tuo preferred this spelling of his name in English, because it conveyed more of the bite of the original sound. Wen I-to, the usual form, he thought absurd and rather commonplace.

beard which was black with red glints in it, having promised himself at the beginning of the Japanese invasion of China that he would not shave until the last Japanese had been thrown out of his country. He was forty-five years old, but in his short life he had been an artist, a poet, a seal carver, an archaeologist, a paleographist, a critic and interpreter of the ancient Chinese classics, an editor, a politician, and the head of the Department of Chinese Literature at Tsinghua University. His first love was painting, which he studied in Chicago and Denver, and he said once that when he discovered that he would never be a great painter, he poured his palette into his poetry. At this time he was chiefly famous for his poetry and his critical reinterpretations of the Chinese classics, especially *The Book of Songs*. But it was not for his poetry or his criticism only that the students looked up to him. There was a fire in him, an extraordinary warmth that was communicated to everyone he met, and at the same time he seemed always a little remote from us, as though he had been chosen by destiny for great things. We spoke of him as a future ruler of China, while not quite knowing what we meant by "ruler." A seat in parliament, a ministry, an embassy? More often we thought of him presiding over a government of the talents, which would take power at the end of the war. These were dreams, but he was a man who set us dreaming.

He lived in poverty in a small cluttered house near the lake, his study being a small cubbyhole with just enough room for a table, a shelf of books, and the instruments with which he carved seals, for he was also one of the most famous seal carvers of his generation. He wore a blue gown, which had been washed so often that it had turned into a strange grayish blue-white color. For weeks he would disappear, and we learned that he was recovering from malaria or typhus. He was dogged by one illness after another.

Wen Yi-tuo was our social conscience, but Chiang Shih-ro, the sociologist, was the gadfly. He looked the part to perfection, being tall and urbane, his calm utterances concealing a passionate ferocity. He was the one who wrote the blistering reports on the state of society which were pigeonholed by the Legislative Yuan and tossed into the wastepaper baskets of Chiang Kai-shek's closest advisers. He lived in a small summer house just behind our converted theater and would sometimes share our meals. "Every government," he said somberly, "must learn the lessons of history, otherwise it goes down to defeat." In the winter of 1943 he was saying that no human power could prevent China from falling to the Chinese Communists, because they alone had studied the history books.

A strange quietness settled on China during the last years of the war: the quietness of fear. The inflation soared, the professors and students became poorer, and some starved to death. Our salaries increased by leaps and bounds, until a full professor found he was earning a million yuan a month with a purchasing power of about fifteen dollars. But it was not poverty that caused our fear: the government was totally incompetent and totally corrupt, without any roots among the people. It had become in all essentials a totalitarian regime, obedient to no purposes except its own.

Nevertheless the Lienta campus was an oasis of peace and scholarship, a place of great beauty and strangeness. One day, taking a short cut home across the grave mounds surrounding the campus, I found myself looking down into an empty grave where there reposed the head of a white horse, which must have been placed there only a few hours before. In the next grave there was another white horse's head. I fled to the North Gate, wondering at the beauty of the dead horses, so fresh and white, in this barbaric landscape, while the American bombers flew overhead and the ancient walls of the city gleamed fiercely in the sunlight.

Sometimes Chinese soldiers from the Burma front came up the long road skirting the university, their clothes in tatters, their faces like skulls, their deep-set eyes glowing with the fevers of the Burmese jungles. The students ran out and gave them milk, and carried them to the local hospitals. Every day there were two or three of these soldiers, and sometimes they came in clusters, leaning on one another. Sometimes they died in the dust of the road, just outside the campus. They died very quietly.

The treatment of the soldiers by their officers had a profound effect on the students, who saw themselves in the doomed soldiers. Wen Yi-tuo attempted to organize a kind of relief expedition, sending students down the road to help the returning soldiers with provisions and medicines, but the local government forbade it, saying it was the task of the Red Cross, not of the university. But the Red Cross did nothing.

When Rose returned from Japanese-occupied China a year after she had set out from Chungking, she painted a disquieting picture of the border. The military officers on both sides had become merchants. Trade flourished at the border posts, and there was no fighting. She reached Peking without any difficulty, disguised as a peasant. One day she appeared at Jacqueline's convent, wearing rags and demanding to see her daughter. The nuns stormed at her and shut the door in her face. She returned to her palace, dressed in her finery, and once more appeared at the convent. This time they opened all the doors and bowed before her, calling her "our little princess," until she reminded them that she was the same person who had come to them in rags after an exhausting journey. Then she took Jacqueline to live in the palace, where they lived quietly and where Jacqueline recovered from the severity of convent life.

Some months later Rose decided to retrieve her jewelry from a bank in Shanghai. She had no difficulty in reaching the bank but had some difficulty in identifying herself. The Japanese police were called in, and she spent the night in the police station and the next day she was interrogated for six hours at the Japanese military headquarters. Somehow she was able to convince them that she had no connection with Chungking. I suspect that she bullied them remorselessly until out of sheer weariness they set her free. They gave her back the jewels they had impounded. Then she returned triumphantly to Peking to prepare herself for the long journey to Kunming.

She was always reckless, and the odds were against her. She went about Peking openly, and it amused her to say exactly what she thought to the Chinese who worked for the Japanese. "To get away with it I had to be absolutely brazen," she said later. One day she slipped out of the palace dressed like a peasant woman. Sewn into her clothes were a diamond necklace, some emeralds, and a solitaire diamond the size of a thrush's egg.

In the summer of 1944 the Japanese were beginning to launch sporadic attacks against the Chinese armies, and she was in danger of arriving at the border in the midst of battles. The Japanese had awakened out of their lethargy in mainland China and planned to drive deep into the southwest to cut the Burma

Road. Ten days after her arrest in Shanghai she was on her way to the south. Five weeks later came the telegram from Chungking: MY TRIP TO THE NORTH HAS BEEN EXCEEDINGLY EXCITING STOP I HAVE SUCCESSFULLY RECOVERED MY FAMOUS JEWELRY FROM THE JAPANESE WITHOUT THE AID OF ANY TRAITOR OR ANYBODY STOP I GOT THROUGH THE BORDER JUST A FEW HOURS BEFORE THE WAR STARTED IN HONAN STOP WHAT LUCK EXCLAMATION MARK.

A few days later she arrived in Kunming, sunburned, wearing a brocaded gown and all her jewelry. Professor Hughes was visiting Chungking, and so we lived in the little balcony of the theater now hung with the tapestries of the Immortals and the running deer, which had once decorated the dark inn in Peipei. Rose came just in time, for I fell ill with one of those mysterious diseases which at various times afflicted most of the professors and students at Lienta. The brocaded gown vanished; she became a nurse in cotton coat and trousers; and I was fed on a diet of jellied blood and raw marrow. Sometimes I thought it would be better to die than to go on swallowing those endless white pulpy strings of marrow. It was the sixth or seventh time that I had been seriously ill in China, but this time the cure came with remarkable speed. "You should have more trust in Chinese medicines," Rose said. "After all, we have been practicing medicine for six thousand years."

I objected that blood and marrow could scarcely be regarded as medicines.

"Nonsense," she replied. "I went to a Chinese doctor, told him your symptoms, and he prescribed blood and marrow. It is as simple as that."

Jon and Mary, her two older children, were now studying in Lienta. At sixteen, Jon looked like a young prince with a disturbing beauty, while Mary, a year older, looked more Spanish than Chinese, dark-eyed, with long black braids and bright red cheeks. Jon had no reserve and would throw himself into every battle, while Mary was all reserve, very quiet, happy only in the shade. She said of herself that she was a dark vase covered by a dark cloth and she did not know what was inside. In fact, she knew herself very well and the dark vase sometimes shone with a blinding light. Her quietness was all the more surprising because she was spectacularly beautiful, while seeming never to be aware of her beauty.

Rose wanted her family around her, and it soon became clear that she was not prepared to live interminably in a narrow corner of a balcony. She demanded at least three rooms, and on this subject she was adamant. I feared for our marriage, for rooms of any kind were quite simply unobtainable in Kunming and she was threatening to return to the small farmhouse near Chungking unless they were provided. At this time I was professor of English poetry and lecturer in Naval Architecture in the Engineering School, and it so happened that one of the Naval Architecture students knew about a White Russian vodka manufacturer who was thinking of leasing two or three rooms in his house near the West Gate. In this improbable fashion we acquired more than we had ever hoped for, for the vodka manufacturer consented to lease four rooms. Two were large, two small, and all of them looked out on a stone-flagged Chinese courtyard with a twenty-foot-high rock garden. The sweet smell of vodka hung over the entire house.

Joseph Shelestian, the owner of the house, was a remarkable character in his own right. The word *shelest* in Russian describes the whispering and rustling of grass or trees in the wind, but no one less resembled his name. His rages were phenomenal, and we would awake in the middle of the night to hear him roaring in the courtyard at the top of his lungs. By selling vodka to the American airmen he had accumulated over a hundred thousand dollars, but this newly acquired fortune, stuffed under his mattress, gave him no peace. He talked about it openly, swore us to secrecy, asked us to name a charity to which he would give it "for the sake of humanity," and then he would fall into weeping fits, saying that everyone was trying to steal it from him and there was no justice in the world. I thought such characters existed only in the pages of Gogol and Chekhov, but he was very real and sometimes terrifying. Once he came storming up the stairs with an ax, loudly demanding my head, and he showed his determination by smashing through one of the panels of the bedroom door. Rose, who had just saved my life with jellied blood and raw marrow, now saved it again by parleying with him through the smashed door. Then for the first time I saw the Rose who had successfully talked her way out of the hands of the Japanese secret police. Half an hour later, having soaked his head in cold water, the vodka manufacturer returned without the ax, announcing that he would perform any act of contrition we demanded. He wept pitifully, spoke of the high cost of producing vodka and the innumerable bribes he had to pay in order to remain in business, and swore that he would turn over a new leaf. If we wished, he would immediately enter the priesthood. "What for was I born?" he asked plaintively. "What for did I come into the world? What for do I make this god-damned vodka?"

The generals, the colonels and the GIs came in increasing numbers, departing with five-gallon drums of vodka. I suspected that the air-force base was awash in vodka. In Shelestian's dining room the generals and the GIs were on an equal footing, no one saluted anyone, and the easy camaraderie between officers and soldiers perplexed and then delighted me. It was unthinkable that English officers would behave in this way. For the first time I saw egalitarian America in action, and if the action consisted of little more than imbibing incredible quantities of vodka, it was nevertheless impressive. As an unlikely guest at Shelestian's parties, I heard stories about life in America which suggested that there were colors I had never dreamed of, shapes and tastes and dramas and confrontations which could exist nowhere else. Why in the world did they speak so much about frankfurters and hamburgers? An American colonel spent an evening describing the days when he was a runner for Chicago gangsters. Another colonel—he was Ilya Tolstoy, the grandson of the great Tolstoy—described his recent visit to Tibet. A GI solemnly handed me a book of poems, and said: "This is the best poetry we have." It was Muriel Rukeyser's *Theory of Flight*, and in the poet's vivid rhythms and urgent imagery I thought I saw the same world the GIs were describing: eccentric, expansive, drenched in color, seething with vital energy. There and then I knew I would make my way to America.

The war that had engulfed the whole world came to an end in August 1945, and a few weeks later it began again in China. The Generalissimo was determined to destroy all real or imagined opposition, and he sent the Chinese Fifth Army to destroy the provincial armies in Yunnan. At the beginning of October civil war broke out in Kunming.

For many weeks there had been rumors of the coming attack on the provincial armies. Some professors at the university,

mostly from the department of history, decided that if this totally
absurd and unnecessary war was visited on us, then we should
at least draw up an accurate record of it. We were, or thought
we were, trained scholars accustomed to disassociate fact from
fancy. We would set down only what we had seen with our
own eyes, and whatever deductions we made would be based
on solid evidence. Altogether six professors took part in the
experiment, and since we all lived in different parts of the city
we hoped to offer a fairly accurate account of the battles. When
we handed in our reports, we found that they had scarcely anything in common, and it would have been absolutely impossible to write a connected story of the fighting from our reports.
In this way we learned of the pitfalls that confront historians.

For five days and nights the gunfire crackled over the city.
The Americans were ordered to remain in their barracks; the
ordinary traffic of the city came to a standstill; the shop shutters
came down. One day the West Gate was defended by soldiers
with white and blue armbands, the next day there were soldiers
with white armbands marked with a V, denoting the Fifth
Army. At the beginning most of the fighting took place around
Green Lotus Lake, near the North Gate, with the Fifth Army
gunners shelling the palace of General Lung Yun, the governor of
Yunnan province. During the second day the fighting veered to
the center of the city, and then spread out unpredictably to the
south and west. By this time people were beginning to come
out of their houses and a few shops were opening their shutters.
On the third day Dr. Mei Yi-chi, the president of Lienta, decided
that a dinner he had planned for some of his professors might
just as well take place. We had just settled down to dinner when
machine gun bullets crashed against the roof, a mortar exploded
nearby, the plaster fell from the walls, and the electric lights
went out. We dived under the table and spent the rest of the
night on the floor.

On the following day it was officially announced that there
would be no more fighting during the day, because "fighting interferes with the peaceful occupations of the people." Large
posters announced that there would be a curfew each evening,
and everyone walking in the streets after the curfew would be
shot. Unhappily there was no precise definition of the word
"evening." We spent the afternoon with Wen Yi-tuo, and sud-

denly realized that evening was coming down. Rose was quite sure the curfew began at nightfall. In the dusk we walked through the deserted streets skirting the lake, aware of the strangeness of this embattled city which seemed to have altered its shape since the fighting began. We could hear machine guns in the distance. We were close to the West Gate, and therefore near home, when a soldier sprang out of nowhere and pressed the barrel of a tommy gun into my stomach. Rose, who was making a profession of saving my life, now saved it again. Something about the appearance of the soldier suggested that he was Huna-nese, and she cursed him fluently in his own dialect. Slowly the barrel of the tommy gun was lowered, while he looked in amazement at the woman who came from his own province. "Is this man a foreigner?" the soldier said. "Yes, and I am married to him," Rose answered, and the soldier shivered with fear, ex-plaining that the Fifth Army had received orders that if they killed any foreigners, then they and their whole families, from the oldest grandfather to the youngest child, would be shot. I said: "It is impossible," and Rose said: "I know Chiang Kai-shek, and even this is possible."

I thought Rose would be elated by her brush with danger, but she collapsed when we reached the house of the vodka manu-facturer. She threw herself on the bed, sobbing, her face white with terror. Less than an hour before, she had been talking gaily with Wen Yi-tuo, discussing the day when we would all be re-turning to Peking. "You do not know how close it was," she moaned. Something snapped in her, and she began to scream. Shelestian came hurrying up the stairs. "What's the matter with her?" he said, and I told him how she had just saved my life. He shook his head sadly from side to side. "I never could understand the Chinese," he said, and went slowly down the stairs to return a few moments later with a jug of vodka. "Tell her to drink it," he said. "It will send her to sleep."

The next day most of the fighting was in the south of the city. The two armies had set up roadblocks along the road out-side the city walls, and the only way to reach the university was through the city. The streets were ominously empty, and if I had been sensible I would have run back to the vodka manufac-turer's house. Machine-gun posts had been erected in the Street of the Forest of Learning, and as I walked along, the barrels turned toward me with a kind of slow and careful precision now familiar to me, because exactly the same thing had happened on a moonlit night in Chungking. My chief feeling was anger at the stupidity of the fighting, but I was also aware of the presence of the Green Dragon. I walked very slowly, as though in a dream, oppressed by a curious heaviness in the air, although it was a cloudless day and the wind was blowing. I passed the lake, where machine-gunners were still firing at the yellow palace, but none of the soldiers paid any attention to me. It was as though I wore a mantle of invisibility. At last I came to the converted theater near the North Gate. As I walked into the theater Professor Wu Mi, the most garrulous and kindly of all the professors in the English Department, shot out of his little cubicle under the stairs and stopped dead in his tracks. "Where have you come from?" he asked. "Don't you know no one is allowed on the streets?"

The fighting came to an end, but the mopping-up campaign continued for many weeks. The governor, Lung Yun, flew to Chungking to make his peace with the Generalissimo and was given a free pardon. The officers and soldiers of the Yunnanese provincial army were less lucky: they were rounded up and shot. One day, two weeks after the fighting had officially ended, I took a short cut from the West Gate through a pine grove. An officer of the Yunnanese army was being marched out under guard, his hands tied behind his back with a thin piece of string. He had the pallor of death, his eyes were glazed, and he was walking remarkably fast. I leaned against a pine tree, sick with fear. A few minutes later there came from the direction of the burial mounds near the university the crackle of rifle shots. There was a long pause, and then the final shot. China was running with blood, and there was no end to it.

The vodka manufacturer's house was kept remarkably clean, but recently there had been an invasion of rats. In the days following the fighting we had trapped and killed all of them, but for some strange reason neither Rose nor I could bring ourselves to kill a silver gray baby rat which had somehow escaped the general massacre. We knew we would have to kill it in the end, but we were tired of killing. There was something extraordinarily appealing about its bright glittering eyes, the delicate fur and the white claws. We were delighted when the little silver head peered out inquiringly from a hole in the wall. A few days later we both complained of headaches, parched throats, extreme lassitude. I lay in bed, fighting off the grinding headaches, sometimes talking incoherently. In three days Rose shook off her lassitude and recovered sufficiently to send for Mary, who bundled me into a ricksha and carried me off to the hospital.

"It's typhus," the doctor said. "I suppose you got it from the rats." And then to Mary: "We'll put him in the isolation ward, but there's not much hope."

THE MURDERS

I lay in a small hospital room in Kunming as though removed from the world, without any desire to live or not to live, scarcely knowing what was happening around me, caught up in a mysterious enchantment. It was, I knew, the enchantment of dying, but this knowledge merely hovered on the edge of consciousness. There was no fear, no pain, no feeling. The poisons circulating through the body seemed to ebb and flow like the waves of the sea, as soft as silk and scarcely more discernible than a mist rising from the sea in the evening. The nurse came and went, the hours passed, dusk gave way to night, the morning came, and there was no sense of time passing.

I spent the days gazing at a plum tree outside the window until I knew every twig and blossom, every curve of every branch, as intimately as I had known a woman. Almost there was no room, no bed, no sky: there was only the flowering tree. I gazed at it for hours, marveling, yet it was not quite marveling, because there was no sense of wonder. The tree was there, very quiet, waving a little in the wind, and it was enough that it was there; and when it vanished at night, this was also enough. During the day everything glowed, and all colors were a little brighter than in ordinary life. At night the shadows glowed, and the eyes of innumerable cats peered through the darkness.

By day there were waking dreams. The spaces between the branches of the plum tree became steppingstones and then a glacier and then a steep snow-covered hill, and people were racing down the hill on skis, and soon the hill became a mountain, all white and glistening with snow, and the skiers were coming down the slopes in brightly colored clothes. Another moment, and the clothes fell away: they were all naked, glowing with health and energy. Then the dusk came again, and there were no more skiers on the mountain.

The doctor came with an enormous hypodermic syringe such

as a clown might use in a comedy played on a stage. The needle went into my arm, and the bright yellow liquid in the syringe went coursing through my veins, then broke through my flesh in the form of sweat. This was uncomfortable, for the doctor had not explained that the bright yellow liquid was boiling hot. During the night all the liquid in my body poured out, and in the morning there was only a dry feverish husk gazing at the plum tree. In the morning the nurse came with three bottles of milk and brooded over me until I had drunk the last drop.

Rose came and looked at me accusingly. She was very pale, very beautiful, very remote. She nodded when the doctor said: "*Bu hao!* It is not good." I said: "I am dying, but it is all right." I was glad when she was gone, because I could then look at the plum tree and see the gaily colored procession of skiers coming down the mountain. Mary came. She was less disapproving, and once she smiled out of pity: the skiers poured out of her teeth and waved to me. An American priest came and recited the Lord's prayer in a voice like thunder, while I wondered how long I would have to endure his presence. Hopefully I would die soon, for his voice gave me an excruciating headache. "Say after me—" he shouted, and recited the Lord's prayer all over again. I remained silent, gazing at the plum tree.

This was the day of the crisis, when the temperature soared and there was almost no pulse. Strangely, I remember that day as one of uncontrollable excitement, the heart beating wildly and exultantly, and I have no memory of a soaring temperature. Afterward there came the slow quiet days of convalescence, the liquefaction of the blood. Colors glowed more brightly than they ever glowed before. A red counterpane, a blue scarf, a bunch of flowers glowed with unparalleled splendor. For a week the world consisted of richly glowing colors. Since then I have always envied people recovering from typhus.

Rose brought me back to the vodka factory in a jeep borrowed from an American colonel. The vodka manufacturer professed to be delirious with joy at my recovery and ordered a sumptuous banquet. Pheasant and roast suckling pig were served, while I watched as though from an infinite distance. Recovery from typhus is a slow process, for the body remains weak and the mind uncomprehending. I enjoyed the golden color of the suckling pig and the green apple in its mouth, and most of all I enjoyed the colors of the faces around the table.

I asked Rose what had happened to the baby rat with the silvery white fur. I learned that it had been killed, and I was sorry.

At one end of the courtyard there was a rock garden about twenty feet high, a tumble of rocks deliberately and carefully built up by the previous owner of the house with wisteria and plum trees planted on it. The planting of the trees was apparently an afterthought. Now, as I gazed at the blossoms, their colors appeared to stream across the courtyard in a steady flow, inexhaustibly brilliant, the reds especially rich and delicate, glowing like red coals. Something of the same thing had happened in the hospital, but now the colors came in massed regiments, blazing as no colors had blazed before. The phenomenon lasted about two weeks. Gradually, as I recovered my strength, the flowers glowed less brilliantly.

From the university came scrolls and small presents to celebrate my recovery. From Wen Yi-tuo came a small seal made of orange stone about an inch high with my Chinese name carved on it and a small lion on top, and the old seal was henceforth abandoned. He was a great carver of seals, and the intricate design carved on the seal was both strong and exceedingly graceful. Better still, he came to dinner one evening with Chiang Shih-ro, and since they were the two people I admired most in the university I thought this was the best present of all. Rose put on her richest brocade gown, red candles were set on the table, the poet and the political scientist talked about Peking, where we would soon be returning, and I wondered how one could possibly be happier, the wars over and the long years of peace lying ahead.

Wen Yi-tuo was saying: "Of course in Peking everything will be much better. There will be real classrooms, not cattle sheds. There will be real dormitories for the students, and better food, and we shall have proper textbooks and our own printing press. Soon we shall be producing real paper, not the miserable stuff we make now. You will have a house on the campus of Tsinghua University—"

On and on he went, describing the new world that would open out for the university once we had all reached Peking. He described our house on the campus with the flaring roof, the red columns, the large study and living room, and my mouth watered, until Rose objected that we already had a house in Peking so large that it could comfortably lodge half the professors at the university. I had never quite believed in her palace in Peking. Now that the war was over, she spoke about it more often and with greater assurance, so that I began to believe that it really existed. Within a few months or weeks the whole university would be making its way to Peking.

"It will probably be months rather than weeks," Wen Yi-tuo said. "The government does not like us and is not doing very much to help us to go there."

I had known for some time that the university was not very popular with the Kuomintang government. The students were clamoring for an end to the civil war which had already broken out between the Kuomintang and the Communists, and they were clamoring even more loudly against the inflation and the corruption in the government. What they wanted was a government of the talents, and they distrusted the Communists as much as they distrusted the Kuomintang. We were still talking about the students and the government when, around nine o'clock, we heard a burst of gunfire coming from the direction of the university. There followed two more short bursts of small arms fire, and then there was silence.

Our first thought was that some drunken soldiers were fighting among themselves, and then that the civil war between the Kuomintang and the local Yunnanese army had broken out again. According to Chiang Shih-ro there had been rumors all week that the Kuomintang garrison commander intended to punish the university. What did they mean by punishment?

"I suppose," said Wen Yi-tuo, "they would like to kill us."

He said this very softly.

"Of course it is quite senseless, like so many other things they do," he went on. "If they kill us, it makes no difference. For every dead professor or dead student, there will be twenty others to take his place. Probably just now they were shooting at the university."

"Deliberately?"

"Yes, deliberately."

"Why? What do they gain by it?"

"They gain nothing, but they do it all the same."

It was the first time anyone had spoken of killing professors or students.

Wen Yi-tuo's instinct was to run to the university and to find out what had happened. Rose urged him to stay the night, but he had a wife and children at home and they would be worried if he did not return. On the other hand, if the military were determined to strike at the university and arrest the leading professors, then it was likely that they had already sent out soldiers to arrest him, and Chiang Shih-ro was in the same danger. So we talked and debated, while the night grew darker and more silent. There had been only three short bursts of gunfire. During the days of our local civil war there had been prolonged bursts of gunfire all day and all night, but this time the outlook seemed even more ominous.

The red candles were flickering and Rose was smiling her most enchanted smile as she hovered over us, pressing more delicacies upon us, saying little, hoping the two professors would stay a little longer, because it was unbearably painful to think of them wandering through the dark streets. Yet they were determined to leave, and it was merely a question of choosing a proper time, in the Chinese manner. At last they stood up, bowed to Rose, complimented her on her cooking, and left. I accompanied them to the corner of the street with three candles in a candelabra. There were a few rickshas about, but they decided to go on foot, taking short cuts.

"You don't have to worry," Wen Yi-tuo said. "We'll get home without being seen."

I was not so hopeful, for it seemed to me that on the very blackest night Wen Yi-tuo could be seen clearly a mile away. He was one of those people who are not overlooked.

We did not sleep that night. Those bursts of gunfire could so easily be explained away, but we did not pretend there were any easy explanations. If some soldiers had shot at the students, then the consequences would be calamitous for the university, but if the soldiers came deliberately, under orders from the Kuomintang generals in Kunming, then the consequences would be calamitous for China, for the students all over China would find themselves in opposition to the government.

The next morning we learned that a mass meeting was being

held on the campus at the time when the shooting broke out. The mass meeting had been arranged by the students, who invited professors of all shades of political opinion to address them. There was nothing in the least subversive about the meeting: the entire spectrum of Chinese political thinking was being presented to students who sat on the grass. Suddenly there was a long sustained burst of machine-gun fire directed over the heads of the students, and some of the bullets clattered onto the corrugated iron roof of the library. The speeches went on, the professors refusing to be intimidated. The microphone went dead, the lamps on the platform went out, and a megaphone from somewhere in the darkness was heard commanding the students to disperse "in the name of the military authorities." Student marshals told the students to stay where they were.

"That was the worst of it," said the student who came to visit us the next morning. "The shooting over our heads was bad enough, but to be ordered to disperse like cattle was quite intolerable. We stayed right where we were."

Dr. Fei Shao-tung, an internationally known sociologist, mounted the platform and began to talk about the civil war. Immediately the machine guns fired again, but this time the angle of fire was considerably lower and the students ducked their heads. "My words must be heard above the sound of the bullets!" the professor shouted. The students cheered, a trench mortar went off somewhere in the mysterious darkness where the soldiers lay concealed, and at this moment someone found an acetylene lamp and carried it up to the platform. "Disperse at once in the name of the military authorities!" came the voice from the megaphone, and then there came a clatter of rifle shots, very brief, as though the soldiers were firing out of habit and no longer had any purpose except to keep themselves awake by firing joy shots. The professor finished his speech, and another mounted the platform to bring the meeting to a conclusion. The students dispersed, pouring out of the main gate or going to their dormitories. Bully boys waylaid them, and there were some small fights. One student was stabbed in the chest and another had his leg broken, and then the bully boys vanished in the darkness.

"If the military governor thinks he can silence us, he is terribly mistaken," the student said. "Now we are on strike, and the military governor says he will use every means open to him to suppress the strike!"

"How?"

"He can try to terrify us, but we cannot be terrified," the student said. "How can you terrify the greatest university in China?"

In the following days the students issued manifestoes, held mass meetings, demanded to see the governor, and set up four or five separate command posts, so that if one group of student leaders was arrested, others would take their place. They were absolutely determined to be heard, and inevitably the issues widened. In theory, everyone in China had the right to freedom of speech and freedom of assembly, and the Republic of China was a democracy ruled by elected officials. In theory, too, no civil war was being fought between the Kuomintang and the Chinese Communists. In fact the Kuomintang government exercised a military dictatorship, and the students wanted a representative government. Above all, they wanted to be heard and the attempt to silence them showed that the government was determined to suppress them. For the first time the government was using naked force against them.

As the days passed, it became clear that the students and the government had embarked on a collision course. Real power was invested in General Kuan Lin-seng, the military governor, who represented the government, and there was nothing to prevent him from suppressing the university. He could send his soldiers into the campus, burn the cattle sheds, the dormitories and the library, herd the students into internment camps, order the professors to leave Kunming, and that would be the end of the university. There was some evidence to show that he intended to do this, but for various reasons the plan was abandoned. Instead he sent armed soldiers into all the colleges and universities in the city "in order to inspire the students with a proper respect for authority." Furniture was smashed, students were clubbed and arrested, professors were threatened, chemistry laboratories were shot up, and books in foreign languages were removed from the library shelves so that they could be examined by the appropriate authorities to see whether they contained subversive thoughts. In this way many books on chemistry and physics were lost.

The armed bands invaded the Teachers Training College on the morning of December 1 and reduced it to a shambles, gutting the rooms and clubbing the students. One of the soldiers hurled a hand grenade, which killed three students. They went on to Yunnan University, and the process was repeated. High schools were also attacked. Finally, the soldiers came to Lienta University and tried to break down the gates, which were defended by students armed with staves. If they had wanted to, the soldiers could have simply climbed over the walls, but for some reason they had decided to congregate around the gate. Someone with a megaphone ordered the students to surrender, as though they were an enemy army. Suddenly four hand grenades were lobbed over the walls, but by good fortune only one of them exploded and only one student was killed. There was a howl of rage from the students, and it looked as though they were about to open the gates and attack the soldiers with staves and bare fists. At this moment a staff car from the local garrison headquarters came down the road and the attack on the university was called off by an officer who immediately sped away. The soldiers retired, and the students rushed the body of the dead student to the nearest hospital, in the belief that there was still some life in him. There were four dead students, about fifty in the hospital, and about two hundred in prison.

On the evening of December 1 it was beginning to look as though the students had been cowed into silence. The students who came to the house looked drained of emotion, exhausted by their long night vigils, almost hysterical with grief. None of the four dead students were studying at the university—three came from the Teachers Training College and the boy who had been killed inside our campus turned out to be a high school student who was visiting his brother—but the university was the rallying point. The government could destroy an obscure Teachers Training College with impunity; it could not so easily destroy a great university unless the students permitted it to be destroyed. There were signs on the following day that the students, far from being cowed, were determined to see that the military governor was punished and that his soldiers would never again dare to attack the university.

I walked to the university. It was one of those days when the skies are high and the air glitters like crystal. The grass on the campus had never looked greener, and the white cattle sheds sparkled frostily, as though they had been hosed down with ice water. Blue-gowned students were milling about. At first I thought nothing had changed, but everything had changed. On every blue gown there was a black armband; in every cattle shed students were writing posters or feeding mimeograph machines or delivering speeches or engaged in earnest discussion with the professors. The Kuomintang flag over the library was at half-mast, and there was an arch of evergreens over the doorway. Inside the library the bodies of the four dead students lay on camp beds festooned with flowers.

There is a general law that if soldiers fire at students they will inevitably kill the least rebellious, the most devoted, the ones who will be most useful to their country. Later, when I was able to compile short biographies of the dead students, I found that three of the dead students were strangely alike, being quiet, studious, handsome, and above average in intelligence. Though they did not know each other, they would have liked each other. Two came from prominent families, two from poor families. Pan Yen, the girl student, was brought up in luxury, but when the war came she escaped from her home and after some schooling joined the army. Yu Tsai, the son of a wealthy Shanghai businessman, made his way to Chungking and joined the army, went back to school, discovered a talent for music, and he was teaching music in a middle school when he was killed. One of his friends said: "He often wept over the fate of China. He praised the passionate spirit of Beethoven and deeply regretted the silence of Goethe." Li Liu-lien was the only son of a poor peasant, and proud of being in a teachers training college. Hsun Chi-chung, the last of the victims, was only seventeen. Very little was known about him except that he resembled any good student anywhere. He had lived too short a life to make very much impression on his friends.

So they lay there in the library, their faces very white, brown blankets drawn up to their waists, their names painted on scrolls, and there were blown-up photographs of them nearby. Though they had names, they had the anonymity of death: they were simply four students whom death had chosen at random. The girl was beautiful, and there was the hint of a smile in the shape of her lips. The smoke from the huge red candles dipped down and hung over the bodies. The students who gathered in front of the camp beds were so ominously quiet that I began to fear they would tear everything apart in their rage against the authorities. The Chungking newspapers published only a brief dispatch about the murders, describing it as a "regrettable incident" and adding that the culprits would surely be apprehended.

Wen Yi-tuo came to the library, looked at the camp beds, and said quietly: "They know very well what they are doing. They will never apprehend the culprits, because they are in the government."

I walked home with him. He was icy calm, with a curious metallic edge to his voice. He said: "If we don't protest, then we are not worthy of being Chinese." When I asked him whether he thought the Generalissimo was responsible, he answered: "People very close to him are responsible. The military governor would never have dared to do this on his own responsibility. One thing is certain—we have come to the turning point. Never again will the students trust the Kuomintang government. We have come to the end of the road!"

"What happens at the end of the road?"

"I don't know. No one knows. The government is so corrupt that it has become unendurable. There is no hope for China unless we get rid of this government."

The students were insisting that the military governor should come to the library and bow to the dead students. They demanded the right to hold a funeral procession through the streets of Kunming. They demanded that the murderers face trial in open court. The military governor rejected all these demands, and when the students went on to demand his immediate resignation, he announced that he had not the slightest intention of submitting to them.

The deadlock continued, with no way out. I thought it would be interesting to meet the military governor and see whether he could not be terrified into sanity. Robert Winter agreed to come with me, and Rose offered to act as interpreter. We sent a message to the general, saying that we would like to see him and he answered that he was quite prepared to meet us for five minutes. We worked out a scenario. If possible, we would arrive at the heavily defended headquarters in a British jeep, with a Union Jack flying, and with someone in uniform armed to the hilt. I went to the British consulate and asked an official for a jeep, a flag and a soldier. He turned bright purple, chewed on his mustache, wrung his hands, and had an apoplectic fit. When he recovered, he said he would telegraph immediately to the ambassador to urge that I should be expelled from China. So we marched up the street and went to the American consulate, where we were greeted more tenderly. A jeep? Of course. An American flag? Nothing was simpler. A Marine would drive the jeep, and another would keep him company. Arrayed in the proper panoply, we drove up to the military governor's headquarters on the edge of the lake.

It was one of those bright mornings in Kunming when the sky seems to be singing. All the trees were in flower, and the lake with its marble camel-back bridges gleamed like frost. The military governor's headquarters was a small palace ringed with barbed wire. The general had been watching our progress from an upper balcony, and he was visibly startled. The flag whipping in the wind was as large as a bedsheet, and the sun glinted off the helmets of the two marines.

A discussion with a Chinese general about the murders he has committed may be expected to follow an unpredictable course. General Kuan Lin-seng was a heavy-set man with thick black eyebrows and the expression of an unusually pugnacious bulldog. It was unlikely that he had ever met any foreigners before, and it was obvious that he was ill-at-ease. Green tea was served while he made a little speech of welcome, and when some officers entered the room, he said gruffly: "Go away. Can't you see I am talking with foreigners?"

At his orders the morning newspaper had contained a long article about the students written by his chief-of-staff. This was military journalism with a vengeance. According to the article there was a secret transmitter in the student dormitories broadcasting to Yenan, the capital of the Chinese Communists. The university was a hotbed of Communist activity. Happily the Kuomintang authorities had their own agents in the university, and they knew where the student ringleaders were to be found and where they concealed their stores of ammunition. Yenan radio had issued instructions to the students to attack public buildings, murder foreigners and create a reign of terror.

It was one of those articles which could only have been written by a military officer who knew nothing about the lives of the students and professors, and cared less. There was no explanation of the murder of the students.

Robert Winter said that to his knowledge the entire article was untrue, there were no Communists in the university, there was no secret transmitter, and no one in the university possessed a radio set except himself. The general smiled indulgently, and said he knew better. Asked to produce the transmitter, he said it had not yet been found. "Everyone knows the university is full of Communists," he said. Robert Winter said curtly: "If you kill any more students, you will certainly create Communists." The general said he was sorry that we did not understand the problem.

He had the look of a man who was supremely content with himself, who had dutifully examined the situation, and had come to the inevitable conclusions. He pointed to the three telephones on his table, and said: "I receive instructions from the Generalissimo three times a day."

"Do you report to him?"

"Yes, of course I report to him."

"Did you tell him everything that has happened?"

"Yes."

"Did you tell the Generalissimo that the girl student Pan Yen, after being cut down with a hand grenade, was repeatedly stabbed in the breast and stomach with a bayonet and then jumped upon?"

"No, I did not tell him that."

"Did you tell him that the names of the soldiers who killed the students are known?"

"No."

"Did you tell him that the students have asked you to bow before the bodies and that you have refused?"

"That is unimportant, because it concerns only my relations with the students."

"Your relations with the students are very important, because they believe you gave the order to kill them."

I think the general was bemused by our arguments and questions, just as we were bemused by his answers and especially by his belief that he was dealing with powerful revolutionary forces in the university and the Teachers Training College. He did not really know what had happened. He was plagued by administrative difficulties, for though he had his own secret agents he had no control over the secret police of the civil governor. A third group of secret police, sent down from the Generalissimo's office, was also operating in the area. Quite obviously the murders were committed by one of these secret police groups, but which one?

Up to this time Rose had been acting as the demure translator, but now quite suddenly she began to cross-examine the general on her own, demanding clear answers to clear questions. Where was he when the murders were committed? When did he hear about them? What orders had he given? How was it that he knew about the secret radio transmitter and had not been able to unearth it? Why was he so certain in the teeth of all the evidence that the university was a hotbed of Communists? Why had he given his seal of approval to the newspaper article when he must have known it was untrue? She leaned forward, cupping her chin in her hand, smiling enchantingly as she asked one deadly question after another. She refused to believe that there were three independent secret police groups: there was only one, and he commanded it, and knew all about it, and was therefore responsible.

"Yes, I am responsible," he said, and scarcely knew what he was saying.

"Responsible for the deaths of the students?"

"Yes."

"Then you should resign—it is altogether too shameful! How can a man live and bear the weight of this responsibility?"

He looked hurt and miserable, for she had wounded him in a place where he could not defend himself. He was responsible for law and order, and must suffer the penalties when law and order are disturbed. In the Chinese fashion, she was turning the tables on him by invoking the idea of "shame." His hands moved restlessly, the sweat pricked up on his forehead, and the bulldog eyes were no longer regarding her steadily. Like a conqueror demanding the utmost submission from the defeated, she repeated the word "shame" until he cried out: "I am not the only one! Everyone blames me, but there are others! No one knows the terrible position I am in!" Then we knew what we wanted to know.

Rose's performance staggered us, for we thought we had gone to the limits of permissible utterance, but she went further. She said things that no one else would have dared to say. It was not enough that he should confess his guilt. She demanded that he expiate his crimes. He listened abjectly while she listed on her fingers the things he would have to do. He must bow before the bodies of the dead students, he must pay an indemnity to their families, he must permit the funeral procession to pass through the streets of Kunming, he must provide an honor guard, and guarantee that none of his soldiers or secret police should be on the streets except for the honor guard, and this was only the beginning, for she went on to demand that he should resign before he could do any more harm. He agreed to all her demands, except the last. Then we left him and drove to the university to report that we had bearded the lion in his den and found him craven like all murderers when they are found out.

Two days later the general came secretly to the campus and bowed to the dead students as they lay in sealed coffins. It was a peculiarly Chinese ritual, and it had the merit of helping to heal the wounds. For some reason the students decided that the bodies should be buried near the library in a marble tomb with a long inscription describing how they had come to their deaths, and many weeks passed before the tomb was completed. When the funeral procession passed at last through the streets of Kunming, General Kuan Lin-seng had been given another command.

Meanwhile the university authorities had decided to keep the students in Kunming through the winter. The great exodus to the north would begin in the spring, and Lienta, the United Universities, would become the separate universities of Peking, Tsinghua and Nankai. In the cattle sheds classes continued, but with a decreasing momentum. I gave lectures on Shakespeare, corrected the students' essays, finished a translation of Shen Tseng-wen's short stories and worked on *The White Pony*, but there was always the sense of living in an enchanted dream world that would soon come to an end. Soon the cattle sheds would be making their way to the north.

In Kunming the lakes were as serene as ever, and the cobbled streets as beautiful as ever, but the city was visibly changing. The Americans were pulling out from the air force base, the government offices were closing. Already Kunming seemed to be shrinking. Soon it would become nothing more than a dusty provincial capital forgotten by the outside world, ruled by an obscure warlord, with grass growing between the cobblestones. We wondered what would happen to the vast airfield on the edge of the lake when the last American airman had left. We wondered, too, what would happen to our campus built on a graveyard, and we hoped it would become an orchard or a rice field, and we knew that in a few months or years not a trace of it would remain.

THE PALACE IN PEKING

Rose had talked so often about her palace in Peking that I felt that I knew it by heart and could walk through it blindfold. I knew that it was enormous and splendid, with endless courtyards opening into one another, with huge marble lions guarding the ornamental gateway, and with ceremonial halls shaded by wisteria trees and moon gates opening into wild gardens of summer flowers. It was called the Palace of the Iron-capped Prince after one of the sons of the Emperor Ch'ien Lung who had distinguished himself in warfare, and it stood on one of those dusty, quiet, tree-shaded streets southwest of the Forbidden City. Someone had once counted the rooms, and there were two hundred and forty.

Those two hundred and forty rooms haunted us when we were living in Chungking and Kunming, where it was sometimes impossible to find any room at all, or at the very best there would be a small rat-infested bedroom in an inn. The palace took on the character of dreams; it was not something one could readily believe in. Like a mirage, it was all the more beautiful because it was unattainable, far away, and perhaps no more substantial than the air. The T'ang poet Li Ho used to dream of ruined palaces after the barbarian invasions, and as he wandered through them at night he would pick up a jade ring, or the bone handle of a fan, all that was left of some vast and sumptuous palace which the barbarians had put to the flames. Sometimes I wondered whether the palace would survive the wars, and it seemed perfectly possible that there would be nothing left of it by the time we reached Peking. It was beyond belief that I would ever live in it.

The difficulty of course was to get there, for Kunming was over twelve hundred miles from Peking as the crow flies and probably twice as far if one traveled by river or by road. Some of the students were already planning to go on foot, while others were preparing to take the roundabout route through Haiphong, then taking ship to Tientsin, which was a little like traveling to the United States by way of Cape Horn. Still others planned to drive to the north in trucks, knowing that the roads were infested by bandits and that they might lose their trucks. Rose decided that the best plan was to go to Chungking by air. From Chungking we would sail down the Yangtze to Shanghai and then take a coastal steamer to Tientsin, or if our luck held, we would fly straight to Peking. Seats on the airplane to Chungking were always hard to get, for they were booked for months ahead.

There was nothing more unpredictable than the Chinese air line. You might reserve tickets two months ahead, and then find that the seats had been commandeered by some government official. This time we were told we could have two seats the following day and there was no likelihood of any more seats for many long weeks. We took the seats, and were sorry. The air between Kunming and Chungking was full of air pockets, the plane floundered through three separate storms, and Chinese generals in full regalia lay on the floor in their ruined uniforms, gasping out their lives and praying fervently to whatever gods they still believed in. Rose, who had no liking for Chinese generals, watched with amused detachment, and if a general rolled too close, she kicked him away gently with her feet.

When I first came to China, Chungking was a ruined, battered, smoke-blackened city shrouded in clammy mists, and seemed to have been erected on a high cliff for no other purpose than to break men's hearts. Now, five years later, it was beginning to look a little like a modern city with four-story buildings, sidewalks, and leveled roads. The telegraph wires were no longer looped and festooned around the telegraph posts; the cinemas and the ice cream shops were doing a roaring business; the buses belching black smoke were no longer tied together with pieces of string. The most notable change had taken place at the Wang Lung Men steps. In the early days these steps were always being carved out afresh with axes; now there was a giant stairway of reinforced concrete glittering in the sun, so new, so polished, so ugly, that it took the breath away.

The new capital of China was Nanking, and now half the

government was there, while the other half remained in Chung-king. The embassies were filled with packing cases, waiting for ships to take them down the Yangtze. Soon Szechuan would become a remote landlocked province far in the interior, forgotten by the rest of the world.

Marshal Feng Yu-hsiang was living in a farmhouse four or five miles from Chungking. The rice was under water, the fields flashed silver, the sun shone. The air was quiveringly alive with birdsong, and Szechuan had never looked lovelier nor more peaceful. He stood outside the farmhouse, wearing the costume of the local peasants, barefoot, with an enormous straw hat on his head and a broom in his hand. He looked like a jovial old peasant, but he was deadly serious. That morning he had received a telegram from the Generalissimo, ordering him to come at once to Nanking.

"I sent him a telegram saying I am ill," he laughed. "What can a man do in Nanking among all those bureaucrats? Besides, it is true that I am ill—ill for China! They are lunatics on both sides, and all they want to do is fight wars. What is the matter with them? We have been fighting each other since 1911, and it is time we stopped."

I asked him what he really intended to do about the Generalissimo's telegram. Would he go to Nanking?

"I shall wait until I have recovered from my illness," he replied, the powerful voice rolling across the fields. "At the moment I am very close to death and my recovery will take a long time."

"How long?"

"Two or three months at least."

He made a croaking sound like a man dying, threw off the enormous straw hat, and stood bareheaded in the sunshine, grinning from ear to ear. He had been working hard in the fields, and his clothes stuck to his skin and his head was shaved smooth, so that he looked like a Tartar chieftain incongruously disguised as a Chinese peasant. He had just written an article calling upon the Kuomintang and the Chinese Communists to come to an agreement and to stop behaving like lunatics. The article would please neither Chiang Kai-shek nor Mao Tse-tung, and he was well aware that by writing it he had weakened his own position as a possible intermediary between them. Though he laughed, he was angry.

"Who do they think they are?" he growled. "They want power. Haven't they had enough? They don't care if another million or another ten million Chinese die, so long as they keep their power. They think they are gods!"

He asked about the students killed in Kunming and said: "It is very simple. The government wanted to terrorize the students into obedience, and they forgot that it is very difficult to terrorize students. It was a calculated act, and this is the government we have to live under."

I asked what the alternatives were, and he answered: "A coalition government. There is nothing else. The Kuomintang must have its teeth pulled, and the Chinese Communists, too. We cannot have two lords of creation."

I went to see him again a few days later, toward evening. He had arranged the farmhouse so that it was like a studio, with a long table for his scrolls and paintbrushes, and when I entered the house he was busily writing a scroll with his spectacles on the end of his nose. The huge wet brush was forming characters a foot high, and I could smell the ink from the doorway. All the time he was humming to himself. Once he looked up, smiled, said: "I am still dying," and resumed painting. On the previous visit I had seen no guards at all, but this time there were at least ten, and they were armed to the hilt.

There was reason for these guards: a surprisingly large number of people opposed to the government and the continuation of the war against the Chinese Communists had recently vanished or been killed. Though he bore the title of Vice-Generalissimo, he was perfectly aware that the title was empty of meaning and his powers were minimal. If he was shot, the government would no doubt blame the Chinese Communists or say it was an accident. He was determined not to be killed and he was determined to use whatever power of persuasion he still possessed. At last he put down the huge brush and read out the scroll: "Let there be peace, only peace, only peace, among the people of China."

"Do you like it?" he asked.

"Yes, very much."

"Then you shall have it."

When the ink was dry, he folded the scroll carefully, saying there was an art in folding scrolls just as there was an art in painting them.

For the first time he looked gloomy, weighed down by an obsessive belief that war was about to break out again in China. He had little hope in General Marshall's efforts to bring peace to the two opposing camps. Chiang Kai-shek and Mao Tse-tung were both in their different ways hoodwinking the Americans, each striving for strategic and political advantages. "General Marshall does not know our passion for intrigue," he said, "but he will learn in time." During the whole evening he only laughed once, and that was when I conveyed Rose's invitation to him to stay in her palace when he visited Peking.

"What should I do in a palace?" he exclaimed. "When I was master of Peking, I threw the young Emperor out of the Imperial City, and I lived in a small bare room with a chair, a table and a bed. What is a palace? A place where you can order servants around and live in luxury, while the rest of China is starving. Do you know what is happening now in Hunan? The peasants are starving and eating the bark off the trees!" And then, seeing that I was obviously hurt, he relented. "Of course I will stay," he said, "but you must give me a small bare room somewhere in the back where no one will pay any attention to me." And then he laughed again, because he well knew that it was unlikely that he would pass unobserved even in Peking.

On the following day I went to see General Marshall, who had just returned from the United States. He was living in T. V. Soong's palatial house, where he seemed completely out of place, for the thick rugs, the overstuffed furniture, and the garish Chinese paintings provided a strange background for a soldier, who was lean as a sword. An extraordinary aura of triumph surrounded him. He was the artificer of victory, and he seemed to move in a world where only victory was possible. He was taller than I expected, the chin firmer, the eyes clearer; his uniform was immaculate, his manners courtly. Rose came with me, and he bowed gravely over her hand. Then, as though to remove himself as far as possible from the sofas and the paintings on the walls, he set three chairs close together in the middle of the room. We talked about the murder of the students in Kunming, the secret police, and Feng Yu-hsiang's fear that the Kuomintang and the Chinese Communists were determined upon an all-out war. He spoke about "the circle around the Generalissimo" with a kind of muted bitterness, the word "circle" emerging from his lips like a steel shaving, and there was even a kind of irony in his pronunciation of "Generalissimo." He had read full reports of the murder of the students, and he knew the powers of the secret police. "I think all the time of the young," he said. "What I am trying to do concerns less the political leaders of the country than the young people of China."

About the truce teams which were attempting to mediate between the Kuomintang and Chinese Communist armies, he said they were admittedly experimental and some other techniques might have to be invented. He knew the risks involved. "If two people are grappling for each others' throats," he said, "then the man who tries to separate them may be set upon by both of them." On this subject he spoke with authority. By this time the number of violations of the truce was in the region of three hundred, which meant that there had been three hundred pitched battles and skirmishes, and countless lives had been lost, at a time when the Kuomintang and the Chinese Communists were theoretically at peace. What would happen if they declared war?

"I hear that the Chinese Communists are well-trained—on the whole better trained than the Kuomintang troops," he said, and then paused abruptly, staring straight ahead, while an extraordinary look of power and authority appeared on his face, and at the same time one immensely long arm rose high in the air, the fingers outspread. For a moment I thought he had gone mad, or perhaps I had gone mad, for he was behaving completely out of character, the face frozen in a mask of authority, the hand shaking violently, as though waving someone away. Suddenly he had become a statue.

I turned to Rose, but she was smiling blissfully. She was wearing her white gown bordered with a thin hem of blue and red ribbons, and as usual she was wearing her diamond, as large as a thrush's egg. Then I realized that she was looking toward the door. I turned and saw a bowlegged Chinese general vanishing down a corridor.

"Who was it?" General Marshall asked, the voice edged with anger.

"It was General Yu Ta-wei," Rose answered serenely. "At least I think it was." And then she added in an even softer voice, "All our generals look alike."

The ice had melted; the look of frozen authority gave way to a grave and courtly smile, while General Marshall turned to her and said: "Sometimes I think our own generals look alike."

The sudden stiffening, the frozen mask, the swift stretching of the hand into the air haunted me during the rest of the interview with General Marshall. It was as though Caesar had suddenly appeared in a room in Chungking. With an imperial gesture he had sent the little general scuttling away, and the fact that it was General Yu Ta-wei, the minister of munitions and therefore the reputed owner of one of the greatest fortunes ever accumulated in China, only added to Rose's pleasure.

Quite clearly the Chinese general had been eavesdropping, and just as clearly General Marshall was alarmed by the failure of his security precautions. Accordingly, the Chinese general was punished by being made to wait an extra quarter of an hour for his interview with General Marshall, while Rose chattered about her life in America and they both chattered about Peking. General Marshall had once served a term of duty in Tientsin, which is only a few miles away.

"But I rarely went to Peking, and I always regretted that I knew so little about it," he said. "In all my life I never saw a more beautiful city."

A few days later Rose was invited to attend the seventieth birthday celebrations of Yu Yu-jen, the venerable head of the Control Yuan, the ministry which theoretically controlled all the other ministries. In fact it had no powers, for Chiang Kai-shek rode roughshod over all its decisions. Yu Yu-jen was a small thin man with a white beard which reached to his waist, and he was famous for his calligraphy, the characters resembling strange twists of barbed wire. Scrolls were presented to him, while Marshal Feng Yu-hsiang, momentarily recovered from his illness, beamed at him and sometimes they held hands. They were the Old Guard, survivors of the early years of the Chinese revolution, and it occurred to me that everyone in the room was very old and an era was passing.

One of those old men was a famous ambassador, small and white-haired, with the expression of a well-mannered fox. Every whisper and gesture suggested ambassadorial discretion. Rose knew him well, for he had been her father's secretary and as a girl she employed him to sharpen her pencils. He was very humble before her, smiling and nodding his head. We stood in one of the corners of the vast reception room. The music of a Chinese lute came from far away, small cakes were being handed around by aged servants, the sunlight poured through the long windows, and there was an atmosphere of calm and decorum. Suddenly Rose was raging at the ambassador, quietly, vehemently, with terrible effect.

"You never obeyed my father's precepts," she said. "My father took you out of nowhere and made you his secretary and you promised always to serve China honorably and truthfully, and now you tell all these lies about China. Once my father caught you out in a lie, and he made you kneel for a whole day in front of a tablet bearing the name of Confucius! Do you remember that? And you are still lying!"

The ambassador seemed to sink into the ground, becoming smaller and smaller. He wrung his hands and the sweat poured out of his face. Rose's rages were terrible to watch, but they were much more terrible to endure. The ambassador lifted up his hands in supplication, while Rose continued to attack him until he seemed to melt and change shape and finally to collapse into a little shapeless heap. When she had wrung the last sigh of contrition from him, she threw him away like a discarded rag.

It was an extraordinary performance, but I was not happy with it. Rose explained that she had followed the traditional Chinese custom. She had chastised him because he was always proclaiming the virtues of the Kuomintang even though he knew that the party was hopelessly corrupt. He had been adopted into the family, and his actions and speeches reflected on the family and especially on her father. "It was an act of family piety," she explained. "Please don't think I enjoyed doing it, but it had to be done. Doing it in front of you made it much worse for him. Also, he won't tell any more lies!"

The next day she flew to Peking, and it was arranged that I should follow a few days later. "I'll go up and air the rooms," she said, and I wondered what it was like to air two hundred and forty rooms.

Peking airport resembled any other small airport in China, and except for a few well-worn DC-3s on the edge of the field there were no other airplanes in sight. The sky shimmered with golden dust from the Gobi Desert, the air was fresh and sweet, the doves were circling in the sky with flutes in their wings. In the distance the high walls of Peking shone biscuit-colored in the afternoon sun, and far away to the west lay the low green hills.

When we came closer to Peking, we saw that the great walls and drum towers were pocked with gray and purple and were already crumbling. Tombs and marble lions stood incongruously in the middle of the ripe maize fields. Rose was saying that just before she arrived, the ornamental gate of the palace had caught fire, leaving the strange sweet smell of *nan-mu* wood lingering in the air. She had sometimes wondered whether the gate was really made of this precious wood, imported from Szechuan, but now she knew for certain. The burning of the gate was evidently an omen, but whether a good one or a bad one she did not know. She believed in prognostications, spells, dream-books, and omens, or rather she believed in them one moment and totally disbelieved in them the next. Instead of the great gate there were now only some stumps of charred wood.

Jacqueline, Rose's twelve-year-old half-French daughter, was waiting outside the palace. She was radiant in a white shirt and black slacks, her cheeks rosy, her hair flying in the gusty wind, her eyes on fire because the long exile from her family was over. The sunlight fell through the leaves of an enormous banyan tree near the gate, splashing on the two guardian lions each resting a paw on a marble ball. Jacqueline was smiling her enchanted smile in the dappled shade. Rose was saying: "Isn't she pretty?" and I heard myself saying: "No, that's not the right word." Jacqueline, hearing only the word "No," uttered a loud wail and vanished into the palace, running from one courtyard to another until at last she took refuge on one of the curving gray-tiled roofs and from there into the branches of an ancient mulberry tree. There we found her an hour later, pale from too much weeping, and we coaxed her down with a dish of ice cream.

Thereafter she was all gaiety and beauty, quietness and grace, moving about the palace as though she alone knew all its mysterious pathways. In Kunming I had imagined her walking among lotus pools in rainbow-colored garments, but instead there was a twelve-year-old tomboy swinging from the branches of the trees. She spoke perfect Mandarin and perfect French, while her English was colored with a strange lilting intonation which was neither French nor Chinese, but a combination of both. She had spent the war years in a convent school, where the nuns were so strict that she found it easier to cry herself to sleep than to stay awake through the long miserable nights. Now she was luxuriating in her freedom.

Rose, too, was luxuriating in her freedom. There had been no servants in Chungking or Kunming: now she commanded the services of the old family retainers who had lived in the palace most of their lives. They dressed in black and walked in thick-soled cotton shoes, and were so silent that I never knew when they entered a room. In time I became completely unaware of their existence as they glided, it seemed, through the interstices of the air. They were the ghosts of the past who never haunted us.

There was scarcely a moment when we were not aware of another ghost, who presided over the entire palace. This was the ghost of Hsiung Hsi-ling, Rose's father, the old prime minister and viceroy of Manchuria, who had once lived there in considerable state. He had been a chunky, well-set man with a broad forehead, widely spaced intelligent eyes, a firm mouth and wispy beard. He was still widely remembered in China, but not for the high positions he had occupied. They remembered him as a superb calligrapher, as a philanthropist who founded a great orphanage in the Western Hills near Peking, and because he had fled to Hongkong when the Japanese offered to make him prime minister of occupied China. He was a man of the old school, with the old Chinese virtues, and not many of them had survived into this century.

Hsiung means "bear," and there was something in his appearance that suggested the relentless energy of a bear, its crushing power and its gentleness. Both these aspects of him

were present in his calligraphy. Rose remembered how he seemed
to go into a state of trance when he began to write a scroll,
his sleeves rolled up, his face suddenly emptied of all expression,
the enormous eyes gazing fixedly at the long strip of paper, and
all the while he was singing tunelessly to himself. At such
moments he seemed to be living in another world altogether,
unreachable. She told other stories of the days when he was
prime minister and sat in the ceremonial hall near the great
ornamental gates waiting for petitioners to arrive. In 1914 it
was still the custom for petitioners to crawl on their bellies to
the seats of the mighty, even though the monarchy had been
overthrown.

We encountered the ghost of Hsiung Hsi-ling everywhere:
his calligraphy, his possessions, were all around us. He had
died in 1938, brokenhearted by the defeat of China by the
Japanese. He had hoped to die in his palace, but he died in
poverty and obscurity in a small hotel in Hongkong.

We were always getting lost in the palace. Once we strayed
from the known paths, we were likely to find ourselves in a
remote unfamiliar courtyard inhabited by Rose's distant relatives, who had come to attend a birthday or some other ceremony,
and stayed on. We discovered that one remote courtyard had
been inhabited by Japanese soldiers who raised the level of
the floor, introduced sliding paper doors, and behaved exactly
as though they were in Japan. We supposed they were deserters
or perhaps bandits who secluded themselves in a courtyard so
far from the street that it was unlikely that anyone would find
them. There had been some fighting among them, for we found
blood-stained uniforms.

I could not imagine a more perfect way of living: the silence,
the curving roofs, the trees everywhere, the sense of a vast composure and serenity, and the presence of Rose and Jacqueline.
Such happiness was almost too great to be borne, and I wondered
whether it could possibly last.

One of Rose's close friends was Princess Dan Pao-ch'ao, who
had been a lady-in-waiting of the empress dowager. She was
then in her late fifties, tall and upright, with enormous slanting
eyes and a mouth which seemed to have been cut out of a rare
stone, so sharp and chiseled were the outlines. Her father was a
Manchu, her mother a Russian, and there was much in her

appearance that reminded one of a Russian ballerina who had grown old with an exquisite grace. Rose and the princess would chatter for hours about ways to retain a youthful appearance, for they were both haunted by age. Arsenic, crushed pearls, rose water, and virgin's milk were eagerly discussed, and when they tired of this they would talk about the old days when the Legation Quarter was alive with young diplomats and Peking was gay with innocent entertainments. The princess could remember the empress dowager vividly, and when she spoke of imperial China in the last days of the Ch'ing Dynasty she had the gift of bringing it to life. She was an excellent painter and she would sometimes show us her paintings with great solemnity.

One morning I drove out to the Temple of Heaven, which was quiet and unvisited in the heat of the day. The huge concentric marble circles and snow-white balustrades flashed in the sun, the blue tiles glittered, the sweet-smelling herbs filled the air, and there was only quietness. To walk there alone was to realize the astonishing brilliance of the proportions of the blue temple and the white altar. It was not only that they were exactly the right distance apart, and were wonderfully constructed to reflect and embellish one another, but what was more important was the spiritual quality of the design, for this white altar was truly an altar and the blue temple at the top of a short flight of steps was truly a temple, though there was nothing at all inside it. Once a thunderbolt tore through the temple roof, armies had fought across the white altar, and both temple and altar had been restored many times, but they still possessed that curiously *untouched* appearance which belongs to all great works of art. Of all the temples I had seen in Peking this was the most moving and the most memorable.

When I returned, Rose and the princess were having afternoon tea. I said I had just come back from the Temple of Heaven.

"I suppose the grass is growing over the altar," the princess said. "No one cares for it nowadays—"

"No, it is well cared for. No grass on the altar, and there's a gardener sweeping everything clean."

"One gardener! Good heavens, in the old days there were hundreds of gardeners! It must have changed a lot since I went there. Of course I haven't been there since the last time the empress dowager implored the blessings of Heaven on the day of the winter solstice. I went disguised as a Manchu official, because there was a law which said that no woman except a reigning empress was permitted to attend the ceremony. It was a long-established law that any woman found at the Temple of Heaven would immediately be put to death, but I went nevertheless. It was terribly cold and my teeth chattered, and once the master of ceremonies began talking to me and I thought the secret was out, but something distracted his attention. I stayed through the entire ceremony and the empress dowager never knew I was there."

"And what if she knew?"

"She would have had me executed on the spot. Of course we expected to be executed if we did anything to displease her."

I doubted very much whether the empress dowager would have executed Princess Dan Pao-ch'ao, who was her favorite. The princess had a gift of laughter, told stories well, and belonged to the inner circle of friends who were rarely separated from her. I envied her for having attended that beautiful and mysterious ceremony.

When China was ruled by the Manchus, it was the custom of the emperor to ride out of the Forbidden City on the night before the winter solstice. No one was allowed out on the streets while he was carried on a palanquin along the straight road leading through the Tartar City to the temple. He came by the light of flares, accompanied by his leopard-tail guards, and the nobles of the court. First, the emperor repaired to the Hall of Abstinence within the temple grounds. Then he proceeded to the blue-tiled temple with the jade stone inscribed with the names of Heaven, and then, moving very slowly and majestically, he made his way along the road leading to the marble altar, where he performed his ministrations, standing alone at the dead center of the world. In the darkness of the night small silken tents were laid on the altar, each tent enclosing some sacred object. The emperor, the tents and the altar were lit by red lanterns. Rolls of pure white scented silk were burned; a pure white ox was slaughtered; the Confucian odes were sung by the priests. For a long time the emperor knelt there, invoking the blessings of Heaven, the jade stone in front of him. He was watching for signs and portents, listening to the voice of Heaven. On this night, and on this night alone, he was believed to be in direct communion with Heaven, which would communicate to him the fortunes of China during the following year. Facing north, about two hours before dawn, his head touching the circle of marble in the center of the altar, he was alone with the alone and deeply aware of his responsibilities to his country. When dawn came, he returned to the palace in the Forbidden City.

Rose, too, had a story about the Temple of Heaven. When her father was prime minister, he accompanied Yuan Shih-k'ai, the President of China, to the ceremony of the winter solstice. The Ch'ing Dynasty had come to an end, but the ancient ceremonies were being revived, although with a republican coloring. The President arrived at dawn in an armored car, wearing a field marshal's uniform. He walked stiffly to the Hall of Abstinence and put on the robe of royal purple adorned with twelve circular dragon designs and then mounted the altar, while armed guards stood around him. Finding himself in such an exposed place, he was frightened out of his wits and called to his guards to come closer, and he performed the ceremony quickly, almost reluctantly, without any feeling for the solemnity of the occasion, always taking care to look in the direction of the movie camera that recorded the scene. An old man, he shuffled across the marble altar without knowing what he was doing, and an hour later he was in his armored car, racing back to the Forbidden City through the silent streets. "It was an absolute farce," Rose said. "He never knew what it meant to worship Heaven."

In 1946 there were still many people alive who could remember the ancient ceremonies, and Peking was still bathed in imperial splendor. Over the gate of the Forbidden City there hung a portrait of Chiang Kai-shek forty feet high, as later there would be a similar portrait of Mao Tse-tung, but no one was under any illusions about the permanence of the Generalissimo's portrait. Peking had watched the warlords come and go, and no doubt there would be many more. The Kuomintang government had taken over large areas of the Forbidden City as though to prove its legitimacy, but it had failed completely to alter the pattern of Peking life. Peking still belonged to the emperors.

In many subtle ways the city came to dominate our lives, and we were content to be its prisoners. It was not only that everywhere you looked there were towers, golden roofs, temples and maroon-colored walls, but the very air possessed a majestic calm, an enchanting ripeness. The sky was an intense blue glittering with the golden sands of the Gobi Desert, and in this light everything seemed a little larger than life. The people walked unhurriedly with a dignity that came from a sense of repose, a consciousness of ancient traditions. Old men, taking their birdcages for a walk, possessed an enviable serenity, and even the ricksha pullers were leisurely. Sometimes, wandering through the winding *hu'tungs,* you would see a red-painted door opening silently to reveal a small courtyard adorned with some strangely shaped rocks, and you would glimpse an ageless and uninterrupted calm. For century upon century nothing had changed in that courtyard: the same children, the same old men, the same wisteria trees.

Foreigners, of course, fell under the spell of Peking without putting up any resistance. Robert van Gulik, who later became famous as the author of Chinese mystery stories, was then the Dutch *chargé d'affaires,* living in splendor in the Dutch embassy. He was tall, heavily built, with the keen scholarly appearance of a youthful professor. Before the war he had accumulated a large collection of Chinese paintings which he sent to Soerabaya in the Dutch East Indies for safekeeping. The entire collection was destroyed in a Japanese bombing raid, and some of the sadness in his features came from a feeling of overwhelming loss. He had no sense of possession. It was simply that he felt responsible for the loss of so many treasures indispensable to the study of Chinese painting. In the twenties and thirties it was still possible to assemble a great collection, but it was becoming increasingly difficult. Now he haunted the antique shops, and since he had very few duties in the Dutch embassy, he was able to spend most of his time building up a new collection. "The great days are over," he sighed. "You simply cannot imagine what it was like in the thirties in Peking."

I was not so sure the great days were over. The thirties, after all, were the time of the Japanese invasion, the fighting in Chapei, the senseless massacres. The Europeans, living in the Legation Quarter, had scarcely raised a finger in protest, happy in their isolation, a cultivated élite protected by Japanese bayonets. I preferred the new Peking, because it was now in the hands of the Chinese. The new rulers were corrupt and incompetent Kuomintang officials, but at least they were Chinese. So we argued, while he displayed his treasures—superb K'ang Hsi vases, an enormous falcon painted on tea-colored silk in the Yuan Dynasty, a Kuanyin carved in painted wood at the end of the Sung Dynasty. The collection was small, but he possessed nothing that was not of the highest quality. When he spoke about Chinese works of art, his voice took on an extraordinary intensity. "I believe," he said, "that there is no art greater than Chinese art. Nowhere else have men been so dedicated to art and all its refinements." Then there were more arguments, for I maintained that Michelangelo and the sculptors of Chartres were infinitely superior to Chinese sculptors and I was weary of the refinements of Chinese jade-cutters.

"You say that now," he said, "but later on, when you have lived longer in Peking, you will know better. Chinese painting and sculpture will cast a spell on you, and you will never be able to escape from them."

Robert van Gulik had known Rose when she was the young darling of the diplomatic corps, and sometimes, while he poured tea on a sunny afternoon, they would both vanish into the past, into the golden haze of an earlier Peking which had remained virtually unchanged since the days of the Emperor Ch'ien Lung. It was not my Peking. I was looking forward to the day when the students would be coming back and I would be teaching again at Tsinghua. There was a new China coming into being, and I hoped there would be no more dictation from the foreign embassies. Like van Gulik, I haunted the antique shops, but on a professor's salary with a wife and three stepchildren to support I rarely bought any antiques.

I wore a blue Chinese gown, partly because it was a sensible thing to wear during the hot Chinese summer and partly because I had grown so accustomed to a gown that I would have felt uncomfortable in anything else. One day, when I called on the British embassy, the gown caused an uproar. Unlike most of the embassies, the British embassy was a former palace built with impeccably good taste, the buildings resembling gilded kiosks set among grass and trees. I spent some time wandering in the gardens. It was an incredibly beautiful place, the air was alive with the singing of birds, and the grass was as green as the grass in England. Finally, I went to call on one of the under-secretaries to discuss some matter so unimportant that I have long since forgotten what it was. The under-secretary was a powerfully built, red-faced man with a military mustache.

As soon as I entered his office, he began to stamp and roar. "I've been watching you through the window!" he shouted. "What do you mean by coming here in a cheap gown! You're a coolie, that's what you are! You're a disgrace to the British!"

"What do you expect me to wear?"

"Coat and trousers, and a clean shirt! You ought to dress like every other decent European! Anyone could tell you're a Bolshie!"

There was a good deal more of it, but he simmered down long enough to discuss my business. As I was leaving, there was another uproar and I was told not to show my face in the British embassy until I learned to dress properly. A heavy man with bulging shoulders, he pressed himself up from his desk and shouted after me: "Get out of here! You're nothing but a damned Bolshie!"

He died a week later, very suddenly. I was not wholly surprised, for I remember hoping I would never see him again. Also, on leaving him, I had invoked the Green Dragon, who may or may not have been responsible for his death. I was told that he had died horribly, in convulsions, and the doctors attending the autopsy were unable to discover the cause of death.

After this experience I kept clear of the British embassy, for fear that it might be necessary to consign other Englishmen to the mercy of the Green Dragon.

Within the Palace of the Iron-capped Prince, life flowed evenly and uneventfully. Jon flew up from Kunming, looking more princely than any prince, striding pleasantly around the courtyards as though he alone had been granted a sense of possession, while he engaged in mysterious intrigues whose outcome was always uncertain and never resolved. I was working on a biography of Chiang Kai-shek, which was not published until a quarter of a century later, and so the mornings were spent tranquilly among mountains of books and loose-leaf folders, but every afternoon there were expeditions to the Forbidden City or the North Lake or the T'ai Miao, the ancestral temple of the Ch'ing emperors. Jacqueline usually accompanied me, and there was nearly always a stop at an ice cream shop. What puzzled me was why she did not become as round as a balloon, for she must have swallowed a ton of ice cream during those after-noon excursions. She explained very simply that she was making up for lost time, for little ice cream had been available during the war.

Americans came to the palace, and occasionally there were visits by high Kuomintang officials and Chinese Communist of-ficials who met secretly in one of the rooms which Rose had set aside for secret meetings. I never learned how she arranged these meetings. These visitors came at dusk or at night, looking absurdly conspiratorial, standing in the courtyard and smoking endless cigarettes until Rose motioned them into the secret room. "They can cut off my head only once!" she exclaimed, when I hinted that she was putting herself in danger. "Anyway, it is better that the Chinese Communists and the Kuomintang talk across a table than start shooting at each other." To have any commerce at all with the Chinese Communists was high treason, and anyone found in Peking with a copy of *The Com-munist Manifesto* or Mao Tse-tung's writings was summarily exe-cuted. As usual, Rose was living dangerously.

I knew very little about the Chinese Communists. For me, they were ghostly men who came to the palace, talked in whispers, and vanished as quietly as they came. I thought they would win in the end because the Kuomintang was irremediably corrupt and incompetent, and any leader who promised to put an end to corruption and incompetence would succeed in overthrowing them if he possessed a small army. The fruit was waiting to be plucked, but it might be ten years before it fell from the tree.

One day an American colonel came to tea. He was a tall, rangy Texan who had fallen hopelessly in love with China, bought Chinese antiques, and was studying Chinese. He had stories to tell about Kuomintang corruption as it affected the United States army that made our hair stand on end, but he was not particularly interested in Chinese politics. What he wanted to do was to travel through all the provinces of China and to see everything that could be seen.

"I've been in China seven months, and all I have seen is Shanghai, Tientsin and Peking," he said. "What I would really like to do is to spend a year just seeing China. Last week I was in Yenan. I went up in the weekly plane, and came back on the same plane. That's not the proper way to travel. I've flown a hundred thousand miles in this war, and now I want to see whether I can still walk a little."

I asked him about Yenan, but all he could remember was a broad yellow valley and the small caves in the hills.

"Why don't you go yourself?" he said. "The plane is always three-quarters empty, and there shouldn't be any difficulty putting you on it."

Two days later, with the help of the American colonel, I flew to Yenan.

JOURNEY TO YENAN

I flew to Yenan in a DC-3 piloted by a young Texan who said he had never flown to Yenan before. When I saw him first he was lying on the grass near the airplane studying the maps, and I remember the green of the maps reflected on his face and the soft Texan voice saying: "Where in hell is Yenan?" It turned out that he was using an old series of maps and Yenan was not marked on them.

That, of course, was the trouble with Yenan: it had no official existence, and had long ago entered the world of mythology. Millions of young Chinese dreamed about it, believing that a new way of life was being hammered out in this remote corner of North China, but very few of them were able to make their way there from the territory ruled by the Generalissimo. Yenan was not a place but a state of mind, a fable, an epic. According to the Kuomintang authorities it was a disease which would have to be stamped out before it spread across the whole of China like an epidemic, and all over Nationalist China suspected Communists were being executed without trial.

Nevertheless Yenan existed, and every week the Americans sent an airplane to this ancient city on the edge of the Gobi Desert partly to bring supplies to the Yenan Observer Group and partly to meet the needs of the truce teams set up by General Marshall. These teams consisted of American, Kuomintang and Communist officers who were sent out whenever Kuomintang and Communist troops clashed, and their task was to apportion the blame and somehow bring peace to the warring armies. It was not a very effective method of preventing war, but it was hoped that with more experience the truce teams would discover new techniques for putting out brush fires. There was still another reason for sending the airplanes into Communist territory. There existed in Peking a delegation of high Communist officials who from time to time returned to Yenan to receive instructions. In theory there existed a state of truce throughout China; in fact the Kuomintang and the Communists were at war. The question to be decided in the next few weeks or days was whether both sides would embark on a full-scale war of annihilation or whether they would content themselves with local engagements designed to extend by a few miles the limits of the territory they had conquered. Either China would be drowned in blood, or there would be interminable brush-fire wars. It was a good time for going to Yenan, for it might be possible to gauge the intentions of the Communist leaders.

A few moments later the American navigator came striding across the airfield, followed by a small straggling column of people carrying paper bags and wicker baskets. The navigator was bringing new maps with Yenan clearly marked and circled in red pencil. A Chinese foreign office official examined our documents, and soon we were all clustered in the DC-3. The bucket seats had been removed and we sat on the floor, with eighteen parachute harnesses swinging on a wire rope above our heads. The Chinese passengers consisted of a doctor, a Red Army general, a girl in a print frock, and four or five soldiers. Apparently none of them had flown in an airplane before and they were all very sick during the journey.

Soon we were flying over the gold-red roofs of the Summer Palace, and a few minutes later we saw the Great Wall winding across the landscape like threads of white lace. Then came the blue mountains, all wrinkled like the skins of elephants, with here and there a space where a peasant had carved out a small farm, while below him the ancient watercourses were no more than white veins on a blue leaf. China looks barren from the air: the endless plains, the endless mountains, and only a few widely spaced hamlets and villages. The mystery, when you are in an airplane, is to discover where the millions of Chinese are living. Have they all gone underground?

The mountains gave way to brown sunbaked crumbling hills and small green rivers that lost themselves among the crumbling valleys. A totally new landscape unfolded, ochre and yellow, a foretaste of the Gobi Desert. The airplane wing swept past a pagoda set majestically on a yellow hill, but there was no sign of any city, only a long yellow valley. Suddenly the airplane came down on a small dusty field, and we were all scrambling out into the blinding sunlight.

The weekly arrival of the airplane usually brought out a small crowd of Communist officials to the airfield. "You'll probably see Mao Tse-tung," the pilot said, but there was no sign of him among the twenty people standing around the airplane. The most surprising person on the airfield was an American major who stepped out of the crowd and said: "I understand you are coming to stay in my cave." I said gratefully: "I don't understand, but I am delighted." For the next eleven days I shared his cave and his food, and wasted a good deal of his time by asking him interminable questions. The American colonel in Peking had sent a radio message saying that I was coming.

The American major was handsome, square-jawed, wonderfully sweet-tempered. As the sole survivor of the Yenan Observer Group sent by the Americans to Yenan two or three years earlier, he was the only representative of a foreign power in the Communist capital. Born in Hawaii of Chinese descent, speaking Chinese, he got along well with the Communists, though he sometimes complained that they gave him little information: the one-man observer group had little to observe. He presided over a radio transmitter, a generator, and a film projector, and every morning he hauled up the American flag outside his cave and every evening he hauled it down again. He had only one serious complaint—he missed his wife, who remained in Hawaii. The cave was a tunnel eight feet high and had four or five wooden bunks. It was absolutely bombproof and even at midday it was wonderfully cool.

From the mouth of the cave the valley of Yenan looked like a place seen in a dream, for the loess hills, flowing gently down to a mile-wide plain, were shaped like golden tents, one tent following another into the remote distance. The valley of the Yen River lay open to the sky, calm and serene, dominated by the pagoda on the highest of the hills. Everything was yellow and bronze and gold. Here and there you might see a red or blue blanket hung over the mouth of a cave, and these colors startled you with their violence. Seeing this valley, you came to understand why the Buddhist monks had inhabited it for centuries. It was such a valley as Van Gogh would have loved to paint, the dust whirling up like flames.

There was something else which was especially charming about the valley. It had the sweetest smell I ever knew in China, a smell compounded of hot sand and grass and parsley and all the scents of summer.

I was still luxuriating in the beauty of the valley when the American major suggested it was time to see some of the Communist leaders. We jumped into his jeep and drove across the sandy valley to a grove of dusty trees. The river presented no difficulty, for at this season it was only two or three inches deep. There were some small farmhouses among the trees, and here we stopped. Yang Shan-k'un, the chief of staff, was sunning himself in his small vegetable garden and tending his tomato plants. We learned that tomatoes were not doing very well this year, but the sandy soil was producing magnificent honey melons.

"Who do you want to see?" Yang Shan-k'un asked, and I said I would like to see everybody, especially Mao Tse-tung and Chu Teh, the commander-in-chief of the Red Army.

Yang Shan-k'un was a Szechuanese, and one of the comparatively few men in Yenan who spoke passable English, although he always looked relieved when an interpreter was present. He made out a long list of people who might be visited. Chu Teh was at the top of the list and Mao Tse-tung at the bottom, and when he came to Mao Tse-tung he shrugged his shoulders and said: "This one is difficult. I'll talk to him and ask him, but I cannot promise anything."

This was disturbing news because Mao Tse-tung was clearly the intellectual leader of the Chinese Communists and it should be possible to learn more from him than from anyone else. Also, he was a poet of some eminence, although only one of his poems was widely known in South China. Before coming to Yenan I had set myself the task of collecting his poems as a means of understanding the man on the theory that a man can hide himself least in his poetry. His poem *The Snow*, written during the previous year, had delighted the professors in Kunming because it seemed to reveal an undisguised romanticism and a deep feeling for the land:

THE SNOW

All the scenery of the North
Is enclosed in a thousand miles of ice
And ten thousand miles of whirling snow.
Behold both sides of the Great Wall—
There is only a vast confusion left.
On the upper and lower reaches of the Yellow River
You can no longer see the flowing water.
The mountains are dancing silver serpents,
The hills on the plains are shining elephants.
I desire to compare my height with the skies.

In clear weather
The earth is so charming,
Like a red-faced girl clothed in white.
Such is the charm of these rivers and mountains,
Calling innumerable heroes to vie with each other in pursuing her.
The Emperors Shih Huang and Wu Ti were barely cultured,
The Emperors T'ai Tsung and T'ai Tsu were lacking in feeling.
Genghiz Khan knew only how to bend his bow at the eagles.
These all belong to the past—only today are there men of feeling.

This poem could be read on many different levels: as an
assertion of his own powers, as a rejection of all past history,
as a masterly summary in a few words of all Chinese history,
all Chinese landscapes. He had evoked the splendor of China
and hinted at greater splendors to come. But what was especially
notable about the poem was its gaiety and optimism, and a kind
of dazzling clarity. Two short poems written during the Long
March were known, but they did not have this gaiety. With any
luck I hoped to leave Yenan with a handful of his poems.

Meanwhile the days passed quickly with visits to the Lu Hsun
Academy, a small university hidden in the caves, where nearly
all the students were young people who had walked hundreds
of miles to reach Yenan, to the hospital, which had also been
tunneled out of the soft loess cliffs, to the agricultural college,
to the prison, and to a kindergarten. But mostly the days were
spent talking with Communist party officials and with survivors
of the Long March. We sat on benches outside their caves, while

they talked about battles that had taken place less than ten years before but already seemed to belong to ancient history. There was, for example, a famous battle at the Ta Tu bridge on the borders of Tibet. It was a very small battle, though a decisive one, and there were three people in Yenan who had taken part in it. All three told their stories, and all were different. It is not only that they differed in minor details, but even in essentials, for memory played tricks on them. Yet the three stories together were far more convincing than any single account of the battle. History, it seems, is ultimately a game played by eyewitnesses.

On the evening of the second day there came a message from Chu Teh, who lived in a cave overlooking a date garden, saying that he had a few minutes to spare and would see me that evening; it would be more difficult and perhaps impossible to see him at any other time in the next two weeks. Since the American major had never seen Chu Teh at close quarters, we drove out in his jeep in the growing dusk. It was dark when we reached the date garden, which was four or five miles to the east. I never learned why he chose to live so far away from the other Communist leaders, but I suspect that he enjoyed his isolation.

Sometimes, as we drove across the sandy valley, we heard the howling of wolves and once the headlights caught the blue glare of a wolf's eyes. We encountered no one during the journey except a ghostly white-turbaned horseman cantering along the river bank. The valley grew dark, the caves disappeared, and the starlings went wild in the cloudless sky. In all the valley there was no sign of movement, no lights shone except for our headlights, and there was only a brooding silence.

We knew we had come to the commander-in-chief's headquarters when we saw the dusty date palms surrounded by a low crumbling wall, a solitary soldier standing at the gate. Telegraph wires were festooned among the date palms, but otherwise there was no indication that this was the nerve center of the Chinese Communist armies. This was the ministry of war; on the gate there was written in large Chinese characters THE GARDEN OF THE DATE PALMS.

While a servant carried a lantern, Chu Teh came down the avenue between the palms to meet us. He was limping a little—

there was said to be something in the local water that made people lame, and a surprisingly large number of people could be seen limping. He was smaller than I had imagined him, and more weather-beaten, with a skin like old wrinkled leather. When he took off his cap, you saw that his hair was thinning, but it was still jet black without a trace of gray, and he had the teeth of a young boy in the face of an old peasant. He looked, in fact, like a farmer who had spent his years tending the feathery date palms.

Beyond the garden lay a short slope to his cave, the largest and deepest I had seen in Yenan, and so sparsely furnished that it resembled an airplane hangar. There were a few wickerwork chairs, a table, three sofas. The wickerwork chairs creaked, the table was rickety because one leg was shorter than the others, and the battered sofas were brutally uncomfortable because the springs stuck out. On the table stood a rapeseed-oil lamp which threw out immense shadows on the curving whitewashed walls.

A soldier came and poured tea into delicate china cups, and because it was growing cold another soldier threw a coat over the general's broad shoulders. He was talking in a husky voice about a battle at Shihpingchieh, north of Mukden, which had come to an end only a week before. This battle is forgotten now, but it had a decisive influence on the history of China. For the first time the Kuomintang and Communist armies engaged in positional warfare. The Kuomintang newspapers, which had no reason to exaggerate the bloodshed, reported that there were 10,000 casualties. It was a full-scale battle lasting a month, with the Generalissimo throwing in tanks and bombing planes and his best troops.

"We have never had a battle like this before," Chu Teh was saying. "Static warfare is something we have always avoided. But the Kuomintang thought they could walk over us. They did not believe we could defend the city, did not realize our strength, and exhausted their energy. We lost ten thousand troops, but they lost more."

The flickering rapeseed-oil lamp shone on his face, which took on the dark reddish brown color of volcanic stone. He looked so much like an old peasant that it was difficult to realize that he was the commander-in-chief of the Red Army and that his decisions had profoundly influenced the course of the battle. I kept thinking of the Kuomintang generals I had met, impeccably dressed, accustomed to luxury, delighting in their power, and totally incapable of inspiring any real loyalty in their soldiers. Chu Teh was a man who obviously inspired loyalty and was totally indifferent to the trappings of power.

He spoke bitterly, with a harsh edge to his voice, about the Kuomintang treatment of prisoners. "They killed all the Communist soldiers who fell into their hands. They were absolutely merciless. As for us, we have no need to kill prisoners. We don't want a war, but when their troops attack us, what else can we do except fight back? There can be no peace with this fascist dictatorship."

A few weeks earlier, before the battle of Shihpingchieh, both sides had declared a solemn truce. It had been broken innumerable times, but the people still hoped desperately that civil war could be avoided. The Chinese were helpless in the face of a new civil war.

"Then there is no hope," I said. "The war will go on for ten more years?"

"There will be war unless there is a coalition government," he said. "We must have democracy, and democracy doesn't mean secret police, dictatorships, tortures, murders and the disappearance of people everywhere."

He still spoke quietly, but when he mentioned the secret police his voice rose. He would mention them again and again, so that the words had the effect of an accompaniment to the conversation which continued for many hours.

The cave was so large, so empty, that it somehow gave the impression of hanging in space. We were enclosed in shadows, and the solitary rapeseed-oil lamp, which was later provided with a brown cardboard shade because the light hurt Chu Teh's eyes, was the center of our existence, the one certain thing among the uncertain shadows. I said something about the flame being as weak and feeble as human life. It was so easy to kill men and so very difficult to give them birth. God knows how many millions of Chinese would die if there was a ten-year civil war! Was it not possible even at this late date to avoid a civil war?

"We want to avoid it," he said, "but we are confronted by a tyranny. Men are strong when they are confronted by a tyranny, and when millions come together, they can burn the tyranny away."

"So the war goes on—"

"Yes, it will have to go on as long as the tyranny endures."

I told him the story about Aristides the Just, a politician in ancient Greece, who was so popular that it was thought best to send him into exile. The British electorate had removed Winston Churchill from office for very much the same reason. But the Chinese had no way to remove their popular leaders. Chiang Kai-shek and Mao Tse-tung had polarized the entire nation, and the civil war was inevitable as long as they remained in power. I asked Chu-Teh whether he was prepared to step down if the commander-in-chief of the Kuomintang armies stepped down. If Chiang Kai-shek would surrender his power to a younger leader, would Mao Tse-tung do the same?

Chu Teh was listening intently, his forehead furrowed with thought. I spoke about the legendary prestige which all these leaders possessed, and how dangerous these legends were, for men cannot choose among legends, but are chosen by them. At first he objected that the leaders were absolutely unimportant: they merely reflected the interests of the political parties: they were servants, not masters. I said they were servants who had taken over the whole house. At last he said: "Yes, if there was a real danger, then I believe both Mao Tse-tung and I would be prepared to leave the field to others."

I was surprised and relieved, but doubted very much whether he really meant it.

He rubbed his chin, grinned, and drank some tea. He told stories about the Long March, and from the dark recesses of the wall he produced his journals going back to the days when he was a young officer. Every day he had written his journal in a remarkably vigorous handwriting. As a result of the wars, a few journals were lost, but the greater part had survived. "Mao Tse-tung keeps no records," Chu Teh said. "No diary, no journal. It does not interest him, and besides there are other people who have recorded what he has been doing from day to day. But the soldiers all keep journals."

Some of Chu Teh's journals looked so frail that they seemed about to disintegrate, but all showed those thick black downward strokes. The recent journals were written even more vigorously than the older ones written thirty years before. He was sixty-five, but he had the handwriting of a man in the prime of life. Sometimes in the journals there appeared poems, for like Mao Tse-tung he was an inveterate poetizer. His journal of the Long March had survived intact, and he supposed rather regretfully that it would one day be published.

The cave grew colder as the night advanced; sometimes the little flame of the oil lamp seemed to die out, only to jerk into life again. He was wide awake, talking about the revolution. For a while I wondered what revolution he was talking about, and it turned out to be the revolution of 1911 when he was a company commander and a devoted follower of Dr. Sun Yat-sen. He had been a regular soldier in the army of the Ch'ing emperor, and he could remember a time when Chinese soldiers were armed with bows and arrows.

"They are always talking about us as though we were guerrillas," Chu Teh said, "but in fact we were trained as regular soldiers. Peng Teh-huei and I were both officers in the Kuomintang army when we defected, and there were many others. We were a real army during the Long March, and we fought positional battles in Hunan, Kweichow, Szechuan and Kansu. We were a real army then, and we are a real army now."

He spoke affectionately of Peng Teh-huei, whom he regarded as the best of his generals, and when he spoke of Mao Tse-tung his face always lit up with a smile, as a brother might smile at the recollection of a brother. Chu Teh looked like an old farmer, and Mao still had about him something of the air of a student, yet they regarded each other as brothers. During the Long March peasants in the remote regions of Southwest China sometimes heard of a mysterious military leader called Chu Mao, whom no one had ever seen.

It was inconceivable that Chu Teh would ever assume any of the postures of power or utter a word out of character. He wore no medals, possessed no uniform except a drab padded cotton coat and trousers, such as might be worn by a peasant, and he seemed to be perfectly at home in the bare cave. When General Marshall flew to Yenan some months earlier, Chu Teh went to the airfield to welcome him. Someone had suggested that he should wear the appropriate uniform of a commander-in-chief. Chu Teh rejected the idea, saying that he absolutely refused to be decked out in any finery, it was totally out of character, and he did not believe that General Marshall would step out of the airplane with ostrich plumes decorating his military cap, gold braid on his sleeve, and medals hanging all over his chest. "I will go as I am," he said. In the end he was provided with a purple cloak with a fox fur collar. He felt so uncomfortable in it that he never wore it again.

In the night, with a lantern, he accompanied us down the long avenue between the date palms. A wolf was prowling along the garden wall, shaggy and black against the starlight; then it jumped down and vanished from sight. As the jeep rolled through clouds of dust, more wolves appeared, but they soon scattered. A cold wind came down the valley, the date garden vanished, there was only the sickle moon, the dark hills, the dark plain. Once a candle gleamed in a cave high up on the mountainside. When the candle went out, the valley looked lonelier than ever.

THE GOLDEN VALLEY

You could wander for days in the golden valley and see nothing more than the peasants making their way to market or some women washing clothes in a stream, or else you would see a solitary horseman riding in the direction of the date garden where Chu Teh brooded over maps; and this horseman with his scarlet saddlecloth, seen at the moment when the sun was setting on the fields of winter wheat, wearing the dust of five provinces on his tunic, seemed to concentrate in himself all the romance of this delectable valley. In the early morning the valley was sunflower yellow, and it was especially beautiful at dusk when bathed in the afterglow of sunset. At night no lights shone and the valley disappeared; there was only the whistling of the wind and the howling of the wolves.

This valley where nothing seemed to be happening was a place where everything was happening. Power streamed from it: power in its most naked form of direct command and implicit obedience. Radio messages were being sent out, food supplies and ammunition were being gathered and distributed, the high command made its decisions, and from all over China people were making their way to join the Red armies already on the march. A hundred million people received their orders from Yenan. But even if you peered into all the caves you would find nothing to suggest the presence of a powerful government. Power was radiating out of Yenan on a scale hitherto unknown in China, and yet the valley seemed to be sleeping.

Partly, of course, it was the sheer beauty of the valley which made it appear so harmless and so vulnerable. The more I explored it, the more it seemed to exist in a painting, being formed out of many shades of yellow, not of substantial earth. The golden hills, the river winding between its sandy banks, the rare trees and the winding mule-tracks, all these appeared to be arranged according to the precise patterns of a Chinese painting in which men appear as minuscule objects seen in the far distance. There was only the blue sky and the yellow valley, and at midday you could sit down on the slope of one of the hills and see no one at all.

One day I climbed up to the pagoda, which was brilliantly clean-cut seen from a distance, but close up was little more than a ruin, the broken tiles lying on the ground. It was ugly and scarred, like a worm-eaten skeleton. There was a little Buddhist temple close to the pagoda, but the rows of life-size plaster Buddhas were in a state of decay. Some had lost their heads, others were armless or legless, while still others looked as though they had been nibbled to death by rats. In one of the cave temples the Communists had established the printing press of the *Liberation Daily:* the steam of the press was melting away the innumerable stone Buddhas crowding the walls. They were Buddhas of the best periods, of the Wei and T'ang dynasties, wonderfully designed, with grave features and arms raised in benediction. The steam press roared and chattered, black and oily, while the jets of steam smoothed out the faces of the statues so that they were almost unrecognizable. In an enormous cave nearby, known as the Cave of the Thousand Buddhas, which is the Chinese way of saying that there were so many they were past counting, there were life-size Buddhas still gleaming with red and green paint, but it was difficult to see them. The cave was being used as a storehouse for bales of the brownish newsprint used for the *Liberation Daily.* These bales were stacked to the ceiling, but by making one's way around them it was possible to see the Buddhas carved with tremendous power and authority at a time when Yenan was one of the great religious centers of China. One Buddha lay in a reclining posture, fingering his stone necklace with one hand and blessing the world with the other; he was about to enter nirvana and this was his last gesture to his bewildered and grief-stricken disciples. Long before the Communists came to Yenan, the Buddhist monks had lived in caves.

I asked the manager of the steam press whether there was some way to protect the Buddhas.

"There are so many caves full of Buddhas," he said, shrugging his shoulders. "It doesn't matter if we lose a few of them."

Someone had pasted a portrait of Mao Tse-tung on the chest

of a life-size Buddha, which thus became a body with two faces resembling the strange monsters found in mediaeval bestiaries.

To reach the printing press it was necessary to make a steep climb up the hillside. At the foot of the hill there was a green-tiled gateway. As I was stepping through the gateway I observed that the head of a Buddha was being used as a doorstop and I picked it up. It was an admirable head, with thick curly hair and an expression of great sweetness and nobility, and it occurred to me that it could have been carved only in the T'ang Dynasty. I carried it back to my cave. Some days later a deputation arrived from the printing press. Someone had observed me carrying it away, and I was told that I was liable to be arrested for "stealing national property." I surrendered the head, and the next time I visited the printing press it was once more being used as a doorstop.

There was, of course, no ministry of fine arts at Yenan, and no one had time to examine or catalogue the treasures in the caves. They said the mayor of Yenan had made a small collection of objects found in the caves, but he was ill and could not be reached. There were poets, musicians and singers in Yenan, but there were no painters or sculptors. Woodcut artists were carving designs with extraordinary skill, and not all of them were propaganda posters. You could see woodcut designs of Mao Tse-tung and Chu Teh, but there were also scenes from everyday life, flowers and landscapes, and you could buy them for a few pennies in the market place.

The market place in the capital of the Communist empire consisted of seven or eight wooden stalls selling paper and envelopes, fountain pens, cigarettes, matches, shirts, dried fish and vegetables. There was the same grayish brown paper which was manufactured all over China in wartime, but was especially porous and friable in Communist China. The cigarettes were very nearly unsmokable and the matches would ignite with a sudden tremendous flare accompanied by a fierce fountain of sparks. The shirts looked threadbare, and only the vegetables gleamed with health on those rickety stalls which the Communists permitted only because it was simpler to permit them than to abolish them. Students and government officials received books of coupons which they exchanged for goods in the few government stores.

One day, while I was buying woodcuts in the market place, a jeep drove past in a cloud of yellow dust. The road was rutted, the jeep bounced unmercifully, the dust rose to the height of a house, resembling a yellow dragon's tail hovering across the valley of Yenan. As the jeep passed, I caught a glimpse of Mao Tse-tung clinging to the handle bar along the side of the jeep. He wore a peasant cap and looked deeply sunburned, glowing with health, and he was smiling as people do when they are hanging on for dear life. Then he vanished from sight, and there was only the yellow cloud of dust whirling across the plain.

I was relieved to know that he was in Yenan, because there had been rumors in Peking that he was on a secret visit to the Soviet Union, and in Yenan they said he was too grief-stricken by the death of two friends in an aircrash to see anyone. The first rumor could be discounted, the second seemed plausible, but the man riding in the jeep did not appear to be sunken in grief. On the contrary he looked robust and happy as he bounced along in the dust.

During the afternoon I went to see Yang Shan-k'un, the chief of staff, and told him I had seen Mao Tse-tung near the market place. He seemed surprised and said Mao Tse-tung was living in deep seclusion.

"He is a man of many moods," Yang Shan-k'un said. "We ourselves rarely know where he is or where to find him. If he is working on his books, he works through the night and sleeps by day. Sometimes he comes down here in the evenings, but without warning. We might see him every evening for a week, but it is equally likely that a month might pass without our seeing him. It is true that he was overwhelmed by grief, and at such times he refuses to see even his closest friends. There is a cave where he goes alone without his wife or children and with only a soldier or a servant to guard him. I have never been in the cave, but I have been told there is not even a bed in it and he sleeps on the bare ground."

It occurred to me that if the members of the Central Committee did not know where to find him, and if he appeared very rarely, and usually only in the evening, there was very little likelihood that I would see him. He had vanished in a cloud of dust, and it was quite possible that I would never set eyes on him again.

I was spending four or five hours a day meeting the Communist leaders and taking down their memories of the Long March, and more and more it was becoming evident that the Long March was an astonishingly complicated maneuver made up of many columns led by men with differing ambitions and out of touch with one another, and the column led by Chu Teh and Mao Tse-tung was only one of many, though the most powerful and the most brilliantly led. Even in those days Mao Tse-tung had acquired a legendary quality which set him apart from other men. There was a remoteness about him, a strangeness as of someone who was not completely of this world, and when they spoke about him there was always a curious reverence in their voices, which was not quite the reverence paid to a great leader but more like the reverence paid to a prophet. If, as Yang Shan-k'un said, he had gone off to a cave alone at a time when he was overwhelmed by grief, he was following a very ancient Chinese tradition. Poet, scholar, hermit—all these went together. There remained the revolutionary who said that all power came from the end of a gun.

That afternoon Yang Shan-k'un offered me the use of a jeep and a Chinese driver so that I could explore the valley. It was a princely gift, for at this time there were exactly two jeeps in Yenan.

"You must take very good care of it," he said. "If anything goes wrong, we will have a terrible time finding replacements."

The driver was a small square-faced Hunanese with rosy cheeks and a look of perpetual astonishment, and what seemed to astonish him most of all was that he was in charge of this beautiful green machine which raced across the valley like a wild stallion. One day we drove to the city of Yenan, bombed flat by the Japanese and resembling a vast field of black cinders, and on the following day there was a long expedition down the valley to attend a *yang-k'o* dance in a grove of trees beside the river. On the way back, taking a corner too rapidly while half-blinded by dust, he drove the jeep over a small cliff, landing among some black pigs. I was able to throw myself clear, but the driver was still in the jeep when it landed among the pigs fifteen feet below the level of the road. He lay sprawled over the driving wheel, dazed and bloodied but not seriously hurt. When he had recovered, he took out a knife and quietly slit the throats of the wounded pigs. The axle of the jeep was broken, and there was blood everywhere.

That was the end of my excursions by jeep, and when I next saw Yang Shan-k'un he gazed at me gloomily, like a judge about to sentence a prisoner. I bore the responsibility of having rendered useless exactly one half of the motor vehicles belonging to the Chinese Communists in Yenan.

"I am sorry," said Yang Shan-k'un solemnly, "but this kind of thing will not bring you favor in the eyes of our Chairman." He spoke in the tone of a man who had hoped for better things. Then he added: "I doubt very much whether he will see you now."

"You mean he will be told about the jeep."

"Of course he will be told about it. We can't hide it from him, and now we shall have to go to endless trouble to repair it. We have no mechanics here, only drivers."

As usual he was sitting on a kitchen chair in the midst of his small vegetable garden. His children were playing at his feet. One was a two-year-old boy who looked like a Chinese doll with pure white skin and brilliant black eyes, while the other was a three-year-old girl dressed in a red jacket and peacock blue trousers with ribbons twined in her long pigtail. She was obviously dressed for some festive occasion, probably her birthday, and since I was now high in his disfavor I thought I might as well talk to his daughter instead. She laughed so much at my execrable Chinese that the ice melted. Once more we were able to discuss the possibility of talking to Mao Tse-tung, who intensely distrusted foreigners and rarely gave interviews. I mentioned the famous interview with Edgar Snow which forms a whole chapter of *Red Star Over China.*

"He was not happy about that interview," Yang Shan-k'un said. "Some mistakes crept in. There were mistakes of fact, and also mistakes of interpretation. He has sworn not to give any more interviews."

"So we are back again at the beginning?"

"Yes, and there is nothing—nothing at all—we can do about it. You probably won't see him again."

On that unhappy note we parted. Dejected, I walked back to

my cave only to learn that a Chinese opera was to be performed that evening in the Yenan theater, a few minutes' walk from the farmhouse where Yang Shan-k'un was living. The American major had seen two or three operas in Yenan and thought they were well acted. "They have made some innovations," he said. "The landless peasants triumph and the landlords suffer terrible defeats."

In the darkness we walked across the valley to the small theater which also served as the meeting place of the Communist Party. It had been built recently and seated about a hundred and fifty people, and was thus considerably smaller than the usual Chinese theater. The opera, which was based on an incident from the novel *All Men Are Brothers*, had already begun when we slipped through a side door and groped around for some empty seats. On the stage a heroic figure, his face painted in heavy red and black grease-paint, wearing a gown of green silk embroidered with dragons, was going through the motions of stepping over the threshold of a house. There was not the least doubt that the man with the red and black face was the captain general of the forces of evil. As he stomped across the stage, singing in a shrill falsetto, he was the incarnation of malevolent pride and savage tyranny. Probably he represented Chiang Kai-shek. We were attempting to work out the symbolism of the scene when we became aware that the man sitting in front of us was turning his head, disturbed by our whispered conversation. The man sitting in front of us was Mao Tse-tung.

For nearly three hours we had an uninterrupted view of the back of Mao Tse-tung's head. It was a good head, well-rounded, the gleaming blue-black hair swept back, the ears large, well formed and fleshy, and there was a small fold of skin rolling above the tight collar of his Sun Yat-sen uniform. But the most remarkable thing about him was that it kept bobbing up and down, weaving backward, forward and sideways, and was never still. He was obviously enjoying the opera. He liked movement, and when there was no movement, when for example a solitary singer occupied the stage, he was likely to gaze up at the side of the proscenium arch which was painted with an immense portrait of him. On the other side there was an immense portrait of Chu Teh. Gazing at his own portrait, Mao Tse-tung seemed to lose himself in long reveries.

For at least half the opera Mao Tse-tung behaved like an excited schoolboy, jumping up and down, enjoying the wild frolic on the stage, but the moment the frolic came to an end he was quite obviously oppressed by an overwhelming sense of boredom and found relief in the contemplation of his own image. He especially enjoyed the great colorful entrances of the heroes, the captains with their nodding plumes, emerald crowns and red-gold robes, who whirled across the stage, wildly waving their riding whips and fluttering their sleeves, but he also enjoyed the scenes in which the peasants, armed with sticks, attacked the citadels of their adversaries. At such moments the crowded stage was given over to choreographed battles of immense complexity.

The music in a Chinese opera is terribly repetitive: the whine of the violins, the clash of cymbals, the tattoo of drums. The soporific quality of the music has the effect of extinguishing one's sense of time, and everything seems to be happening in an eternal present. The background was a blue sheet lit by powerful lights, and the unchanging blue sheet burned into the eyes. This, too, produced a curious numbing effect on the onlooker, who soon found himself wholly at the mercy of the performers, believing in the truth of everything they did, even those things that were demonstrably fictions. A girl comes to the front of the stage and opens an imaginary door with a quick twist of her fingers, or a carriage drives up—we know it is a carriage because two men come forward, each bearing a yellow banner on which a carriage wheel is painted. The general mounts the carriage by lifting one leg. After a while these conventions become not only acceptable but completely convincing: the carriage constructed out of two banners becomes far more real, far more compelling, than any carriage made of wood and paint.

There was a wonderful moment when the son of the rebel general falls into the clutches of the landlords. He says he is only a poor peasant but the landlords are suspicious and attempt to examine his hands. To trick him, the landlords engage him in the finger game, the very noisy and exhausting guessing game that accompanies all Chinese drinking bouts. In this game the two contestants throw out their hands with or without extending their fingers, and each has to guess how many fingers are going to be extended or whether no fingers will be extended.

The son of the rebel general plays the game in such a way that they never have a chance to examine his hands. This comic interlude was played so well that the whole audience was roaring with laughter and excitement, and Mao Tse-tung nearly bounced himself out of his seat. At the end the peasants were triumphantly slaughtering their enemies and singing at the top of their voices, while the red flags waved and Chiang Kai-shek knelt before them, pleading for his life. Then the lights on the stage went out, and in the darkness Mao Tse-tung slipped away. For a moment we saw him bowing to his friends in the darkness outside the theater, and then he was gone.

Two days later I sat behind him again in the large cave belonging to the Yenan Observer Group. The American major sometimes showed films flown up from Peking, and Mao Tse-tung was invited to see the film *A Walk in the Sun* describing the adventures of American soldiers behind the German lines in Italy. A screen was stretched against the back of the cave and a projector stood near the cave mouth. There were four armchairs and about a dozen cane-bottomed chairs. Mao Tse-tung arrived with his wife and two children, and the moment they sat down in the armchairs the film began.

A Walk in the Sun was one of those films in which Hollywood demonstrated its mastery of the unreal and the inconsequential. The American soldiers were seen wandering helplessly across an imaginary Italian countryside, at odds with one another, without any concerted plan. They hole up in a small villa, fight their way out, and then wander aimlessly across the countryside. At the beginning Mao Tse-tung kept bobbing up and down, but after a while his head sank back against the armchair never to rise again. Unlike the Chinese opera, the film gave an impression of total unreality so that it was impossible to believe that the soldiers or the landscape ever existed. When it was over Yang Shan-k'un and Mao Tse-tung engaged in a whispered discussion of the film, and a few minutes later Yang Shan-k'un came over and said: "The Chairman would like to know whether the Americans really fight like that." I said I was sure they did not. They had won great victories in pitched battles; they did not wander aimlessly about the countryside. All the time Yang Shan-k'un permitted an ironical smile to play on the corners of his lips.

Since those days I have been haunted by the thought that Mao Tse-tung's contempt for American fighting power may have had its origin on that evening when he saw a strangely disorganized film in a cave in Yenan. The "paper tiger" was manufactured in Hollywood. Three years later when vast quantities of American arms fell into his possession, and when he rode in triumph through Peking on a captured jeep followed by a column of American tanks, he would inevitably think all the less about American fighting power, although the captured armaments were prizes taken from the Nationalist armies. Yang Shan-k'un returned to Mao Tse-tung, whispered something and then beckoned. Then for the first time I shook hands with Mao Tse-tung, his wife and the two children. Handshaking was evidently a concession to western custom, and Mao Tse-tung had no liking for it. One shoulder went up, the hand came out awkwardly, and he seemed relieved when it was over. His wife, a former actress, shook hands more naturally, and the children shook hands very solemnly. They were about six and eight years old, dressed in warm woolens against the cold nights, and they had slept through the film.

The children were rosy-cheeked, and Mao Tse-tung's wife was much prettier than Madame Chiang Kai-shek. There was an unaffected naturalness about her. She wore black slacks, a painted blouse, and a heavy western coat, and all her movements were graceful. Unlike Mao Tse-tung, who spoke only Hunanese and could scarcely be understood by anyone from the other provinces, she spoke in Mandarin, the language of Peking.

Because it was growing dark, the American major began to haul down the American flag which flew above his cave, and as Mao Tse-tung stood there at the cave mouth he seemed to be absorbed in watching the slow descent of the flag. Finally, it was carefully folded up and placed inside the cave. Mao Tse-tung watched every movement made by the American major, as though engrossed by the ritual.

While he was waiting for his jeep to arrive—the one remaining jeep belonging to the Communists in Yenan—I asked Yang Shan-k'un whether I could have a talk with Mao Tse-tung. After all, I was now one of the world's authorities on the back of Mao Tse-tung's head, for I had twice sat behind him, and it was time to study him face to face. The message was conveyed to Mao Tse-tung, who thought about it for a few minutes, stroked his chin, and said: "Perhaps." It was not quite the answer I had been hoping for.

I was beginning to wonder whether I would ever come closer to that elusive and perplexing man who seemed to hold the destiny of China in his hands. I had seen him three times, shaken his hand once, and spent at least four hours minutely examining the back of his head. I had very little confidence in his "perhaps," and it was beginning to look as though I would return to Peking without asking him a single question or receiving a single reply.

A DINNER WITH MAO TSE-TUNG

In the early mornings the sun slanting over the yellow hills exploded in purest sheets of gold. About all this wide valley there hung a particular splendor, as of a place which is beautiful and still virgin, seen in the early morning of the world. I would wake up on the hard bunk inside the cave and see the yellow light pouring through the cave mouth and wonder whether the day could possibly be as beautiful as the previous day. Then, washing in a canvas bucket just outside the cave, seeing the crested hills, the shadowy caves in the distance and the river no more than a small stream wandering leisurely through golden sands, I would find myself saying: "It can't possibly be true." Day after day the sun shone against the perfect blue skies, and every day the valley became more beautiful.

All through their history the Chinese have been haunted by the thought that they might one day come upon a perfect landscape. Hills, valleys, rivers, streams, orchards, all these would be in harmony. There would be pathways leading to small houses hidden in groves of trees, and there might be a boat floating casually on the river, but the works of men would have only a small place in the landscape. So it was in Chinese paintings, and so it was in the valley of Yenan. Sometimes you would see some women washing clothes in the river or some men in drab blue uniforms climbing the roads carved out of the loess hills on the way to their caves, but just as often you would see no one at all. When a cart came along the valley, the wheels bit deep into the dust and threw up enormous yellow clouds like huge feathers. Then the feathers would be blown away in the wind, and there was only the valley, depth upon depth of yellow. When there was no wind, the feathers would simply hang there, gradually disintegrating and crumbling under their own weight.

But it was at noon that Yenan really achieved its greatest beauty, for then the whole valley shimmered in the haze and the hills seemed to grow larger, magnified by the heat, quivering as a landscape quivers when seen through fumes of boiling lead. There were noons when it seemed that the valley must inevitably melt, so great was the heat pouring out of the sultry indigo-blue sky. At such times people took refuge in the caves, which remained cool even at midday, and the animals clustered in what little shade remained. The gates of the ancient city of Yenan were still standing, and at midday you would see old men squatting in the shade of the gates and smoking their pipes, gazing across the valley with eyes like slits. In all that immensity nothing moved, nothing stirred. There was only the heat.

In the afternoon life flowed back again, and sometimes you would see the farmers climbing the steep paths to the fields of winter wheat on the hills, or someone making his way from one cave to another. Life was curiously leisurely in the valley. Only toward evening, in some mysterious way, the valley seemed to quicken with life—the life of decision, of orders and commands and summary judgments. In the depths of the caves the seeds of power were germinating.

Apart from the handsome American major I was the only foreigner in Yenan. The Communists denied that there were any Russians in the valley, and I never saw any. Yang Shan-k'un said there had in fact been a Russian in Yenan three or four months ago: a veterinary surgeon urgently summoned to put down a disease among the local horses. I found no reason to disbelieve him.

Shortly before I left Yenan, Yang Shan-k'un sent a message across the valley inviting us to dinner at the "foreign office." This was the small building with the rice-paper windows, little more than a shack, which stood near his farmhouse. When we arrived at the farmhouse, there was no sign of the chief of staff. His children were playing in the garden, and a bored soldier on guard duty was picking his nose and gazing at the distant hills. We went on to the "foreign office," a room just large enough to hold a round blackwood table. Surprisingly, the walls were decorated with photographs of Chiang Kai-shek, President Truman and Prime Minister Attlee. There was also a portrait of Mao Tse-tung. The photograph of Attlee had been blown up from a magazine and bore only a faint resemblance to the prime minister.

It was not a particularly inviting place, although from the appearance of the four portraits it was obviously the chief reception room in the Communist capital. Cobwebs hung from the wall, there was dust everywhere, and there was the musty smell of a room which has not been aired for a long time. Clearly the "foreign office" was rarely used, for there were few foreign visitors. As we entered, some soldiers were wiping the dust off the table.

We were not told the names of the other guests who would be invited, and assumed that the dinner party was being given by Yang Shan-k'un in his capacity as unofficial foreign minister. The soldiers were laying out six places round the table, and soon three Chinese professors who had flown up from Peking entered the room. With Yang Shan-k'un, the young American major and me this meant that we were all properly supplied with bowls and chopsticks. Suddenly the soldiers began to race about, orders were shouted, more bowls and chopsticks were hurriedly placed on the table, and a moment later Chu Teh and Mao Tse-tung entered arm-in-arm. Mao Tse-tung was wearing a brown Sun Yat-sen uniform, very new and crisp, and evidently uncomfortable, while Chu Teh wore a gray padded cotton uniform. He was limping heavily and smiling his broad smile of a *bon paysan*. A moment later Mao Tse-tung's wife arrived, greeting everyone with an enchanting *"Nin hao"* (How are you?) and she was followed by Peng Teh-huei, who was also wearing a new crisp uniform. Suddenly Yang Shan-k'un and one of the Chinese professors vanished. It was like a game of musical chairs, with the professor and the chief of staff losing out, or perhaps there was not enough room for them at the crowded table. When finally we sat down to table there was Mao Tse-tung, the American major, Chu Teh, two Chinese professors, myself, Peng Teh-huei, Madame Mao Tse-tung and an interpreter.

I remember thinking that this small dinner party in a small house in Yenan had something in common with one of those fabulous balls described by Tolstoy in *War and Peace*. The generals come together at the invitation of the emperor, frolic for a few moments, and then depart. In my mind there was no doubt at all that these men without badges of rank were the future emperors and princes of China.

Over a dinner of boiled meat, lettuce and maize, Mao Tse-tung, prompted by one of the Chinese professors, began to talk about the Long March in a low, feminine voice. They had asked him for his own experiences. Instead he talked about Chu Teh. "It was extraordinary," he said. "Chu Teh was the only one who had the courage to go through the grasslands twice. The rest of us felt we were lucky enough if we succeeded in traveling across them once." Sometimes he smiled at Chu Teh, and there would come from the commander-in-chief of all the Red Armies a growling reply or a boyish laugh. It was growing dark, and one by one the people in the room seemed to disappear in the thick wheeling shadows until at last the electric light from the American generator on the other side of the river came up, blinding us all in its yellow glare. The sun sets quickly in North China, the high loess hills glow for a moment as though turned to beaten gold, then the darkness falls. The valley of Yenan becomes strangely silent, and the only sound comes from the distant howling of the wolves.

The elderly professors listened to Mao Tse-tung's stories with an air of discreet politeness, which concealed their excitement. Madame Mao Tse-tung listened even more attentively, for she had married him long after the Long March and there were many things he had not told her. On this occasion she wore a thick woolen sweater and black trousers, and looked surprisingly young and pretty, carrying herself with a natural dignity. Once she said: "Did this really happen?" and he smiled at her indulgently, almost protectively, as though to show that it was possible to survive even more terrible hardships.

In the legend of the Long March no incident was more famous than the ascent of the Great Snow Mountains, and the professors questioned him about it.

"I was terribly ill during that time," he said. "We seemed to be climbing up vertical sheets of ice, and I have no idea how I survived. Some fell down the mountainside and perished from the cold. Sometimes in the plains it was just as bad, for we were surrounded by mystery and horror. We did not know where we were. We had no maps. There were places where no one had ever been before, places so solitary we thought we had reached the end of the world. I don't know where my strength came from, for day after day I remember marching without any sleep. Day after day, endlessly." When I asked him what was his worst memory of the Long March, he answered: "The cold —the terrible cold."

But in this warm room, by the light of the electric lamps, everything seemed warm, secluded, very friendly. We drank rice wine from little cups shaped like eggcups. There were the inevitable toasts drunk with grave solemnity. Mao Tse-tung rose and drank a toast to England, and this was probably the only time in his life when he drank such a toast. I replied with a toast to the Eighth Route Army, whereupon the American major drank to the health of Mao Tse-tung. Suddenly Ying-kuo and Mei-kuo, England and America, became friendly presences in Yenan, to be admired and cherished for their sacrifices against the fascist powers. From time to time Mao Tse-tung stood up and leaned across the table to place choice tidbits in our bowls, for he was very much the host conscious of his responsibilities. Sometimes, too, he would laugh gently at Peng Teh-huei, who suffered from ulcers and therefore was permitted to eat only gruel and drink only milk. Later Peng Teh-huei would become commander-in-chief of the Chinese Army in Korea, and later still he would be drummed out of the Communist Party.

When dates and pears were served, Mao Tse-tung remembered his hunger during the Long March. They killed their horses and pack animals for food. Starvation threatened them. Of all the places he had traveled through, he remembered most the grasslands—those immense fields of waist-high grass growing out of marshes. In this borderland near Tibet the Red Army very nearly came to grief. "The best fighters we ever faced were the aboriginals," he said. "We learned to respect the Miaos, the Fans, the Mis and the Huans. They were determined to prevent us from getting through, and we were just as determined to go through their territory, and so, when we could, we bargained with them, but often we had to fight them." Then a little later, smiling ironically, he said: "We owe a great debt to the Generalissimo for driving us into these strange regions, which we would never otherwise have seen." He was fascinated by the extraordinary changes in scenery: every day there was an entirely new landscape. One of the professors asked him what was the most extraordinary thing he saw during the journey. He said: "Some fish in a river near Tibet. We waded out, and the fish came streaming toward us. They were not afraid, because there had never been any fishermen in the river." Then someone asked him how they had managed to come through unharmed, and he answered: "The vast territories of China and the backwardness of everything."

Backwardness became the theme of a sermon, and indeed he resembled a priest sitting over a Sunday dinner and remembering the adventures of his youth in a primitive country. By "backwardness" he meant the lack of organization, the nature of the primitive societies they passed through, the unpreparedness of the enemy. Chiang Kai-shek never committed his own shock troops in the battles against the Communists, but instead ordered the armies of the provincial warlords to attack them, and the warlords had no very great liking for Chiang Kai-shek. Psychologically, the war was won before it was engaged. "There was never a moment when we were not absolutely certain we would win through," he said.

In fact, there were many moments when the Red Army was in terrible danger. Mao Tse-tung admitted that at first he was paralyzed with fear when the first bombing planes came over, dropping bombs on the thin column of Red Army soldiers. Then, seeing what little damage they did, he rationalized the experience, coming to the conclusion that China in its vast immensity could absorb millions of bombs without any notable change in the appearance of the landscape. The Chinese Communists learned very early not to be afraid of tanks, armored trains and airplanes. They had a supreme contempt for them, relying on guns and knives. The battle, the real battle, was being fought for people's souls, and in that battle tanks, armored trains, and airplanes had very little meaning.

As he described the Long March, Mao Tse-tung sometimes spoke excitedly, waving his hands, and the color mounted in his cheeks, so that he resembled the rebel leader in the Chinese opera we had seen a few days previously. In the opera the rebel leader came leaping onto the stage with a firebrand in his hand while simultaneously the whole stage was bathed in the glare of saltpeter flames. The castles of the landlords went up in flames. So now, while we ate his succulent pears, we became increasingly aware that Mao Tse-tung was splitting up into many distinct personalities. He was the romantic revolutionary on fire with revolutionary ideas, but he was also the retiring scholar and the calm spectator of events and the author of the opera which he had dreamed up during long studious nights. He was a man playing several parts, and no one would ever know what compulsion drove him to becoming so various. Scholar, revolutionary, student, military strategist, poet, propagandist—he was all these, but he was considerably more. Those soft hands held China in their steel-like grip.

We all watched him closely, hoping that at any moment he would reveal his real self—a gesture, a sudden illuminating sentence, an anecdote which would tell us more about him than we had ever known. Instead, there was a smiling host lifting an eggcup to his lips. There was no electricity, no suggestion of extraordinary powers, no charisma. When the Generalissimo enters a room he is accompanied by his private electric storm; you are instantly aware of a crackling in the air, and if he comes from behind, you wheel round to confront him. Mao Tse-tung had slipped into the room very casually, without ostentation, without a storm.

The young American major took some flashlight photographs and then he gave the camera to a Chinese soldier, who had never held a camera before. Some trick of the flashlight produced a photograph in which Chu Teh looks ferocious, while Mao Tse-tung appears as gentle and reserved as a young girl.

Suddenly the electric light went out and in the darkness Mao Tse-tung called for oil lamps. As the lamps were lit, there came a brief moment when his huge shadow went racing across the wall, rippling over paper windows and crowding the ceiling; and seeing the shadow, we thought we had seen the real Mao who had eluded us throughout the dinner.

The party came to an end, the chairs slid back, the table was cleared, and one by one the guests departed, while Mao Tse-tung accompanied each to the door. He had said during the dinner that he would talk with me afterward, and I remained behind. When he returned, he looked grim, his dark eyes glowing and his mouth set in a hard line. Yang Shan-k'un had said he hated being interviewed and had sworn he would never permit himself to be interviewed again, but for some reason he had relented. He threw his legs astraddle a chair, leaning his arms across the top of the chair, half his face lit by a rapeseed-oil lamp, the other half lost in the shadows. I asked him about his poems, especially the poem *The Snow*, which had been printed in Chungking and was now famous all over China.

"I wrote it in the airplane taking me to Chungking to see the Generalissimo," he said. "Then I gave it to a friend, urging him to let no one see it. He immediately published it without my permission." He said this without anger or bitterness. "I don't like my poems," he went on "They're bad—terribly bad! I only write poetry to waste time."

I said that the students at Lienta knew his poem by heart. Two or three other poems were known and they were circulated in manuscript. He smiled incredulously and said: "They have no business wasting their time with these poems."

Through General Marshall's good offices there had come about a period of truce between the Kuomintang armies and the Red Army, but the investigation teams were continually reporting small battles and skirmishes. Could anything be done to prevent war from breaking out? He snapped: "Yes, the Kuomintang should stay in their own territory and leave us alone. They are always committing acts of treachery. Are we supposed to sit back and let them do whatever they please?"

"So the fighting goes on?"

"Yes, the fighting goes on. The people who are fighting us don't want democracy at all. There won't be peace until they learn what democracy is. It doesn't matter how many tanks and airplanes they send against us. We are not afraid of them."

I asked him what the Red soldiers would do when confronted with heavy tanks supplied by the Americans.

"We'll tear them apart with our bare hands," he said, and threw out his hands and feet like a Chinese boxer.

He looked deadly serious. There was nothing theatrical in the gesture. For many months I had been convinced that the Red Army would conquer the Generalissimo's armies, and at that moment I knew for a certainty that their victory was inevitable. I could not imagine a Kuomintang general saying those words.

The civil war in Spain had raged for two and a half years and a million people had been killed. If there was a civil war in China millions upon millions would be killed, because civil wars are more deadly than foreign wars. Was it worth while to fight a war which would produce multitudes of dead?

He answered that civil war in Spain could not be compared with civil war in China.

"In the first place the situation in Spain is quite different to the situation in China," he said. "There were only eight million people fighting against Franco, but the Chinese liberated area numbers a population of a hundred and thirty million. The Spanish Republic fought for three years, while we have been fighting for twenty-one years. As for the dead, you should ask the Kuomintang, who kill and mutilate the Red Army soldiers who fall into their hands. We did not bring this war on China; they forced it on us. From the very beginning up to now we have desired peace and we do not want this war to be prolonged."

He was angry when he spoke about the heavy equipment given to the Kuomintang by the Americans. Originally intended for use against the Japanese, it was being turned against the Red Army.

"We are losing too many men," he said bitterly. "Even though we capture most of the equipment sent against us, the price is too high. Better if they stopped sending supplies to the Kuomintang. There are people abroad who do not want or approve of democracy in this country: these people are acting with the consonance of the reactionaries of China. Let them know that whatever happens, even if we are faced with mechanized war, we shall win in the end."

We spoke about England and I reminded him that there was a socialist government in a country that had never known a real socialist government before. The heavy industries were owned by the state, social programs hitherto unthought of were being introduced by the government, socialism was being practiced in a country which had changed its government without bloodshed. He shook his head. He did not believe that England had become truly socialist. "They took over the heavy industries only because they need them for export," he said. "If they were really socialist, then it would be impossible to explain their foreign policy. They are still in India—"

"They have promised to go, and will go."

He looked at me as though I was a child.

"They will never leave—never," he said. "It is absolutely impossible!"

"Nevertheless they are going. The prime minister has said so, and no one in England doubts his word."

"They will stay."

"No, you are wrong!"

Mae Tse-tung's face reddened to anger, but he was too good a host to take offense. However often I insisted that the days of British colonialism were over, he refused to believe it. I told him the story of Lieutenant-General Sir Philip Christison, commanding the British troops landing in the Dutch East Indies, who announced: "I have not come to give this country back to the Dutch." Mao Tse-tung was incredulous, shaking his head from side to side. Such a statement could not possibly be reconciled with Communist theory; therefore it could not have been made; therefore it was untrue. He had never heard of Sir Philip Christison and did not know that British troops had landed in Java.

While Mao Tse-tung held fast to the rigid outlines of Communist theory, it was clear that within the theory there were infinite possibilities of adaptation and change. One moment he would say that war against the Kuomintang would result in an inevitable Communist victory, and five minutes later he would say that in a civil war neither side would win and it was better to have a coalition government. I do not think he had yet decided to launch a full-scale civil war; he was still seeking, if half-heartedly, for a way out. "There are some people abroad who hope to extend the civil war in China—they are doing everything they can to extend the war," he said. "But on our side we do not want war, and we look forward to the time when all democratic elements in all countries are united in a common aim for peace. It is as simple as that."

But of course it was never simple, and he was only too well aware of the complexities of politics. Suddenly, because we were being confounded by complexities, he began to talk about English poetry. He had read Byron and Shelley, and there had been a period when he studied English earnestly, though apparently without much success. He recognized some English words, and once he asked the interpreter to repeat in English what I had said, and repeated the words one by one, very slowly. He knew the names of countries. Ying-land, Indi-yar, Amer-eeka, Ro-shar—he spoke the words heavily, harshly, as though he liked none of them but was compelled to live with them on the same planet. From English poetry it was a short jump to Chinese poetry. I asked him once more if I could see more of his poems, but he said: "They are stupid, and you must not pay any attention to them. They are *ma-ma-hu-hu*." That delightful word means "something of no importance whatsoever."

We had been talking for over an hour and there was now some danger that he would vanish before I asked him the most important question of all. Would it not be better if the great legendary figures who dominated Chinese politics departed from the scene? China was polarized between Chiang Kai-shek and Mao Tse-tung, and if both retired there was always the possibility of a compromise solution. Let the lesser men debate and come up with their own ideas. Was he prepared to leave, if this was best for China?

Mao Tse-tung was not disturbed by the question. Indeed, he seemed to be expecting it, and it is possible that he had discussed it with Chu Teh, who had been asked the same question.

"I am no one," he said. "Why should I leave the country? A single man can do nothing. If the Generalissimo died tomorrow, the situation would be exactly the same: the same rotten society would go on. And if I died tomorrow, the Communist Party would be exactly what it is today."

I do not believe this theory of "no one." Mao Tse-tung had become a legend, larger than life, almost godlike. People spoke of him as though he were infallible and possessed superhuman powers, and sometimes they spoke in the same way about the Generalissimo. The two superhuman powers were on a collision course which would involve all China in destruction. It was not too late. If they left the scene, the Chinese would have a breathing space.

"I am no one," he repeated, "and the Generalissimo is no one. We are nothing, the social forces are everything."

A Chinese, when his visitor departs, will sometimes ask him for criticism. Following this custom, the visitor is expected to mingle blame with blandishments, saying for example that the host has been unwise in spending so much time with an unworthy visitor and that he has been altogether too indulgent.

Mao Tse-tung was not a man who would be pleased by blandishments. So I said there were two criticisms. First, the Communist radio was always saying that the Kuomintang consisted of vile, bloodsucking, treacherous bandits, and the Kuomintang radio said the same about the Communists. In theory, there was a truce between the two sides. Could not there be a verbal truce as well? There cannot be a reasonable discussion between two people screaming at each other.

I had thought this question was the least offensive of all, but it was the one which made him most angry. He spoke heatedly and impatiently, and in the light of the rapeseed-oil lamp on the table, his face, blood-red, seemed to swell ominously.

"I admit our propaganda is very bad," he said. "We are not properly trained for it. Nevertheless, when we use those adjectives, you must understand that they are perfectly true. The Kuomintang consists of criminals. That is why we are fighting, and we cannot tolerate any longer their infinite corruption and the way they treat our soldiers who have fallen into their hands."

The second criticism was briefer. I had been in many offices and caves, and seen many maps of China hanging in them, but I had not seen a single map of the world. I had the impression that the Chinese Communists totally disregarded the rest of the world.

"It is true that we do not know enough about the outside world," he replied. "It will come in time, this knowledge that you speak about. Remember that for most of our lives we have been too busy fighting to pay any attention to the rest of the world."

Saying this he looked up, as though he expected to see a map hanging on the walls of the "foreign office," a map of the world brightly colored with all the countries in their proper places. But there were only the shadows whirling in the dark room lit by a single lamp.

For a few more minutes he talked about England, which he seemed to understand better than he understood the United States, saying: "There is one good thing about England—the English are not helping to extend the war in China. We will remember that." Then for a while he looked down at his black cotton slippers, as though lost in some dream or other, or perhaps he was exhausted by the long interview. I remembered one last question I wanted to ask him. The Chinese philosopher Lao Tzu said that "government should be as simple as cooking little fishes." Did he agree with this? He smiled and said: "You may be sure that when the Communists are in power, government will be as simple as cooking little fishes."

Shortly afterward he left, wandering up the road to his cave, the heavy sloping shoulders, the blue-black glossy hair, the bowed figure colored with the blood-red light of a lantern carried by a soldier walking behind him.

A few days later I left Yenan. Until the very last day the valley lay golden in the sun, but on that morning the low gray clouds came drifting in from the east and the rain was already falling when we reached the airfield. There is sun nearly all the year round in Shensi, a hard glittering baking sun which hardly changes in intensity, though the seasons change. Now the rain fell, and the yellow hills turned grayish-green, as though dissolving in the rain. Mao Tse-tung had come to the airfield wearing sandals and blue padded cotton clothes, with a blue workman's cap worn low over his forehead. "I have come to see you off," he said, but this was persiflage, though it was meant kindly. Once again there was the strange handshake with the elbow lifted high, and once again I asked for his poems. "They are so stupid," he said. "You really mustn't pay attention to them—they are *ma-ma-hu-hu.*" There was a small group gathered around Mao Tse-tung. Chu Teh, Peng Teh-huei, Yang Shan-k'un, and a few others were being drenched in the rain.

The DC-3 gathered speed along the small runway, and through the windows we saw the future emperor and princes of China clustered together, and they looked like a group of peasants in an abandoned field, which was slowly turning silver in the rain.

PEKING SUMMER

In the Palace of the Iron-capped Prince, life went on at a leisurely pace. Summer came in with a vengeance. The skies were royal blue, blue mingled with gold from the dust of the Gobi Desert, and there were only small puffballs of cloud that soon melted in the heat. Then the summer rains came, and for a few hours there were thunderous downpours. Afterward the sun came out more strongly than ever, and there was the pleasant whispering sound of the waters trickling away. Peking after the rains gleamed like golden ice.

The storms were spectacular. There were days and nights when you would have thought the city would be washed away in the rains, or at the very least all the roof tiles would be blown away. The courtyards became lakes, the streets became rivers, the trees bent as though they were being lashed by tropical hurricanes. But in fact these storms did very little harm, and even the ricksha pullers, bowling along at an incredible pace, seemed not to be aware that the streets were three inches deep in water. Sometimes at night we heard crackling explosions, as a roof was struck by lightning and a few tiles clattered to the ground. But these storms gave a quickening flavor to the lives of the people of Peking, who seemed almost unnaturally calm and unhurried.

It was the time when the market places were filled with melons, the red flesh so succulent that we found ourselves eating them all day long. The large black seeds were also succulent. The melons, cooled in an icebox, were very juicy, but lacked the delicate flavor of Szechuan melons with their suggestion of honey, strawberries and lemons. A Peking melon, like Peking itself, possessed a certain stateliness and grandeur; it was a full meal; and we gorged ourselves. One could exist quite happily in Peking on a diet of melons, hot tea and *mant'ou*, the creamy white bread of North China, and if in addition there was an occasional serving of Peking duck, so much the better.

As for Peking duck, many opinions have been held and much has been written about them, nearly always in superlatives. My own opinion was more conservative, for though I was prepared to agree that no other food could be compared with it, and that the ambrosia of the gods was almost certainly Peking duck, I was not prepared to agree that it can be eaten only in Peking. I have tasted duck cooked in the Peking fashion in Chungking and Kunming which was just as good as the duck served in the drab restaurant off Morrison Street which is universally regarded as the proper home of Peking duck. The restaurant was dirty, the service was poor, the duck took two hours to come to the table. The truth was that we never found any good restaurants in Peking.

In Kunming I had imagined that life in Peking would be ceremonial, with brilliant festivities taking place every week. I imagined processions moving at dusk through the palace court-yards, acolytes bearing spirit lamps, and much worshiping of ancestral tablets. In fact, there were no ceremonies at all except on the anniversary of Hsiung Hsi-ling's death. On that day his silver-framed photograph was hung above an altar heaped with bowls of fruit, and in the center of the altar stood the ancestral tablet surrounded by joss-sticks. The relatives would come and kneel before the tablet, and there would be a brief ceremony supervised by a Buddhist priest. Very late in life the old Viceroy had married for a second time. His bride was a middle-aged schoolteacher with a rather severe expression, who wore spectacles, dressed drably in black and spoke in a high-pitched voice. Rose had no particular liking for her widowed step-mother and although devoted to her father, she had no patience with ancestor-worship. Consequently she held herself a little to one side, permitting the ceremonies to take place in the palace, but otherwise showing very little interest in them. The relatives were greeted politely but without enthusiasm. When I said I intended to see the ceremonies, she shrugged her shoulders.

"They will probably want you to kowtow before my father," she said. "After all, you are his son-in-law, and it will be expected of you."

It occurred to me that I had no objection to kowtowing before

the old Viceroy, who smiled with gentle benignity from the
large photograph set up on the altar.

"If you are not careful," she went on, "you'll find that you
are the ceremony."

But nothing of the kind happened, for we stood in the wings,
a little to one side of the altar, admiring the thick red candles,
the bowls of glistening fruit and the Buddhist priest who began
chanting in an interminable singsong, calling upon Buddha to
protect and preserve the soul of the departed. Then one by one
the relatives came to the altar, fell to their knees, and kowtowed,
their heads touching the floor. There were about twenty relatives, most of them elderly. Three or four of them, according
to Rose, were living in obscure corners of the palace, and it
was not surprising that I had never seen them, because they
rarely went into the street, but lived out their completely
sheltered lives within the palace walls.

"They came here long before the war," Rose was saying. "It
must have been to attend a birthday celebration given by my
father, or perhaps he was simply honoring the entire family. In
the thirties there were three or four of these celebrations, and
we had to put up hundreds of people. Some of them stayed on,
and some of them were not relatives at all."

Rose sighed, for the management of the palace had fallen on
her shoulders. She did not know all the people who were living
there, and whenever she penetrated into the courtyards far
from the main entrance there was always a sound like the whispering of leaves as people scuttled away to their hiding places.
Then, when she had gone, they would return quietly and take
up residence again in the quiet shady courtyards which were
rarely penetrated.

Meanwhile the priest was still chanting and some incredibly
old people came and kowtowed before the altar. At last it was
the turn of Rose's stepmother. *Bump, bump, bump* went her
head on the stone floor. Again and again she prostrated herself
in the ancient manner. When she rose at last, there was a bruise
on her forehead as though she had smeared herself with blue
paint. There was more chanting and then Rose gave the visitors
some food and hurried them away. Later in the day the servants
dismantled the altar and carried away the fruit. The ceremonies
were over for another year.

"What I don't understand," Rose said, "is how she could demonstrate her love for my father by bumping her head on the floor."

A week after I returned from Yenan the same American colonel who put me on the plane to Red China called again. He enjoyed showing us the latest curios he had bought, and he liked wandering round the palace. Just as he was about to leave, he said very casually: "There is a plane leaving tomorrow morning for Kalgan. If you would like to go, it is already arranged."

I spent a week in Kalgan, which the Chinese Communists occupied shortly after the surrender of Japan, thus taking possession of a vast munitions dump abandoned by the Japanese, many factories, a railhead, and a strategic position across the Great Wall. Kalgan—the name comes from the Mongolian *kalga*, a gate—was the gateway to Mongolia and all the riches of the Mongolian plains. During the Japanese occupation it was ruled by a puppet, Prince Demchukdongrob, a descendant of Genghiz Khan, whose palace lay in the shadow of the craggy blue-black mountains dominating the city. The prince, who was the titular leader of the Mongol Horde, had fled, and his palace was now occupied by General Nieh Jung-chen, the military governor of the whole region.

General Nieh was the most cultivated Chinese Communist I ever met. He had studied chemical engineering in Paris and Belgium, spoke French with only a trace of an accent, and carried himself with the air of a man who knew precisely what he was going to do at every moment of the day. In conversation Mao Tse-tung and Chu Teh were inclined to hesitate, to backtrack, to announce a theory only to change it in mid-passage. They were rough-hewn and full of knots. General Nieh had a mind like a rapier, clean and straight. He had the features of an intellectual, a fine forehead, dark eyes, a straight nose, and well-carved lips. He might be taken for a professor of science, which is what he had once hoped to be. In fact he was one of the most daring and ruthless of the Chinese Communist leaders, and he had led the vanguard in the Great March.

Few foreigners came to Kalgan, and for the moment there was little fighting in the neighborhood. I therefore saw a good deal of General Nieh, who paced about his preposterous palace filled with gewgaws left by the prince's wives and concubines.

"You understand," he said, "I have not the least desire to live in this palace. For a Communist, a palace is the ultimate absurdity. I haven't touched any of the prince's property, though I am occasionally tempted to make a big bonfire in the courtyard. I have a feeling that a good deal of this stuff may be valuable, and in the end we shall probably decide to convert the palace into a museum."

He talked about the French books he had read long ago. He had seen especially attracted by the works of Romain Rolland, and wondered whether he was still writing. He remembered the poems of Verlaine and recited them softly. "I intended to become a scholar, and instead I became a bandit," he said. Others in Kalgan regarded him as the most scholarly of the Chinese Communist generals and pointed to the fact that most of the important Chinese Communist novelists, poets and playwrights had left Yenan and were living in Kalgan. Ai Ching, the poet, and Ting Ling, the novelist and short story writer, were living in the outskirts of Kalgan and writing furiously. One gathered that there were disadvantages to living in Yenan under the impatient eye of the Master. Mao Tse-tung's judgments on literature were likely to be caustic, and he usually had excellent reasons for making them change their style, their subject matter, and their plots. In Kalgan they could write more freely.

How freely could they write? Ai Ching thought he could write as freely as he pleased. It would never occur to him to write a poem in praise of Chiang Kai-shek or the bankers of Shanghai, and he thought it highly unlikely that he would write a poem in praise of Mao Tse-tung. On the other hand he was committed to writing poetry for peasants and soldiers and much of it took the form of propaganda for the Chinese Communists. "It isn't intentionally propaganda," he said. "This is the way it comes out. The poems encourage them to live, to fight and to die for their country. It is very simple poetry."

He was a lyrical poet and a very good one. Originally he intended to be a painter, went to France, and earned a living painting pottery. He spent only a few years in France, but it was enough for him to acquire a deep knowledge of French poetry. He returned to Shanghai, joined a small study group with vaguely leftist leanings, and was promptly arrested by the French police in the International Settlement, thrown into prison, and very nearly starved to death. The experience turned him into a Communist, and when he was finally released he made his way to Yenan, where he organized resistance groups against the Japanese. It was a fairly typical career for a young writer in China. What was not typical was his lyrical gift, his power to write verses which Chinese students learned by heart and mimeographed all over China. If you asked a Chinese student in Kunming who was the greatest living Chinese poet, he would answer: Ai Ching. It did not in the least concern them that he was a Communist, and in fact there was nothing in his poetry to suggest that he was. His poetry had a naturalness, an inevitableness, that made it immediately comprehensible to the young. One verse, a fragment of a longer poem, was characteristic of his work:

> Winter is lovely in no color.
> Winter is lovely for no birds sing.
> In the winter forest a solitary walk is happiness.
> I will be like a hunter, lightly passing over,
> Nor do I think I will gain anything.

In the South we imagined him middle-aged, bearded, stooping a little as he wandered from one village to another singing his poems. We thought of him as a Chinese Whitman, a sage in homespun, exotic and garrulous. Instead, he was singularly young, handsome, deeply tanned, with a fine forehead, enormous eyes, and a chiseled mouth. He carried himself with an almost princely dignity, and when he grinned, which was often, he looked like a schoolboy. He wore a thin blue cotton suit and a blue cotton cap, and he walked with the springy stride of a man who knew exactly what he wanted to do with his life.

The name of Ting Ling was equally famous in Kuomintang China, although she too had spent the war years in Yenan. She was known chiefly for her love stories, and she occupied in Chinese letters a position roughly corresponding to that of D. H. Lawrence in the West, for she was the innovator, the first to speak of sexual love in human terms. Her characters were the feverish, rather decadent, westernized Chinese of Shanghai, among whom she had grown up. She knew them intimately and was able to describe them with passion and accuracy. After the Japanese invasion of China she turned more and more to writing about the peasants. Finally she abandoned novel-writing and wrote reportages about life in the Communist areas.

The image we had formed of her in the South was based largely on the impression conveyed by her early novels. Tall, intense, perhaps beautiful, certainly sensual and very feminine, given to wearing frilly costumes. Instead, she was short, plump, bespectacled, with the face of a happy owl. She had a gay laugh, and I think that of all the people I met in Red China she was the most at ease, happy in her writing and in love with the egalitarian society which she believed she saw around her. "We are all equal here—that is what makes life so full of joy for me," she said. Some, of course, were more equal than others, and when the Chinese Communists came to power both Ai Ching and Ting Ling were punished for their failure to follow the party line.

Even the Chinese Communists felt the strangeness of Kalgan. The sharp-bladed blue-black mountain cut across the sky, looking wildly improbable on the edge of the desert. The Japanese had fled, but they had left their traces in temples and ceremonial gates. One ceremonial gate led to a temple which served as a depository for the ashes of the Japanese dead. One day I went to the temple with General Nieh, who had never visited it. There were mountains of soft white ash, and we walked among them without quite realizing what they represented, for they resembled mountains of salt and had the consistency of powder. The general's uniform was white with the powdery ashes when we left the temple, and he was shaking his head and saying: "I did not know we had killed so many."

The American airplane came at last, and as the only passenger I had a seat in the cockpit. The pilot this time was a Virginian who enjoyed nothing better than aiming his airplane about twenty feet below the crest of a mountain, counting on the updraft to carry him over the top. He enjoyed playing this game. I enjoyed it less, but after the sixth or seventh attack on the mountain I became fascinated by the way the airplane shuddered and leaped over the edge with only a few inches to spare, like a spirited horse leaping over a fence. "Of course," the pilot exclaimed, "you can do this kind of thing once too often!" I was more grateful to him when, approaching Peking, he decided against all the rules to fly low over the yellow tiles of the Forbidden City. As we streaked over the ancient palaces, the sun struck the roofs and turned them into molten gold, and all Peking seemed to melt in the golden blaze.

There followed long days of "tiger heat," when Peking lay in the blue flames of a furnace and the gold sands of the Gobi Desert swept across the cloudless sky. The heat was terrible, but it was also invigorating. The ricksha pullers continued to run with the speed of galloping horses, but when we went into the streets we took care to walk in the shade.

One morning, reading the newspaper, Rose gave a sudden cry, and the newspaper fell out of her hand.

"Wen Yi-tuo has been killed," she said in a voice I had never heard before.

The delayed report described how the poet had been killed just outside his house in Kunming by four gangsters equipped with American revolvers fitted with silencers. His son, who was standing nearby, saw the men approaching and shouted: "Let me die for you, father." He threw himself on his father's body, and they pumped four bullets into him while he lay there. From his hospital bed the boy told a strange story of how the assassins stood over him and said before shooting him: "We must shoot you to save our lives, but we will not kill you. Later, when you have recovered, you may take revenge on us." It was as though the old feudal China had survived into the modern age. As for the assassins, no one reading the newspaper account could have any doubt that they belonged to the Kuomintang secret police.

For me and for a whole generation of Chinese students Wen Yi-tuo represented the very best of China. He knew the West, for he had studied painting at the Art Institute in Chicago and later at the University of Colorado, but he was more quintessentially Chinese than anyone else I had known. Those austere, powerful and gentle features I had encountered many years before in the paintings of Buddhist saints found in the Tunkuang Caves and now in the British Museum. Robed in purple, he would have resembled a priest. Instead, he wore a thin blue gown, usually torn and patched. He was the man people went to when they were in trouble, and all China was in trouble. They killed him because he possessed all the elements of a national leader, because he was becoming widely known, and because the students would have followed him to the ends of the earth.

It was one of those bright sunny days when the courtyard flashed gold and green, but the air became dark with horror. We knew that if they dared kill Wen Yi-tuo, then no one was safe and there was no end to the killing in store for China. The Kuomintang press announced that there would be an official inquiry, the culprits would be punished, and the family of the dead poet would be granted a pension; and nothing more was ever heard of the inquiry, and the murderers were never arrested. In one of his most famous poems Wen Yi-tuo described the feudal China of his childhood as a ditch of stagnant water:

Here is a ditch of dead and hopeless water:
No breeze can raise a ripple on it.
Best to throw in it scraps of rusty iron and copper,
And pour into it the refuse of meat and soup.

Perhaps the copper will turn green as emeralds,
Perhaps the rusty iron will assume the shape of peach blossoms.
Let grease weave a layer of silky gauze
And bacteria puff patches of cloud and haze.

So let the dead water ferment into green wine
Littered with floating pearls of white foam.
Small pearls cackle aloud and become big pearls,
Only to burst like gnats to rob the vintage.

And so this ditch of dead and hopeless water
May boast a touch of brightness:
If the toads cannot endure the deadly silence,
The water may burst out singing.

Here is a ditch of dead and hopeless water,
A region where beauty can never stay.
Better abandon it to evil—
Then perhaps some beauty will come out of it.

Now the ditch of dead water was fermenting and boiling, and no one knew what strange monsters would emerge from it.

I thought of this stagnant ditch a few days later when Rose suggested that we visit the Hunting Park in the Western Hills. For seven centuries Chinese emperors had hunted deer and wild boar in the park, and through all that time it had remained an imperial preserve to be visited only by permission of the emperor or one of the officers of the court. Then, about 1915, Rose's father had acquired the Hunting Park and transformed it into an orphanage, building schools, dormitories, workshops and porcelain kilns among the silver birches. "But the best thing of all," said Rose, "is a spring that bubbles out of the ground—the purest water in all China."

The spell of Peking held us in the city and we rarely journeyed outside its walls. Suddenly we borrowed a jeep and drove out to the hills which looked purple-gray from the city, but were green and sweet when we came to them. This particular part of the hills was called Hsiang Shan, the Fragrant Mountain, and long before we reached the orphanage there came the sweet smell of the flowers. The hills were well-watered, flowers grew everywhere, the great silver birches towered into the skies, and far away we could see the monasteries nestling on the slopes. It was one of those rare summer days when the air was limpid and cool. Rose wore her white summer gown trimmed with a thin red ribbon at the hem. It was the same dress she had worn when we were married.

When the prime minister bought the Hunting Park for three hundred taels, which he raised among his friends, he intended to build enough dormitories to house at least a thousand orphans. "China is a country of orphans," he said, "and if we had a Hunting Park ten times as large we could not begin to look after them." In fact, there were never more than three or four hundred orphans living there because there was never enough money to support them and during the war years the orphanage had simply ceased to exist. A handful of caretakers had lived there, supporting themselves by selling off the furnishings and whatever else could be sold. The paths were weed-grown, some of the tiles had fallen from the roofs, the houses had no furniture at all, but they were still solid. There were perhaps twenty houses altogether, and they were all strangely clean as though washed by recent rains.

In some of these houses the photograph of the prime minister still hung from the walls and there were scrolls bearing his calligraphy, that bold and exuberant calligraphy which was once famous all over China. In the photographs he looked wonderfully alive with his perky tuft of beard, a half-smile playing on his lips, his eyes glowing. He seemed to be present, and Rose talked about the days when she had walked hand in hand with him through these groves of pine, birch and acacia.

"He was so happy here—he was like a boy," she said. "What he liked most of all was to escape from Peking, wander in the woods, and talk to the orphans. Sometimes there were archaeological expeditions. Once they found an ancient bronze caldron which had turned bright green with age. The Peking Museum wanted it, but he refused to part with it. On the place where it was found he erected a stone plinth and riveted the caldron to it. "It belongs to the Hunting Park," he said, "and this is where it will remain."

We found the green caldron standing alone in an alleyway' of silver birches. Full-bellied, glowing like a fruit and dappled with sunlight, it stood there in magnificent isolation. Not far away was the spring of pure water, which made a little rushing sound as it came welling out of the earth. Rose knelt beside it, cupped her hands over it, and drank deeply. Then I knelt and drank, and it was true that the water was cool and pure beyond any water I had known. Then she drank again, looking very solemn, as though performing a rite, until her face was splashed all over and there were dewdrops in her hair.

"They say those who drink the water can never go far away," she said, laughing.

In a few days I would be leaving for India, England and America. I wanted to see what the world was like outside China: a six-month journey around the world, returning to Peking early the following year. Rose did not like the idea, for she had dreamed that I would never return. I laughed at her fears, and we were not thinking about the journey around the world as we walked through the Hunting Park. We came back to the spring and drank the pure water as though we were feasting on wine.

I flew to Shanghai and called on Madame Sun Yat-sen, who was living in a large mansion on the outskirts of the city. The mansion was guarded by soldiers with fixed bayonets, and heavy chains were wrapped around the great iron gates. She wore a white gown, and was far more beautiful than Madame Chiang Kai-shek, who was her sister. She lived in great comfort, in rooms filled with flowers, and in each room there was at least one armed guard. She said quietly: "Of course I expect to be shot by the Kuomintang secret police."

She had married Dr. Sun Yat-sen, the father of the Chinese Republic, when she was a young woman and her husband was middle-aged. Now, more than twenty years later, she still had the appearance of a young woman, and she smiled like a girl. Tea was served. It was chrysanthemum tea, of a soft amber color, the petals floating on the surface. While sipping the tea, she launched into a long diatribe against Chiang Kai-shek. "They say he walks in his sleep, but it is intolerable that he should go sleepwalking at this time. China is in terrible danger of civil war. The Kuomintang and the Communists must lay down their arms—it is shameful that we should be fighting each other now that the war against Japan is over."

She spoke about the Kuomintang generals who commandeered the relief supplies sent by UNRRA and sold them for their own profit. Her husband had founded the Kuomintang party in order to overthrow the corrupt Manchu Dynasty, and now the party itself was riddled with corruption. I said: "It has been like this for a long time." She shivered, for suddenly it had grown cold. A storm was brewing, the rain was drumming on the roof. "A long time," she murmured, looking out of the window at the flowers turning and twisting in fierce gusts of rain, and then she said: "There can be no solution unless they both lay down their arms and unless the Kuomintang cleanses itself. As you know, I have written a manifesto telling them in the name of my husband to make peace, and now the Kuomintang regards me as a Communist agent. What do they gain?"

I said I would soon be leaving for India and would see Nehru. She immediately called a servant, asked for pen and paper, and wrote a letter to him in English, pausing to ask how to spell the word "discipline." I was handed the letter and told to give it to Nehru with her love.

She was simultaneously a mature woman and the girl who had never grown up. One moment she was complaining about her wretched living conditions, although she was obviously living in exquisite comfort, and the next moment she was talking sensibly about the hospitals she had founded, the censorship, the secret police, the students, and her own unavailing attempts to stop the war. Once she said: "Dr. Sun Yat-sen would have cursed both sides and put himself between Chiang Kai-shek and Mao Tse-tung to stop the fighting." Sometimes, as she spoke, she lowered her head and her voice dropped to a whisper.

She got up, rearranged the flowers in their massive vases, walked up and down the fantastically beautiful Chinese carpet, and seemed close to tears. She said: "It won't end. it won't end— I believe they will go on fighting for twenty years."

On the following day I flew to Nanking and called on the British ambassador. I told him about Yenan and about Mao Tse-tung's intransigence and about the massive power of the Red Army. His thin lips were pursed together in an expression of total disbelief.

"Ah, the Red Army," he said. "Tell me, how many soldiers of the Red Army did you see in Yenan?"

"Only one. He was a courier riding along the valley to Chu Teh's headquarters."

He seemed vastly relieved, as though a great weight had been lifted from his shoulders.

"One soldier?" he exclaimed. "One soldier! Did I hear you correctly? Take it from me, if the Kuomintang army and the Red army ever come to grips with one another, there will be nothing left of the Communists!"

At that time Marshal Feng Yu-hsiang was living in Nanking. By the purest chance I arrived at his villa on a day which had great significance for him: it was his sixty-fifth birthday, the day when he was automatically retired from the army. He was still a Marshal, and was still addressed as Vice-Generalissimo, but the titles were devoid of substance, for he was no longer a member of the Supreme Military Council. "Better that I should not be!" he said. "The Generalissimo is moving his troops about as though they were his own private army. He is determined to smash the Communists, and in the process he will destroy all of China. He doesn't realize that everything has changed now that the Pacific War has come to an end."

He was speaking English better than ever, and looked wonderfully fit, the heavy face bronzed by the sun, the dark eyes gleaming. Gradually the melancholy that had settled on him with the realization that he had been ousted from the last vestiges of power gave place to mischievous good humor.

"So you are going to India? What shall we do? You know I have no patience with people who give feasts, so I will give you a little feast. An egg? Two eggs? No, it must be something quite extraordinary. Shall I read you a chapter of the Bible? We must do something quite extraordinary to celebrate your departure!"

"Something quite extraordinary" took the form of a boat ride on the lake. But Vice-Generalissimos cannot simply go down to the lakeside and enter a boat. First, a guard was sent out to choose a boat with the proper specifications: it must be quite simple, with no silk curtains or cushions, and it must be docked at a place were there were no crowds. Secondly, there was the question of what disguise he would wear, and this was solved when he decided to wear a peasant's costume and an enormous wide-brimmed hat which would conceal his features. Thirdly, we would need provisions. Fourthly, we must find a map of the lake and decide upon the itinerary. It was all worked out like a military campaign.

All these preparations took some time, and it was late in the afternoon before we reached the lake and jumped into a very large boat moored at some distance from the usual mooring place. On the whole he disapproved of the boat, which was altogether too large, and there were too many silk cushions and too much fancy scrollwork. But no one had observed him entering the boat and he was prepared to make the best of it. Soon he was chanting poems while gazing up at the sky. The first stars came out, and red lanterns appeared on all the other boats, but he thought there was some advantage in not lighting our lanterns. In this way we glided among the lotuses, keeping as far as possible from the other boats, the lake very quiet and still, so that one had the illusion of gliding through a dream.

For a while he talked about Wen Yi-tuo, whose books he had read. He said: "We have a proverb in China: 'A clear sky and lotuses are like scholars,' and we mean by this that the scholar is pure and virtuous. When a scholar is killed, then the light of the sky goes out."

It was growing so dark that he finally agreed to light one of the red lanterns. The chanting and the singing went on, and when the boat was caught among the reeds he leaped out and pulled it away. He said: "You shouldn't be surprised. I've always had to think of boats and pontoons. Now I am going to study water engineering. It is terribly important. Think what will happen when we harness the power of the Yellow River and the Yangtze River."

"Are you serious?"

"Yes, quite serious. I am going to America. I shall look at all the dams and the great waterways. It will be a long trip, perhaps a year or two."

Even then I was not quite sure whether he was serious. If he was going to America, it was probably to escape from the appalling atmosphere of Nanking, the stifling bureaucracy, the ever-present secret police. "No more politics!" he said. "I want to be a student, only a student!" When I still demurred, he said: "I will become a scholar of waterways."

A few weeks later he sailed for America and traveled up and down the country studying the waterways. In the summer of 1948 I met him several times in New York, but he was no longer the pure scholar of waterways. He had become a political figure again, rallying the opposition against Chiang Kai-shek. He wore his military uniform without badges of rank. One evening I was summoned urgently to his apartment. There were mountains of luggage all round him. He said he was taking the night train to Montreal and from there he would take ship to England. For an hour I was kept busy writing letters of introduction to friends in England. He was in good form, laughing as uproariously as ever, relating his adventures in America, saying over and over again how much he had enjoyed his visit. From England he would go on to France and Germany, for he had still not completed his study of waterways. What about his pronouncements against Chiang Kai-shek? "One can do two things at once," he said. "One can study, and one can also hope for peace in China." He gave me some photographs of himself and a book of his poems. He had written an autobiography, and he hoped it would be published in America. He came out in the street to help me find a taxi, and in the light of the street lamp he was larger than life. I never saw him again.

Some days later I read in a Boston newspaper: "General Feng Yu-hsiang, known as 'the Christian General,' and his eldest daughter were accidentally burned to death on the Soviet ship *Pobeda* as it was steaming toward the port of Odessa. It is believed that the General was operating a projector in the forward part of the ship, when the film caught fire. An inquest will be held."

I can make nothing of this report from the official Tass agency. I know that he never operated a film projector in his life. I know that he would never have said he was going to Canada and England unless he genuinely intended to go there. When I think of him now, I see him on his sixty-fifth birthday wading in the Nanking lake and lifting the boat out of the reeds with his shoulders, and in the light of the bobbing lantern he looks like an ancient denizen of the lake, pirate or seagod, so powerful that he could have held up the sky.

That night I stayed in his villa, and on the following day flew back to Shanghai. Then, after being shuttled from one functionary to another to have my passport stamped, I flew to Calcutta.

A SMALL MASSACRE

India was another color, another sky, another planet. Coming down low over the green hills of Assam, having left the Salween, the Irrawaddy and all the rivers of China behind, we were aware that the sky had not so much changed its color as changed its substance. The air was smoky yellow, clotted with the dust of innumerable plains, not watery and transparent as in China. Silver stream after silver stream flowed into the Bay of Bengal, but everywhere we looked the sea was yellow. For fifty miles out to sea there flowed the yellow detritus of the plains and the mud of the Ganges.

It was dusk, the "cowdust hour," when we landed at Dum Dum airfield far in the outskirts of Calcutta. A brilliant yellow haze, soft at the edges, shadowed the field, where the bombers lay in rows, rusting now, for the wars were over. When we stepped out of the airplane, the heat burned into our faces like acid, and the dust choked us. Walking across the airfield, I began to wonder why I had left China with its cool skies and golden palaces for this hothouse of smoking dust, the earth steaming after the rains and the dust thickening the air.

In Singapore there were Sikhs in colored turbans and small wiry Tamils moving with astonishing grace, but at Dum Dum there were neither Sikhs nor Tamils. The British were in charge: polite, brisk, well-laundered, with gleaming buckles and gleaming ribbons on their chests, absurdly sure of themselves. They were direct, and this puzzled me, since for nearly five years I had taught myself to speak in the Chinese manner, indirectly, with deliberate hesitations and half-apologies, and I was still bowing to everyone I met. It took six months before the habit was finally cured.

The British saddened me: I had forgotten that they were so brisk and so ugly. I remembered the British military attaché in Chungking who thought the Chinese face the most beautiful in the world, and Western faces were like two potatoes glued together. They were efficient, but they seemed scarcely human. More human were the Indians, inelegant in their dhotis, wrinkled white cotton skirts looped up between their legs, their faces so dark and seamed that they might have been carved out of mahogany, and the whites of their eyes were stained with yellow. They were so thin that the bones stuck out through their skins. These Bengalis had none of the grace of the Tamils or the martial bearing of the Sikhs, and they were weighed down with poverty.

A Bengali, who must have been about sixty, with a dark knotted face and a day's growth of spiky white beard, whispered: "Taxi, sahib," and one look at him convinced me that he could no more drive a taxi than pilot an airplane. The weight of centuries bowed his shoulders. His eyes were pools of viscous yellow, his lips were wet, his hair an indeterminate white. He wore a soiled shirt, and one lean leg was bare, while the other leg vanished in the dusty folds of his dhoti. There was no grace in him, but he had a grave dignity and stood out from among the other poor Bengalis as one who was imperturbable and passionless, for he did not care whether I would take his taxi, but kept on muttering: "Taxi, sahib," as though by instinctive habit. Finally, I got into his taxi and immediately regretted it, for the springs coiled up through the threadbare cushions, the paint was peeling, and the engine coughed menacingly.

In later years I wondered often why I had chosen him, when there were twenty others to choose from. Of all the Indians I have ever known he was the one whose face and features are most clearly stamped on my memory. His name, he said, was Das Gupta, but that is a name he shared with thousands of other Bengalis, thus reducing him to the ranks of anonymity.

He was a good driver and his taxi was unworthy of him; he was not what he seemed to be. He spoke in a soft musical voice about his family, his wife and five daughters, all of them married now, and his life in a crumbling tenement somewhere in the east of Calcutta. He was sorry he had no sons, but the girls had given him pleasure. Besides, with girls, there was no need to provide money for education and they had married well. So he talked, while the light faded, and I gave myself up to the contemplation of the crowds of Indians in the streets, their movements, the beautiful gestures of their hands, the way they held their heads.

In his throaty singsong voice Das Gupta said: "We'll take a short cut, sahib, if that is agreeable."

We drove through a working-class district where the washing was hanging out to dry and the hot smells of urban India filled our nostrils. Suddenly there was a piercing yell, a knife flashed, and we could see people fighting just in front of us. White gowns and shirts and dhotis were turning scarlet. Although it was dusk, we could see clearly. Two mobs were hacking at each other with knives and swords; there was the sharp smell of blood, and the screaming was so high-pitched that it was almost inaudible. There was blood on the knives: it was astonishing how quickly a shirt could turn red. No doubt the driver could have backed the taxi, but that would have meant knocking down the crowd gathering behind us. Instead, he blew on a police whistle, pressed down hard on the accelerator, and carved through the two mobs at each other's throats. We could feel the thump of bodies against the taxi, and the people in front of us seemed to be made of elastic as they jumped out of our path, while others appeared to come floating up from under the wheels.

We had seen enough to know that we had witnessed a small massacre. We did not know how much we had added to the massacre, but it was inconceivable that we could plow through such a mob without killing anyone. It was all over in less than a minute. We lurched around a corner on two screaming wheels and came into a street where nothing whatsoever was happening except that people were walking calmly along the sidewalk. Das Gupta still had the police whistle clenched between his teeth. The whistle was on a chain around his neck, and at last he let it drop.

"I apologize, sahib," he said gravely. "I use the whistle because the horn does not work. Please don't tell the police commissioner."

I promised not to tell the police commissioner, and asked him whether massacres were common in Calcutta.

"Unfortunately, sahib, they happen nearly every day. It is very regrettable, but the Hindus and the Muslims are—" He shook his head helplessly, but no words came. When we reached the hotel in the center of Calcutta, he said: "I apologize for taking the short cut, sahib. In future I will always go the long way." I reflected that within half an hour of landing in India I had seen a small massacre in a crowded street and met a courageous Bengali.

That night I sat in a vast room in the hotel, while a metal fan wheezed overhead, and black moths hurled themselves at the lamps. Outside my door a servant in a dusty blue turban sat cross-legged, waiting to run errands for me, and if I opened the door and walked down the immense corridor, I would find servants sitting outside every door. Calcutta, it seemed, was a city of servants, wheezing fans, black ants, black moths, and massacres.

I knew what I wanted to do in India, and Calcutta had little part of it. There were four men and eight places I wanted to see. The men were Gandhi, Nehru, Jinnah, and Jinnah's second in command, Nawabzab Liaquat Ali Khan, who was thought to be the intelligence behind Jinnah's rhetoric, the man who was shaping the idea of Pakistan and giving it form and substance. The eight places were Delhi, Agra, Fatehpur Sikri, Daulatabad, Aurungabad, and the sculptured caves of Elephanta, Ellora and Ajanta. I did not see Gandhi, but I saw Nehru, Jinnah, and the Nawabzab. They said of Gandhi that he was unreachable and would see no one, and it was probably true.

Three days later in Delhi I sat in an overstuffed chair with ornate gilded armrests in the Nawabzab's mansion. "Nawabzab" was a princely title, and he lived in princely magnificence. There were Chinese vases on delicately carved mahogany tables, the deep-piled carpets were so soft you could drown in them, and there was a vast clutter of tables, carvings, silver-framed photographs and knickknacks.

He was the first Indian prince I had ever met, and he looked the part to perfection. He was heavily built, jowly, obviously accustomed to snapping out commands and seeing them instantly obeyed. He wore white trousers under a long pearly-gray kaftan with gold buttons going down the full length of it. The eyes were clear behind thick spectacles, which magnified them, and he had a lawyer's voice, throwing emphasis where he pleased. He said he was ill and tired, and would grant me no more than ten minutes, and went on to speak for nearly two hours about the necessity of Pakistan, the crimes of the Hindus, the appalling ignorance and general imbecility of the British Raj, and the indifference of the world's leaders to the real problems of India. He marshaled ideas with the ease of a practiced speaker, but all the ideas led to Pakistan.

"Of course, the trouble lies with the pernicious caste system of the Hindus," he said, as though stating a fact almost too obvious to be mentioned. "You must start from there—all the evils that come from stratification, the lords and masters at the top and the sweepers at the bottom. We have nothing in common with the Hindus, for there is not the least stratification among us. I am the brother of every Muslim, and we are all equals in the sight of God, but the brahmin is not the equal of the sweeper.

"So we have two totally different societies, and there is absolutely nothing in common between them. Our customs, our food, our ways of life and worship are so different that we might be peoples belonging to different worlds. I ask you, what have we in common with them? Must we be everlastingly exploited by them, or fobbed off with empty promises? What power will we have if Congress rules India? We shall have the power to be exploited, yes, mercilessly exploited by the Birlas and the Tatas, with their huge industrial empires. They support Congress, because it is to their advantage, but we have no millionaires supporting us."

On the table, in a square frame, lay a map of India hammered out of a sheet of silver with large curiously shaped inlays of green enamel. All of Bengal, and most of northwest India from Karachi to Kashmir were in green enamel, together with Assam. About a third of India was labeled "Pakistan." He had been tapping on this silver-green map with his heavy fingers, and now he turned it round and showed it to me. It was beautifully made, with all the mountains and rivers clearly indicated, the silver and green flashing in the sunlight coming through wide windows: just such a toy as a Mughal emperor might carry about with him in his travels to remind him of the extent of his empire. But the map was strangely faceless, for not a single city or province, nor any word except "Pakistan" appeared on it. I said: "If Pakistan breaks off from India, there will be a terrible bloodletting."

"What is bloodletting?"

"The shedding of blood."

He laughed softly.

"There will be bloodshed, of course. The Hindus have forced it on us."

The strange thing was that he spoke almost lightheartedly, as though this was the least important problem facing him.

I said I had seen a small massacre in Calcutta within half an hour of arriving in India.

He had been leaning back in his sofa, like an emperor among cushions, and now he leaned forward and interrogated me about it. Where had it happened? Who had attacked first? How many were killed? I replied briefly, but I could answer none of his questions, and was led to understand that I had seen nothing more dangerous than a scrimmage on a football field. He had been a famous football player in his youth. He said: "You must expect a few broken noses when people are so profoundly antipathetic to each other."

"It will get worse," I said, "unless someone decides to stop it. It's not a question of broken noses, but killing women and children. China is in the midst of a civil war, and soon it will be India unless you stop it. I am told you have the power to stop it."

He muttered something about "things have gone too far," and blamed the British cabinet mission for raising such high hopes, while leaving most problems unsolved. "Three weary old men came here, promised one thing to the Muslim League and something else to Congress, and left us to solve our own problems," he said. "Well, you can be sure we will find some way to solve them. We are warriors and we shall give a good account of ourselves."

"That means civil war raging through India?"

"Yes, unless they give us Pakistan."

Already in his imagination Pakistan existed, and the evidence for it lay in the silver-green map on which his fingers drummed so relentlessly. His belief in Pakistan was so firm that you felt he had lived with it all his life. In fact, the idea of Pakistan was scarcely more than twelve years old, having been conceived by an Indian Muslim, Chaudhary Rahmat Ali, while living in England in 1933. Originally it was thought of as a federation of Muslim states including the Punjab, Afghanistan, Kashmir and Sind. The original river had overflowed its banks to include Bengal and Assam. Already, on that summer day in Delhi, there could be heard the preparatory creaking of an entire subcontinent about to be torn into fragments.

The Nawabzab raised his hands in a gesture of princely benediction.

"I am afraid you are much too easily frightened," he said. "You evidently don't understand the Muslim mind. If you did, you would not be so insistent. India is not China or Palestine. We will manage our affairs well enough."

I said I was afraid that the men with the knives would arrange their affairs too well.

"You have seen a fist fight and you think all India will soon be exchanging blows," he said. "You're quite wrong! We shall have Pakistan, with or without the help of Mr. Gandhi or Mr. Nehru. Then with Pakistan as a basis we shall be able to employ our energies in building up our own cultural and economic life without fear of Hindu exploitation."

"So you are determined on civil war?"

"No, we are determined on Pakistan!"

Those words, so often repeated, resembled the classic chorus in an ancient tragedy. He was saying: "Whatever the cost, we shall have what we want." I said: "The cost is a war of annihilation. It is much better to wait and hope for something better." "You are wrong," he answered. "We have little time, and Pakistan cannot be delayed." And then a little later, near the very end of the conversation, he said: "We may have a united India one day, but it is impossible to think of it now!"

As we walked out in the hallway he put his hand heavily on my shoulder and said: "What should I do? Tell me. I am responsible for a hundred million Muslims. Surely I have no right to commit them into bondage! You do not know how mercilessly the Hindus exploit our people!"

We stood for a few moments in the flowering garden, where some six or seven Hindu gardeners were scything the lawn and cultivating the flower beds. The Nawabzab looked old and exhausted, with an unhealthy yellow color. Although it was high summer, Delhi seemed suddenly cold.

Conversations with powerful political figures are nearly always fragmentary, like pieces of mosaic scattered over the floor. They are inclined to repeat themselves, so that the same piece of mosaic is continually turning up. Politicians, by the nature of their craft, must necessarily perform continual exercises in self-justification, reminding themselves that they are still alive, still incarnating political ideas, still performing the appropriate ritual gestures. They betray themselves by their silences and their smiles. The Nawabzab smiled often, and especially when the thought of massacre occurred to him, but he was not smiling when he said he was responsible for a hundred million Muslims.

I had left China with the knowledge that only a miracle could save it from civil war; now I knew that India, too, was doomed to be torn to pieces. The Nawabzab had no feeling or understanding or sympathy for people. What he wanted was power, and in the course of time he got what he wanted. He became Pakistan's first prime minister and was later killed by one of his own people.

Delhi enchanted me, and not only because it was full of magnificent monuments. Das Gupta, with his absurd police whistle, had taught me a healthy respect for the Indians, and I enjoyed wandering about aimlessly in the bazaars and along the crowded streets, watching them as they went about their affairs. "To see the true light," wrote Meister Eckhart, "man must become blind and strip God naked of things." But in India the nakedness of the mind is confronted with the luxury of things: every stone concealed a million ants, every field and tree was overripe, and every sky was potentially full of fruitful clouds. The sheer luxury of India, after the long years of privation in China, made me dizzy.

Here there were no more language difficulties, and it was no longer necessary to carry baskets full of money, for the inflation had not reached India. There were English bookshops, English uniforms, English banks, English was spoken in half the shops, which were full of things unavailable in China. Half of our happiness in China lay in our poverty. Now half of my happiness lay in the knowledge that the shops were full of things I could buy. It was beyond belief, but it was so. Peace had come, and the world was mercantile again.

The Red Fort at Delhi and the Taj Mahal at Agra were designed with a sumptuous elegance which at first dismayed me, and then took possession of me, as I realized how studied and deliberate they were. Elegance was married to a cunning intelligence: the Indians played on their intelligence as though it were a musical instrument. Chinese art was essentially frontal and linear—the curve of a roof against the sky, the white circle of the Temple of Heaven to be observed from some mysterious Tree of Heaven high above it—and the faces and bodies of people had little place in it. Indian art, on the contrary, showed an extraordinary understanding of the intricacies of space, and the human form was everywhere in evidence from the dancing Nataraja, the lord of the world enclosed in a ring of flame, to the statue of the youthful Buddha whose calm meditations scarcely denied the beauty of his flesh. Seen in the light of a full moon the Taj Mahal was an abstract portrait of grief, the sunken archways representing sunken eyes. To see it on a moonlit night with scudding clouds racing across the heavens, the marble gleaming and then fading, so alive, so feverish, is to see it in its ultimate grandeur.

So, too, at Fatehpur Sikri, the rose-red city built by the Emperor Akbar to honor the birth of his son, there was the sense of a purely human grandeur. The emperor's private chamber, where he sat enthroned on a column in the center, was small and unpretentious except in its elegance. The vast courtyards and soaring throne chambers of China were absent. The marble palaces in the Red Fort at Delhi were the size of cottages. In the most delicate of these palaces the Emperor Shah Jehan ordered that there should be inscribed the words: "IF THERE IS A PARADISE, IT IS THIS, IT IS THIS, IT IS THIS!" Here the emperor sat enthroned, robed in the purest white silk patterned with gold flowers, and the immaculate beauty of the setting was merely an ornament for his majestic presence. There were no towering walls or archways, no immense flights of steps. The doors were man-size, the roof was comfortably close to one's head, and if you stretched out your arms you could almost touch the facing walls.

I confess I preferred the Mughal emperors to the Chinese emperors. At Fatehpur Sikri the Emperor Akbar seems to be vividly present, a gruff, kindly man with thin eyebrows and the slanted eyes of his Mongol ancestors, limping a little, sometimes wearing European clothes, smiling gently as he engaged in discussions on the nature of God with Jesuits, Buddhists and

Hindus. He was a good listener, which is rare among emperors. I liked him all the more when I discovered a portrait of his concubine, the Princess Meriam, high up on the wall of one of the palaces. She was wearing a green gown and lifting a flute to her lips against a background of woodlands and streams, and she smiled entrancingly.

I knew that if I stayed more than a few weeks in India I would become its prisoner. Delhi delighted me because the streets were wide and shaded with trees, because even the beggars had noble faces, because the museum was crowded with statues unlike any I had ever seen. There was little grass in China, and here there were whole fields of it. The dawns and the sunsets were more richly colored, the noons were brighter. Life in Delhi was being lived with a feverish intensity, and it seemed incredible to me that only a few days before I had been walking through the calm streets of Peking.

Bombay, with its red-brick Victorian Gothic buildings, lacked Delhi's imperial splendors, but it was even more feverish. I raced around the city, looking at shops and museums, and on the second day had a fainting spell in a market place. Suddenly brightly colored vegetables came cascading up, while I went sinking to the ground. I remember an old Indian fruit seller with a gray spiky beard, toothless and smelling of toddy, squatting beside me while I lay there. He had a look of compassion, shaking his head slowly. I rose unsteadily, and hurried back to the Taj Mahal Hotel, where the maharajahs and rulers of the princely states were holding a conclave. The timing was perfect, for as I hurtled down a corridor and turned a corner, covered with the juices of squashed vegetables, I was met by a solid mass of jeweled maharajahs and their gold-braided aides. Never had a proletarian scattered so many maharajahs!

The fainting spell was disturbing, and I decided to see a doctor. Someone recommended a certain Dr. Berger. They said he was a refugee from Germany, well known for his vast knowledge of medicine and absolutely reliable. He was especially famous as a diagnostician and since he spent a long time with his patients you were likely to spend hours in his waiting room. I made an appointment for three o'clock and arrived five minutes early.

My heart sank, for the waiting room was filled to overflowing with the most exotic creatures I had ever seen. There were three or four Arabian sheiks each accompanied by his entire family. The sheiks wore spotless white robes with golden headropes and gold-hilted daggers at their waists. They looked exactly like the Meccan princes described by Lawrence of Arabia, dark-skinned, predatory, fiercely aristocratic. The door opened, a nurse appeared, one of the sheiks, limping a little, swept into the surgery, his white robe billowing behind him. I calculated that it would probably be forty-eight hours before I would see the doctor.

About half an hour later the sheik emerged smiling, evidently well pleased with the news he had heard from the doctor. He made a short speech in Arabic, and everyone listened intently, craning forward. At the end of the speech the Arabs rose in a great swirl of white draperies, chattering loudly as they made their way to the outer door. I was still sitting there open-mouthed with happy astonishment when the nurse tugged at my sleeve and said the doctor would see me.

The doctor was a small man with heavily lidded eyes and a faintly ironical smile. He looked very capable, very alert, and very down to earth. I asked him about the sheiks.

"They always travel with their families," he said. "In the early days they all crowded into the surgery—wives, children, grand-children, armed guards, everyone! It took a long time to teach them to come in one by one."

I described my symptoms while he nodded patiently. I went on to describe my medical history. Malaria, tuberculosis, typhus: a fairly uneventful history. He was interested in typhus, for people do not often recover from it, but seemed guarded and amused by the fainting spell. After a thorough physical examination he said: "I can find absolutely nothing wrong. Come back tomorrow and I'll have a report on the blood samples. Now tell me about China."

What chiefly interested me, however, was India, and after submitting him to a desultory description of Peking with some passing comments on the valley of Yenan, I kept asking him so many questions about India that he threw up his hands and said: "I am a doctor, not a politician. You'd better meet the politicians. If you come to my club I'll introduce you to them."

At his club that evening nearly everyone seemed to be a

politician. There were maharajahs, judges, generals and ministers of state, such a galaxy of officials that it seemed that all the governments of India, past, present and future, were gathered there. I observed that they all listened intently to the quiet doctor with the ironical smile. I learned that Dr. Berger was well known for possessing precisely those qualities which are absent in politicians, and his very gentleness and unassertiveness made him seem strong and assertive amid that boisterous crowd of politicians vying for power or already in positions of power. The doctor moved among them with an air of extraordinary authority, no doubt because many of them were his patients.

A fat maharajah was fingering his necklace of pearls as though they were worry beads; a man with a heroic mustache reaching to his ears was proclaiming that British justice was the foundation stone of independent India; a heavily bearded Sikh with a blue turban was saying that Gandhi belonged to the past and would serve no useful purpose in the future. Someone was saying: "The winds of change have come to India," as though it was something that had occurred to him only at that moment. A judge of the High Court, an Englishman with a pointed gray beard, was relating how he had just sentenced an Indian coolie to death by hanging, and he hoped, by God, that the wretched coolie would not die instantaneously. The Indians around him applauded. They were all drinking rather heavily and they enjoyed each other's company.

"What do you make of them?" the doctor asked, as we were leaving the club.

I said: "They are all playing games."

"Of course," replied the doctor, and there was no irony in his voice. "What did you expect of them?"

"I don't believe Nehru and Jinnah are playing games."

"Of course not. They are playing for higher stakes—stakes that the people you saw this evening could never dream about. As it happens, they are both in Bombay. Would you like to meet them?"

I said I had a letter from Madame Sun Yat-sen to deliver to Nehru.

"That makes it easier," the doctor said. "When you come for the results of the blood tests I'll try to have everything arranged for you."

The doctor was as good as his word. The next day, when I called at his office, I found two notes. The first said that Jinnah would see me on the afternoon of August 14 and Nehru would see me on the afternoon of the following day. The second note said the blood tests were negative, and went on: "Sleep eight hours, don't spend too much time in the sun, and take an hour's rest every afternoon." I had a clear day before seeing Jinnah and decided to go to the island of Elephanta, which lies six miles off the shore of Bombay.

It was a blustery day, for the monsoon was coming. The wind whipped up white waters, and quite suddenly India seemed to have lost all its colors. When we came close to the island of Elephanta it was wreathed in gray mists and resembled a rocky island off the coast of Scotland. A pathway led along the shore, all pebbles and shingles and wet knee-high grass. The palms bent in the high wind, and green pigeons flew up at our feet. All the way to the caves there was the sound of birdsong.

The Dutch traveler Jan Huighen van Linschoten wrote in his *Discours of Voyages into ye Easte and West Indies* published in 1579 that the caves of Elephanta contained carvings of "Elephants, Lions, Tigers, and a thousand other such-like wild and cruel beasts, also some Amazons which are so well and workmanlike cut that it is strange to behold." Once, it is true, there were elephants standing guard at one of the mouths of the caves, but they have long ago been removed to the Bombay Museum. As for the lions, tigers and other cruel beasts mentioned by Van Linschoten, they seem never to have existed, for all the surviving images are carvings of the gods. One imagines that he entered the caves briefly by the light of a guttering candle and saw what he wanted to see, heraldic lions and tigers crouching in the darkness. But there is no doubt that he saw Amazons, for they are still there. They are the twelve-foot-high androgynous gods, each with one breast, dancing and summoning the worlds into existence.

The traveler, climbing up the winding path that leads to the caves, is haunted by the splendors that have not yet been discovered. One suspects that there may be many more caves, and we know that two entrances to the caves are choked with detritus. Somewhere in that labyrinth there may still be discovered the tomb of the princess, the daughter of King Banasura, who dedicated herself to perpetual virginity and was rewarded after many years with a shower of heavenly gold. Yet, while the silver ropes of rain fell from the palms and the shingle crackled along the weed-grown path, while the storm blew overhead and the ship which had brought us from Bombay rocked crazily at the landing stage, we were more than content with what we saw.

Once you have passed the entrance to the caves, you enter a world of mysterious activity, where even the gods who are not dancing give an impression of being about to spring from the walls. Someone once brought up a cannon and blasted away at these carvings. Here and there heads, arms and legs have been lopped off. It scarcely makes any difference. Panel after panel shows the god Shiva performing various dances. Usually the dance is controlled, the fury masked, the passion stilled. On one panel, huge and austere, he performs an abandoned dance, his elephant-hide cloak hurled backward in the air, his broadsword uplifted, and from his neck there descends a necklace of skulls which crashes against the bronze plates girding his loins. One of his many arms rings a bell summoning the other gods to dance with the same fury. This sculpture of Shiva is a thing of astonishing power.

The subtlest and most violent gestures find their expressions in these caves. The most subtle of all is the Trimurti, the three-headed god, of whom we see only the high crowns, the heads and the shoulders rising out of the rock. The shoulders thrust up like a wave; power surges through them, but it is not power so much as the purest divinity which shines from those faces. One head, of great authority and beauty, confronts the onlooker, while the others are carved in profile. This central face is one of the world's greatest masterpieces. It is such a face as one sees in dreams, very full, suffused with thought, possessing a brooding majesty and a perfect serenity. In a moment the god will breathe, he will speak, and out of his breath and his speech there will come the creation of new constellations, new universes.

Here, at some time in the seventh century, a sculptor of genius had portrayed an absolutely credible divinity, a great glory shining from his face. Perhaps for the first and last time Eternity had been carved in stone.

Most of the world's great works of art are not to be found in museums; they are in the places where they were first painted or carved or built. On the island of Elephanta statue after statue had been carved in an age of towering artistic creation. Above all, there was the Trimurti, so powerful, so august, and so beautiful that it seemed to have been carved by the gods for their own delectation.

While we were walking through the labyrinth of caves, the storm was gathering. As we ran down the winding pathway, the sky grew darker and it was almost indigo blue when we reached the landing stage. The rain was falling, the trees were bending in the wind, and the seas were white and fuming. By the time we reached Bombay the monsoon rains had begun in earnest, and the whole city was drowning in the ferocious downpour. All night the rains thundered down, and in the morning the skies were clean and pure.

THE GREAT LEADERS

The house of Mohammed Ali Jinnah was more like a palace than the residence of a brilliantly successful lawyer. It stood at the end of a great driveway shaded by palms, gleaming with marble and colored stone. There were vast and opulent houses in the Malabar Hill district of Bombay, but Jinnah's house was the most opulent of all. To his followers he was known as Qaid-e-Azam, "the great leader," and his utterances were nearly always couched in the tones of an emperor addressing his subjects. In August 1946 Pakistan was still a dream, and there was still some hope that India would not be torn apart by Muslims and Hindus. Jinnah was the man who hoped to preside over the birth of a new nation by cutting it away from the living flesh of India.

In China I had read some of his speeches and knew him to be austere, sharp-tongued, intolerant. Even the Muslims feared him, found fault with him, and spoke of his arrogance. They also spoke of his charismatic quality: when he entered a room or a meeting, the air became electric and regal, and they said his silences could be as terrible as his utterances. Dr. Berger said it would be a mistake to see Nehru before seeing Jinnah. "Jinnah will shock you, Nehru will calm you," he said, and I wondered why. Nehru's rages were famous, and it was said of Jinnah that with a single glance he could turn a man into stone.

Beyond the sentry at the iron gate and the cluster of armed policemen lay the waving palms and the misty outlines of a house resembling a wedding cake. The sentry telephoned to the house, and after a proper delay I was permitted to walk down the immense driveway past an army of gardeners tending his flower beds. Then up the marble steps, to be received by a major-domo in scarlet, who bowed low and said that the Qaid-e-Azam was in conference and would perhaps be delayed. "Only a few minutes, sahib, only a few minutes," the major-domo said.

I therefore settled down for a wait of about half an hour, admiring the marble columns, the potted palms, the mirrors reaching to the ceiling, and the ormulu clock on the mantelpiece. It
might have been the palace of a maharajah except that there
were no tiger skins. Through the wide french windows the misty
green garden seemed to stretch to the horizon.

There were silver-framed photographs of King Farouk and the
Shah of Persia on a low table near the fireplace. The photographs
were puzzling because I could not remember an occasion when
Jinnah had encountered either Farouk or the Shah. But what was
still more puzzling was the fact that it was very cold in this
enormous room and the marble floor was especially cold; from
below the floor there came the faint whispering and whistling
sound of water. For the first and last time in my life I was in a
house cooled by flowing water.

About five minutes later Jinnah emerged from the long dark
hallway which stretched to the rear of the house. He was thinner
and darker and smaller than I had expected; the eyes were
feverish and deep-sunken; the nose pointed; the mouth like a
trap. He wore a black coat, black-striped trousers, a white waist-
coat, and the high starched collar was the purest white, and so
were the cuffs which darted out from his sleeves. On a black
ribbon an eyeglass, like a medal, dangled on his chest. Immaculately attired, he looked more like a tailor's dummy than a
political leader.

He called for the scarlet-coated major-domo, asked whether
I would like a whisky and soda and ordered one for himself.
This, too, was puzzling, for it was three o'clock in the afternoon,
too early for serious drinking. While we waited for the whisky
to appear, I said I had seen a massacre in Calcutta and feared
that India would soon drown in a bloodbath. I had come from
China, and it was equally clear that the Chinese were in danger
of the same fate. Surely it was the duty of politicians to avoid
bloodshed. I said: "Would you agree, Mr. Jinnah, that politics
is the art of preventing people from murdering each other?"

He gave a frosty smile, carefully crossed his thin legs, toyed
with his eyeglass, and said: "That is one definition, but there
are many others."

"What would be your definition?"

"A famous Englishman said politics was the art of the possible.

A politician should do all that can possibly be done for his people."

"Then surely the most useful thing is to prevent them from quarreling among themselves. There are all these massacres, and very little is being done—"

"You must understand that these massacres have been going on for a long time. You are fresh to India, and you do not know our history. We are two nations forced to live together by the British. We did not ask to live with the Hindus, we had no control over it, and we have no desire to live with them any longer. If the blame for these massacres lies anywhere, it lies with the British!"

By this time the whisky had arrived on a silver tray, and he poured out a full half-glass, adding a sprinkling of water, and I did the same. Dr. Berger had told me that Jinnah was under medical care and for some months had not touched any alcohol. In fact he drank two half-glasses of whisky in a little less than an hour.

I said: "It is not a question of blame. It is a question of what can be done to prevent further massacres. Can you do anything? Can Nehru do anything?"

I have observed that politicians habitually fail to answer questions, and that it is almost the mark of a successful politician that when he is asked a question, he gives a totally irrelevant answer and embarks on a long discourse on a subject as far removed as possible. So when I asked Jinnah whether there was any possibility of bringing calm to the violence of India, he answered with a long tirade about the cows wandering aimlessly through the streets of Bombay, holding up traffic and otherwise impeding the march of progress.

"The Hindus reverence the cows," he said. "We eat them. We don't worship animals. Animal worship is the religion of a primitive people at a very low level of religious life. The Hindus are just as aimless and spineless as these cows wandering about in the market place and eating whatever they can find on the stalls and making messes wherever they please. If you want to understand the Hindus, you must see them in their relationship with the cow. We do not live in the same world. We are a martial people, and they are a timid, fearful people."

I said that when Muslims and Hindus massacred one another,

the Hindus gave as good as they got, and there was not the least evidence of their timidity. The danger of the present confrontation lay in the fact that both sides were reckless and inclined to kill first and ask questions afterward. The memory of the massacre in Calcutta was very fresh in my mind, and since it was unlikely that he had ever seen a massacre at close hand, I told him what it was like. He seemed to flinch, because it was not pleasant.

I said: "If you would tell all the Muslims: 'Go in peace, do not kill the Hindus,' and if Nehru tells the Hindus: 'Go in peace, do not kill the Muslims,' then at least there will be far fewer people hacked to pieces. Will you say that?"

"Why should I say that?" he answered angrily. "Why should I? Why should that question be addressed to me? You don't know the real situation. The Muslims are outnumbered by the Hindus. They never attack. They are set upon by fanatical Hindus, and of course they defend themselves. Do you expect them to sit still with folded arms when a frenzied mob attacks them?"

He sprang up from his chair and began to recite a long list of massacres in which the Muslims had suffered and the Hindus alone were responsible, giving dates and places, the numbers of people slain, the number of women deflowered, the number of children thrown into the wells. He evidently knew the list by heart, and he flung out the words with a proper emphasis on the name of the town and the numbers slain, but there seemed to be no conviction in his voice. He had not seen these massacres. These were towns and numbers to be employed with dramatic effect, and he gave to each of them a sharp, spine-chilling intonation. He was walking up and down the carpet, as in previous years he had marched up and down in front of a jury box, but now there was something about him of the caged animal with the carpet as his cage, for never once did he permit himself to walk on the bare marble floor. He went on:

"You cannot deny that these massacres took place—there is incontrovertible evidence—they are a part of history. We have suffered long enough! That is why we must have Pakistan at whatever the cost! Today India is ruled by British bayonets and Hindu knives."

"The bayonets are leaving soon—"

"Exactly. We shall be left to the mercy of the Hindu knives, and that is no mercy at all! We must have a wall between us. That is why Pakistan is necessary."

When I talked again about the massacre in Calcutta, he said: "Are you afraid of a little blood, Mr. Payne?"

"I am afraid of a lot of blood," I said. "I believe that on both sides in India political leaders are exasperating the situation, not healing it. If you would only say to the Muslims, 'Go in peace,' then there might be some hope."

"There is hope for Pakistan," he said grimly.

I asked him if there was any message he would like to give to the West.

"There is only one message to give them," he snapped. "Tell them to pay the least possible attention to Indian affairs, and let us settle the issue among ourselves."

"By war?"

"By war, or by other means."

"If it is war, then it is a ten years' war."

"Then let it be so. God will favor his own."

"What if the war is not decisive? What if it ends as most civil wars end, in the total bankruptcy of India?"

"Money, wealth, has nothing to do with it," he shouted. "Whatever happens, there must be the separation between the Muslims and the Hindus. If this entails the bankruptcy of our country, that is a small penalty to pay for the sake of honor. The Muslims have no regard for money, but they have a high regard for honor."

I asked him if he was prepared to step down if Nehru stepped down.

"Why should I?" he said sharply. "I have earned my position. Why should I step down?"

I spoke again about the war between the Muslims and the Hindus, the war that seemed so inevitable and so close, and he said: "We shall win, because we have spiritual weapons."

Strange that an English-trained Muslim lawyer should speak the words of Gandhi.

When I left him, I knew that nothing in the world would dissuade him from plunging India into a bloodbath, and that millions would die as a result of his decisions, for he was insensitive to human suffering. He had "earned" his position, and this gave him the right to wield incalculable power over the destinies of peoples. The pale ghost among the marble columns wanted power for himself alone.

On the following day I called on Nehru, who was staying in the house of his sister, Krishna Hutheesing. Dr. Berger had waved his magic wand, opened the doors, and vanished with a beneficent smile. The Hutheesing house had a high wall and a wild garden, and resembled a small, well-kept, middle-class house in England. There was a narrow hallway with the inevitable umbrella stand and coat rack, and everything smelled of English wax: almost one expected to find a framed photograph of Scarborough on a May morning. There was none of the oppressive luxury of Jinnah's palace: no marble floors, no servants in brocaded uniforms. At the top of the stairs was Nehru's study overlooking the garden. A nondescript servant led me to the study and then vanished.

The study was small, one wall covered with books. There were entire rows filled with the yellow-jacketed books of the Left Book Club, and he had obviously bought every single one of these books as they came out. There was *The Seven Pillars of Wisdom* by T. E. Lawrence, much thumbed and much read. All the modern English poets were there, and there was Edgar Snow's *Red Star Over China*. But it was not so much the books that attracted my attention as the enormous silver-framed photograph that stood on a carved teakwood table. I had expected a photograph of his father or his wife, but there was none. The photograph in the silver frame was a magnificent study of the Buddha at Anuradhpura in Ceylon, beautiful and commanding, taken in such a way that it bore a distinct resemblance to Nehru himself.

It was quiet and peaceful in the study, the only sound coming from the trees brushing against the windowpanes, the branches so thick with leaves that one could scarcely see the garden below. From far away there came the muffled voice of someone speaking on the telephone: the voice would go on, then stop, then go on again. A gardener was cutting a grassy patch in the garden with a scythe, and the low moaning sound of the scythe only made the silence deeper. This was Nehru's room where he worked and received visitors and gazed out of the window, and it was not much larger than a prison cell;

and I began to wonder whether he had deliberately selected this small room for his own because he had spent so many years in prison. Here he had written his autobiography, or rather he had put the finishing touches to it. Here, when the day's work was over, he read late into the night, and there was no telephone to disturb him. So the minutes passed, and there was no Nehru: only the long silence of a summer's day.

There was nothing to do except to wait patiently and to examine the library. I pulled down *The Seven Pillars of Wisdom* bound in red calfskin: there were penciled annotations on nearly every page. There was a volume of Dylan Thomas' poems— more penciled annotations. There was a row of books on political science and economics, and scarcely an annotation anywhere. It occurred to me that one could learn a good deal about Nehru by looking at his library, and certainly there were more English poets than anyone could have expected. Chaucer was there; so was Shakespeare; and there were perhaps a hundred English poets, with Auden and Spender having pride of place. Already I was beginning to understand Nehru better.

Half an hour later I heard a rustling sound and turned sharply to see him emerging from a long book-lined corridor. He wore a white tunic and jodhpurs and the inevitable white Congress cap, and there was a red rose in the second buttonhole of his tunic. He was smaller than I expected, and walked with a kind of dancing step. His eyebrows were dark, the mouth long and sensitive, and the eyes were like the eyes in Mughal paintings, very deep and tender, though they had about them the sadness which you see in nearly all Indian eyes. As he came into the room he raised his hands to the level of his heart in the Hindu gesture of salutation, and when I replied awkwardly in the same way he gave a smile that was so feminine, so entirely without guile and so full of a mysterious charm that my knees trembled. He was very much the Nehru I expected, the adored leader of countless millions of Indians. He sat down in the window seat, took off his white cap, perhaps because it was a very hot day, and immediately he was transformed into another Nehru altogether. Instead of the youthful and smiling man of so many newspaper photographs, there was an old bald-headed man with a fringe of white hair above the ears. He looked very ancient, very careworn.

When I gave him the letter from Madame Sun Yat-sen, he put on his spectacles, and there was another transformation— he looked older still as he bent over the letter. I wondered how many more transformations there would be before the afternoon was over.

Since I had helped to write the letter and knew it by heart, it was amusing to watch him reading, now pursing his lips, now smiling faintly. He asked how she was, and I said she was in good health and good spirits. He said: "Is she safe?"

"As safe as anyone can reasonably hope to be. She is surrounded by guards."

He was not convinced.

"I think she is in danger," he said. "She has ties with the Communists."

He spoke of his meeting with her in Chungking and how much he admired her. She was the most beautiful of the Soong sisters, and the most intelligent. He had kept up a fitful correspondence with her over the years, usually through mutual friends, and he wished he had come to know her better, because she was one of the few Chinese he could understand. "I don't understand the Chinese," he said. "Probably you have to learn the language before you can understand them. I was impressed by the Generalissimo, but I could not fathom how his mind worked. I read a great deal about him before I met him, but nothing I read corresponded to the impression he made on me. I saw someone driven by a fierce hatred against the Japanese, a hard, inflexible man whose only aim was to drive the Japanese out of China."

"Too often he hated the Chinese."

"That may be so. You must remember that China is an old patriarchal civilization and the patriarch expects to be obeyed. I suppose he hates the Communists as much as he hated the Japanese."

For a while he played with the idea of China as the great patriarchy, but finally he threw up his hands in despair.

"I can't make them out at all. I see—I think I can see—what is happening in all the other countries of Asia, but China is a complete mystery to me. We have sent one of our best ambassadors there, and I study all his reports, but I still don't understand them." He pointed to his bookshelves. "I have fifty books on China, but they do not help me. Who is going to win—Chiang Kai-shek or Mao Tse-tung?"

"Mao Tse-tung."

"You are quite sure?"

"Yes, because the peasants and the students are on his side, and everyone is sick to death of Kuomintang corruption."

Nehru was not in the least convinced. The Kuomintang had well-trained troops, American advisers and unlimited supplies of American tanks and airplanes; they would crush the Chinese Communists until their towns and villages were nothing but smoking ruins. He spoke as though he was almost sorry for the Chinese Communists, who were fighting a losing battle, and he seemed to think that Madame Sun Yat-sen was in great danger, because she had chosen the losing side. I had asked Mao Tse-tung what would happen when his troops were confronted by tanks, and he answered: "We'll tear them apart with our bare hands." I said: "A man who talks like that cannot be beaten. He knows exactly what he wants to do and how to do it. He is even more inflexible than the Generalissimo."

"No," said Nehru. "When he said that, he might have been boasting."

As he spoke, the transformations were continually taking place. He could laugh like a child, and the next moment he had the brooding severity of an old man. He spoke with a kind of crisp lilt, the Indian intonations superimposed on the subtle accents of an educated Englishman, and yet he obviously derived pleasure from the spoken language, enjoying its rhythms and shifting emphasis, placing the accentuation exactly where he wanted it, so that when he said that Madame Sun Yat-sen has ties with the Communists, the emphasis on "ties" embraced many subtle possibilities, and when he said "boasting," it could be understood as an ironic commentary.

He asked what places I had seen in India, and a moment later he was saying: "You must go to Kashmir. It is the only place where you can wander about in the woods and forget the world's troubles." He said this so sadly, with such an air of weariness, that a wound seemed to be opening. I said: "What is it that attracts you to Kashmir especially?" He answered: "The silence and the peace."

The interview was obviously coming to an end, but there

was still one more hopeless game to play. I told him about the interview with Jinnah, who was even more inflexible than Chiang Kai-shek. Jinnah had stormed and raged against the Hindus. I had seen one massacre in Calcutta, and it was as clear as daylight that there would be many more, for Jinnah had spoken as though he would cheerfully murder the Hindus and go to any lengths to impose Pakistan on India. There seemed to be only one solution. If Jinnah and Nehru would both step down, there might be some hope of a compromise worked out by lesser political figures. India had become polarized around the names of the legendary figures. It was a familiar argument by now, but it had not lost its force. It was obvious that millions of people were going to die because Chiang Kai-shek and Mao Tse-tung had acquired legendary powers, for no one dared to argue with them and they alone made the decisions which led to peace or war. It was obvious that if they vanished from the scene, peace could be patched up between the warring factions, but while they remained alive there was no hope for peace.

I said: "If Jinnah stepped down and if you stepped down, wouldn't it be better for India in the end?"

He looked startled.

"Why do you say that?"

"Because it is the same problem in China—the people have become polarized around the leaders."

There was a long pause while he gazed at the photograph in the silver frame.

"Jinnah will never step down," he said quietly. "As for me, even if I wanted it—and sometimes I want it very much—there is no possibility of escape. I would feel that I was deserting my country."

It was hopeless to insist; hopeless to suggest that the desire to wield power might be only another aspect of "no possibility of escape." Unlike Mao Tse-tung, who said it would make no difference whether he was Chairman or not, because he was merely the product of social forces, Nehru saw himself as one who could not escape his obligations and who must inevitably occupy the seat of power. He was very determined, very proud, and very certain of his aims. When I went on to talk about the massacre I had witnessed within half an hour of arriving in Calcutta, he simply waved his hands, as though these massacres were commonplace.

I said: "I am sure it will get worse. The hatred in Jinnah's voice—"

"There has always been hatred in his voice," Nehru answered. "This is nothing new."

As he spoke, he was gazing at the photograph in the silver frame as though lost in it, finding in those powerful brilliant features a reflection of his own; and I was reminded of Mao Tse-tung studying his own portrait painted on the proscenium arch of the theater in Yenan. Pride assailed him, as it assailed Mao Tse-tung, and in both of them there could be discerned the sharp cutting edge of power. They were much more alike, much closer to one another, than they knew. It was not only that they had acquired the force of legends and could scarcely see themselves outside the context of their own legends, but they were both dedicated to the attainment of power without any calculation of the cost to others, for "the others" inevitably became the servants of the legend.

Finally Nehru rose, smiled his enchanting smile, and said: "Everything will come out for the best."

He did not know, and would not know until the evening, that one of the most terrible massacres visited upon the Indians was taking place while we were talking. On the previous day Jinnah had issued the order for "direct action" to his followers in Calcutta. With absolute contempt for human lives he commanded the Muslims in Calcutta to stage a massive uprising, and for four days the streets ran with blood. From August 15 to 18 the Muslims armed with knives and guns fell on the Hindus, who not unnaturally defended themselves. Throats were slashed, bellies were ripped open, armed gangs prowled the streets. It was the worst massacre in Calcutta in living memory.

I left Nehru with a feeling of bewilderment and uneasiness, for he was like quicksilver, elusive and strangely remote. He resembled a scholarly chessplayer who would not hesitate to sacrifice the pawns, rooks, knights and bishops in order to check-mate the adversary. He was much harder than I had imagined, and there was very little earthiness in him. Jinnah resembled an enraged mediaeval emperor, while Nehru was a man of our time, with the sensibilities of our time, but ultimately possessing little sympathy or understanding of people. A cold flame burned within him, and as long as he lived it would not go out.

That evening Dr. Berger gave a small dinner party in his house set among high trees overlooking the sea. The house was plainly and modestly decorated, and so gave an impression of great calm. The moon came out and all of Bombay was bathed in silver. I chattered away about Nehru and Jinnah, and about the appalling prospects for India if they remained in positions of power. The doctor smiled his gentle, ironical smile, and beyond the open windows Bombay lay quiet and peaceful as a lake in a forgotten village.

THE GREEN DRAGON AGAIN

The rain came down again, drumming on the roof of the third-class carriage taking us from Bombay to Aurangabad. It was the night train, and before we set out from Victoria railroad station we felt the peculiar atmosphere of despair which descends on all Indian trains at night. We were all sodden from the rains, steam rose from our clothes, there were puddles everywhere, the air smelled of urine. The lights flared up, flickered and went out while we were still traveling through the outskirts of Bombay. Half an hour later they came on again, but so feeble that the greenish bulbs gave only enough light to illuminate themselves and a small fan-shaped area immediately beneath them. In this eerie darkness, swaying violently, the train hurtled eastward across the plains with its cargo of dead men and women.

Dead they assuredly were, for they neither talked nor grimaced nor moved, but assumed the attitudes appropriate to the dead. They were greenish-gray, like cadavers, and their mouths hung open and their heads lolled strangely. The violence of the storm, the roar of the thunder, had silenced them. If they were not wholly dead, they were dead to the world. It was beyond hope that they would ever awake.

One should not, if one can possibly help it, travel third class on an Indian train at night. It is not only that dacoits have an unpleasant habit of murdering people on trains or holding up an entire train for ransom, but one can very easily die of the prevailing despair that seeps into the body like a poison from the moment you board the train. Exhausted by poverty and hunger, clutching their small possessions, they had no sooner boarded the train than they flung themselves down on the seats where they remained motionless, as though dead or in a trance. A young soldier from the Nizam of Hyderabad's army sat beside me. "They are very poor," he murmured, and shook his head slowly from side to side.

To say they were very poor was to say nothing at all: they had lost all hope, the night and the storm offering them no solace at all. One wondered whether they knew where they were going, or whether they had simply climbed on the train in a state of unconsciousness, so that it was all one to them whether the train took them to Aurangabad or Delhi or the Malabar Coast. The men with their crumpled dhotis, the women with their saris and tight blouses which left the waist bare, were so ghostlike in the frail light filtering from the electric bulbs that their shaking seemed unreal and their occasional groans seemed presumptuous. Since they were dead, what right had they to disturb the long Indian night?

When at last the storm came to an end, they woke up, whispered, grunted, gazed out of the window at the bright stars, smiled, and went to sleep again. The roaring and drumming of the rain had acted as a soporific. The windows were shut tight, yet somehow the rain had poured in, and the intolerable heat only increased now that the storm had come to an end: no one dared open a window. After the storm the train picked up speed, rocketing through the night, ejecting a stream of sparks, shuddering and swaying more violently now that it no longer had the storm to contend with, while the young soldier spoke sorrowfully about the poverty of the peasants and how difficult it was to understand what was happening in India. "Tell me, where are we going?" he said, and I thought he was talking about this maddened train taking us to Aurangabad.

I learned more about India from the young soldier than I had learned from Nehru, Jinnah and Liaquat Ali Khan. He was about twenty-four, with fine clear-cut features, a small mustache, heavily lidded eyes. He was dressed neatly and carried himself well. He had spent a good deal of his life asking himself unanswerable questions. I learned from him that even quite reasonable people in India were terrified of the future, did not know where to turn, distrusted their rulers, and felt they were doomed to suffer the consequences of centuries of misrule. He was glad the British would soon be leaving India, but that was only the beginning. He would have liked to see the princely states abolished, and he would have been happy if all the politicians were placed on a ship which was sunk somewhere in the Indian Ocean. "They don't care," he said. "If only they would learn to care—"

We arrived at Aurangabad just before dawn, when the small city lay under a deep purple sky and was still sleeping. The people who had been no more than sodden cadavers on the train jerked into life, shouted, smiled, ran up and down the platform, poured water on their faces and babbled merrily.

Aurangabad lived on its past. Once it was an important town, and the Emperor Aurangzeb had stayed there when he was the Viceroy of the Deccan, and then gradually it faded into obscurity. There were some Buddhist caves in the nearby hills, but those heavy Buddhas had been carved in an age when sculpture was no longer a living art.

On the outskirts of the town stood the mausoleum which Aurangzeb erected for his favorite wife. Fantastic mausoleum! Gleaming white in the early morning sunrise, it resembled the Taj Mahal to perfection—the same dome, the same arrangement of minarets, the same garden leading to the portal of the sanctuary. Yet, here and there, one could detect minute differences. The minarets were a little too abrupt, a little too heavy, the dome was not quite the right shape, and there was no green river behind it to give it perspective. The soaring grace, the delicacy and the assurance were lacking, and the architects had included in the design of the new mausoleum a hint of Aurangzeb's ferocious cruelty.

For three hundred years the Mughals, of Turkic and Mongol origin, had ruled over India, and everywhere they established their courts they built majestically. No one ever built palaces, mosques and mausoleums with such splendor. The Emperor Aurangzeb, or, to give him his full name and titles, Aurangzeb Muhayyi-ud-Din Alamgir, Ornament of the Throne, Preserver of the Faith, Grasper of the World, had ruled over India for fifty years, and there was scarcely a day when he was not plotting some outrageous crime. He murdered his brothers, poisoned his father, and made life very nearly impossible for everyone around him. He died at the age of eighty-nine, writing in his will that he desired his funeral expenses to be paid "out of the sale of the quilted caps I have made with my hands, and furthermore the Korans written in my own hand shall be sold and the money shall be distributed among the poor." The quilted caps sold for 10 rupees each, and the sale of the Korans brought only 805 rupees.

His tomb lies in the village of Roaza, a few miles from Aurangabad. It is a drab village lost among the hills. There was a grave surrounded by a marble screen, with no inscriptions. Some small *subja* flowers, with their musky-sweet scent, were planted at the head of the grave. Somehow it was appropriate that he should lie there, just as it was appropriate that the Emperor Shah Jehan, his father, should lie with his queen, Mumtaz Mahal, in the Taj Mahal in Agra, with its infinity of marble screens and glistening mosaics. Aurangzeb died in the misery of repentance, knowing full well that he deserved an obscure grave. While he was dying, he wrote to one of his sons: "I die and carry with me the fruit of my sins. I have committed so many crimes, and do not know what torments will be visited on me."

My plan was to visit the nearby caves of Ellora and then to swing around and make the forty-mile journey to the caves of Ajanta. Under that bright maddening sky I expected miracles, and they came soon enough. A few miles along the road to Ellora we came to a shrine beside a quiet pool. There was nothing remarkable about the shrine except its perfect beauty. It was perhaps ten feet high, with a small dome, the greenish stone was flaking away and the roots of an ancient banyan tree were curling through the broken walls. We stopped the car to see whether we could find anything more about the Moslem saint who had been buried there, but we found no inscriptions. Some green pigeons sat on the gnarled branches of the banyan tree, and the summer pool quivered in the freshening wind. The lonely beauty of the place gave us the impression that we had stepped into another age, into the long distant past, far from human habitations. While we were lingering there beside the pool, some girls came down to bathe, but seeing us they laughed and made their way to some swings hanging from another banyan tree a short distance away; and when we set off for Ellora, we heard their laughter and the sound of splashing.

When I think of India now, I remember the small green shrine beside a green lake, and the perfection of the dome's reflection in the water. The girls who came flocking to the pool did not break the spell, for time had come to an end in a moment of perfect peace and serenity.

But what had happened to the caves of Ellora? "Another five miles, sahib," the young Moslem driver was saying, fingering his sparse beard with one hand, while lightly touching the wheel with the other, but he had said this so often that I no longer believed him. He was graceful and elegant, and he enjoyed talking about the virtues of the Moslems and the incalculable vices of the Hindus. "When you live among them, you see what terrible people they are!" he lamented. "Such buffoonery! Such drinking of toddy!" As for the caves, since they were carved by Hindus, they were obscene beyond belief, all of them equally detestable. If only the Hindus were converted to Islam there might be some hope for them.

Suddenly we were in the presence of the caves hidden for so long by the protecting hills. In fact, they were not caves. The face of the cliff had been torn open and carved into the shapes of palaces and temples. Generations of monkish sculptors, armed with chisels and hammers, had honeycombed the mountain, filled it with giant guardian gods and goddesses, thus asserting the triumph of the human spirit over brute creation. Every hundred years or so a new cave was carved out of the cliff. The Hindus, the Jains and the Buddhists rivaled one another in making sumptuous habitations for their gods, pretending that the rock was wax, pouring their own vitality into stone. There is a mile of temples under the shadow of that immense cliff, one temple beside another, one spectacular row of ten-foot gods beside another. The Hindu caves with their dancing Sivas, the lovers at their play and the gods in their eternal tumult, offer a prodigious window into the Hindu mind. An angel, high up on the sheer rock face, takes flight. There is a superb energy in the angel, and it is this energy, radiating from the assembled gods, which distinguishes Indian art from all other arts. Energy is Eternal Delight! Never was there such a tumultuous explosion of human vigor, so many clean dancing limbs, such a robust feeling for the human body in violent action or in absolute stillness! These flying buttresses, these life-size elephants carved out of stone, the legendary lions and leaping angels are merely the decorations of a heavenly palace. But what is most appealing about these sculptures is that they were created by men who were deeply and continuously aware of the presence of the gods, for otherwise they would not have been able to carve them with so much authority.

The young driver, of course, was impatient to return to Aurangabad.

"Too many caves, sahib," he complained. "We have no time, no time." He went on hopefully: "Perhaps we go Ajanta tomorrow. It is a very long journey, and the roads are bad!"

The roads, as it happened, were the best in India, for although the Nizam of Hyderabad was notoriously miserly, he took the greatest care of the roads in order to police his state, and the only cars we saw on that bright summer day were the black police vans belonging to the security forces of His Exalted Highness. We drove along winding red roads past shepherds' huts and ancient crumbling fortresses. Once, at a turning in the road we came upon the carcass of a dead bull with some twenty vultures perched on its back and at our approach they rose heavily in the air with a creaking and snapping of their leathery wings, so defiantly ugly, so menacing, that they darkened the sky.

Ajanta, reached in the afternoon, was a small unkempt village with perhaps three poverty-ridden streets. Some naked children were playing in the dust, while their mothers fanned themselves with palm leaves. Beyond the dusty village the landscape opened out, the trees were a brighter green, and there was a sudden freshness in the air, as though after a long journey overland we had come in sight of the sea.

But there was no sea, only a small winding river where the reeds waved in the wind and small fat jays flew lightly over the lotuses. Deer ran through the forest glades; you saw their bright eyes flashing, and the white scuts, and then they were gone. At the foot of a cliff the river widened among feathery oleanders, and there were mudbanks where the brown goats pastured. Hawks, wheeling above the cliffs, flashed in the sun, and sometimes their shadows fell on the white river. The hawks have been there since the world began; so have the oleanders; so have the deer. High up on the cliffs, overlooking the horseshoe-shaped valley, lies a necklace of caves.

There are twenty-nine caves at Ajanta, dating from the first century B.C. to the seventh century A.D. All are Buddhist, and some are shaped like temples, while others resemble low-roofed palaces. While Ellora gives an impression of heroic adventure, the caves of Ajanta suggest a meditative calm. Ellora shouts, Ajanta whispers. A brow of the cliff overhangs these caves, and you are scarcely aware of them until you come close to them. Indeed, for over a thousand years men lost sight of them. In the early years of the nineteenth century a party of British officers out tiger shooting stumbled upon them and found a tigress and her cubs in one of the caves.

On this day I had the caves to myself, for visitors come infrequently. The old Hindu attendant, with a face like a dark walnut, was fast asleep, his head on a stone, the sunlight pouring down on him. I had no heart to disturb him and went from cave to cave, until it became clear that I would never see the paintings unless I woke him. Only four caves have paintings, only one is filled with paintings in a fair state of preservation, and this one was so dark that it was necessary to seek his help. He went into a little shed and brought out a powerful lamp fitted with a reflector and a length of electric cord. Inside the cave he plugged in the cord, and the cave was lit up.

The first impression was of green, red, orange and yellow streamers shooting across a room not much larger than an ordinary dining room. There were at least twenty scenes painted on the walls of the cave, but it was some time before the eyes could separate the individual scenes. Angels, demons, bulls, lovers, processions moved across the dancing walls, and always there was the Buddha in the attitude of blessing or meditating. In ancient times the light came from polished mirrors set outside the mouth of the cave, and no doubt this light was more diffused than the beam of the powerful electric lamp. The demons taunted the Buddha; young women in transparent garments clung to him; ambassadors paid him tribute; the bulls locked their horns above garlands of sunflowers and poppies; the lovers smiled, and the priests made offerings of fruit and flowers.

At last when the eyes become accustomed to these fresh vivid colors, and when the paintings have arranged themselves in an orderly pattern, then the majesty of this room with the painted columns becomes apparent. All is ripeness and tenderness. Here and there the paint has flaked away, but no great harm has been done. Beyond the further wall another cave

opens up, and there is a large statue of Buddha of no particular
distinction. Clearly the statue was not carved at the same time
as the paintings, and just as clearly all these frescoes were
painted by a single artist of genius. The light moves across the
wall, picking up a bird in full flight or the face of some traveler
from beyond the Himalayas or a girl gazing enraptured at her
lover.

Greatest of all the figures is the Buddha Padmapani, "he who
holds the lotus." No one knows exactly which of the many
Buddhas he represents. Is he the young prince who left his palace
to embark on a life of meditation and devotion, or is he the
ageless emperor of the world offering his blessings? He stands
there in innocence and beauty, an imperturbable smile playing
on his lips, a crown upon his head, his shining body naked to
the waist, and he wears a necklace of pearls and carries a blue
lotus in his hand. He has emerged from a red-walled palace,
and there is about him the power and grace of the greatest gods.
What is extraordinary about him is the reality with which he
is invested. He is about to move, about to speak, about to dance,
and yet he does none of these things. He trembles in his meditation on the edge of mystery, and in a moment he will shatter
the earth to fragments or create it anew. The palm trees wave
in the wind, a blue swan flies low above his head, and the
world rejoices.

"If a man speaks or acts with pure thought," says the early
manual of Buddhism called the Dhammapada, "happiness follows
him like a shadow that never leaves him, and if he acts with evil
thought, then pain follows him, as the wheel follows the tread
of the oxen drawing the farmcart." It is significant that the
Buddhists should have thought of happiness as a shadow. But
there are no shadows at all in these paintings glowing with the
colors of luxuriant life, scarlet and emerald and turquoise blue.
Divested of the love of all created things, yet in some mysterious
way conspiring with creation, the youthful Buddha proclaims
from the jeweled cave the beauty of the visible world—so beautiful that it is almost beyond belief.

While I was still gazing at the Buddha Padmapani, there came
a sound of roaring in my ears, a green fire poured into the cave,
and a moment later the Green Dragon was standing there. He
was grinning from ear to ear, his eyes glowed like cats' eyes,

his green tail was a thousand light-years long, and his claws, as they gripped the rock, made a sound like iron striking iron.

"What are you doing here?" I asked, surprised by his sudden entrance into the cave.

"I might ask you the same question," he replied pleasantly. "The caves of Ajanta are my favorite abode, for those artists are among the most superb creators who ever lived on the earth. I sometimes come here to remind myself that there was once some hope for humanity."

"You mean there's no hope now?"

"Not very much, I am afraid. We gave them this beautiful earth to play with, and all they do is kill each other. But I haven't come here to discuss the non-existent future of the human race. As soon as I saw you here, I thought it was time we renewed our acquaintance. I thought we might draw up an inventory of your affairs. You made a lot of mistakes of course. I don't suppose you really learned anything by meeting Hitler. You were deadly wrong about Singapore, and before that you were wrong about Republican Spain. You should have known they didn't have a chance, and that you would always be on the losing side. You really thought that Wen Yi-tuo and Feng Yu-hsiang between them would be able to put China on her feet. You were right about Communist China, but I don't suppose that helped you very much. I showed you the great leaders, and you were fascinated by their power and their ruthlessness. You overestimated them, but I don't want to harp on your errors—"

"That's exactly what you are doing," I said bitterly.

"Nonsense! There were one or two things I approved of. I especially approved of your marriage to Rose and your Chinese palace. I liked the way you walked up to the machine guns, but you wouldn't have done it without my help. I liked the way you talked to the dictators, but then again you knew I was there. You were impudent—it is a quality I approve of. You traveled across China and India, and I approve of that, too. I observe that you are very happy in India. Is there anything I can do for you? Would you like to marry an Indian princess?"

"No, I am still married to a Chinese princess."

"In the realms we live in," said the Green Dragon sagely, "a few marriages more or less do not make any difference. If you would like an Indian princess, I have only to twitch my whiskers and there will be a whole army of painted and caparisoned elephants and slaves carrying her up the valley of Ajanta. I remember you said once that you envied the gentlemen in the British Museum Reading Room who spend their time fetching books for the readers. You said you envied them for being among books all the time. No more action, no more running about the earth—just books and dreams. Is that what you want?"

"Yes, yes, yes," I said.

"Then you shall have it," the Green Dragon said, and he wagged his tail and we walked out of the cave together.

INDEX